MW00844257

# John Keats' Medical Notebook
# Text, Context, and Poems

ENGLISH ASSOCIATION STUDIES, 6

HRILEENA GHOSH

# *John Keats' Medical Notebook*

## Text, Context, and Poems

LIVERPOOL UNIVERSITY PRESS
THE ENGLISH ASSOCIATION

First published 2020 by
Liverpool University Press
4 Cambridge Street
Liverpool
L69 7ZU



British Library Cataloguing-in-Publication data
A British Library CIP record is available

ISBN 978 1 78962 061 0

Typeset by Carnegie Book Production, Lancaster
Printed and bound by CPI Group (UK) Ltd, Croydon CR0 4YY

The position of the hand in dissecting should be the same, as in writing or drawing; and the knife, held, like the pen or pencil, by the thumb and the first two fingers, should be moved by means of them only; while the hand rests firmly on the two fingers bent inwards as in writing, and on the wrist.

(*The London Dissector* (1811), 1)

# Contents

*Acknowledgements* ix
*Abbreviations* xi
*A Note on Texts* xiv

Introduction 1

**John Keats' Medical Notebook: An Annotated Edition** 19

1 John Keats' Medical Notebook: An Overview 87

2 John Keats' 'Guy's Hospital' Poetry 119

3 Keats' Medical Milieu 150

4 John Keats at Guy's: Scholar and Poet 173

5 *Endymion* and the Physiology of Passion 203

6 'The Only State for the Best Sort of Poetry' 233

Conclusion 269

*Bibliography* 271
*Index* 285

# Acknowledgements

I thank Keats House and the City of London Corporation for permission to reproduce the written text in Keats' medical Notebook. I also thank King's College London for permission to quote from materials in their archive. Grants from the Charles Wallace Trust of India, the Inlaks Shivdasani Foundation, the Keats Foundation, the Keats-Shelley Association of America, the Keats-Shelley Memorial Association and the University of St Andrews enabled me to research and write this book: I acknowledge their contributions with gratitude.

I am indebted to the staff at the following institutions for helping me to access material in their care and answering my many questions: the British Library; Keats House, especially Ken Page and Sofie Davis; Keats-Shelley House, especially Giuseppe Albano; King's College London, especially Diana Manipud and Lianne Smith; London Metropolitan Archives; National Library of India; National Library of Scotland; the Non-Catholic Cemetery for Foreigners in Testaccio, Rome, especially Amanda Thursfield; Special Collections Department, University of St Andrews; St Andrews University Library and Trinity College Cambridge Library, especially Jonathan Smith.

An earlier version of Chapter 2 appeared in *John Keats and the Medical Imagination*, ed. Nicholas Roe (Palgrave Macmillan, 2017), 21–41, while an earlier version of some sections of Chapter 6 appeared in *Keats's Places*, ed. Richard Marggraf Turley (Palgrave Macmillan, 2018), 31–52; I'm grateful to the editors for allowing me to reproduce this previously published material.

Nicholas Roe read multiple drafts of this book with meticulous attention and great good humour, offering astute criticism each time. John Barnard shared his immense knowledge of Keats' medical career with me, and read parts of the manuscript, as did Katie Garner and Richard Marggraf Turley. R. S. White offered information on nineteenth-century medicine with unstinting generosity. Sukanta Chaudhuri spared valuable time to discuss editorial practice. Their generously shared knowledge has enriched every page of this work, and I'm grateful to them all. Malabika Sarkar encouraged me every step of the way: my gratitude to her is boundless. For offering advice and responding to specific queries I thank Amlan Das Gupta, Carly Stevenson, Emily Rohrbach, Fiona Stafford, Gordon Bottomley, Greg Kucich, Heidi Thomson, James Grande, Janine Utell, Janis McLarren Caldwell, John Williams, Jonathan Mulrooney, Matthew Rowney, Meiko O'Halloran, the late Michael O'Neill, Peter Dale, Peter Mackay, Richard Alford, Sarah Wootton, Sean Francis Hughes, and Tom Jones.

At Liverpool University Press, I am particularly grateful to Jenny Howard for her initial interest in this book, and to Christabel Scaife for taking it forward with continued enthusiasm. The suggestions offered by the two anonymous readers for the press were gratefully received and incorporated in various ways; I thank them for their time and attention, and for improving this book.

My friends and family have helped in various ways; I am especially grateful to Aart Murray-Carlsson, Aritra Chakrabarti, Aveek Sen, Craig Anderson, Douglas Christie, Doyeeta Majumdar, Edward Burke, Elena Sischarenco, Lav Kanoi, Lisa Griffin, María Merino Jaso, Priyanka Nandy, Sandeep Mancha, Somnath and Subhasree Basu, and Vinayak Das Gupta for advice and encouragement along the way. Ranjan Gupta and Pamela Leporati hosted me on research trips more times than I can count; Indra Das reminded me – one author to another – that there was more to life than writing. Costantino Mattioli and Theodosia Michou welcomed me into their family and their home; Vittorio Mattioli cheerfully accepted Keats into his life and proof-read parts of this book. My parents, Amit and Anindita Ghosh, have been unwavering in their support – I am grateful to them for that, as for all else.

# Abbreviations

*Manuscripts*

JKMN — John Keats, John Keats' medical Notebook [MS]. K/MS/01/002: Keats House/London Metropolitan Archives.

Waddington — Joshua Waddington, *Lectures on Anatomy; And The Principal Operations of Surgery: Delivered at the Theatre, St Thomas's Hospital; between the 1$^{st}$ of January, and the 1$^{st}$ of June 1816; By Astley Cooper Esq$^{re}$. Vol 1$^{st}$* [MS]. GB 0100 G/PP1/62/3. King's College London.

*Printed*

BT — John Barnard, '"The Busy Time": Keats's Duties at Guy's Hospital from Autumn 1816 to March 1817', *Romanticism* 13.3 (October 2007): 199–218.

CCC — Charles Cowden Clarke, 'Recollections of Keats', *The Atlantic Monthly* 7.39 (January 1861): 86–101. Courtesy of Cornell University Library, Making of America Digital Collection.

*CH* — *Keats: The Critical Heritage*, ed. G. M. Matthews. New York: Barnes and Noble, 1971.

*EB* — *Encyclopaedia Britannica*. Online Edition: Britannica Academic. <https://academic.eb.com/levels/collegiate> (accessed 19 November 2018).

Forman — *John Keats's Anatomical and Physiological Note Book printed from the holograph in the Keats Museum Hampstead*, ed. Maurice Buxton Forman. Oxford: Oxford University Press, 1934; reprint New York: Haskell House, 1970.

*GA* — Henry Gray and H. V. Carter, *Anatomy Descriptive and Surgical*. London: John W. Parker and Son, 1858. Commonly known as Gray's *Anatomy*.

*JK* — Robert Gittings, *John Keats*. London: Heinemann, 1968.

*KC* — *The Keats Circle: Letters and Papers 1816–1878*, ed. Hyder Edward Rollins. 2 vols. Cambridge, MA: Harvard University Press, 1948.

*KW* — George A. R. Winston, 'John Keats and Joshua Waddington Contemporary Students at Guy's Hospital', *Guy's Hospital Reports* 92 (1943): 101–10.

*LD* — *The London Dissector; or, System of Dissection, Practised in the Hospitals and Lecture Rooms of the Metropolis…*, 3rd ed. London: John Murray; J. Callow; E. Cox; T. Underwood; and Edinburgh: William Blackwood, 1811.

*LJK* — *The Letters of John Keats 1814–1821*, ed. Hyder Edward Rollins. 2 vols. Cambridge, MA: Harvard University Press, 1958.

*LM* — Robert Hooper, *Lexico-Medicum; or Medical Dictionary; Containing an Explanation of the Terms … Selected, Arranged, and Compiled from the Best Authors*, 4th ed. London: Longman, Hurst, Rees, Orme, and Co.; Scatcherd and Letterman; J. Cuthell; Cadell and Davies; Baldwin, Cradock, and Joy; Highley and Son; Cox and Son; J. Callow; T. and G. Underwood; G. and W. B. Whittaker; Ogle, Duncan, and Co.; G. Mackie; J. Anderson; Burgess and Hill; Stirling and Slade; and Edinburgh: Fairbairn and Anderson, 1822.

*Mem* — John Flint South, *Memorials of John Flint South*. 1884; Fontwell: Centaur Press, 1970.

*NL* — Nicholas Roe, *John Keats: A New Life*. New Haven, CT/London: Yale University Press, 2012.

*ODNB* — *The Oxford Dictionary of National Biography*. Online edition, 2004. <http://www.oxforddnb.com/> (accessed 19 November 2018).

*OED* — *Oxford English Dictionary*. OED Online, 2018. <http://www.oed.com/> (accessed 19 November 2018).

| | |
|---|---|
| *Poems* | *The Poems of John Keats*, ed. Jack Stillinger. London: Heinemann, 1978. |
| *PP* | Donald Goellnicht, *The Poet-Physician: Keats and Medical Science*. Pittsburgh, PA: University of Pittsburgh Press, 1984. |
| *RMJK* | Hermione de Almeida, *Romantic Medicine and John Keats*. Oxford/New York: Oxford University Press, 1991. |
| *RoW* | Charles and Mary Cowden Clarke, *Recollections of Writers*. London: Sampson Low, Marston, Searle and Rivington, 1878. |
| *Texts* | Jack Stillinger, *The Texts of Keats's Poems*. Cambridge, MA: Harvard University Press, 1974. |

# A Note on Texts

All quotations from Keats' poetry are from *Poems*, unless otherwise indicated. Quotations from Keats' poems, Shelley's *Adonais: An Elegy on the Death of John Keats*, and Milton's *Paradise Lost* are cited in text. All quotations of *Paradise Lost* are from John Milton, *Paradise Lost*, ed. Alastair Fowler (London/New York: Longman, 1968, 1971; reprint 1992). Quotations of *Adonais*, including from Shelley's 'Preface' to that poem, are sourced from the texts presented in Anthony D. Knerr's *Shelley's* Adonais*: A Critical Edition* (New York: Columbia University Press, 1984). All references to *OED*, *EB*, and the *ODNB* are to their online editions, accessed 19 November 2018.

Waddington's notes are cited from my transcriptions of his manuscripts, using the page numbers he gave them: he wrote his manuscript volumes (with very few exceptions, and none in the sections quoted here) on the rectos only. He numbered his rectos regularly and consistently, using odd numbers; conceptually, therefore, his versos must have constituted the even-numbered pages. Therefore, when a page range is offered in citing any of Waddington's manuscripts, the versos within that range are blank.

# Introduction

John Keats, the poet of *Endymion*, 'Ode to a Nightingale', and *Hyperion*, is admired all over the world. It is less well-known that he was a trained and skilled surgeon who studied at Guy's Hospital, London, from October 1815 to March 1817, while simultaneously making his way as a poet. From the many notes he would have made in lectures and classes, one notebook survives and is currently held by Keats House, Hampstead, and the City of London Corporation. This document remains the only record we have in Keats' own hand for this formative period in his development. Keats' medical Notebook is important for two reasons. First and foremost, it contains notes taken by Keats: thus, it represents a tangible material link to the poet, and analysis of it provides insights into his medical and anatomical knowledge and how this may be related to his poetry. Secondly, it is an important documentary source for the history of medicine: it provides first-hand evidence of what trainee surgeons in early nineteenth-century Britain were taught at one of the leading London teaching hospitals, and as such it represents the cutting edge of British scientific education at the time.

Over the two centuries since Keats' death his poems and letters have been edited many times, most recently by Jeffrey Cox and John Barnard.[1] It is strange, therefore, that the medical Notebook has received scant editorial attention – the only previous edition of it dates from 1934, and is not annotated – and only intermittent scholarly and critical discussion.[2] The fully annotated edition presented in this book has been newly transcribed and edited from the manuscript, and is

1 *Keats's Poetry and Prose*, ed. Jeffrey N. Cox (New York/London: W. W. Norton and Company, 2009); *Selected Letters*, ed. John Barnard (London: Penguin, 2014).

2 Forman.

the foundation of and companion to the chapters of commentary that follow. The commentary ranges from an exploration of Keats' poetic creativity while at Guy's Hospital through an account of the medical milieu within which he lived and worked and a close analysis of his manuscript medical Notebook to explorations of how *Endymion* and the poems in the 1820 volume were inspired and shaped by Keats' medical knowledge and experience. Throughout the book, I return to the contents, imagery, language, and form of Keats' medical Notebook, showing how it illuminates the poetry he wrote while at, and after leaving, Guy's Hospital. At the same time, this book is also in constant dialogue with the insights of literary and critical studies on Keats and Romantic literature that have come before it, supplemented – wherever possible – by reference to unpublished manuscript sources and publications dating from Keats' lifetime.

It is an irony that the importance of Keats' medical training to his poetry was acknowledged in such powerful terms during his lifetime and then ignored by critics for the rest of the nineteenth century. The devastating efficacy of John Gibson Lockhart's medically themed attack in his essay on 'The Cockney School of Poetry IV' provoked Keats' friends and admirers to suppress as far as possible any idea that Keats' medical knowledge may have influenced his poetry, while simultaneously promoting Shelley's magnificent apotheosis of him as 'Adonais' – 'burning through the inmost veil of Heaven, / … like a star' (466–67).[3] It was only in the twentieth century that critical attention focused on the influence Keats' medical knowledge might have exerted on his poetry. Two major biographies published in the early years of the twentieth century – by Sidney Colvin and Amy Lowell – explored the significance of Keats' medical training to his biography and also referred to the existence of his medical Notebook.[4] However, it was only in 1925 that William Hale-White, in a pioneering essay on 'Keats as a Medical Student', devoted significant attention to the Notebook as a manuscript in its own right.[5] His intervention,

3 John Gibson Lockhart ['Z'], 'Cockney School of Poetry, No. IV', *Blackwood's Edinburgh Magazine* 3.17 (August 1818): 519–24.

4 Sidney Colvin, *John Keats His Life and Poetry His Friends Critics and After-Fame* (London: Macmillan, 1817); Amy Lowell, *John Keats*. 2 vols (Boston/New York: Houghton Mifflin, 1925).

5 William Hale-White, 'Keats as a Medical Student', *Guy's Hospital Reports* 75 (1925): 249–62.

followed by Maurice Buxton Forman's publication of *John Keats's Anatomical and Physiological Note Book printed from the holograph in the Keats Museum Hampstead* (1934) – the only edition prior to the one in this book – ensured that subsequent commentaries could not ignore this manuscript. Since then, a level of specialized interest has been focused on it, albeit of less intensity than is accorded to Keats' literary manuscripts or other aspects of his biography.

Acknowledging this aspect of Keats scholarship, my first chapter offers an overview of Keats' medical Notebook, discussing its provenance, describing it as a bibliographic object, and investigating some of its more puzzling aspects. It explores Keats' engagement with his medical studies at the time he took the lecture notes, as evinced by this surviving Notebook, and finds him an attentive and successful student: he took care to keep legible notes and frequently annotated and cross-referenced them, revealing a degree of interest in his medical studies that counters traditional accounts of his indifference or disinterest. Keats' medical Notebook was a dynamic repository of evolving knowledge to which he returned again and again: the chapter considers the only previously published edition of it, as well as its treatment in popular publications, including the major Keats biographies.

Pioneering research into the topic of 'Keats and Medicine' was conducted by Charles Hagelman in the 1950s, culminating in his doctoral thesis 'John Keats and the Medical Profession' (1956), which was concerned to 'describe medical training in the early nineteenth century, to point out its relationship to Keats' medical training, and to explore its significance in [Keats'] poetry, his life and his after fame'.[6] He was one of the first critics to note that, in the light of George Winston's 'invaluable study, based on heretofore unpublished manuscript material' comparing the medical notes of Keats with his fellow student Joshua Waddington's, it was 'clear that Keats' anatomical and physiological notebook, edited by M. Buxton Forman and published by the Oxford University Press in 1934, must be re-edited'.[7] Almost 30 years later, Donald Goellnicht's seminal study *The Poet-Physician: Keats and Medical Science* (1984) focused

6 Charles Hagelman, 'John Keats and the Medical Profession' (PhD diss., University of Texas, 1956), 1.

7 Hagelman, 'Medical Profession', 344. Winston's 'invaluable study' is a reference to *KW*.

attention for the first time on the extent to which Keats' poetry drew directly on his medical knowledge and vocabulary.[8] These are foundational works on 'Keats and Medicine', and this book is in continuous dialogue with their insights: my second chapter – in attempting to recreate Keats' hospital schedule – has drawn particularly on them, as well as on more recent recuperative work by R. S. White, John Barnard, and Nicholas Roe.[9] This chapter considers the poems Keats was writing during the period when he was also taking down the notes in his medical Notebook at Guy's Hospital, October 1815–March 1817. Looking at Keats' poems in terms of their dates of composition, juxtaposed with events in the hospital calendar and in his biography, reveals patterns of sociality and conviviality that tie in with the quantity and sometimes the quality of his poetic compositions. Keats' attitude towards poetry underwent a significant change after he successfully passed his licentiate examination in July 1816. I have drawn on analyses of Keats' friendships by Ronald Sharp and Richard Holmes,[10] as well as biographies of the poet and accounts by Keats' friends themselves, to show that his living arrangements in London reflected his waning commitment to Guy's and growing interest in poetry to 'gain [a] Living'.[11] I also explore Keats' fellow student Henry Stephens' 1847 account of Keats at Guy's in the context of his developing fame in the nineteenth century, to show that the only surviving first-hand account from a fellow medical student was influenced and to some extent distorted by myths already gathering around 'the Poet John Keats'.[12] Here, I have developed my argument from the work of J. R. MacGillivray and Susan Wolfson.[13] The chapter traces Keats'

8 *PP*.

9 R. S. White, '"Like Esculapius of Old": Keats's Medical Training', *Keats-Shelley Review* 12 (1998): 15–49; *BT*; Nicholas Roe, 'Mr. Keats', *Essays in Criticism* 65.3 (July 2015): 274–88.

10 Ronald A. Sharp, 'Keats and Friendship', in *The Persistence of Poetry: Bicentennial Essays on Keats*, ed. Robert M. Ryan and Ronald A. Sharp (Amherst: University of Massachusetts Press, 1998), 66–81; Richard Holmes, 'John Keats the Well-Beloved', in *The Long Pursuit: Reflections of a Romantic Biographer* (London: William Collins, 2016), 219–41.

11 *KC*, I, 307.

12 *KC*, II, 206.

13 J. R. MacGillivray, *Keats: A Bibliography and Reference Guide with an Essay on Keats's Reputation* (Toronto: University of Toronto Press, 1949); Susan

development into the physician–poet he became at Guy's Hospital, from his initial recourse to poetry as a distraction to his recognition that poetry might be a possible career choice and a panacea for the miseries of the world.

My third chapter offers an account of the London teaching hospitals of the early nineteenth century to show how, as a medical student, Keats had privileged access to the intellectual capital that would eventually inform and enrich his poetry. Drawing upon previous work in this area, notably Hermione de Almeida's *Romantic Medicine and John Keats* (1991), which addressed 'the fundamental intellectual issues of Romantic medicine ... as these find focus and exemplary conceptual expression in the poetry and aesthetic theory of Keats', the chapter also relies on hitherto unpublished contemporary manuscripts to complete the picture.[14] The important – and vexed – question of the source from which Keats' medical notes derived is addressed, and my account draws upon archival evidence to resolve some long-standing mysteries, including the dates for the lecture series that Keats attended.

The fourth chapter also concerns Keats' lecture courses, opening with a detailed textual comparison, including statistical analysis of lexicography, between Keats' notes and those kept by his fellow student Joshua Waddington. These prove that the two sets of notes derived from the same source and reveal that, although Keats has essentially the same information as Waddington, his habits of concision, reorganization and cross-referencing mean that they are presented in a different – indeed, distinctive – form. The chapter finds that some characteristic features of Keats' mature poetry are prefigured in his medical notes: striking imagery, verbal rhythms, and 'poetical concentration' (as Leigh Hunt described it) are all typical of Keats' medical thought.[15] Close readings of some of Keats's most accomplished poetry – 'Ode to a Nightingale', *Hyperion* and its reincarnation *The Fall of Hyperion*, and the late poem 'This living

J. Wolfson, 'Keats enters history: Autopsy, *Adonais*, and the fame of Keats', in *Keats and History*, ed. Nicholas Roe (Cambridge: Cambridge University Press, 1995), 17–45.

14 *RMJK*, 4.

15 James Henry Leigh Hunt, *Lord Byron and Some of His Contemporaries with Recollections of the Author's Life, and of His Visit to Italy* (London: Henry Colburn, 1828), 266.

hand' – reveal the medical underpinning for much of his greatest poetry, in content, vocabulary, and style.

New Historicism, with its interest in the interactions between cultural context and literary creativity, led to renewed critical interest in Keats' medical career, and with it in his medical Notebook. Marjorie Levinson, in *Keats's Life of Allegory: The Origins of a Style* (1988), argued that Keats' socio-economic position – including his training as an apothecary – and his consequent feelings of disempowerment and class alienation had a profound influence on his poetics.[16] Nicholas Roe interpreted Keats' alienation differently in *John Keats and the Culture of Dissent* (1997), showing how his medical training empowered Keats to adopt a poetic idiom at once scientifically aware and politically subversive.[17] Alan Bewell devoted a chapter of *Romanticism and Colonial Disease* (1999) to Keats' imaginative response to the spectre of dreadful contagion from the east, and Alan Richardson, in *Romanticism and the Science of the Mind* (2001) discussed Keats' poetic debt to contemporary developments in neurology.[18] In *Keats's Boyish Imagination* (2004) Richard Marggraf Turley explored how Keats appropriated his medical vocabulary for poetic, political, and therapeutic ends.[19] James Allard's *Romanticism, Medicine and the Poet's Body* (2007) considered the effects that Keats' exposure to the 'bodies' at Guy's Hospital had on his own depiction and conception of the human body.[20] Nicholas Roe's discovery in 2015 of a contemporary newspaper account describing Keats acting in his role as a dresser shows that this is a field still rich for investigation.[21] It is also one that still arouses general interest: the topic of the 2017 Keats

16 Marjorie Levinson, *Keats's Life of Allegory: The Origins of a Style* (Oxford: Basil Blackwell, 1988).

17 Nicholas Roe, *John Keats and the Culture of Dissent* (Oxford: Clarendon Press, 1997).

18 Alan Bewell, *Romanticism and Colonial Disease* (Baltimore, MD/London: Johns Hopkins University Press, 1999); Alan Richardson, *British Romanticism and the Science of the Mind* (Cambridge: Cambridge University Press, 2001).

19 Richard Marggraf Turley, *Keats's Boyish Imagination* (London/New York: Routledge, 2004).

20 James Allard, *Romanticism, Medicine and the Poet's Body* (Aldershot: Ashgate, 2007).

21 Roe, 'Mr. Keats'.

Memorial Lecture, delivered at Apothecaries' Hall, London, was 'How did John Keats's Medical Training Influence his Poetry?'[22]

My penultimate chapters, which focus most closely on Keats' poetry, have been informed and enriched by this wealth of scholarship. They also draw upon recent criticism exploring how various aspects of culture and biography, psychology, and literary creations interacted and inspired each other in the Romantic period. Denise Gigante's insights in *Taste* (2005) and its follow-up *Life* (2009), which explored how profoundly artistic creation is influenced by the conception of physiological processes and organic forms, undergird my argument in this book that Keats' knowledge of anatomy and physiology influenced his creativity.[23] Robert Mitchell's *Experimental Life* (2015), examines how Romantic writers appropriated the concept of experimentation in their works, and informs my analysis of the creative inter-currents between Keats' medical notes and his known interests outside the field of medicine, in history, mythology, politics, and poetry.[24] In the popular press, Richard Holmes' *The Age of Wonder* (2008) explored how, for the Romantics, 'science' and 'art' were fluid terms applied to creative activities that inspired wonder and fear alike: my book is an argument that for Keats, as a man and a writer, creativity was fluid – and that the qualities that made him successful as a medical student were the qualities that, applied differently, enabled him to write 'verses fit to live'.[25]

Chapter five focuses on *Endymion*, the only long poem Keats ever completed, written immediately after he left Guy's Hospital and therefore at a time when his medical experience was fresh in his mind. Reading *Endymion* through the contents of Keats' medical Notebook allows a fresh perspective on the physiology that underlies

22 Sean P. F. Hughes and Sarah Hughes, 'Keats Memorial Lecture: How Did John Keats's Medical Training Influence His Poetry?', *Keats-Shelley Review* 31.2 (September 2017): 136–46.

23 Denise Gigante, *Taste: A Literary History* (New Haven, CT/London: Yale University Press, 2005); *Life: Organic Form and Romanticism* (New Haven, CT/London: Yale University Press, 2009).

24 Robert Mitchell, *Experimental Life: Vitalism in Romantic Science and Literature* (Baltimore, MD: Johns Hopkins University Press, 2013).

25 Richard Holmes, *The Age of Wonder: How the Romantic Generation Discovered the Beauty and Terror of Science* (London: HarperCollins, 2008); *Poems*, 102.

and informs the poem's depictions of passion. I have drawn upon Noel Jackson's investigation of the relationship between sense-perceptions and aesthetic experience to show how Keats' medical experience affected his poetic creativity and how contemporary critical responses to the poem recognized and responded to this.[26] The chapter concludes with an exploration of Keats' knowledge of Romantic medical ethics and how this informed his delineation of the figures of healers in *Endymion*. My account reveals how the physiological treatment of passion in *Endymion* gives the work its distempered life: the poem showcases Keats' extraordinary ability to convey extreme emotional states through anatomical description and medical vocabulary. This is a characteristic feature of Keats' best works and imparts to them their enduring vitality; it is also one that draws directly on the vocabulary and contents of his medical Notebook.

The final chapter of this book concerns the last collection of poetry Keats published in his lifetime, *Lamia, Isabella, The Eve of St Agnes, and Other Poems*, exploring it from two different but related perspectives. The first part of the chapter discusses the circumstances in which Keats composed the poems that made up his 1820 volume, showing how, at every turn, questions related to health, disease, medicine, and death forced themselves upon his attention. My approach draws upon Anne Mellor's methodology in her pioneering *Mary Shelley: Her Life, Her Fiction, Her Monsters* (1988), where a comprehensive account of the author's work was presented by combining techniques of analysis and insights derived from a range of fields, including gender studies, psychoanalysis, biography, and literary criticism.[27] This part of the chapter is recuperative, exploring how the lived experiences of biography fundamentally influenced the poetry that came out of it, and evaluating the extent to which these infiltrations were consciously allowed. To this end, I also analyse the publication history of the 1820 volume, the appearance of which owed much to extra-literary circumstances – with George Keats' financial troubles providing the initial impetus and the precipitous decline of Keats' own health

26 Noel Jackson, *Science and Sensation in Romantic Poetry* (Cambridge: Cambridge University Press, 2008).

27 Anne Mellor, *Mary Shelley: Her Life, Her Fiction, Her Monsters* (London/New York: Routledge, 1988).

clinching the decision to publish. In its concluding part this chapter reads poems from the 1820 volume – including *Isabella*, *The Eve of St Agnes*, 'Ode to a Nightingale', and 'Ode on Melancholy' – in the light of the contents of Keats' medical Notebook and through the lens of contemporary medical developments, showing how these works function as knowing interventions in prevalent medical debates. My analysis is informed by contemporary medical publications in the nineteenth century as well as by modern literary criticism, particularly medico-literary readings of Keats' poetry as is found, for example, in the recent collection of essays *John Keats and the Medical Imagination* (2017).[28] The combination in this final chapter of a biographical investigation with close readings of the poetry reveals that, without the medical crises and adverse circumstances that characterized his life during 1819–20, Keats' greatest poems might never have been composed. Their conception owed much more to his medical training than is realized, and their form and vocabulary were significantly influenced by the contents of his medical Notebook.

Taken as a whole, then, the book moves from a new edition of Keats' medical Notebook, through editorial commentary and elucidation, to a critical consideration of how the Notebook and his medical career helped shape the poetry Keats wrote while at Guy's Hospital and in the years after.

## On the Edition

Keats' medical Notebook is characterized by a complex but mostly coherent layout in terms of the arrangement of notes on the page and across the volume. In this edition I indicate details of bibliographic interest, including the positioning of Keats' marginalia in relation to the rest of his text through editorial intervention or, where Keats uses them, by reproducing Keats' own symbols for cross-referencing his marginalia with his notes. That said, editorial interventions have been kept to a minimum, and I have not attempted visually to reproduce the effects that the distinctive formatting of Keats' notes present. Inevitably, this means that aspects of the

28 Nicholas Roe, ed., *John Keats and the Medical Imagination* (Cham: Palgrave Macmillan, 2017).

visual impact of Keats' presentation are lost. This is unfortunate, for the peculiar visual appearance of some of these pages immediately and powerfully underlines the fact that Keats' medical Notebook was a working document that developed over a period of months. Keats used it as a repository for practical information and also to work out ideas and associations arising from that information. He evidently reread and added to his notes (at least while he was still at Guy's), supplying annotations and attempting to cross-reference passages. Furthermore, reproducing Keats' handwritten notes in type makes for a consistency in appearance that is not evident in the manuscript: across the Notebook Keats' handwriting changes, is rushed or cramped, evens out, or grows more careful. These effects are of significance – as the chapters of commentary will show – but the distinctive features of Keats' 'living hand', apparent in my illustrations, are regrettably lost in this edition to the uniformity of type. Reproducing Keats' medical notes in an annotated edition is a compromise, but, short of producing a photographic facsimile, I believe that this is the best solution.

Keats' medical notes are distinctively ordered across and through the volume: this aspect of the medical Notebook requires some explanation. Keats wrote his notes from both the front and the back end of his Notebook; at both ends he opened with a section from 'Lect$^{r}$ 4'. I have used the capital letters F and B in front of the folio numbers to indicate, respectively, whether the sequence starts from the front of the Notebook (F) or the back (B). The layout of Keats' Notebook is therefore idiosyncratic, all the more so in that these two sections of Lecture 4 were not the first entries Keats made in it. He had already started writing notes headed 'Lect$^{r}$ 1' at folio 2 recto from the front (Ff2r), and then proceeded to 'Lect$^{r}$ 2$^{nd}$. On the Blood', which he started writing at Ff3r.

Keats did not, however, arrange a straightforward sequence of successive lectures – first, second, third, and so on. In an utterly baffling twist, Ff2v – the page opposite the one on which Keats wrote his notes for 'Lect$^{r}$ 2$^{nd}$' – had been written on *before* he started to transcribe this second lecture. This is apparent because, in addition to the notes on Ff2v being unrelated to the subject of 'Lect$^{r}$ 2$^{nd}$. On the Blood' opposite (at Ff3r), when Keats ran out of space for his 'On the Blood' notes on Ff3r he opted to continue along the outer margins of Ff2v, turning the Notebook horizontal (i.e. in 'landscape') and writing around pre-existing material. Still unable to set down all he had to write there, he then returned the page to its original vertical, 'portrait', position, and wrote along the bottom margin of Ff2v, once again working around pre-existing writing. He did not turn the page to Ff3v because it, too, already had notes on it, and so the same pattern repeats for 'Lect$^{r}$ 3', which Keats started writing on Ff4r. When he ran out of space he continued writing along the bottom margin of Ff3v (with the page still in the original 'portrait' position) and then along the outer margin (with the page horizontal, in 'landscape') of the same page. The notes on Ff1v, Ff2v, and Ff3v appear to be linked to each other – they are the only three pages in the entire document to which Keats assigned page numbers, denoting them in sequence '1', '2', and '3'.[29] Why this separate sequence occurs, and why Keats chose to abandon it, is not clear, but Keats does continue to make use of his page numbering for these pages in his cross-references throughout his medical Notebook, as the text of the edition will show.

As already mentioned, Keats' material culled from 'Lect$^{r}$ 4' commences on the first page of the Notebook from the front, at Ff1r. It then continues ('Lect$^{r}$ 4 continued') at the back of the Notebook, at folio 1 recto (Bf1r). Thereafter, Keats proceeded to write continuously and in numeric sequence of the lectures, moving inwards from the back of the Notebook. He misnumbered Lecture 7 as 'Lect$^{r}$ 6' at Bf2v, having already written out 'Lect$^{r}$ 6' from Bf2r. He continued with this numbering sequence until he started 'Lect$^{r}$ 10' at Bf4v, where he corrected himself: thus, though the numbering gives the impression that Lecture 9 is missing from the notes, in reality all the lectures are represented, but with lectures 7–9 being numbered 6–8. Keats stopped numbering his lecture notes after 'Lect$^{r}$ 12' at Bf6r, although he continued writing steadily until Bf7r. Thereafter he left Bf7v blank, then inserted notes on bones at Bf8r. Bf8v and Bf9r contain notes on ligaments. A comparison with his fellow student Joshua Waddington's fair copy of notes indicates that

29 It is unclear which lecture(s) these notes derive from, or even if they derive from lecture(s). There are no obvious correlates for them in Joshua Waddington's notes. Given that, on occasion, Keats consolidated material from across several lectures (see Chapter 4), it is possible to hazard a guess that the notes on Ff1v, Ff2v, and Ff3v represent a collation and drastic summarization of the contents of Lectures 3–17 in Waddington; however, the fact that Keats has separate lecture notes for Lectures 3–15/16 renders this both unlikely and baffling.

this sequence contains notes up to and including Lectures 15 or 16: as Waddington has them, 'Structure of Bones, continued: Of Cartilage; Of Ligament' and 'On Diseases of Joints', respectively. After a discussion of afflictions of ligaments at Bf9r there follows 123 blank pages, and then the notes written from the front of the Notebook.

At Bf9r Keats stopped writing from the back of his Notebook and also abandoned his sequential progress through the lectures. At folio 4 verso from the front (Ff4v) he headed his notes 'Of Osteology' and proceeded to enumerate and, subsequently, describe the bones in the human skeleton. From Ff4v he wrote only on the verso for two pages (Ff5r and Ff6r are blank), then on both versos and rectos for Ff7 and Ff8, before reverting to writing on versos only until Ff19. At Ff19 he writes on both recto and verso (commencing his notes on 'Syndesmology' at Ff19v), but from Ff20 to Ff24, where the notes break off, he writes only on versos again. Keats headed the notes commencing Ff23v 'Sphlanchnology' and apparently completed his note-taking at Ff24v with the 'Structure of the Heart'. After Ff24v there are the 123 blank pages up to the point on Bf9r where the text from the back of the Notebook broke off.

It is important to state here that, though I believe the Notebook to have been rebound at some point, this distinctive layout is not the result of pages being disordered during rebinding.[30] There is an internal coherence to the arrangement and progression of the notes, immediately evident upon perusal, that rules out any possibility that this structure was accidentally imposed by a third party (as would be the case with a botched rebinding, for instance). I do not attempt to explain the more baffling aspects of the ordering of Keats' notes except to suggest that, though all the notes belong to the same lecture series, they were not all taken at the lecture theatre: Keats appears, on occasion, to have returned to his Notebook to annotate a set of notes already written.

30 The volume has 'Keats Anatomical Notebook' in gold lettering on the spine. It was part of the Dilke Collection bequeathed to Keats House, but Keats House has no extant records of having rebound it. Ken Page speculates (personal correspondence, 22 May 2014), and I concur, that this rebinding was probably arranged for by Sir Charles Dilke, at some point before the bequest to Keats House. I am indebted to Ken Page of Keats House for checking the Keats House records for the Dilke Collection for evidence of a possible rebinding of this Notebook.

The transcription in this edition starts from the back of Keats' medical Notebook: the first notes transcribed are therefore those of 'Lect$^{r}$ 4 Continued' at Bf1r, after a description of the contents of the inside back cover (Dilke's book plate and sketches of skulls). I chose to transcribe from the back because the text from the back of the Notebook follows a more obvious sequential pattern than the text from the front, and also presents fewer complexities of page layout. Starting from the back allows the reader to become familiar with the manner of Keats' note-taking and provides a more accessible introduction to the form and content of this text. It also offers a way forward sequentially through the lectures that Keats' notes at the front of the volume do not. Reading from the front, Keats' notes move to the back of the Notebook midway through 'Lect$^{r}$ 4'; the ordering of the notes means that proceeding sequentially through the folios has 'Lect$^{r}$ 4' preceding 'Lect$^{r}$ 1$^{st}$'; there are intervening notes on other material at Ff1v, Ff2v, and Ff3v; and once Keats resumed writing from the front at Ff4v ('Of Osteology') he had ceased to order his notes according to the chronology in which the lectures were delivered – an issue discussed in detail in Chapters 3 and 4. On occasion Keats' layout may seem incomprehensible, yet I have found that there is usually a pattern and logic to his sequencing. Accordingly, readers with the opportunity to accustom themselves to the manner of Keats' note-taking by perusing the less unusually ordered lectures from the back will gain a sense of the overarching method that exists even in apparent disorder. Additionally, Keats' notes from the front of the Notebook feature more marginalia and over-writing, and therefore the pages have a more intricate layout: in consequence, there is more editorial intervention in the text of these notes. Reading from the back allows readers to focus on Keats' notes without having to navigate the editorial interpositions within the body of the text that necessarily feature in the pages and notes with more marginalia and an intricate layout.

Within the text of Keats' notes – as already stated – editorial intervention has been kept to a minimum and is used almost exclusively to indicate Keats' emendations and cross-references, and to clarify page layout. The bulk of editorial annotation and commentary is in the footnotes. Some of these are concerned with aspects of layout that the edition does not reproduce visually. Others supply bibliographic information or help clarify cross-references made by Keats within his notes. Most of my annotations, however, offer contextual information on the medical notes. Many of these concern anatomical features, and here I was forced to confront an inconvenient aspect of medical history: many anatomical names and terms that were used by Keats remain current today, albeit with radically different meanings than in Keats' time. While the signifier remains the same, at some point between the early nineteenth century and the present day what it signifies has changed – therefore what Keats *meant* in writing a certain term may be quite different from what that term means today, and the term currently used for what he meant is often different from the one he *wrote*. For example, in Lecture 8 (misnumbered 'Lect^r 7') at Bf3r, Keats discusses 'Reticular Membrane'. In the early nineteenth century this meant any membrane or tissue in the human body that was 'interwoven like a net', and Keats' notes reflect this.[31] In modern usage, however, the term refers exclusively to a structure within the cochlea of the inner ear – and if the notes were read with this meaning in mind they would appear incomprehensible. On other occasions, Keats – writing in a hurry – makes mistakes: from what he writes it is clear that he meant to write something other than what he wrote. The most complicated instances result from a combination of these two scenarios: Keats makes a mistake in the term he *meant* to write, and the term he meant to write means something entirely different in modern medical usage. For example, at Ff17v Keats, listing the '[p]arts which pass through the different [f]oramina' of the skull, writes of 'The Foramina lacera'.[32] The early nineteenth century knew the 'Foramina Lacera' as '[a] pair of foramina in the basis of the cranium, through which the internal jugular veins, and the eighth pair and accessory nerves pass'; however, based on the structures Keats identifies as passing through it in his list, this is clearly not the foramen he meant.[33] He appears to have meant the opening now known as the superior orbital fissure, which Keats usually refers to in his notes as 'Lacera Orb. Sup.' or 'Lacera Orp. Sub.'[34] He does write about the 'Foramina lacera' – as understood by the early nineteenth century – later in this same list, but mistakenly calls it 'Foram. lacera basis cranii' there.[35] This term was used at that

31 *LM*, 758.
32 JKMN, Ff16v, Ff17v.
33 *LM*, 363.
34 JKMN, Ff12v, Ff14v, Ff13v.
35 JKMN, Ff17v.

time to refer to the aperture known as the jugular foramen in modern usage. 'Foramen lacerum', meanwhile, currently refers to a triangular hole at the base of the skull (which fills with cartilage after birth) first described in 1869.[36] This is a particularly convoluted case, but it is not a unique instance in Keats' notes. When any of these scenarios occur I have indicated as much in the footnotes and – where appropriate – provided a definition or additional information drawn principally from *Lexico-Medicum; or Medical Dictionary* (1822) and the *London Dissector* (1811), supplemented by the first and the current edition of Gray's *Anatomy* (1858 and 2015, respectively).

Where the context of a word in Keats' notes supplies sufficient locational information I have not attempted further clarification. The aim of these annotations is to provide enough contextual information to make Keats' medical notes comprehensible for a reader who does not have specialized medical knowledge, but they cannot and do not substitute for a trained knowledge of anatomy. I do not believe that specialist knowledge is necessary to understand, study, or appreciate this manuscript, but nor can I pretend that my annotations serve as a substitute to such in-depth knowledge. Notes are intended as signposts to assist understanding, pointing to sources of more detailed information and, where appropriate, to visual sources.

Before Henry Gray published the first edition of his *Anatomy Descriptive and Surgical* in 1858 illustrative anatomical diagrams in medical textbooks were not labelled on the page. Instead, illustrations were keyed to an index at the back of the book – an arrangement that was both impractical and inconvenient. Gray's *Anatomy* revolutionized medical publications by providing for the first time clear textual explanations for anatomical illustrations. Despite Henry Gray's *Anatomy* being published almost four decades after Keats' death, I refer readers to anatomical diagrams in this work rather than to earlier (and more obscure) nineteenth-century sources. In doing so, I have ascertained in each instance that the diagram presented in the first edition of Gray's *Anatomy* is compatible both with early nineteenth-century medical knowledge as well as the contents of Keats' notes (as far as this can be determined) by checking against contemporary reference material. Similarly, my rationale for

36 Michael Tauber, Harry R. van Loveran, George Jallo, Alberto Romano, and Jeffrey Keller, 'The Enigmatic Foramen Lacerum', *Neurosurgery* 44.2 (February 1999): 386–91.

referencing the first (1858) – rather than the modern (2015) – edition of Gray's *Anatomy* lies in the fact that medical knowledge, including knowledge of anatomy, has changed vastly in the last 150 years. The medical training that Keats received had far more in common with Henry Gray's medical world than with modern medicine.

Throughout the text of the edition, square brackets indicate editorial interventions. This includes bibliographic details, such as folio numbers, to point out pages left blank, or any other textual notes (for instance, to indicate the continuance of the notes of a single lecture across several pages). Conjectural readings are offered within square brackets and followed by a question mark, thus [?]. I have exercised caution in conjecturing readings: I have only done so when I'm sure that this is the word Keats intended. In more difficult instances, I have reproduced what I can read on the page, even if the sense behind the words/letters is not evident. Unless otherwise indicated, Keats' spellings, capitalization, punctuation, and spacing between words have been reproduced as found in manuscript. Keats was apt to run the words 'to be' together, so that they read 'tobe', but on occasion other words were also treated similarly: for instance, he has 'Bloodvessels' for 'Blood vessels' and 'Glandis' for 'Gland is' (both at Bf2r). In cases where words have been misspelled/misspaced or otherwise changed into forms not instantly recognizable I have offered an annotation for the first occurrence, but where the word intended is immediately clear to the reader – as, for instance, in Keats' habitual misspelling of 'absorption' as 'absorbtion', or his habit of adding an 'e' to the end of words (e.g. writing 'withe' for 'with' or 'bothe' for 'both') – I have refrained from additional intrusive commentary.

Where Keats' hand-writing is illegible I have inserted three plus signs, +++; two pipes, | |, with or without text between them, indicate lacunae in the text resulting from tears, stains, fading of ink, and so on. Keats' own insertions are indicated within curly brackets {}; his deletions are represented by strike-throughs; and his over-writing within pointed brackets, < >. Symbols within rounded brackets, thus (•), represent Keats' own annotations for his marginalia; numbers within rounded brackets, such as (1), represent the page numbers Keats gave some – but not all – of the pages. An asterisk or tilde within square brackets, [*] or [~], represent my editorial interventions to indicate the positioning of Keats' marginalia where Keats himself has not indicated their position relative to the main body of text.

Where Keats' marginalia change direction with relation to the page – i.e. on pages where some of his marginal notes are written with the page vertical in 'portrait' mode, and some with it in horizontal, 'landscape' mode – I have indicated textual direction by changing the font: marginalia in 'portrait' is in **bold font**, while that in 'landscape' is in *italic font*. Where necessary, two or more of these editorial symbols have been combined to accurately indicate the state of the text in manuscript. Page divisions in the medical Notebook are indicated in this edition by an em-dash at the centre of the page.

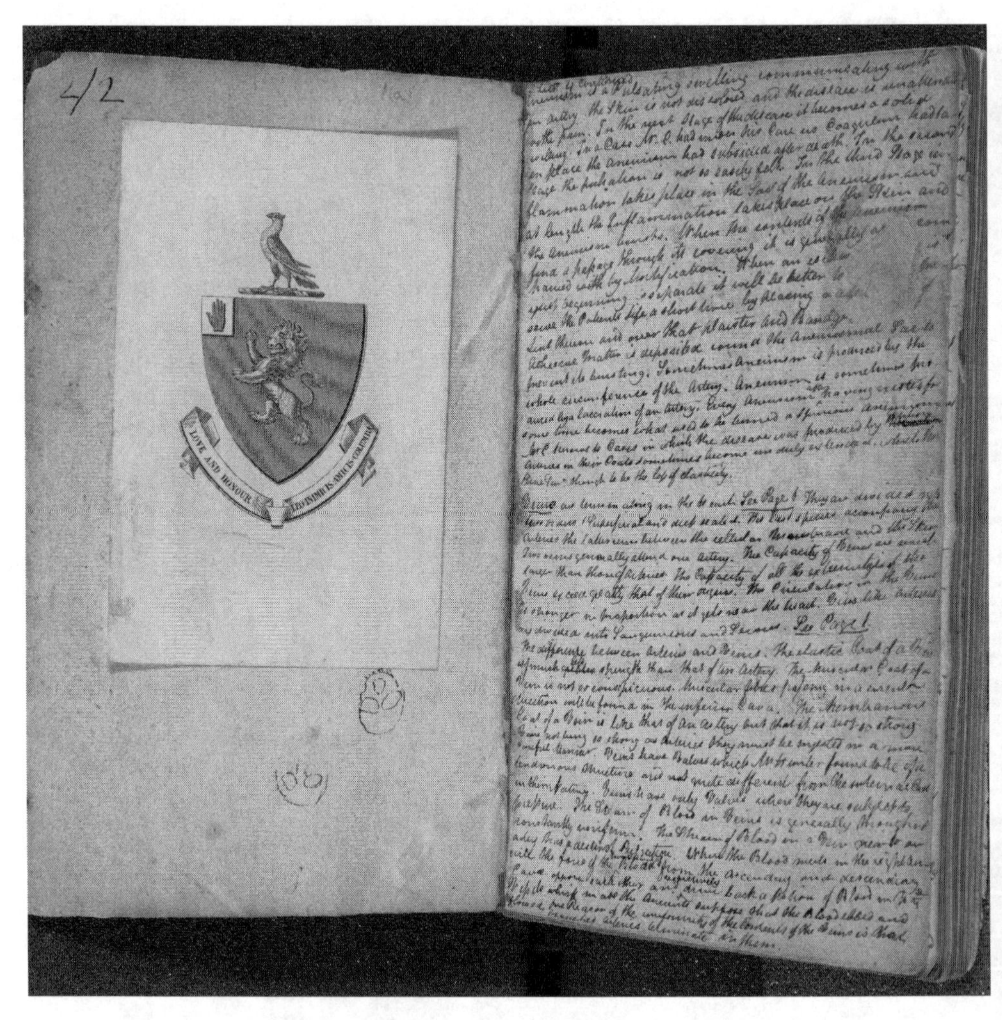


**Figure 1:** Inside back cover, featuring Sir Charles Dilke's bookplate and a pair of upside-down skulls, and Bf1r on which Keats has written his 'Lect$^{r}$ 4 Continued'. From 'John Keats' medical Notebook'. Image © City of London, Keats House, Hampstead.

# John Keats' Medical Notebook
## An Annotated Edition

**Key**

*Editorial emendations*

+++ text illegible

[?] editor's conjectural reading

| | lacuna in text (tears/stains, etc.)

[ ] editor's insertions

[*] and [~] editor's symbols to denote positioning of marginalia

[Bibliographic details supplied by the editor in square brackets].
All footnotes supplied by editor.
Unless otherwise stated, references to *GA* in the footnotes are to anatomical diagrams.

*Keats' emendations*

{} Keats' insertions

~~Keats~~ Keats' deletions

< > Keats' overwriting

Symbol within brackets, thus (•) Keats' own annotations for marginalia

Numbers within brackets, thus (1) Keats' page numbering

**Bold font** Keats' marginalia written with the page vertical (i.e. 'portrait' format)

*Italic font* Keats' marginalia written with the page horizontal (i.e. 'landscape' format)

[Inside back cover: see Figure 1]

2/2[1]
Dilke's book plate
[two (upside-down) drawings of skulls]

—

[Back folio 1 recto = Bf1r: see Figure 1]

Lectr 4 Continued

Aneurism is a Pulsating swelling communicating with an artery. The Skin is not discolored and the disease is unattended |w|ithe pain. In the next Stage of the disease it becomes a solid |s|welling. In a Case Mr C.[2] had under his Care no Coagulum had taken place the aneurism had subsided after death. In the second Stage the pulsation is not so easily felt. In the third Stage inflammation takes place in the Sac of the Aneurism and at length the Inflammation takes place on the Skin and the aneurism bursts. When the contents of the aneurism find a passage through its covering it is generally a| |companied ~~with~~

1 The purchase price of 2s. and 2d. is written in the top left corner in black ink in an unidentified hand.

2 Unless otherwise specified, by 'Mr C.' Keats always means his lecturer, the surgeon Astley Cooper (1768–1841). Cooper was apprenticed to his uncle William Cooper at Guy's Hospital but switched his apprenticeship to Henry Cline Senior of St Thomas' Hospital, who encouraged him to attend John Hunter's lectures. Cline became a close friend, and influenced Cooper with his democratic politics. In 1789 he appointed Cooper his Anatomy Demonstrator, and in 1791 invited him to share lecturing duties on his course on anatomy and surgery. Cooper was appointed surgeon to Guy's Hospital in 1800 and remained at that post till 1825. He was a popular lecturer and an outstanding operator, widely considered the best surgeon in Britain – his most famous surgery was the first successful application of an aortal ligature (1817). His many publications reflected his twin passions for anatomy and surgery, and a number of body parts bear his name (for example Cooper's ligaments in the breast). Cooper's overarching presence in Keats' time at Guy's Hospital is discussed throughout this book. For an excellent modern biography see Druin Burch, *Digging Up the Dead: The Life and Times of Astley Cooper, an Extraordinary Surgeon* (London: Chatto and Windus, 2007).

by Mortification. When an eschar[3] | | is just beginning to separate it will be better to | | preserve the Patients life a short time by placing a dossil[4] | | of Lint thereon and over that plaister and Band{a}ge. | | Adhesive matter is deposited round the Aneurismal Sac to prevent its bursting. Sometimes Aneurism is produced by the whole circumference of the Artery. Aneurism is sometimes produced by a laceration of an Artery. Every Aneurism {after} having existed for some time becomes what used to be termed a spurious Aneurism. Mr. C. knows 10 Cases in which the disease was produced by ~~+++~~ {Exertion}. Arteries in their Coats sometimes become un duly extended, which Mr Cline Sen$^{r}$[5] though[t] to be the loss of elasticity.

Veins are terminating in the Heart. See Page 1[6] They are divided into two orders. 1 Superficial and deep seated. The last species accompany the arteries the latter runs between the cellular Membrane and the Skin. Two veins generally attend one artery. The Capacity of Veins are much larger than those of arteries. The Capacity of all the extremit~~y~~{ies} of the Veins exceed greatly that of their origins. The Circulation in the Veins is stronger in proportion as it gets near the heart. Veins like arteries are divided into Sanguineous and Serous. See Page 1.

The difference between Arteries and Veins. The elastic Coat of a Vein is of much ~~greater~~ {less} strength than that of an Artery. The Muscular Coat of a Vein is not so conspicuous. Muscular fibres passing in a circular direction will be found in the inferior Cava. The Membranous Coat of a Vein is like that of an artery but that it is not so strong. Veins not being so strong as Arteries they must be injected in a more |c|areful Manner. Veins have valves which M$^{r}$ Hunter[7]

3 'A brown or black dry slough, resulting from the destruction of a living part' (*OED*).

4 'A plug of lint or rag for stopping a wound' (*OED*).

5 Henry Cline, Senior (1750–1827), was appointed surgeon to St Thomas' Hospital in 1784 and continued there until his retirement in 1812, when he was succeeded in the post by his son, also Henry Cline (d. 1820). A former student of John Hunter's, he taught Astley Cooper, and remained his friend and collaborator after the latter's appointment as surgeon to Guy's. A democrat, Cline Snr numbered among his friends the reformers John Thelwall and John Horne Tooke. He was a skilled surgeon and a man of great integrity, well-loved by students and patients alike. In 1805 he published a book *On the form of Animals*.

6 Ff1v, which Keats numbered as '1'.

7 John Hunter (1728–1793), surgeon and anatomist, began his career as assistant

found tobe[8] of a tendonous structure and ~~not~~ quite different from the internal Coat in their Nature. Veins have only Valves where they are subject to pressure. The Stream of Blood in Veins is generally throughout constantly uniform. The Stream of Blood in a Vein near to an artery has a distinct Pulsation. Where the Blood meets in the right auricle the force of the {two streams of} Blood from the ascending and descending Cavae oppose each other and {respectively} drive back a po[r]tion of Blood in to $y^e$ Vessels which made the Ancients suppose that the Blood ebbed and flowed.[9] One Reason of the uniformity of the Contents of the Veins is that branched arteries terminate in them.

—

[Bf1v]

Lect$^r$ 5 Diseases of Veins. The Veins of old Persons are apt to become varicose[10] and this where the greatest column of Blood – the Valves loosing their power is the cause of the disease. The Blood by this

to his elder brother William (also a surgeon: see n23), before being appointed surgeon to St George's Hospital in 1758. In 1760 he accepted a commission with the army as a staff surgeon, seeing action in Portugal during the Seven Years' War. Hunter's interests encompassed comparative anatomy and physiology, and his reputation as an experimental anatomist brought rapid election as a Fellow of the Royal Society in 1767 (his key research publications were then still in the future). He was appointed Surgeon-General to the Army (1770), published *A Treatise on the Natural History of Teeth* (1771), and became Surgeon-Extraordinary to George III (1776). His other major publications include *A Treatise on the Venereal Disease* (1786), *Observations on Certain Parts of the Animal Oeconomy* (1786), and *A Treatise on the Blood, Inflammation, and Gun-Shot Wounds* (1794; for more on this work see Chapter 3). His pupils included many luminaries of nineteenth-century medicine and surgery: Edward Jenner, William Blizard, John Abernethy, Henry Cline Senior, Anthony Carlisle, and Astley Cooper, all of whom became protectors of his legacy and applied his precepts in their own practice. Hunter's influence on British medicine – especially surgery and anatomy – is impossible to overstate, and he remains a towering figure in the history of anatomical studies.

8 For 'to be'. Keats frequently ran these words together, resulting – as above – in 'tobe' and, unless otherwise indicated, his original spelling, punctuation, and spacing have been retained throughout this edition.

9 See *GA*, 630 for a diagram of the Right Auricle of the Heart.

10 'Of veins: Unnaturally swollen or dilated' (*OED*).

Means is not kept from gravitating to y$^{e}$ foot the Consequences are Scabrous[11] Skin and Ulcers. The remedy Pressure By Rollers. To the Cuticle, Lotions as Lime Water and Sp. Vini[12] by this Means you diminish the Size of the Exha|lan|ts.[13] The Ung$^{ts}$[14] Hyd. Nit. Ung$^{t}$ Hy$^{d}$. Nit. oxy$^{d}$. may be [then?] | | used. This is entirely a local complaint therefore the | | Constitution should not be weakened by Purges on | | the contrary {it} should be nourished. ~~Ulcers have been~~ | | It has been advised and practised to cure Ulcer by tying the Vein but as this is extremely dangerous it is now disused. If the Vein should burst, the Patient should be placed in a recumbent posture and a roller applied.

The Aneurismal Varix produced by pricking an Artery through a Vein. The Lancet[15] is pushed through the Median Vein and punctures the Brachial Artery.[16] In a Week or ten Da|ys| the Vein begins to enlarge and pulsates like an Aneurism. If you make pressure above on the Artery and below on the Vein it will disappear. It is fed both ~~with~~ {by} Artery and Vein. There is a constant hissing noise The Brachial artery becom|es| twice its natural size – the Veins are not enlarged. The reaso|n| of the Enlargement of the Arteries is that ~~a fresh unusual stream of Blood is~~ the Blood is transmitted with unusual facility. Treatment. Bandage. No Operation as the disease seldom becom|es| of that consequence. The plan to be pursued after an Artery being pricked is first making pressure in hope of adhesion. If you do not succeed and a pu[l]sating swelling appears in the Cellular Membrane an Operation ~~to~~ will be necessary – this tying the Brachial above the Elbow upon the inner side of the Biceps. The most general Varix is diffused there is however a Species which is local and forms a Sac on the Vein like an a|ne[u]|rismal Swelling.

—

11 'Rough with minute points or knobs, as distinguished from unevenness of surface: esp. ... *Physiology*' (*OED*).

12 Probably ethyl alcohol.

13 An exhalant vessel or organ is 'one that transfuses or conveys (blood, etc.) in minute quantities' (*OED*).

14 Unguents, plural of unguent, meaning 'an ointment or salve' (*OED*).

15 'A surgical instrument ... usually with two edges and a point like a lance' (*OED*).

16 Both blood vessels are in the arm.

[Bf2r]

Absorption is a process which performs 3 Offices 1[st] Removal of Blood. This done by taking foo[d] the nutritive part of wh|[ich]| is removed by the absorbent vessels and poured in the form of Chyle[17] into the Mass of Blood. See page 1.[18] A change is constantly going on in the Body during its growth. Those Fluids which cease to be useful are taken up by the absorbents. They take the Cour|[se]| of the Veins and are divided into superficial and deepseated – there are generally two absorbents to one artery. They arise from different parts. 1[st] Interior of the Intestines when they arrive at the outer side of these they divide into numerous Branches filled with Chyle. These are called the Lacteals, they do not differ from other Absorbents 2[nd] From the surface of the Skin the whole of which is loaded with Absorbents 3[rd] From the cellular Membrane into the network of which a fluid is exhaled, which is taken up by Absorbents. 4[th] From all the larger Cavaties of the Body as Peritoneum Pleura &c[19] 5 From the interior of the excretory ductes of Glands. They have two terminations Those of the left Side ~~the greatest part~~ from the Abdomen Organs of generation principal part of the Chest, left Arm left size[20] of the head and Neck and lower extremities. On the right side are from the right side of the head and Neck the right Arm the right lung and part of the liver. Absorbent Vessels may be traced into Veins. In the teeth and bone they arise from Bloodvessels.
Lect[r] 6
Absorbents. The Absorbent Vessels are extremely thin, yet anatomists have given them two Coats. When the Thoracic duct[21] is enlarged from disease it is said that Muscular fibres may be seen – But it is proved that they are muscular by the Contents of an abso[r]bent

17 '[T]he white milky fluid formed by the action of the pancreatic juice and the bile on the chyme, and contained in the lymphatics of the intestines' (*OED*). *EB* defines it as 'lymph laden with fat'.

18 See n6.

19 A list – Keats has neglected to use commas.

20 For 'side'.

21 'The THORACIC DUCT may be seen passing from the abdomen into the thorax, between the aorta and the right crus of the diaphragm' (*LD*, 41). In anatomy, the term 'crus' is applied to parts appearing in pairs or sets and having some resemblance to legs. Diagram at *GA*, 427.

Vessel being emptied at the time that pressure is made upon it & the Capacity of increase of Action in them which may be done by Stimulants. They are able by their power to burst themselves. The inner coat resembles that of a Vein but that it is much stronger. There are {~~sometimes~~} Valves in the Thoracic duct and when found they are ~~two~~ found in pairs. They differ from the Veins in having Valves generally diffused with the exception perhaps of those of y$^{e}$ Brain. If an Absorbent have been inflamed, after death it will appear red. Mr. C. has never seen their Vasa Vasorum.[22] They differ from the Veins in having Glands. The Glandis generally an oval form firm texture, brown color and varying in size from a pin's head to the end of the little finger. They are highly vascular, they have Cells which on being pressed gives out a milky fluid. Those Absorbents which pass from a Gland are called the Vasa efferentia, those to the Gland the Vasa afferentia and those going over the Vasa circuita

—

[Bf2v]

The Absorbed fluid is taken by the Vasa circuita when the Gland is diseased. The Absorbents are sometimes enlarged taking a cel[lu]lar Appearance. Functions and Diseases. Till within these few Years that they were considered a kind of Veins. From the white fluid exuding from them they were called Lymphatics. We are indebted to D$^{r}$ and M$^{r}$ J. Hunter[23] for what we know concerning these Vessels. One of the Experiments of M$^{r}$ J. Hunter was tying the biliary duct of a dog, the absorbent Vessels of the liver of which was found on examination

22 Nutrient blood-vessels that supply the walls of large blood-vessels, found in both arteries and veins.

23 'D$^{r}$ … Hunter' is a reference to William Hunter (1718–83), physician, surgeon, anatomist, and man-midwife, appointed Physician-Extraordinary to the Queen in 1762. Hunter commenced his anatomical lectures accompanied by demonstrations for medical students in 1746; he continued these for the rest of his life, eventually founding (1767) the anatomical school at Great Windmill Street. He had an interest in comparative anatomy, was a Fellow of the Royal Society, and is credited with having established the anatomy of the gravid (i.e. pregnant) uterus in humans and the relationship between the maternal and foetal blood systems in the placenta. He frequently collaborated with his younger brother John over the course of their careers: for more on John Hunter see n7.

tobe gorged with bile. This clearly proves them absorbents. They do not only absorb fluids but also the solids of ye Body. But it is tobe enquired ~~when they~~ whether the solid parts do not undergo solution before passing into the Absorbent Vessels. No doubt. In a patient upon whom Mr Cline was going to operate for Cataract the point of the Knife (which accidentally was broken off and remained in the Cornea) was absorbed. The Bases of the Teeth are absorbed. Carbon is not soluble in the animal fluids and therefore the Marks of tattooing are never removed. The Absorbents are continually at Work. They pour out more by the extreme Vessels than the Abs[or]ptions take up, and in this way is accomplished the growth of the Body – In the Adult the action of the absorbents and arteries is equal. In age the Absorbents take away more than the Arteries can renew and thus the decrease of ye Body. It has been supposed that Absorption took place on the surface of ye Body but this is greatly doubted unless under friction. The fluids contained in ye Absorbents are Chyle and Lymph[24] and nearly resembles Blood in its Nature. See Page 2nd.[25] There is a great difference between Vegetable and Animal a portion of each put into Phials the fi[r]st does not become putrid for some Weeks, the latter does so in a few hours. This was first noticed by Dr Marcet.[26] The Structure made up of animal Chyle as the Muscle of a dog will undergo decomposition much faster than the Structure formed from Vegetable Chyle as that of the Sheep. Analysis. Sp. G.[27] from 1021 to 1022. Contains 892 parts of Water Albumen[28] 93. fibrin[29]

24 'A colourless alkaline fluid, derived from various tissues and organs of the body, resembling blood but containing no red corpuscles' (*OED*).

25 Ff2v, which Keats numbered 2.

26 Alexander John Gaspard Marcet (1770–1822), physician and experimental chemist of high repute, who served as physician to Guy's Hospital (1804–19). His systematic study of urinary calculi led to the identification of a new type, composed of xanthic oxide. He helped popularize his collaborator Jöns Jacob Berzelius's work on animal chemistry. From 1807 till his retirement, Marcet – along with his colleagues William Babington and William Allen – offered lecture courses on chemistry accompanied with practical demonstrations; Keats almost certainly attended at least one of these courses.

27 Abbreviation for 'Specific Gravity'.

28 Albumen, also spelled albumin, is a type of water-soluble protein and can, in various forms, be found in blood serum, milk, egg whites, and plant seeds.

29 In the early nineteenth century the term was interchangeable with 'coagulable lymph', i.e. the whitish substance necessary for blood to coagulate.

8 Salts 7. Vegetable Chyle 936 Water. 50 Albumen. 6 Fibrin 8 Salts. The Proportion of solid Matter. Animal 95 parts in a thousand vegetable 78. The Lymph coagulates as the Chyle and separates into 2 parts Serum and Crassamentum.[30] The difference between Lymph and Chyle is that in the Chyle has alone white particles. Lect^r 6. The Glands are supposed to be assimilating Organs. A Poison in passing through a Gland is so altered that it does not affect the Glands beyong.[31] All except oily substances undergo a remarkable change on being received into the Body.

—

[Bf3r]

In promoting the action of the Absorbent Vessels, Mercury is the best means tobe employed – Pressure also is very effectual. All Medicines producing Nausea promote Absorbtion as Digitalis, Antimony &c When purgatives are given in proportion as there is excretion, the Absorbents increase the action. Upon this principle Elaterium[32] is used in dropsy[33] Stimulants will produce Absorbtion. A Node will best be removed by a Blister: acting at the same time upon the Constitution with Mercury – Friction is very effectual. M^r Grosvenor's[34] Practice has been a highly useful One. At the same time that this Gentleman employs friction he directs the Joint to be moved about. Diseases. The Absorbents are very frequently diseased. In Age their Coats become opaque and white which occasions a same state as in the Arteries. People of warm Climates have very large absorbents – in them the thoracic duct is twice or thrice the size as that of an European. They are liable to disease from irritation or absorbtion of Poisons. When inflamed they will

30 'The solid jelly-like part of coagulated blood, consisting of fibrin with blood-corpuscles entangled in it; the clot, coagulum' (*OED*).

31 For 'beyond'.

32 A purgative and emetic composed from the extract of the wild, or squirting cucumber; 'the most powerful cathartic in the whole materia medica' (*LM*, 570).

33 'A preternatural collection of serous or watery fluid in the cellular substance, or different cavities of the body' (*LM*, 440).

34 John Grosvenor (1742–1823), surgeon and, from 1795, editor of the *Oxford Journal*. He enjoyed an immense practice in Oxford and the surrounding areas and was especially successful in treating stiff and diseased joints by massage, a technique he first used with success on his own diseased knee.

sometimes suppurate – in the lower extremities scarcely ever in the upper – inthe Glands and not in the Vessels. The Poison of Venus[35] will by absorbtion inflame the absorbent Gland though it does not affect the Vessel by which it is conveyed. The Absorbent Vessels leading from a Cancer to an absorbent Gland should be removed. They sometimes undergo ossification. Mr— met with a Thoracic ductin[36] this state. ~~The Can~~ The thoracic duct is sometimes obliterated in Scrophula.[37] The glands are becoming enlarged on irritation and Poisonous substances being absorbed. The Poison of Scrophula is of a curdly nature and does not become organized which may be seen under the adhesion of a Gland enlarged by Scrophula. The Absorbents of the Mesentery[38] and the Bronchi[39] have frequently large deposits of Earth.

(Reticular[40] Membrane)

Lect[r] 7. It has been said that the reticular Membrane is not sensible but this is evidently a fallacious opinion and which any operator must find to be so. The reticular Membrane must be considered a secreting Membrane the operation of which is by exhalents. It sometimes forms an extended Membrane as the Tunica Vaginalis, Peritoneum, Pleura Pericardium &c. When a Membrane becomes extended a Cavity is produced. The reticular Membrane enters into the composition of the Body so as to unite the different parts and the parts themselves are conglomerated by it. It is found upon Chemical Examination that it consists of Gelatine.[41] The cells of the Membrane

35 Possibly a reference to either syphilis or gonorrhoea. The early nineteenth century was unsure if these were different stages of the same ailment or different diseases, though the evidence suggests that Astley Cooper believed the latter.

36 For 'Thoracic duct in'.

37 'A constitutional disease characterized mainly by chronic enlargement and degeneration of the lymphatic glands' (*OED*).

38 Usually refers to the tissues that attach the small intestines to the back of the abdominal wall. See *GA*, 599.

39 Passages in the respiratory system conducting air into the lungs. In the diagram at *GA*, 649 they are labelled 'Bronchial Tubes'.

40 'Interwoven like a net' (*LM*, 758). In the early nineteenth century, any membrane with an interwoven structure. In contemporary use, found in the cochlea of the inner ear.

41 'The substance which is the basis of the jellies into which certain animal tissues

all communicate freely with each other. This is seen in Anasarca.[42] This is the reason why an oedematous[43] swelling is the first swelling of dropsy. This may be the result of some organic disease. Diseases of the Heart, Liver, &c increases the serous[44] secretions. The Water becomes effused because the Blood does not find itself a way by the Veins by which a congestion is thrown upon the Artery the consequence of which an increased action of the Exhalents. The fluid formed in Dropsy is more watery than serum.

—

[Bf3v]

When Water is collected in the lower extremities if the constitution be strong enough inflammation will take place and ulceration will be the consequence, but if it be weak Mortification will take place. In these cases where the Surgeon would assist Nature by making small punctures, the Punctures should not be made too distant from the Heart as upon the inner side of the Thigh and the Scrotum. The Surgeon should exercise his Judgment in ascertaining whether he shall accelerate mortification by puncturing. Air is sometimes extravasated[45] and this in two modes one by secretion in the reticular membrane itself – Emphysema[46] ~~the i~~ is more commonly produced in cases of injured Ribs where the Lungs have been hurt. Emphysema in itself does not produce any ill effects in a few days the Air becomes absorbed. The Extravasation of Air proves the communication between the different parts of the ~~body~~ {reticular membrane}. Blood is sometimes extravasated and appears to undergo a process of solution in the Serum. This is called Echymosis. The fatty Membrane

(skin, tendons, ligaments, the matrix of bones, etc.) are converted when treated with hot water for some time' (*OED*).

42 A type of dropsy. See *LM*, 49–51 for more.

43 'Of the nature of oedema', with an 'oedema' defined as '[o]riginally: †a fluid-filled tumour or swelling (*obsolete*). In later use: the localized or generalized accumulation of excessive fluid in tissues or body cavities' (*OED*).

44 'Of or pertaining to serum; consisting of or containing serum; of the nature of serum. *Pathology.* Involving or characterized by an effusion of serum. *Anatomy.* Secreting or moistened with serum, as a membrane' (*OED*).

45 Let out or flows out.

46 The condition of air being present in tissue or body cavities where it is not normally present.

is composed of distinct Cells. Fat is found on the less moveable parts of the Body. It is found in the Posterior part of y$^e$ Body more than the Anterior with the exception of the Abdomen. The Cellular Membrane when loaded with Adeps[47] is considerably vascular. Every cell of fat may be considered as a little gland in which Arteries terminate of deposit the Adeps. There is no means of its being removed but by Absorbtion. Fat is not in a solid but in a fluid State in the living Body and this is the reason why steatomatous[48] swellings fluctuate. In some Animals it is fluid after death as in the whale. The Uses of fat are to provide soft ~~parts~~ {beds} for delicate Structures and to secrete nourishment for Animals when by illness or situation they cannot take food. Fat by its accumulations sometimes produces disease. Lect$^r$ 8. Nervous System.

The external part of the Dura Mater[49] is rough and vascular, the inside is smooth and secretes a fluid to lubricate the surface of y$^e$ brain. Its Processes support different portions of y$^e$ Brain. It serves the purpose of an external periosteum[50] – serves to keep the brain from press|ure| Its Sinuses[51] return the Blood from y$^e$ brain. The ~~Pia Mater~~ {Tunica Aracnoidea}[52] is intimately connected with the ~~Arachnoi~~ | | {Pia Mat} dea[53] in some particular parts so as to lead to the opinion of their being two laminæ[54] of the same sort. It is not vascular. The Pia mater is y$^e$ most vascular of all y$^e$ Membranes. Its vessels are derived from 2 Sources – The internal Carotid and the basilary.[55] The Arteries differ in their structure from those in other parts, they

—

47 'Animal fat; lard. In early use also: †adipose tissue' (*OED*).

48 Resembling or related to a 'steatoma': '[a]n encysted fatty tumour' (*OED*).

49 'The dura mater is a thick and inelastic fibrous membrane' (*GA*, 447) which surrounds the brain and spinal cord.

50 'A close and dense network of compact blood vessels, which ramify in a fibrous membrane, is termed the periosteum' (*GA*, 3).

51 In this instance, receptacles for blood.

52 The arachnoid membrane is a 'thin membrane of the brain, without vessels and nerves, situated between the dura and the pia mater, and surrounding the cerebrum, cerebellum, medulla oblongata, and medulla spinalis' (*LM*, 73).

53 For 'Pia Mater', which is located beneath the arachnoid membrane, and separated from it by the sub-arachnoid space.

54 Plural for 'lamina': '[a] thin layer of bone, membrane or other structure' (*OED*).

55 Both are arteries.

[Bf4r]

have no elastic coats, which prevents ~~the~~ a superabundant circulation in the Brain. It has of late been thought the the Convolutions of the Cerebrum expand on the accumulation of Water. The Medullary substance seems tobe composed of fibres. – The ventricles differ from other Cavaties in that in all others vapor is found before it has been condensed but in the recent and warm Brain Water is discovered. The Medulla oblongata[56] is formed of 4 Columns two from the Cerebrum and ~~2~~ 2 from the Cerebellum. From y$^{e}$ Medulla Oblonga[ta] proceeds the Medulla Spinalis.[57] The Spinal Marrow is composed of 2 Columns – of late it has been {said to have been} discovered that these at the upper part cross each other. The Spinal Marrow is enclosed in Membranes answering to those of y$^{e}$ Brain. There is a communication under the Dura Mater down to the extremity of y$^{e}$ Spinal Marrow. In this Canal a watery fluid is secreted and in Spina Bifida[58] it here accumulates. Bifid Spine occurs at the junction of y$^{e}$ Sacrum[59] with y$^{e}$ vertebrae. If this disease be left to itself it enlarges to an enormous size and draws out the nerves from the Medulla Spinalis. The Tumor has a Pulsation communicated {to} it from y$^{e}$ Brain. The fluid it contains is completely limpid.

The Mode of Treatment is either palliative or radical Mr C treated one Case like a Hernia. Pressure is salutary and when it has been long applied it cannot be dispensed with. No hope of Cure from this ~~par~~ practice. M$^{r}$ C. has never seen a patient continue to live without pressure. The other mode is puncturing with a Needle – M$^{r}$ C. advises not using the Lancet for that purpose. M$^{r}$ C. the intervals being one or two days for seven days without inflammation (This disease is generally connected with Hydrocephalus)![60] Inflammation was at length produced and the opening closed by adhesion. The Arteries of the Spinal Marrow are derived from the Vertebral. There is a sinus Venosus on each side of the Spinal Marrow which returns the blood,

56 Located in the brain stem, it is the cone-shaped mass of nerve cells responsible for involuntary functions.

57 Spinal cord.

58 'A tumour upon the spine of new-born children immediately about the lower vertebræ of the loins, and upper parts of the sacrum' (*LM*, 332).

59 A bone of the pelvis: diagrams at *GA*, 13–14.

60 'Dropsy of the brain. Dropsy of the head' (*LM*, 433).

it passes out through the 7$^{th}$ Cervical Vertebra into the Sub-clavian.[61] The Nerves of each side of the Brain are supposed to arise from the part in which they are discover, this opinion arises from the Symptoms in injuries of y$^{e}$ Cranium. If there be any elasticity in Nerves it is tobe imputed to the cellular Membrane – which enters into their Structure. Nerves are composed of numerous Cords this is still the Case in the smallest. They take a serpentine direction. They arise by numerous branches from the Substance of y$^{e}$ Brain – there is however a contrary opinion extant. The Dura Mater does not accompany the Nerves to any distance – they are however covered with Pia Mater. The Nerves frequently meet and form a Plexus:[62] Nerves also form Ganglions[63] – these are found to differ in Structure from Nerve – they are much more solid – are of a light brown Color. The interior of a Ganglion is not of a fibrous Structure.

—

[Bf4v: see Figure 2]

Lect$^{r}$ 10. Physiology of the Nervous System. The 1$^{st}$ office is that of Sensation, it is an impression made on the Extremities of the Nerves conveyed to the Brain. This is proved by the effects of dividing a Nerve. After a time the sensation of a Nerve will return as it unites – in a small nerves 2 or 3 Months will be required for its reunion – 12 Months for a large one. It will require more than 8 Months for the Suborbitary[64] to be restored to organization. ~~Thos~~ The Patriot K.[65]

61 Artery.

62 '[T]he union of two or more nerves' (*LM*, 701).

63 'In anatomy ... a natural knot-like enlargement, in the course of a nerve' (*LM*, 374).

64 Probably the infraorbital nerve, which runs along the lower edge of the orbits (sub-orbit?), but possibly the supraorbital nerve.

65 Tadeusz Kościuszko (1746–1817), Polish army officer and statesman of international repute, also known as as 'Thaddeus Kosciusko'. He first gained recognition for his participation in the American War of Independence, by the end of which he was made a Brigadier-General in the US Army and given American citizenship. His subsequent leadership of nationalist and liberal forces during the insurrections in Poland (1794) secured his fame, and his refusal to compromise his liberal principles when threatened with exile made him a hero for those – such as Keats and Leigh Hunt – who espoused liberal politics. Keats left some space after the words 'The Patriot K.' in the manuscript.

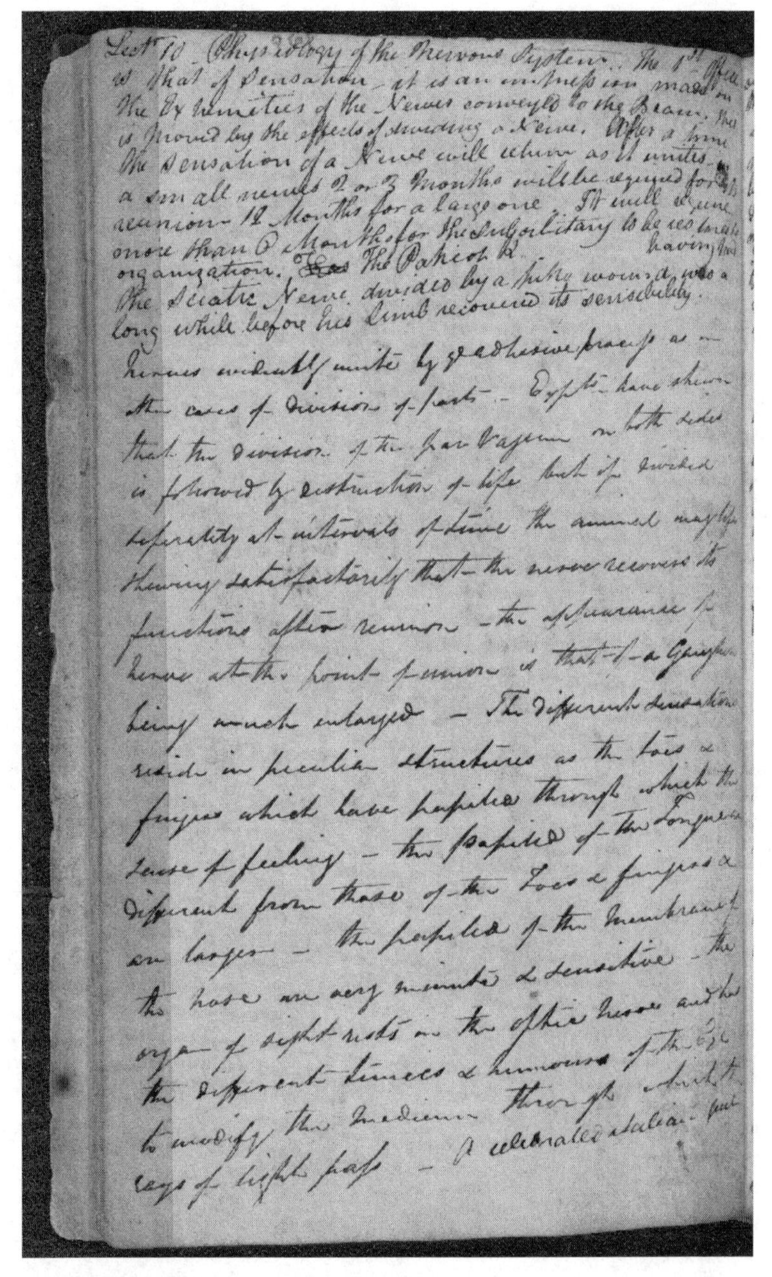

**Figure 2:** Bf4v, 'Lect$^{r}$ 10', which features 'the Patriot K.' (nine lines down from the top) as well as an apparently different hand in the lower two-thirds of the page. From 'John Keats' medical Notebook'. Image © City of London, Keats House, Hampstead.

having had the Sciatic Nerve[66] divided by a pike wound was a long while before his limb recovered its sensibility.
Nerves evidently unite by y$^{e}$adhesive process as in other cases of division of parts.– Exp$^{ts}$[67] have shown that the division of the par Vagum[68] on both sides is followed by destruction of life but if divided separately at intervals of time the animal may life showing satisfactorily that the nerve recovers its functions after reunion – the appearance of Nerves at the point of union is that of a Ganglion being much enlarged – The different sensations reside in peculiar structures as the toes & fingers which have papiliæ[69] through which the sense of feeling – the papilliæ of the Tongue[70] are different from those of the Toes & fingers & are larger – the papiliæ of the Membrane of the nose are very minute and sensitive – the organ of sight rests in the optic nerve and has the different tunics & humours of the Eye to modify the Medium through which the rays of light pass – A celebrated italian[71] put
[Continued at Bf5r]

—

[Bf5r]

out the Eyes of a Bat and turned it loose into a Room and found that it did not strike itself against the Parieties.[72] In irritation made in the middle of a Nerve the Sensation is felt at its extremity sometimes at its origin. The Sensation will sometimes be conveyed to the Brain

66 'A branch of a nerve of the lower extremity, formed by the union of the lumbar and sacral nerves' (*LM*, 792); diagram at *GA*, 527.
67 Abbreviation for 'experiments'.
68 The vagus or the pneumogastric nerve – also called cranial nerve X – which mediates parasympathetic control of the heart, lungs, and digestive tract.
69 Plural of 'papilla': '[a] small nipple-like protuberance on or in a part or organ of the body' (*OED*).
70 *GA*, 548.
71 Lazzaro Spallanzani (1729–99), an Italian physiologist best known for his experimental contributions to the study of animal reproduction. He also conducted extensive experiments with bats and concluded that they used some other sense than sight to navigate in darkness.
72 Parietes = paries: '[t]he wall of an organ, structure or cavity of the body' (*OED*).

and thence to the Extremities. The Sensation of the foot being asleep is in consequence of pressure made on the Sciatic Nerve. Sensation returning. Pins and Needles. Injuries may happen so quickly that sensation has no time to be communicated. The Pain is proportioned to the degree of quickness o~~f~~{r} slowness of Wounds being inflicted. The Nerves were once supposed to assist in the nourishment of ye Body – a limb will not increase if the Nerves be destroyed – yet the Foetus will continue to grow without Brain. Mr C believes that ye Nerves support the organization of the Body, but do not directly afford it nourishment. Volition is the contrary of Sensation it proceeds from the internal to external parts. It does not reside entirely in the Brain but partly in ye spinal Marrow which is seen in the Behaviour of a Frog after having been guillioteened.
Of Involuntary Powers. They are supported by the nervous System and do not depend upon ye Brain. Of late an opinion has been held that involuntary Action depended upon the Spinal Marrow. Le Gallois[73] injured the spinal Marrow in different parts and found in the different parts a deadening of the organs which received Nerves from them. If you destroy the Spinal Marrow too suddenly the Shock will occasion immediate death. The Action of ye Heart will continue after ye destruction of ye Spinal Marrow, Mr C. believes that the powers of parts are supported neither by ye Brain nor the M.S.[74] {but} by their particular Nerves. <u>Sympathy</u>. By this the Vital Principle is chiefly supported. The function of breathing is a sympathetic action – from irritation produced on the beginning of ye Air Tube affects yeAbdominal Muscles and produces coughing. Sneezing is an instance of complicated sympathy. We need not say any thing about the sympathy between the Breast and ye uterus. Upon this most of ye diseases of the Body depend. In diseases Medical Men guess, if they cannot ascertain a disease they call it nervous. They are often disordered in function, and anatomy cannot discover a corresponding breach of Structure. They are sometimes subject to tumours – Tic dol~~o~~{eu}reux.[75] Mr C. has seen but one dissection of

73 Julien Jean César Legallois (1770–1814), a pioneering French vivisectionist whose work helped define, identify, and correlate the neurological centres that control specific functions of the body.

74 For 'Medulla Spinalis' = spinal cord.

75 Tic douloureux = trigeminal neuralgia, characterized by brief – often unpredictable – attacks of severe pain along the trigeminal nerve.

this disease – the nerve on the affected side was slightly smaller than that on ye other. there is no inflammation. It is a disease in which the power of the Nerve is diminished, being therefore directly opposite to inflammation. In Palsy[76] no difference with respect to structure can be discovered – some say they are on ye affected side rather smaller. Volition is sometimes present while sensation is destroyed. In a Gentleman who had lost sensation and yet had powers of Volition, it was observed that he could grasp and hold a substan|ce| while his whole attention was directed thereto, but on his turning to a fresh occupation the substance dropped.

—

[Bf5v]

It is supposed that Ganglia are giving power to Nerves which give involuntary Action. The opinion of late years entertained concerning the Cause of nervous energy was started by Mr J. Hunter. He examined ye Body of a Gymnotus Electricus[77] he found it provided with abundance of Nerves {sufficient} to account for its electric properties. From this he inferred that the Nerves were conductors of electric fluid. ~~Cavallo~~ {Galvano}[78] found that a action of ye ner|ve| was produced by applying Metal thereto. The present opinion therefore is that a fluid, like that of the electric is secreted in ye brain which is thence communicated along the Nerves. Lectr 11. Muscles. They are fibrous ~~M~~ Structures endowed with contractile Power during {life}. Their number ~~now~~ {near} 500. Both extremities of a Muscle sometimes move their respective Attachments. The fibres are taking very different directions to their Tendons. A Muscle is called a half penniform when the Tendon is situated at one side. Sometimes the Tendon is between 2 sets of fibres and is called a Penniform. Sometimes there are several Tendons and the fibres pass with the same obliquity as in the half penniform and is called the

76 'Paralysis or paresis (weakness) of all or part of the body, sometimes with tremor; an instance of this. In earlier use, frequently with *the*. Now chiefly with distinguishing word' (*OED*).

77 The electric eel. Also known as *Electrophorus electricus*, of the family Gymnotidae.

78 Luigi Galvani (1737–98) investigated the nature and effects of electricity on animal tissues.

complex penniform. Where the fibres pass in the same directions of the Tendon and then the Muscles are called Recti. When the Fibres pass in a circular the Muscle is called sphincter. Mucles are named from 3 Circumstances. 1st Form as Biceps and Triceps. ~~2nd From~~ Digastric 2 From their Uses as Flexor, Extensor &c 3 in Consequence of attachment as Sterno Clido mastoideus. Structure. They are composed of fibres disposed ~~of~~ in Bundles – there is great Similarity between a Muscles and a Nerve. ~~the~~ The red color is not an essential to the action of Muscles. The Arteries distributed to them are very Minute and numerous – the arteries have corresponding Veins. Absorbent Vessels cannot be injected in Muscle except in the diaphragm and upon the Heart, but that they have absorbent po|w|er is shown from ulceration. With regard to Nerves in Musc|le| they are like the Arteries and Veins extremely minute. Its sensibility therefore is not exceedingly acute. It has been suppose|ed| that Muscular fibre was hollow and that when the Muscle was in action by being emptied and filled with Blood.

Tendon. Is very different from Muscle – it is inelastic and possesses a Silvery appearance. Different in chemical Comp[79] from Muscles. The whole of a Tendon may be converted to Gelatine. It is very little vascular and on this account possesses the least living power and hence wounds in these Parts are so extremely dangerous. Lock Jaw[80] is frequently the result of injuries in these Structures. For this reason it is extremely dangerous to amputate above the wrist joint. Tetanus is frequently arising from lacerated wounds of the finger.

—

[Bf6r]

Absorbents have never been injected in Tendon: still they have absorben|t| Powers. Nerves exist in them so sparingly that it is doubted whether the[y] possess at all Sensibility. The Membrane which covers the Tendon possesses great Sensibility. The interior of Tendons in a State of Inflammation possesses feeling. Tendon is extremely strong – muscular fibre will be torn through before the ~~ten~~ Tendon will give

79 Abbreviation for 'composition'.

80 Also called tetanus: an infection caused by the bacillus *Clostridium tetani*, characterized by rigidity and muscular spasms. The muscles of the jaw are almost invariably affected, hence the name lockjaw.

way. Aponeurosis[81] of Fasciæ.[82] A very strong one the Fasciæ lata connected with the Tensor Vaginæ Femoris. Fascia is a tendonous inelastic structure, Membrane is elastic. The use of Fasciæ is to bind down Muscles together giving them thereby additional Strength. Saculus mucosus is a tendonous Bag lined with a membrane similar to the Sinovial, – they are situated between Tendons and bones and by the mucilaginous[83] fluid they secrete prevent frictions. There is a large one under the Tendon Patellæ. The~~ir~~ use of tendons is to occupy a small space for passing over Joints. Lect$^{r}$ 12. ~~An~~ Experiment shows that Muscle does not swell or diminish when in action. If a Man throw his Muscles into action while in water it will not rise in the Vessel. As far as it can be discernd Muscles when contracting their fibres are thrown into a Serpentine course. Action requires subsequent relaxation. By attending to this dislocations are replaced Muscles are voluntary, involuntary or ~~f~~{m}ixed. The Muscles of the Abdomen maintain the peristaltic motion.[84] There a mixed Muscles as those of respiration. If a nerve going to a Muscle be cut through the voluntary Motion is destroyed but it may be excited to action by stimuli this action from stimuli cannot be continued for many days. ~~When~~ A Muscle has a vis Tonica[85] which causes it to rest in the smallest possible space. This is the reason why a face becomes distorted in Hemiplagea.[86] No part of the

81 'A tendinous expansion' (*LM*, 69).

82 Plural of 'fascia': '[a] thin sheath of fibrous tissue investing a muscle or some special tissue or organ; an aponeurosis' or '[t]he substance of which this is composed' (*OED*).

83 'Containing, secreting or coated with mucilage or other viscid substance', with 'mucilage' defined as '[a] viscid fluid in an animal's body, or secreted by an animal; *esp.* mucus; (also) synovial membrane' (*OED*).

84 Involuntary movements of the muscles of the digestive tract that occur in progressive wavelike contractions.

85 '[W]hen a muscle is divided, its parts contract; or when the antagonist muscle is cut, the undivided muscle draws the parts into which it is inserted into a fixed situation. Thus, if the biceps muscle be divided, the triceps keeps the arm constantly extended; if the muscles on one side of the face be paralytic, the opposing muscles draw the face to their side. This contraction, which used to be called the *vis tonica*, … will continue an indefinite time … '. Astley Cooper, *A Treatise of Dislocations and Fractures of the Joints*, ed. and enlarged by Bransby Blake Cooper (Philadelphia, PA: Lea and Blanchard, 1844), 18.

86 '[P]aralysis of the muscles of the lower face, arm, and leg on one side of the body' (*EB*).

Body would maintain its ~~Power~~ figure if it were not for the vis tonica by which the antagonists act +++ If you lay bare the Sciatic nerve after an amputation and stimulate it the Muscles will begin to quiver. They are sometimes the subject of spasms either {(x)} occasional and in common cramps or permanent – this is difficult to remove – the best treatment, (which is known by the Case of a Boy in S^t Thomas who had contracted fingers) is by Electricity. When Muscles have been long out of use they become fatty. This will sometimes be the case although the Muscles around will be in a natural state. Cellular Membrane is a common seat of Inflammation – adhesive Matter is thrown into the reticular membrane and obliterates the Cavaties by which it looses its mobility. The substance thrown out in inflammation is albumen.[87] If the inflammation do not stop the Blood vessels become affected and pus is secreted which collects together into a Cyst. The next thing is an absorbtion of the surrounding parts by pressure. At length by the Skin becoming absorbed the Matter becomes discharged. When the cellular Membrane becomes killed the disease is Carbuncle. There are also Inflammations
(x): **In these Cases the Spasms should be resisted. A ligature is of great use.**

—

[Bf6v]

of the Cellular Membrane as Fungus Haematodes.[88] Cancer is an inflammation which is common at first but having a peculiar Species of excretions depending on the state of Constitution. These are steatomato|us| Swellings of y^e cellular Membrane in which the Cells are enlarging and filling with fat. In removing these the smalles[t] Portions must not be left. An Encysted swelling is frequent. M^r C. has seen 9 in the same Person. Of Glands. Various fluids are produced in y^e Body differing from Blood as the Bile tears &c. These fluids are secreted by Organs call'd Glands which are

87 See n28.
88 A type of cancer, contemporarily also referred to as 'soft cancer' or 'spongoid inflammation', and the subject of a well-known monograph by James Wardrop, *Observations on Fungus Hæmatodes or Soft Cancer, in Several of the Most Important Organs of the Human Body* … (Edinburgh: Constable and Co., 1809).

divided into conglobate and conglomerate. Conglobate are those of a smooth surface as y^e^ kidneys: The conglomerate are uneven being a number of Bodies bound together by cellular Membrane. Secreting organs may be divided into three kinds 1^st^ As the Pleura Peritoneum Mucous Membrane &c[89] |2|^nd^ Follicles are pores as those in y^e^ tongue and tonsil gland 3^rd^ The large glands having an excretory duct in them such as the Liver, Kidneys &c. Structure of Secreting Membranes Arteries are sent to these membranes which terminate in 2 ways 1^at^ By orifices in one part in which the fluid is secreted 2^nd^ into Veins by which the Blood is brought back. The Structure of follicles is much the same only the Blood is thrown into cylindrical Tubes and brought back to y^e^ veins. Structure of Glands. They are among the most vascular Structures of y^e^ Body and are generally furnished with a Capsule[90] – some parts are more vascular than others – Arteries going to them are named from the organ to which they are going, or from the function they are to assist in performing – they are sometimes entering into the substance of Glands as in the Kidney and sometimes distributed on y^e^ surface of Glands as in the Testicle. The Structure of Arteries in Glands is different from their Structure in any part of y^e^ Body – the Arteries terminate in veins, these veins come from that part of the Gland where the Arteries enter. In y^e^ Liver the Vena Portæ performs the function of an Artery. Excretory Ducts are peculiar Structures. They are glandular, have no elastic Coat, generally Muscular which may be known from their Action. Their glandular Structure consists in y^e^ mucous Membrane. If a sore be produced in this Membrane it is difficult to heal – an ulcer in y^e^ Bladder frequently destroys life as the Urine is so continually irritating. The Mode of Treatment is to introduce a flexible Catheter and keep y^e^ Bladder continually empty.

—

[Bf7r]

The Ducts[91] of Glands are frequently terminating in Cells as the Ureters terminating in y^e^ Bladder, the Duct of the Liver in y^e^ Gall

89 A list – Keats has forgotten to put commas.

90 '*Physiology*. A membranous integument or envelope; a bag or sac' (*OED*).

91 '*Physiology*. A tube or canal in the animal body, by which the bodily fluids are conveyed. Formerly used in a wide sense, as to include the blood vessels and

Bladder – animals whose stomachs are continually full have no Gall Bladder as y^e^ Horse.
The Use of Glands The opinion now generally entertained is that the fluid produced depends upon the action of Arteries {not veins} – Fluids when agitated in a particular Manner will change their nature and that the Gland performs an operation similar to Churning by which Cream is changed into Butter and Butter milk – If the Action of Vessels be changed different fluids will be produced as in Salivation, Diabetes &c. Nerves are supposed to contribute to this operation, which is proved by the secretion being stopped in those Glands the Nerves going to which have been divided. The means of increasing secretion is by Stimuli as Snuff to y^e^ Nose, Purgatives to y^e^ intestines – Stimuli are either specific[92] as Calomel, Aloe &c. Mercury is specific by acting on the Salivary Glands. There is a sympathetic secretion as in the Breast, Tears &c. The Passions of y^e^ Mind have great influence on the secretions, Fear produces increase Bile and Urine, Sorrow increases Tears. Diseases of Glands Inflammation frequently attacks Glands – if it extend over the whole Gland the secretion is Stopped, but if it be not diffused over the whole Gland, the part free from disease will continue to secrete. Inflammation produces the same consequences in Glands as in other parts.

—

[Bf7v = Blank]

—

[Bf8r]

The Animal Matter of which Bone is composed – Gelatine is organised. The Bone of a young person maybe reddened by injection. The Arteries are of small Size but numerous and are accompanied by Veins. Absorbents exist although they cannot be injected for there is no part in which Absorbtion goes on in greater nicety than in Bone. For Example. The Growth ~~of the~~ and Enlargement of Bone from youth to Age by Absorbtion of the interior and deposit of Bony Matter without. In many diseases of Bone there is great Absorbtion.

alimentary canal, but now applied more strictly to the vessels conveying the chyle, lymph, and secretions' (*OED*).

92 'A remedy that has an infallible efficacy in the cure of disorders' (*LM*, 829).

It is clearly shown in Persons who have died under Salivation [*sic*]. It is known that the interior of the Bones is supplied with nerves, but it is doubtful whether the Shell is. Diseased Bones possess great sensibility. The Cellular structure of the interior of Bone is lined with a Medullary Membrane supporting the Medulla in separate Ba[ses?] the same as the Membrane of the adipose substance. This Membrane is freely supplied with Blood and hence the Branch which enters the Bone is called the Medullary artery – it commonly enters the Middle of the Bone and divides into two branches which go to each end of the Bone. The Minute dividions[93] of these communicate with those of the Periosteum.[94]

<u>Appendages to Bones</u>. Cartilage is fibrous, elastic and Compact. It may be converted into Gelatine. There are 3 kinds of Cartilege. 1st Supplying the place of Bone in early Youth 2nd Those which supply the place of Bone in the Adult and 3d the Articular Cartilage.[95] The Cartilage which supplies the Place of Bone in Children is vascular. Diseases of Cartilages are extremely difficult to cure as in noli me tangere.[96] There [are?] loose Cartilages in the Body as in the Jaw. At the Knees the two semilunar Cartilages.

—

[Bf8v]

Ligament is a fibrous white shining and inelastic structure generally proceeding from bone to bone to unite them to each other. There are 2 arrangements longitudinal from Bone to Bone transverse to unite the|m| first. It possesss very little vascularity. Mr C knows no distinction in the Structure of Ligament and Tendon. There are Vessels passing through Ligament to the subjacent Membrane. Haller[97] denies its sensibility. Mr C thinks this not exactly the fact,

93 Possibly a misspelling for 'divisions'.

94 See n50.

95 'The form of cartilage which enters into the formation of joints' (*GA*, 133).

96 'Under the name of *Noli me tangere* have been confounded *Lupus* and the cancerous affections of the face'. [Pierre-Louis] A[lphée] Cazenave and H. E. Schedel, *A Practical Synopsis of Cutaneous Diseases, from the Most Celebrated Authors, and Particularly from Documents afforded by the Clinical Lectures of Dr Biett* (Philadelphia, PA: Carey, Lea and Carey, 1829), 324.

97 Albrecht von Haller (1708–77), Swiss biologist, who made prolific contributions

– The inner side of the Capsular Ligament is lined with sinovial Membrane.[98] The Sinovial Membrane is extremely vascular and from the exhalent Vessels the Sinovia is poured out. What was formerly called the sinovial Gland is nothing but adeps. If the Sinovial Membrane be inflamed the Person is unable to extend his Limb. It possesses considerable Sensibility. D^r Woolaston[99] found in 100 parts of Sinovia 11 parts fibrin[100] 4 Albumen,[101] Muriat[102] f{a}nd Carb of Soda[103] and phosphat of Lime.[104] When a Joint has been wounded the synovial Membrane becomes inflammed and its secretion is increased and continually exudes preventing the Union of the Wound – the irritation produces suppuration from the Synovial Membrane no adhesive inflammation takes place – the Matter distends the Joint. When this suppuration occurs it continues a long time on account of the surrounding parts being so long before they granulate therefore the ulceration which takes place destroys them. The Granulations which arise from Bone restore these parts. Matter does not always issue from one opening but from many Therefore from these concurring Circumstances wounds of Joints are often attended with either the loss of Limb or Life, and when most favorable the restoration is very slow. For the Treatment endeavor in y^e first place to heal the external Wound before the synovial Membrane becom|es| inflammed. Cartilaginous substances are often found in Joints – they are found tobe bone surrounded by Cartilage and are at their first formation connected to the Joint

to physiology, anatomy, botany, and embryology. He was able to prove from experimental evidence that irritability was a specific property of the muscles while sensibility was a specific property of the nerves.

98 '*Synovial Membrane* is a thin, delicate membrane, which invests the articular extremities of the bones, and is then reflected on the inner surface of the various ligaments which connect the two articulating surfaces. It resembles the serous membrane in being a shut sac, but differs in the nature of its secretion, which is thick, viscid, and glairy, like the white of an egg; and hence termed *synovia*' (*GA*, 134).

99 Charlton Woolaston (1733–64), physician to Guy's Hospital and subsequently to the Queen's Household.

100 See n29.

101 See n28.

102 'A salt of muriatic (hydrochloric) acid; a chloride' (*OED*).

103 Carbonate of soda, or sodium carbonate.

104 Phosphate of lime, or tricalcium phosphate.

by a peduncle.[105] This is afterwards broken and then the substance becomes loose, these sometimes get between the Bones and occasion frequent stumbling of the Patient.

The Operation of removing those Bodies is extremely dangerous from the irritation and inflammation of the synovial Membrane +++ and 2 by the incision into $y^e$ Joint.

—

[Bf9r]

A knee cap Bandage may be worn with a strap above and below the Patella[106] so as not to confine the Joint but merely this loose substance by which evil consequence may be prevented. Joints are affected with a Rheumatic Inflammation accompanied with a swelling occasioned by an effusion of a mucilagenous[107] fluid from the synovial Membrane – the Joint is frequently loose from an elongation of the Ligaments. Treatment. No puncture should be made. Stimulants, as the Empl Ammoniaci c̄[108] Hy reg in Straps rest being at the same time enjoined – if this should not succeed blisters should be applied and kept open: the Constitution should be attended to ~~it~~ The Complaint will generally yield to this treatment. – Gouty inflammation frequently attacks the Joint producing what ~~is~~ are call'd chalk Stones which are composed of uric acid – Gouty habits and Stone in the Bladder are often found together. These Substances in the Joint frequently ulcerate when the white substance protrudes it may be touched with nitrate of Silver.[109] Gouty affections seldom occasion constitutional irritation or suppuration: in the Treatment the stomach should be principally attended to. Joints are frequently affected with scrophula[110] this occurs in debilicate Constitutions

105 By 'peduncle', Keats meant a narrow part connecting one part of the body to another, larger part. In modern anatomical usage, the word refers almost exclusively to connections between parts of the brain, or, more generally, to bundles of nerve fibres connecting parts of the central nervous system.

106 'The knee-pan. A small flat bone, which, in some measure, resembles the common figure of the heart, with its point downwards, and is placed at the fore part of the joint of the knee' (*LM*, 660). Diagram at *GA*, 116.

107 For 'mucilaginous': see n83.

108 For 'cum' [Latin].

109 Silver nitrate.

110 See n37.

suffering from chronic disease existing from birth not brought on by improper living and habits – this disease arises from inflammation of the synovial Membrane occasioning a thickening of the Ligament and a change in the Membrane – this terminates in the suppuration and absorbtion of Cartilage.

–

[Bf9v = Blank]

–

[Inside Front cover]

425
in my catalogue
Ch. W. D.

John Keats [signature]

–

[Front folio 1 recto = Ff1r]

Lect$^{r}$. 4. Arteries continued from page 3 Physyology of Arteries and their diseases. Circulation of the Blood. The Bloo|d| brought to the right auricle by the venæ Cavæ from thence it is fo|r|ced by the contraction of the hear~~d~~{t} into the right ventricle whence it passes into the pulmonary Arteries to circulate through the lungs, from which it is ~~difused~~ {carried} by the Pulmonary Veins into the left auricle from whence it is forced into the left Ventricle and next it passes into the Aorta.[111] Arteries are either in a state of Systole[112] or Dyastole.[113] When the force of the Blood is thrown upon an Artery it elongates and convolutes. Pulsation does not take place exactly at the same time at y$^{e}$ Extremities and at the Heart. Arteries are always full

111 See n9.

112 'The phase of the heartbeat during which the heart contracts, expelling blood from the heart into the arteries; a contraction of this nature' (*OED*).

113 Now usually spelt 'diastole': 'dilation or relaxation of the heart or an artery (or other pulsating organ in some lower animals), rhythmically alternating with the *systole* or contraction, the two together constituting the *pulse*' (*OED*).

that is they adapt themselves to their contents. The change of place produced on a colum of Blood by the force of the hearts contraction, constitutes pulsation. The Pulse at Birth is 140. at one Year 124 at 2 Years 110 At 3$^{ys}$ 96 at 7 86 at Puberty 80 in an adult 75 at 60 Years 60. In some Persons thoug|h| healthy the Pulse is remarkably swift or slow. The slowest pulse Ast. Coo[p|er|?] heard of was seen by M$^{r}$. Stocker[114] and D$^{r}$. Cholmondly,[115] this was in general 20 and sometimes 28 or as low as 14 – this without disease. If there be in Fever a determination of Blood to the Head the Pulse will increase. Heat readily increases the Pulse – the warm bath will elevate the Pulse to 120. Cold on the contrary will diminish soon reduce it, diminishing the diameter at the same time. If ~~from~~ a Man h| | pulse have an quick unhealthy irritable pulse, the cold bath will sooth the Pulse, lowering it with respect to quickness ~~but~~ {and} increasing its diameter. Wine although stimulant gives to the Body great additional Strengt[h]. Stimulus when applied where there is gre|at| |d|ebility is a Tonic. In Typhus Stimulants will reduce the pulse, Digitalis considerably diminishes the frequency and force of the Pulse. The Pulse is quick or slow in proportion to their Size. In the Dog it is 130 in the Horse 32. The Arteries after death the Arteries are found empty, they have power of expelling the Blood in the last Struggles of Life – this is a proof that the Arteries have a muscular Coat. <u>Arteriotomy</u> is principally performed on the temporal Artery. It is done by making an oblique incision over the Artery and puncturing its Coats. D$^{r}$. Jones[116] observed that inflammation will take place to seal |[a]| divided Artery, in 6 Hours. If inflammation do not take place fr|om| debility of Constitution secondary hemorrhage will take place. Coag|u|lum is not concerned in the ultimate union in inflammations. Diseases. 1$^{st}$ Ossification of its Coats this in general happens

114 Richard Stocker (*c.*1761–1834), apothecary at Guy's Hospital while Keats was a student there.

115 Henry James Cholmeley (1777–1837), physician to Guy's Hospital, who shared lecturing duties with James Curry on the course on 'Theory of Medicine, and Materia Medica' while Keats was enrolled at Guy's.

116 John Frederick Drake Jones, author of *A Treatise on the Process Employed by Nature in Suppressing the Haemorrhage from Divided and Punctured Arteries, and on the Use of Ligature; concluding with Observations on Secondary Haemorrhage* (1805). His work contributed to understanding bodily reactions to haemorrhage and the natural process of blood clotting.

in the large|r A|rteries – small arteries are sometimes ossified. It is the constant effect of Age and it seems that nature protected the Arteries by a deposit of Bone. The Young who lead a life of Intemperance are subject to ossification. Those who have been much addicted to Study from Keeping up a continued determination of Blood to the Brain, have often the Vessels of that part ossified. It frequently obliterates an artery and thereby renders the part beyong[117] subject to mortification. When the smaller arteries are ossified there is more danger from oss|ification. The Seat of ossification| is between the Muscular and |+++ Coat.|

—

[Ff1v]

(|Fro|m Above) Cartilage is first deposited. It is deposited in patches along the Striæ[118] of the Muscular Coat.

(|1|)
There are two original Arteries Viz Pulmonary and Aorta.
They have five terminations
[*] In Veins
In Arteries by Anast.[119]
In Exhalents
[~] In Cells &
In [A]Glands or Secret. Duc[t].
Arteries have three Coats
Elastic, Muscular & Membranous.
There are six Veins
Four Pulmonary &
Two Venæ Cavæ
Some Anatomists add two others.
The Coronary & Vena Port.

117 For 'beyond'.

118 Plural of 'stria': '[a] small groove, channel, or ridge; a narrow streak, stripe or band of distinctive colour, structure, or texture; *esp.* one of two or of a series' (*OED*).

119 Abbreviation for 'anastomosis': '[f]rom (*ανα*, trough, and *ςομα*, a mouth.) The communication of vessels with one another' (*LM*, 51).

Veins have three Origins
    1$^{st}$ From Arteries
    2$^{ly}$ From Cells &
    3$^{ly}$ From Sinuses as in y$^{e}$ Brain
Veins have three ~~Origins~~ {Coats}
    Elastic Muscular & Membranous
The Uses of the Absorbents are three
    To form new Blood
    To prevent dropsical accumulat|ions|
    To Model the Body during growt|h|
[*] **A. A Gland is a collection of Absorbent Vessels, Arteries &c. having an excretory duct.**
[~] **See P.3.f.2**[120]

–

[Ff2r: see Figure 3]

Lect$^{r}$ 1$^{st}$.
1 Anatomy – Knowledge of Structure
2 Phisiology – – of the Functions of Parts
3 Pathology – – of the Diseases.–
The Structure of the Body is general or particular.
The general, the diffusion of Arteries, Veins, Absorbts
Particular as in the Lungs where a particular Structure is added to these Organs.
Divided into 3 Parts    1 Those for {(x)} Loco Motion
    2 Those to support Life
    3 Those for the propogation of Species
Example of those for {(x)} 1 Bones, Cartilage, Ligament, which differs from Cartilage in being inelastic – The Membrane lining the Capsular Ligaments secrete Sinovia. Muscle which is tipped with tendon and possesses contractile Powers and Arteries, Ligamentum Sub flavum[121] & elastic Powers of Loco Motion.

120 This is apparently a reference to some other document or printed source, rather than a cross-reference within the medical Notebook, since none of the material on Keats' page 3 appears to be linked to Keats' subject here.

121 Keats appears to mean 'Ligamenta flava', or the interlaminar ligaments that connect the neural arches of the vertebrae in the spine to each other and support the flexibility of the spinal column. At Ff3v he refers to this as 'the Elastic Ligament as in the Spine'.

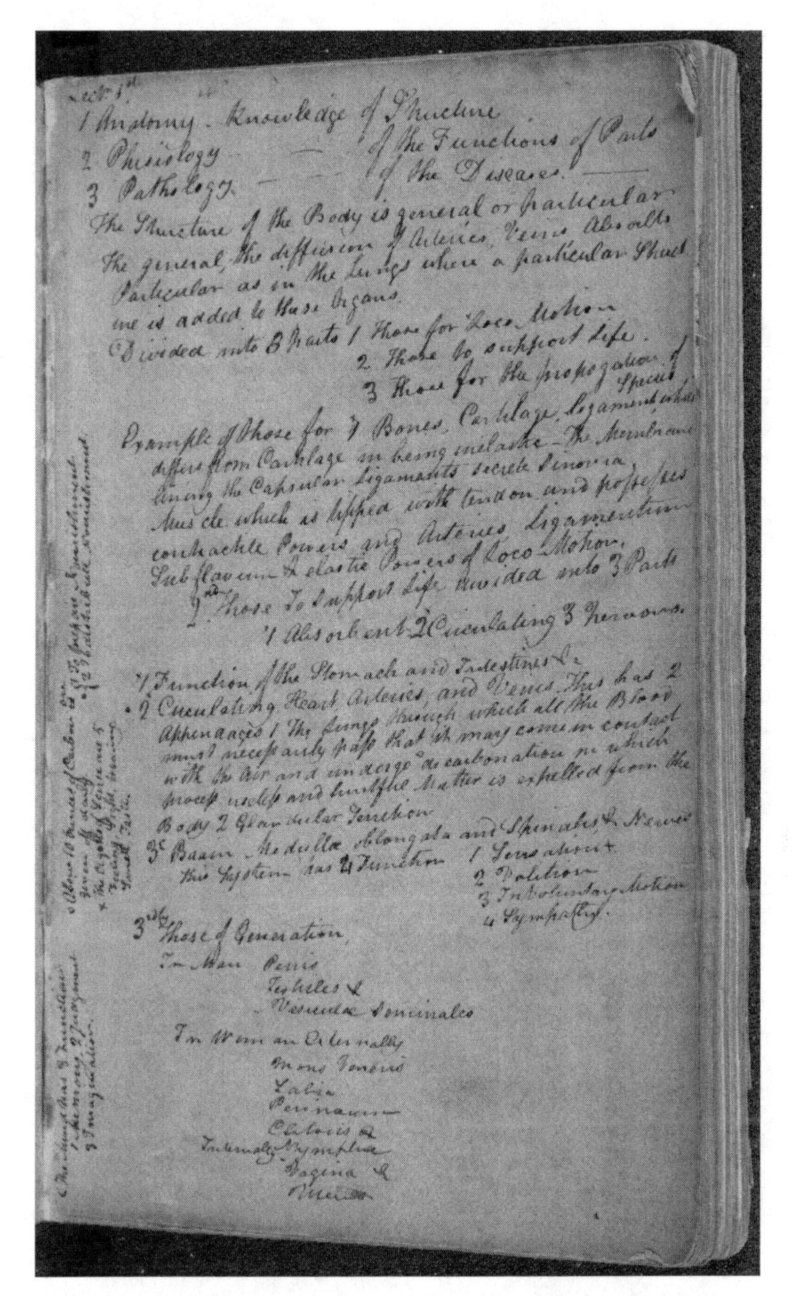

Lect^r 1st

1 Anatomy - Knowledge of Structure
2 Physiology — of the Functions of Parts
3 Pathology — of the Disease. —

The Structure of the Body is general or particular the general, the diffusion of Arteries, Veins Absorbts Particular as in the Lungs where a particular Structure is added to these Organs

Divided into 3 Parts 1 Those for Loco Motion
2 Those to support Life.
3 Those for the propagation of Species

Example of those for 1 Bones, Cartilage, Ligaments which differs from Cartilage in being inelastic - the Membrane Among the Capsular Ligaments secrete Sinovia, Muscle which is tipped with tendon and possesses contractile Powers viz Arteries Ligamentum Subflavum & elastic Powers of Loco-Motion.

2nd Those To Support Life divided into 3 Parts
1 Absorbent 2 Circulating 3 Nervous.

1 Function of the Stomach and Intestines &c
2 Circulating Heart Arteries, and Veins this has 2 Appendages 1 The Lungs through which all the Blood must necessarily pass that it may come in contact with the Air and undergo decarbonation in which process useless and hurtful Matter is expelled from the Body 2 Glandular Function
3c Brain Medulla oblongata and Spinales & Nerves this System has 4 Function
1 Sensation
2 Volition
3 Involuntary Motion
4 Sympathy.

3rd Those of Generation
In Man Penis
Testicles &
Vesiculae Seminales
In Woman Externally
Mons Veneris
Labia
Perinaeum
Clitoris &
Internally Nymphae
Vagina &
Uterus

**Figure 3:** Ff2r, 'Lect^r 1st', showing Keats making extensive use of marginal notes and cross-referencing, as he revisits this page to build up his 'database' of information. From 'John Keats' medical Notebook'. Image © City of London, Keats House, Hampstead.

$2^{nd}$. Those To Support Life divided into 3 Parts

{(x)} 1 Absorbent 2 {(x)} Circulating 3 Nervous

{(x)} 1 Function of the Stomach and Intestines &c.

(♦) 2 {(x)} Circulating. Heart, Arteries, and Veins. This has 2 Appendages 1 The Lungs through which all the Blood must necessarily pass that it may come in contact with the Air and undergo (◊) decarbonation in which process useless and hurtful Matter is expelled from the Body 2 Glandular Secretion

3(c) Brain Medullæ oblongata and Spinalis, & Nerves

This system has 4 Function 1 Sensation (x)<br>
2 Volition<br>
3 Involuntary Motion<br>
4 Sympathy.

$3^{rdly}$ Those of Generation,

In Man Penis<br>
Testicles &<br>
Vesiculæ Seminalis[122]

In Woman Externally<br>
Mons Veneris<br>
Labia<br>
Perinæum<br>
Clitoris &<br>
{Internally} Nymphæ[123]<br>
Vagina &<br>
Uterus

(♦) { *1 To prepare Nourishment*<br>
*2 To distribute Nourishment*

(◊) *Above 10 Ounces of Carbon ~~is~~ {are} given off daily.*

(c) *The Mind has 3 Functions*<br>
*1 Memory, 2 Judgment*<br>
*3 Imagination.*

(x) *The Organs of Sense are 5*<br>
*Feeling, Sight, Hearing,*<br>
*Smell, Taste.*

—

122 *GA*, 679.

123 Also known as labia minora.

[Ff2v]

(2)
<Th>e Functions of the nervous System are Sensation, Voluntary Motion & Involuntary Action.–
<T>here are three different kinds of Glands.
    Membranous, Follicular & Ductiform.
The Uses of the cancellated[124] Structure <of> the Bones are three
    1st To give Lightness to them
    2ly To enlarge their extremities for the attachment of Muscle
  & 3ly The formation of Joints.
There are three different Kinds of Cartilages
    1st That which supplies the place of Bone in the Adult subject
    2ly That which does the same in the young subject &
    3ly The Articular.
They have three Uses.
<1st> To prevent the effects of Friction
<2rd> To allow of the process of Ossification
<3rd> To adapt the ends of the Bones to each other and take of the Shoks on falling.–

[Continuation from Lecture 2nd at Ff3r in the left-hand margin]
*lated in 3¾ hours and with it in ¼ hour according to Mr Huson's*[125] *Experiment. Mr Hunter*[126] *who thought || Blood possessed Vitality thought it underwent a change like the contraction of Muscular Fibres at the time of death The Muscles do not relax and the Blood does not coagulate in an Animal killed by lightening. Mr C's opinion is the Blood is preventing from coagulating by nervous energy. The Uses of Coagulation are 2. 1st The solids thereby*

124 'Having a cellular structure formed by fine interlacing fibres and plates running in all directions, and separated by minute labyrinthian cavities, as in the less compact tissue of bones' (*OED*).

125 William Hewson (1739–74), noted surgeon and anatomist, a close associate of the Hunters. He is principally remembered for his researches on the lymphatic system, and on the properties of the blood which – as Keats notes – contributed to understanding the process of coagulation and the form of red corpuscles.

126 For a discussion of John Hunter on the vitality of the blood, see Chapter 3.

[Continued from above, along the bottom of the page]
**are formed 2$^{nd}$ in Case of injury it Seals bleeding arte- Arteries. The Blood undergoes a remarkable Change under inflammation the red particles Subside and the Fibrin is separated.**

—

[Ff3r]

Lect$^{r}$ 2$^{nd}$ On the Blood. The Blood appears on its flowing fro|m| the Blood vessels appears to be of an uniform appearance but |in| the space of 10 Minutes it {begins to} become~~s~~ separated into Serum and Crass|a|mentum. Quantity of Blood in the Body cannot be ascertained. The Quantity given out before death is in weight from 1/16 to 1/20 of the whole Body. Of the Heat of the Blood. The Body exceeds in heat the surrounding atmosphere. The heat of the Blood is supposed to be from 98 to 100 degrees. The heat of venous and arterial Blood is the Same. This M$^{r}$ C. ascertained by introducing a bulb of a thermo[me]ter into the left {ventricle} and right auricle of a dog. The Blood undergoes a change from its florid in passing through the extreme vessels into the Veins and is occasioned by passing through minute passages. The Specific gravity 1045 to 1000. Different parts of the Blood. Serum is a transparent fluid of saltish taste and greenish color it is heavier than Water. The Serum becomes lighter as the crassamentum becomes decreased. It coagulates at 160 degrees. When consolidated it is divided into Albumen which is the solid substance and a small quantity of fluid called serosity. The Serum containing solidity forms the finer and colourless textur|e| of the Body. Serosity is a solution of Albumen with Alkali according to M$^{r}$. Brandt.[127] ~~There is~~ Serum is composed of 110 parts Wate|r| 75 Albumen 15 Salines. Serum has various appearances – sometimes it is clouded which is of the nature of Chyle and is intermixed with the Serum and is Chyle not yet converted into Blood. It sometimes is converted into a Substance resembling Milk with a Crea|m| on its surface M$^{r}$. Huson found this of the Nature of Milk. Serum contains

127 Probably a reference to William Thomas Brande (1788–1866), who in 1813 had been appointed Professor of Chemistry to the Society of Apothecaries. Brande was influenced by Humphry Davy to pursue a career in chemistry and in 1813 succeeded him at the Royal Institution. He continued lecturing there until his retirement in 1852.

a quantity of Salts which are Muriates of Soda and Potash, Carbonate and Sulphate of Soda, Phosp[h]ates of Soda and Lime, Subphosphate of Iron and sometimes Sulphur and Magnesia.
Of the Crassamentum[128] The Solid part begins to form in about 4 Minutes but continues much longer to concentrate and press out the Serum – after 24 hours or much longer time the contraction of the Crassamentum is going on. The Coagulum is composed of Fibrin and red Particles. Coagulated Lymph is not the fibrous part of the Blood. Fibrin is so called from being composed of fibrous particles. Coagulation of the Blood. The first idea is that it is kept fluid by heat. This however is fallacious for it will coagulate in a heat superior to that of the human Body. 120 degrees will coagulate it instantly. The 2 opinion was tha|t| rest was the Cause, it will however coagulate though kept in Motion and Blood in the livving will remain a considerable time at rest without coagulating. Huson thought that the Air was much concerned in the Process. It may certainly has a small share in it but as Blood when extravasated into cavaties of the Body coagulates it cannot be a principal cause. Blood without the access of Air coagu
[Continued in left margin of Ff2v]

—

[Ff3v]

(3)
<There> are three kinds of Ligaments,
Capsular or Bursal
Lateral, and Crucial. The Elastic may be reckoned a fourth.
<There> are four kinds of Joints,
By Sutures, By Capsular Ligament
By intervening Cartilages, and
By the Elastic Ligament as in the Spine.
<The> Periosteum has three Uses
1st. As a Bed for the Ramification of Vessels going to Bone.
2nd To unite the Epiphyses[129] of Bones {to} their extremities &
3rd To lessen the friction of Tendons and Muscle on Bones and for the Attachment of Muscles. —

128 See n30.
129 Plural of 'epiphysis': '[a]ny portion of bone growing upon another, but separated from it by a cartilage' (*LM*, 328).

[Continuation of Lecture 3 at Ff4r, along the bottom of the page.]
**The Red Particles are a recent discovery. They a much heavier than the other parts of the Blood. They appear to be made up Bladders not completely full. They are not globular, ~~but of an oblong~~ They have the Power of Changing their figure that they may more easily enter the Vessels. They cannot enter into all the Vessels – are of slow formation. The red particles are less abundant in an inactive animal than an active one. Their Size is supposed by Dr Wollaston[130] to be 1/4000 part of an inch.**
**Echymosis[131] is generally the result of rupture of Blood vessel. ~~When~~ The cellular membrane is {sometimes} torn and the Blood collects into a clot under the Skin in bothe <t>hese Cases do not use the Knife but trust to Absorbtion, <u>nless the Clot be very large and all other means fail. Sometimes Extravasated Serum cannot be Absorbed.**

[Continuation from above, along left-hand margin]
*Petechiæ[132] are of the Same Nature <of> {as} Echymosis but proceed from weakness of vessels – After Typhus it is better not to give Stimuli too suddenly. Be upon your in Bleeding from the appearance of the Blood. A Buffy appearance is produce[d] by hurried action as well as inflammation. ~~Debility~~ Be principally directed by the state of the Pulse – a hard pulse indicates Bleeding especially when combined with a cupped appearance.*

—

[Ff4r]

Lectr 3. Arteries are elastic tubes which convey the Blood to different parts of the Body. They generally take a central course where they are safe from injury. It is also the shortest course they can take for distribution. They are always found on the concave surface of Joints. They are sometimes superficial, as the Groin, the Wrist (the Radial) the Ulnar is easily injured. In some parts they take a tortuous course as in the lips, the Brain. The principal use

130 For 'Woolaston' see n99.

131 Usually spelt 'ecchymosis'.

132 Plural of 'petechia': '[a] red or purple spot that mostly appears in contagious diseases, and resembles flea-bites' (*LM*, 674).

of this is to slacken the force of the Circulation which especially in the brain necessary – which is farther guarded against by their passing through foramina. The Spermatic is tortuous in its Course. In the Uterus it lessens the danger of Hamorrhage. Arteries form Angles which are larger or smaller in proportion to their distance from the heart. The angles are more acute in proportion tothe distance from the Heart and as the vis a tergo[133] is not so strong at a distance from the Source of Circulation these angles are adapted for a more ready transmission of the Blood. Arteries are divided into Serous and Sanguineous. See Page 1 fol. 1.[134] The Anastomosing of Arteries in very important and its great advantage is that upon the Obliteration of a Vessel the Anastomosing vessels carry on the Circulation.[135] There is no part of the Body in which the circulation of the Blood will not be carried on after the obliteration of a Vessel except the Subclavian.[136] All surfaces discharging fluid of a watery kind are supplied with exhalens as well as on the surface of the Skin. The Arteries terminating in excretory ducts have their Contents changed into peculiar fluids. See Page 1. f. 1.[137]
The Use of the Elastic Coat is to assist in Circulation and thus, the force of the Blood +++anes the Tube and the elastic coat contracting pushes on the Blood. It is by the elastic Coat that the Cylindrical form of the Arteries is preserved. There is every probability of the existence of a muscular Coat as it appear from several Circumstances that Arteries must have an independant Action as in Blushing. The inner Coat of an Artery alone gives way on the application of a Ligature – it is upon this principle that narrow ligatures are now used. Arteries have their Vasa Vasorum – these are not derived from the vessels they supply. Absorbents and Nerves are distributed to Arteries.

—

133 '[A] force operating from behind; a propulsive force' (*OED*).

134 An apparent reference to Ff1v, which Keats numbered as '1'.

135 See n119.

136 The subclavian artery arises from the arteria innominata (or brachiocephalic artery) on the right and the arch of the aorta on the left, and continues till the outer border of the first rib.

137 See n134.

[Ff4v: see Figure 4]

## Of Osteology.[138]

The Skeleton is divided into
Head, Trunk and Extremities.
The Trunk is divided into
Spine, Pelvis and Thorax.
There are twenty four Bones composing the Spine which which are divided into three Classes
7 Cervical[139]
12 Dorsal[140]
5 Lumbar[141]
—
24
—
The Parts of each Vertebra are a Body and 7 processes
Two superior Articular oblique
Two Inferior D° D°
Two transverses &c
One Spinous Process &c
a large hole in each for the passage of the Spinal Marrow.
The Cervical differ from the dorsal in having hollow instead of flat surfaces on their upper parts, and being rounded below. In having their articular processes very ~~deep~~ oblique, their transverse processes short, and spinous process bifid,

—

[Ff5r = Blank]

—

138 'The branch of anatomy or comparative anatomy that deals with the skeleton; the scientific study of the development, structure, arrangement, etc., of bones' (*OED*).

139 *GA*, 6–7.

140 *GA*, 8–9.

141 *GA*, 10.

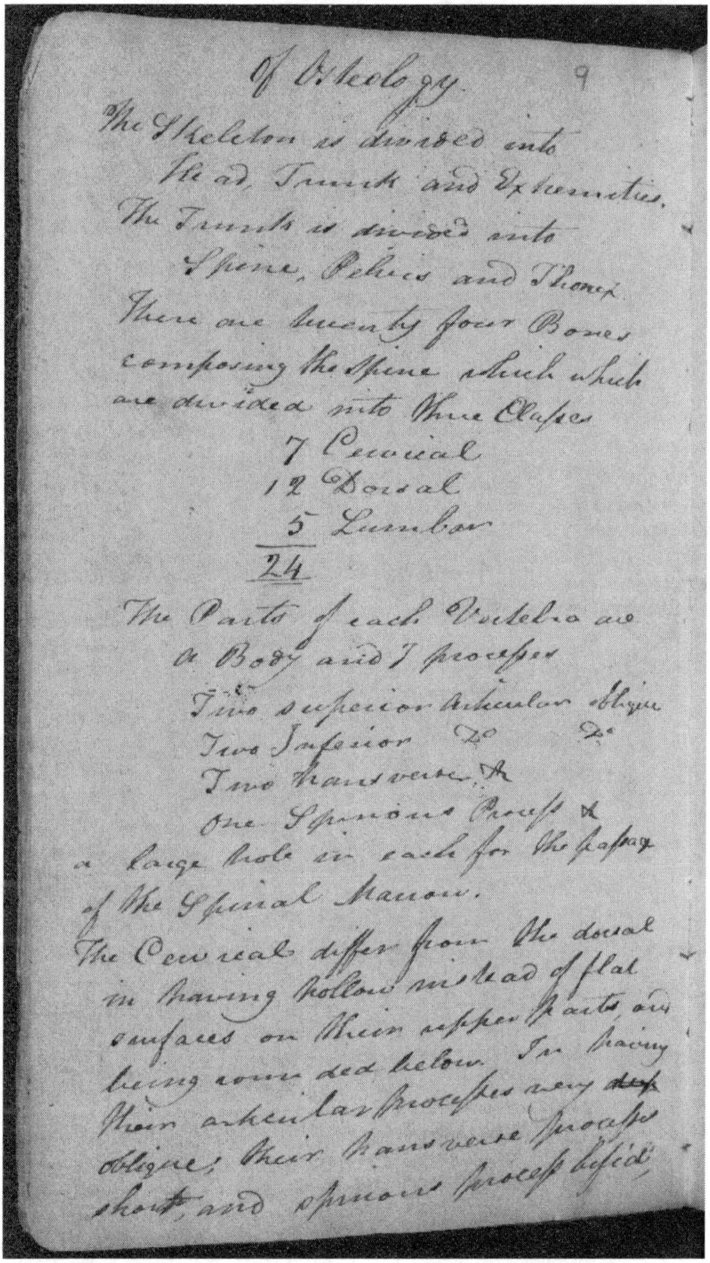

Of Osteology. 9

The Skeleton is divided into
Head, Trunk and Extremities.
The Trunk is divided into
Spine, Pelvis and Thorax.
There are twenty four Bones
composing the Spine which which
are divided into three Classes
7 Cervical
12 Dorsal
5 Lumbar
24
The Parts of each Vertebra are
a Body and 7 processes
Two superior Articular oblique
Two Inferior Do Do
Two transverse &
One Spinous Process &
a large hole in each for the passage
of the Spinal Marrow.
The Cervical differ from the dorsal
in having hollow instead of flat
surfaces on their upper parts, or
being rounded below. In having
their articular processes very ~~deep~~
oblique; their transverse processes
short, and spinous process bifid.

**Figure 4:** Ff4v, 'Of Osteology', featuring the handwriting that Colvin thought belonged to 'some other student'. From 'John Keats' medical Notebook'. Image © City of London, Keats House, Hampstead.

[Ff5v]

but more particularly in having holes in their transverse Processes for the transmission of the Vertebral Arteries.

The Dorsal Vertebræ are formed with their Bodies rounded on y$^{e}$ fore part with their superior & inferior surfaces flattened with their articular processes nearly perpendicular. The two upper having their surfaces for articulation turned backwards. The two lower forwards. Their spinous processes are long and bent downwards and are hollow underneath – the spinal Canal is rounded.
The Dorsal Vertebræ are not all alike. The 1$^{st}$, 11$^{th}$, & 12$^{th}$ differ from the rest; having whole articular Surfaces for the 1$^{st}$, 11$^{th}$ and 12 Ribs; and having their transverse Processes wanting.—[142]

The Lumbar Vertebræ are known by the Bodies of each being very large and of a somewhat oval Shape – Their upper articulatory processes have their faces turned towards

—

[Ff6r = Blank]

—

[Ff6v]

each other, their lower ones from each other. Their Transverse processes are long & slender, their spinous Processes short and straight – the spinal Canal small & of a triangular shape.

The 1$^{st}$. Cervical Vertebra differs from the Rest in its being a mere bony ring, its Body being wanting; In having an articulatory surface for the dentiform process of the 2$^{nd}$ Cervical; in having two deep concave articulatory sockets above for the Condyloid Processes of the Os Occipitis, and two flat articulatory surfaces below to rest and rotate on on the 2$^{nd}$ Vertebra, and in having a Groove above for the lodgement of the Vertebral Artery.[143]

142 *GA*, 9.
143 *GA*, 6.

The 2nd Cervical differs from the Rest In having a tooth like or dentiform Process rising upwards from the body of the Bone. This Process is received into the first Vertebra, and is confined there by a Ligament running across it, which keeps it in its place. Around this Process the first Cervical moves, thus performing the rotatory Motion of the Head.[144]

The 7th Cervical Vertebra differs from the 1st Dorsal; In having holes in the

–

[Ff7r]

Transverse Processes for the transmission of the Vertebral Veins from the spinal Marrow, and in its not having any Articulatory surfaces for the Ribs.
The 7th Cervical differs from the rest in not having its spinous process bifid.

There being so many Bones to form the Spine fits it for great exertions of Strength without much motion in any one Joint. It is thus contrived because great Strength and extensive motion are incompatible in the same Joint. There being 24 Bones with half an inch extent of Motion to each, a Movement one foot in extent can be made among the whole, at the same time the Spine remains excessively Strong.[145]

The Bones of the Pelvis are 4
Two Ossa Innominata[146]
Os Sacrum[147] &
Os Coccigis[148] –
In the young Subject each Os Innominatum is divided into three Bones,
Ileum, Ischium and Pubis.[149]

–

144 *GA*, 7.
145 *GA*, 17.
146 *GA*, 77–78.
147 *GA*, 13–14.
148 Labelled coccyx in the diagrams at *GA*, 16.
149 Keats has misspelled 'ilium' as 'ileum'. Ilium is a bone in the hip joint; ileum is a part of the small intestine.

[Ff7v]

The Muscle that naturally fills up the Venter of the Os Ileum is
The Iliacus internus.[150]
The Artery that passes on the inner side of the tuberosity[151] of the Ischium is the
Internal Pudendal
The Acetabulum[152] is formed by the unio|n| of 2/5 Ileum, rather more than 2/5 Ischium and rather less than one fif|th| Pubis.
By the Union of the Os Ischium and Pubis is formed
The Foramen ovale[153]
The Bones that form the Sacrum in the young Subject are
Five united by four Cartilages
{The Os Coccygis[154] is divided into 4 in the young subject the upper bone is united to the sacrum by Cartilage and has two artic|u|lar and 2 transverse Processe|s|}
The Bones of the Thorax are 37 in Number, 12 Dorsal Vertebræ (x) 24 Ribs and the Sternum.
The Number of the true Ribs are 14 the rest are false.
The Sternum is formed of three parts,
The first and second are Bone – the third is Cartilage

—

[Ff8r]

|T|he Ileum[155] is sometimes frac[t]ured it may be ascertained by moving the Crista[156] with the hand. The Bone should be kept from

150 Keats misspelled 'ilium' as 'ileum'. The internal surface of the ilium 'presents anteriorly a large smooth concave surface called the internal iliac fossa, or the venter of the ilium; it lodges the Iliacus muscle' (*GA*, 78). The venter is labelled as 'Internal Iliac Fossa' in the diagram at *GA*, 78.

151 In anatomy, a tuberosity is a large irregular projection of bone. For a description of the tuberosity of the ischium, see *GA*, 80. For a diagram, see *GA*, 81.

152 *GA*, 77.

153 More commonly referred to as the 'obturator foramen' in modern usage. Diagram at *GA*, 77.

154 See n148.

155 For 'ilium'.

156 Crest of the ilium, or iliac crest. Diagram at *GA*, 77.

being acted upon by the Muscles – Bandages should be employed so as not to make pressure. The Patient requires support rather than depletion.
M$^{r}$. C has never seen a fracture of the Ischium alone.
(x) The 11$^{th}$ and 12$^{th}$ Ribs are more straight than the rest. They are not attached by cartilage to the Sternum and have no passage for intercostals. The Ribs increase in length to the 7$^{th}$ and decrease to the 12$^{th}$. They gradually increase in Motion as they descend

If a hernia be protruded on the outer side of the Spinous process of the Pubis it is femoral if on the inner it is inguinal. Fracture of the Pubis is not uncommon and are frequently attended with rupture of the Bladder and when it so happens recovery is scarcely to be expected. M$^{r}$. C has seen one do well where the Bladder had not been injured. It is best to introduce a Catheta to prevent if possible extravasation[157] into the Membranes.
The Thigh bone is dislocated downwards when the head is found in the foramen Ovale, backwards into the ~~Dorsum Ilei~~ Ischialic Notch,[158] upwards into the Anterior tract of the Dorsum Ilei.[159]
There is a great difference in y$^{e}$ form in the Sacrum – sometimes the lower part is bent at right Angles owing to a deficiency in the Earthy deposit.
The Os Coccygis serves as a support to the Viscera and is moveable to give an easy exit to &c. &c.
The Pelvis of the Male and female – the female has the Ilei[160] farther apart. The Aperture of the Male Pelvis is longest from before backwards that of the female from side to side on the upper Cavity. In the female outlet of the Pelvis the Tuberosities of the Ischii[161] are farther distant than in the Male. P The Viscera of the Abdomen in the Natural position of y$^{e}$ Body are no placed in a line withe the Pelvis. A K{n}ife passed through the Body above the Pubis would touch the extremity of y$^{e}$ Coccȳx.

157 'The escape of an organic fluid … from its proper vessel into the surrounding tissues; an instance of this' (*OED*).
158 Also referred to as the great sacro-sciatic notch, labelled as such in the diagram at *GA*, 77.
159 'Ilei': the plural of 'ilium' is actually spelled 'ilia'.
160 See n159.
161 Plural of ischium.

In Case in which it is necessary to let out any fluid from beneath the Ribs the puncture should be made just above the upper edge of the Rib or there will be danger to injuring the intercostal Artery.[162]
The first Rib differs from the rest in having more curve, in having but one tubercle[163] and one articular surface[164] with the Vertebra. On its upper surface it has a notch for the passage of the subclavian[165] – the knowledge of this is very useful in bleeding of the upper extremities.

—

[Ff8v]

The Number of Articulatory Surfaces[166] of the 2nd Bone of the Sternum are

7. 1st. A half articulatory surface for the 2nd Rib
A whole art. surf.[167] for the 3rd
– – – – – – – – – – – 4th –
– – – – – – – – – – – 5 –
– – – – – – – – – – – 6 – and

A half art. surf. for the 7th besides an articulatory surface for the 1st Bone of the Sternum, and another for the ensiform Cartilage.

The Bones of the Shoulder are
The Clavicle[168] & Scapula.[169]
The Parts of the Scapula are the Dorsum, Venter, Spine, Processus Acromion – Articulation for the Clavicle – Fossa supra spinata, Superior Costa, Inferior Costa – Basis, Superior Angle, Inferior

162 An artery of the thorax, arising from the aorta and the subclavian. See *LD*, 190 for more detail.
163 'A small rounded projection or protuberance on the surface of the body or a body part, esp. a bone or tooth' (*OED*).
164 '[T]he extremity of every bone is perfectly adjusted to the end of the bone with which it is connected; and this connexion is termed their articulation' (*LM*, 85). Any skeletal surface that naturally makes direct contact with another skeletal surface is an articular surface.
165 See n136.
166 Articulatory Surface = articular surface.
167 Abbreviation for 'articular surface'.
168 *GA*, 85.
169 *GA*, 87 and 88.

Angle, Glenoid Cavity, Tubercle for the long head of the Biceps Muscle, Coracoid process, Cervix and Notch.

—

[Ff9r = Blank]

—

[Ff9v]

The Parts of the Os Humeri are
Head, Neck, Greater Tubercle, Lesser Tubercle, Groove for the Tendon of the long head of the Biceps: – at its inferior extremity are 2 Condyles and 2 depressions and 2 articular surfaces; one for the Ulna called the Trochlea, the other of a rounded shape for the Radius. On the inner side of the Trochlea is the internal Condyle, within which is a groove for the lodgement of the cubital Nerve.[170]
The Processes of the Ulna are,[171]
The Olecranon which lengthens its upper part – below this is its Coranoid[172] Process, and between the two is a double articulatory surface for the Os Humeri – on the outer side of the Coronoid Process is an articulatory surface for the head of the Radius. Its inferior extremity is round and lengthened by the styloid process – it has an articulatory surface on its side for the Radius, but of itself it forms no part of the wrist Joint.

—

[Ff10r = Blank]

—

170 'A long cylindrical bone, situated between the scapula and fore-arm' (*LM*, 424). Diagrams at *GA*, 92 and 94.
171 *GA*, 96 and 99.
172 'Processes of bones are so called, that have any resemblance to a crow's beak' (*LM*, 259). For the ulna, it is 'a rough triangular eminence of bone which projects horizontally forwards from the upper and front part' (*GA*, 97).

[Ff10v]

The Parts of the Radius |are|
The Radius has been divided into Head, Body and Extremity. On its head are two articulatory surfaces; one on its upper part concave to receive the articulatory surface of the outer condyle of the Os Humeri the other at its side to roll on the Ulna. Below the head of the Bone is a contracted part called its Cervix and immediately below this a prominence of bone called its Tubercle, for the attachment of the Tendon of the Biceps flexor Cubiti.

Its inferior extremity is broad and expanded, having an oval articulatory surface for the three first Bones of the Carpus, Scaphoid Lunare & Cunieforme. and on its inner side is an articulatory surface for the Ulna. On the outer side of its inferior extremity is a process called the Styloid.[173]

The Radius is united to 4 Bones the Ulna,[174] the Scaphoid, the Lunare[175] and the Cunieforme.

—

[Ff11r = Blank]

—

[Ff11v: see Figure 5]

The Bones of the Hand are
Divided into three parts
Carpus, Metacarpus and Phalanges

| | |
|---|---|
| The Carpus consists of | 8 Bones |
| The Metacarpus of | 5 |
| The Phalanges of | 14 |
| Making | 27[176] |

The Number of Bones that form the Wrist {are} Eight. They are placed in two rows

173 *GA*, 96 and 99.
174 *GA*, 96 and 99.
175 Keats wrote 'Lunare' for 'lunate' or semi-lunar. Diagrams at *GA*, 104 and 106.
176 *GA*, 104 and 106.

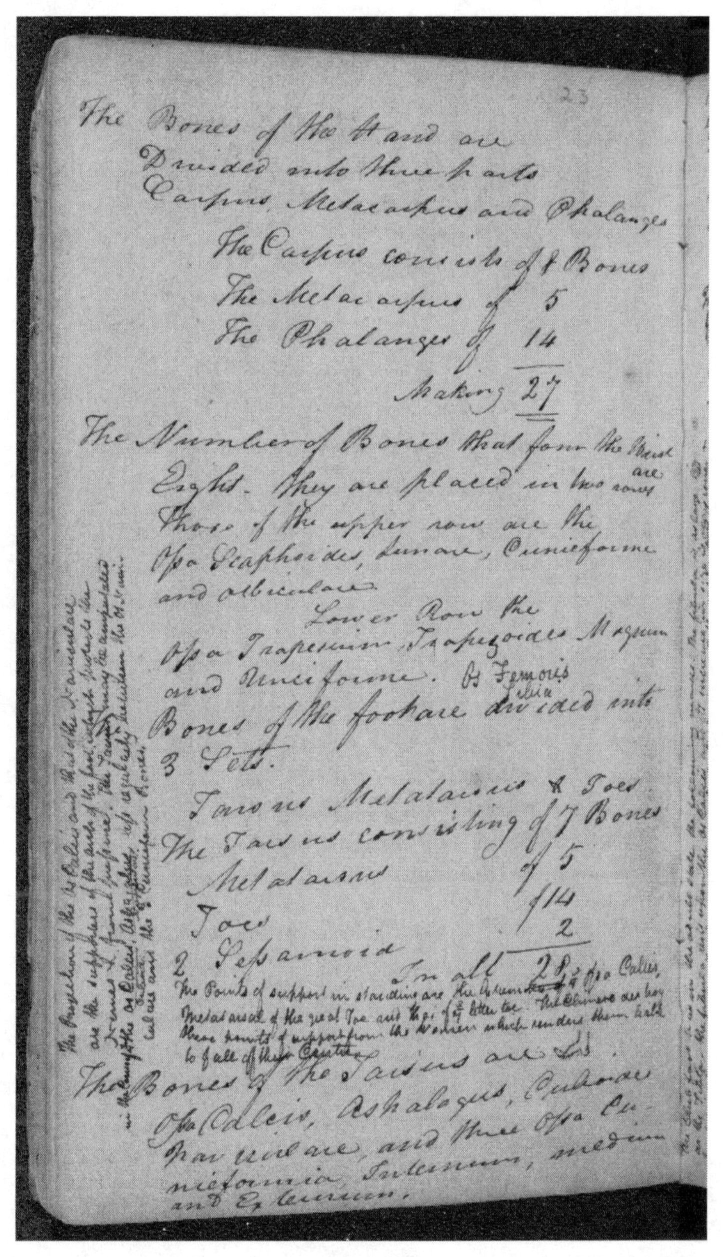

The Bones of the Hand are
Divided into three parts
Carpus, Metacarpus and Phalanges
The Carpus consists of 8 Bones
The Metacarpus of 5
The Phalanges of 14
Making 27
The Number of Bones that form the Wrist
Eight. They are placed in two rows
Those of the upper row are the
Ossa Scaphoides, Lunare, Cuneiforme
and Orbiculare
Lower Row the
Ossa Trapezium, Trapezoides Magnum
and Unciforme. Os Femoris Tibia
Bones of the foot are divided into
3 Sets.
Tarsus Metatarsus & Toes.
The Tarsus consisting of 7 Bones
Metatarsus of 5
Toes of 14
2 Sesamoid 2
In all 28
The Bones of the Tarsus are Seven.
Os Calcis, Astragalus, Cuboides
Os Naviculare, and three Ossa Cuneiformia, Internum, medium
and Externum.

**Figure 5:** Ff11v, where Keats writes about the bones of the hands and feet, and draws a foot at the end of the fifth line from the bottom of the page. Note how the marginal annotations are clearly inserted within and over the main text. From 'John Keats' medical Notebook'. Image © City of London, Keats House, Hampstead.

[*] Those of the upper row are the Ossa Scaphoides, Lunare,[177] Cunieforme and Orbiculare.
Lower Row the Ossa Trapesium, Trapezoides Magnum and Unciforme. {Os Femoris Tibia}
<The> Bones of the foot are divided into 3 Sets.
Tarsus Metatarsus & Toes.
The Tarsus consisting of 7 Bones
Metatarsus of 5
Toes of 14
2 Sessamoid 2
In all 28[178]

[~]
<The> Bones of the Tarsus are [here a foot has been drawn]
Ossa Calcis, Astralagus, Cuboides Naviculare, and three Ossa Cunieformia, Internum, medium and Externum.[179]

[*] *The Projection of the Os Calcis and that of the Naviculare are the supporters of the arch of the foot, which protects the Nerves &c. from pressure. The Tarsus may be amputated in the Course of the Os Calcis, Astragalus, less regularly between the Os Naviculare {Cuboid} and the 3 {Navicula[re?]} Cuneiform Bones.*
[~] **The Points of support in standing are the the Extremi<ties of> ye Ossa Calcis, metatarsal of the great Toe and that of ye little toe. The Chinese destroy these points of support from the Women which renders them liable to fall off their Centre.**

—

[Ff12r]

The Tibia and fibula are frequently broken – the ~~Fibula~~ {Tibia} more frequently than any bone in ye Body. The Tibia from it situation is very subject to compound fracture.[180] Many taild Bandage. and

177 See n175.
178 *GA*, 123 and 126.
179 *GA*, 123 and 126.
180 'The Tibia ... is situated at the anterior and inner side of the leg, and, excepting the femur, is the longest and largest bone in the skeleton. It is prismoid in form, expanded above, where it enters into formation with the knee joint, and more slightly below' (*GA*, 116).

splints. The fracture of y$^{e}$ fibula is more difficulty to discover – it is in general broken a few inches above the Malleolus[181] and a crepitus[182] will be discovered on rotating the foot.

The Magnum forms a Joint with the Scaphid[183] and Lunar[184] Bones which form a Cavity to receive its head.[185]
The Carpus forms an Arch to protect the Vessels and Nerves from Pressure. It is an example of great strength combined with extensive Motion.
The Articulation of the Thumb differs from all others in the Body having a double pulley once from before backwards.[186]
[*]

The Projection of the Bones over the Articulations of the Phalanges[187] <m>akes it necessary to make a lateral entrance into the Joint in amputating:
There are 2 sessamoid bones on y$^{e}$ first joint of the Thumb[188] and may be considered as small patellæ.
The Condyles of the Os femoris[189] have a much greater extent of Motion behind than before.
The Head of the thigh bone becomes in age depressed. This is the case in children with the rickets[190] ~~which~~ from the same cause are produced arched and bent Bones. Sometimes the Bone is unnaturally straight and is then in greater danger from Accident.
The Os femoris is subject to 3 kinds of fractures 1$^{st}$ Throu|gh| the Middle Treatment, taild Bandage 3 Splints, with the Heel resting and the Knee elevated 2$^{nd}$ Neck of the Bone – this occurs in elderly

181 By 'Malleolus', Keats appears to mean the 'malleolus externus', i.e. the lower extremity of the fibula.
182 Cf. 'crepitation': 'the noise and sensation observed in the grating together of the ends of fractured bones' (*OED*).
183 Scaphoid.
184 See n175.
185 *GA*, 104 and 106.
186 See *GA*, 108–09 for a detailed description of this joint.
187 Bones of the fingers.
188 *GA*, 106.
189 *GA*, 111 and 113.
190 See 'Rachitis' in *LM*, 741–42 for details.

people. Mr. C. says that in this Case no union ever takes place M^r. Abernethy <is> however of a contrary opinion. M^r. C. thinks that a <f>racture through the[191] Trochanter major has been mistaken <f>or fracture through the Neck.
<The> Patella[192] is united to the femur by Muscle and to the Tibia by Ligament. When fractured it unites by ligament.
[*] *The Club foot has in the adult state the following marks. The fibula is as large* [circular doodle here – a flower?] *as the Tibia – the fibula rests upon the Os Calcis and its increase in size is occasioned (x) by being borne upon. The bearing is upon the Os Cuboides and the extremity of the metatarsal Bones of the little Toe. The Astragalus is curved.*
**(x) The deformity is easily remedied if undertaken a Month after the Birth of the Child. The foot is placed in a tin Splint. The Cause Mr. C thinks is an unnatural shortness of the Gastrocnemius and the Tendon Achillis[193] drawing up the Os Calcis.**

—

[Ff12v]

The Number of the Bones of the Cranium are eight. Os Frontis,[194] Two Ossa Parietalia.[195] Two Ossa Temporalia,[196] Os Occipitis[197] The Ossa Sphænoides[198] & Ethmoides.[199]
The Sutures of the Cranium are five

191 John Abernethy (1764–1831), surgeon to St Bartholomew's Hospital, London, 1787–1827. A protégé of William Blizard (1743–1845), surgeon, and a student of John Hunter (see n7), Abernethy was a noted medical practitioner (numbering among his patients Samuel Taylor Coleridge) and lecturer. He served as Professor of Anatomy and Surgery at the Royal College of Surgeons between 1814 and 1817, becoming embroiled in the Vitalism Debates in the process; for details refer to Chapter 3.

192 See n106.

193 See *GA*, 292 for the normal position of these two.

194 *GA*, 25 and 26.

195 *GA*, 23 and 24.

196 *GA*, 28 and 29.

197 *GA*, 19 and 21.

198 *GA*, 33 and 35.

199 *GA*, 37.

Cornonal, Sagittal, Lambdoidal[200] Squamose[201] and Transverse.[202]

The Anterior Division of the Cranium

This Division is bounded before by the Os Frontis,[203] at the back part by the anterior Clinoid Process. In the Middle is the Crysta Galli on ~~th~~ each side of which is the cribriform plate and to the outer sides of this the 2 orbitar plates.[204] Above the Chrysta Galli is the Spine of the Os frontis, and between the Spine and the Crysta Galli is a Foramen[205] called the Foramen secum.[206]

The Foramina in the Middle division of the internal Basis of the Skull.

There are 6 pair viz

Foramen Optica to transmit The Optic Nerves and opthal. Artery

— Lacera orb. Sup[207] — — 3rd[208] 4th[209] 1[|st|?] 6[|th|?] of 5th[210] & 6 [|+++|][211]

200 These three are at the vertex (upper surface) of the skull.

201 This appears to be a reference to the suture at the base of the skull, usually called the squamo-sphenoidal.

202 The transverse suture extends across the upper part of the face.

203 Also called frontal bone.

204 For a more detailed description see 'anterior fossa', *GA*, 55–57, and the diagram at *GA*, 56.

205 'An opening or orifice, a hole or short passage, for the protrusion of an organ, or for the performance of organic functions'. The plural form is 'foramina' (*OED*).

206 Labelled 'Foramen Cæcum' in the diagram at *GA*, 56.

207 Apparently a reference to the superior orbital fissure, labelled in the diagram at *GA*, 56 as 'Sphenoidal fissure'.

208 Cranial nerve III, or oculomotor; also referred to as motor oculi in the nineteenth century.

209 Cranial nerve IV, or trochlear.

210 '1[|st|?] 6[|th|?] of 5th': cranial nerve I is the ophthalmic but it does not pass through the superior orbital fissure. The '1st … [of] 5th' may refer to the first part of the fifth nerve: i.e. the three branches of the ophthalmic nerve (or cranial nerve $V_1$) of the trigeminal nerve or cranial nerve V, which pass through this fissure. However, the trigeminal nerve has only three major branches so the '6th of 5th' that Keats has here appears to be a mistake. In addition to the nerves mentioned by Keats, the fissure also transmits the superior and inferior divisions of the ophthalmic vein.

211 Cranial nerve VI, or abducens.

| | |
|---|---|
| – Rotunda –– | 2nd branch of 5th[212] |
| – Ovalia – – | 3rd branch of 5th or inf. Max[213] |
| – Spinosa – – | Dura Materal Art.[214] |
| – Carotica – – | Carotid Art. |

—

[Ff13r]

|S|ometimes an elevation of the Os Occipitis extending as far as |t|he Sutura Lambdoidalis which gives the Junction with the |O|ssa Parietalia the appearance of a depression – Surgeons have been |d|eceived by this variation and have trephined[215] to their sorrow.
|T|he frontal Sinusus communicate with ye Nose and are supposed to assist in forming the voice –
Fractures of the Os Frontis may be assisted by trephining except in two places, upon the Spine and upon the frontal Sinus.
If a fracture take place on the Spine apply the trephine to one side and elevate –
If the outer table of the frontal Sinus be depressed there is no need to trephine –
In the young subject the Os Frontis is frequently fractured, in the Adult more frequently the Parietal upon the whole surface of which ~~mav~~ the Trephine may be applied – except the sagittal Suture – the anterior and inferior ~~and~~ angle from danger of wounding the Dura Materal Artery – nor can it be done at the inferior and posterior angle withou|t| wounding the Lateral Sinus –
The Os Occipitis is but rarely broken – when so a very small part is accessible to the Trephine – that part which can be trephined must be done so laterally on account of the perpendicu|[lar]| ridge – The whole line drawn from the summit of the to the Middle of the Nose and the perpendicular ridge of the Os Occipitis is objectional to the Trephine for the above mentioned Reasons.

212 Superior maxillary.

213 Inferior maxillary.

214 Now known as the meningeal artery.

215 Transitive verb, meaning 'to operate upon with a trephine'. A trephine is '[a]n improved form of trepan, with a transverse handle, and a removable or adjustable sharp steel centre-pin which is fixed upon the bone to steady the movement in operating'. A trepan is 'a surgical instrument in the form of a crown-saw' (*OED*).

M$^{r}$. Whitfield[216] trephined on the temporal Bone – the temporal Muscle should be divided in the direction of its fibres.
The Sphenoid is never broken by itself but the fractures continue from other Bones – There is no part where the Sphenoid Bone can be trephined except where it joins the anterior and inferior angle of the Parietal Bone – It has never been and probably never will be trephined –

—

[Ff13v]

The Foramina in the posterior division of
The Skull's internal Basis
Three pair and a single one
Foramina Auditiva – for the Audit. Nerve[217]
– Lacera Basis Cranii — Int. Jugular[218] and 8$^{th}$ pair[219] and the nervi accessorii[220]
– Condyloidia — — — 9$^{th}$ pair or Sub.Ling[221]
~~en~~ Magnum Medulla oblongata, Verteb|ral| Arteries. Sub.occip| |[222] and Nerous access|or|[223]

Thus the Foramina at y$^{e}$ internal Basis of the Skull are 9 pair and a single one

| | |
|---|---|
| 1$^{st}$ Foramina | Optica |
| 2 — — | Lacera Orp Sup[224] |

216 'R. Whitfield, Apothecary to St. Thomas's Hospital when Keats was at Guy's' (Forman, ix).
217 Auditory.
218 Internal jugular vein.
219 Consists of three nerves: the glosso-pharyngeal, pneumo-gastric, and spinal accessory.
220 Spinal accessory nerve, usually considered a sub-division of the eighth pair in the nineteenth century (*GA*, 496–97), now known as cranial nerve XI.
221 The condyloid foramen transmits the lingual nerve. The sublingual gland is lodged in the sublingual fossa of the inferior maxillary bone at the jaw.
222 Probably 'Sub-Occipital'.
223 Probably a misspelling: he seems to have meant the spinal accessory nerve.
224 Apparently a reference to the superior orbital fissure, labelled in the diagram at *GA*, 56 as 'Sphenoidal fissure'. See nn207–11.

3 — — Rotunda
4 — — Ovalia
5 —— Spinosa
6 —— Carotica[225]
7 —— Auditiva
8 —— Lacera Basis Cranii
9 —— Condyloidia
10 Foramen Magnum

The Anterior division of the internal Basis of the Skull.
It is bounded on the fore part by the Os Frontis behind by the Pterygoid Processes of the Sphenoid bone.[226] In the Middle of this division is placed

—

[Ff14r = Blank]

—

[Ff14v]

the Ethmoidal Bone[227] & from the Centre of this is proceeding the nasal plate of the Ethmoid, which when united with the Vomer[228] one of the Bones of the face forms the Septum Narium.[229] To the outer side of the Nasal plate {(x)} are the ethmoidal Cells,[230] to the outer side of these are parts of the Ethmoid termed the ossa Plana[231] further outward still are the 2 orbitar Cavaties which are bounded on the outer side by the two external angular processes.

(x) of the Ethmoid is the superior turbinated bone being part of the Ethmoid – exterior to the Nasal plate & [a hand pointing upwards – an 'indicator' hand – drawn here]

225 Carotid canal.
226 *GA*, 33.
227 *GA*, 37.
228 'It is a slender thin bone separating the nostrils from each other' (*LM*, 938).
229 Nasal septum.
230 These are found at the edges of the ethmoidal notch of the frontal bone. They are depicted, but not labelled, in the diagram at *GA*, 26.
231 See 'os planum' in the diagram at *GA*, 37.

In this Division are 3 pair of Foramina
1st Foramina Optica
2nd – Lacera Orb sup.
3rd – Rotunda
The Middle Division of the external Basis of the Skull. It is bounded on the fore part by the Pterygoid Processes of the Sphenoid Bone, and at the back part by the styloid Processes of the Temporal Bone.[232]

–

[Ff15r = Blank]

–

[Ff15v]

In the Middle of this division is observed the Azygos portion of the Sphenoid Bone for the attachment of the Vomer, and behind this an articulatory surface, for the Cuneiform process of the Os Occipitis.[233]

The Pterygoid Processes are placed laterally & they have an Internal and an External Plate – behind these are the spinous processes, which gi|ve| name to a Foramen – to their outer sides are the two Zygomatic processes situated to the outer sides of the depressions for the lower Jaw, which uniting with the process of the Ossa Malarum[234] form the Zygomatic Arches.[235] At the root of the Zygomatic process is a depression for the Articulation of the Lower Jaw.
In this division are 6 pair of Foramina.
1st The Foramina Pterygoidea
2nd –– Ovalia
3rd –– Spinosa
4th – – Carotica
5th Iter a Palato Ad Aurem
6th Meatus auditorius externus.

–

232 *GA*, 31.
233 *GA*, 19 and 21.
234 *GA*, 45 and 46.
235 Cheek bones.

[Ff16r = Blank]

—

[Ff16v]

The Posterior Division of the external Basis of the Skull.

It is bounded on the fore part by the Styloid Processes of the Temporal Bones, and behind by the Os Occipitis. In the Middle of this division is found the Cuneiform process of the Os Occipitis. On the outer sides of this the two Condyloid processes which rest on the Atlas or 1st Vertebra[236] – on the sides are the Petrous portion of the Temporal Bone.[237] To the outer side of the Condyloid process|es| are the styloid and these are surround|ed| by sheath like processes called the Vagi|nal|[238] Further outwards are the 2 Mastoid or Maxillary Processes, at the roots of which are the Fossa digastrica.[239]

The posterior part is divided into 2 Ridges the first small for the attachment of the Recti and obliqui, the other large for the Complexus and Scaleni.[240]

The Foramina in this Division are

4 pair and a single foramen
1st Foramina Lacera Basis Cranii
2nd — — Condyloidea
3rd — — Stylo Mastoidea
4th — — Condyloidea Poster[241]
and the Foramen Magnum

The Parts which pass through the different Foramina
1st – The Foramina Optica are formed to transmit the optic Nerves to the Retina & the ophthalmic Artery.

—

236 *GA*, 6.
237 *GA*, 29.
238 *GA*, 31.
239 *GA*, 28.
240 These are muscles located at the back and base of the skull, and along the spine.
241 Posterior condyloid foramen.

[Ff17r = Blank]

—

[Ff17v]

2nd The Foramina lacera[242] to transmit the 3rd the fourth, the first Branch of the 5th and the 6th pr of N[s?][243]
3rd Foramen Rotund to transmit the 2nd Branch of the 5th pair or superior maxillary.
4th Foram. Oval. to transmit the 3rd Branch of the 5th or inferior maxillary –
5th Foram. Spinosa to transmit the Dura Materal Artery or Spheno Spinalis.
6th Foram. Carotica to transmit the Intern Caroti|d|[244]
7th Foram. Auditiva to transmit the Auditory |Nerves|
8th Foram. lacera basis Cranii to transmit the internal Jugular Vein & 8th pair of Nerves or Pars Vaga & the Nervus accessorius.[245]
9th Foramen Condyloidea to transmit the 9th pair or Sublingual[246] or gustatory going to the To|ngue|
10th The Foramen Magnum for the passage of the Medulla oblongata 2 vertebral Arteries and the Nerviaccessorii.[247]
The other Foramina at the external Basis of the Skull are 1st The Foramina Pterygoidea to transmit a reflected portion of the 5th pair which unites with the grand Sympathetic.

242 *LM* defines 'Foramina Lacera' as '[a] pair of foramina in the basis of the cranium, through which the internal jugular veins, and the eighth pair and accessory nerves pass' (*LM*, 363). However, based on the nerves this aperture is transmitting, Keats here appears to be referring to the superior orbital fissure. He refers to the 'Foramen Lacera' as defined in *LM* in the eighth item on this list, using the name 'Foramen lacera basis Cranii'.

243 The superior orbital fissure, which transmits the oculomotor (cranial nerve III), the trochlear (cranial nerve IV), the ophthalmic (the first branch of cranial nerve V – or trigeminal – and denoted as cranial nerve $V_1$), and abducens (cranial nerve VI). See nn208–11.

244 Internal carotid artery.

245 The spinal accessory nerve. It leaves the skull through the jugular foramen, having travelled along the inner wall after entering the skull through the foramen magnum.

246 Mis-writing for lingual nerve.

247 The spinal accessory nerve; see n220.

2nd The Foramen or iter a Palato ad aurem is for the Eustachian Tube.[248]
3rd The Meatus auditivus externus for the passage of Sound.[249]
4th The Foramen Stylo Mastoideum to transmit the portio dura of the 7th pair of Nerves.[250]
5th Foramina condyloidea posteroia to transmit the Veins from the Sinuses of the Dura Mater.

—

[Ff18r = Blank]

—

[Ff18v]

The Bones of the Face are in number
Fourteen viz Ossa Nasi — 2[251]
— Maxillar sup. 2[252]
— Malarum — 2[253]
— Palati — 2[254]
— Turbinata inf 2[255]
— Unguis 2[256]
Os Vomer 1[257]
— Maxil. Inf 1[258]
—
14
—

248 'Iter a Palato ad aurem' is the eustachian tube. Its passage – or foramen – is through a groove that lies between the petrous part of the temporal bone and the great wing of the sphenoid. See diagram at *GA*, 31.
249 Shown in the diagram at *GA*, 56.
250 The facial nerve.
251 *GA*, 39.
252 *GA*, 41 and 42.
253 *GA*, 45 and 46.
254 *GA*, 47 and 48.
255 *GA*, 49.
256 *GA*, 44 ('The Lachrymal Bone').
257 *GA*, 50.
258 *GA*, 51 and 52.

The Bones of the Orbit are in number

| | |
|---|---|
| Seven viz | Os Frontis |
| 3 Bones of y^e Head { | – Sphænoides |
| | – Ethmoides |
| | Os Malæ[259] |
| 4 of the Face { | – Maxil. Super[260] |
| | – Palati & |
| | – Unguis |

—

[Ff19r: see Figure 6]

The Ductus ad Nasum[261] is formed ¾ in the Os Maxillare sup | | and ¼ in the Os turbinatus inferior.
The Dens sapientiæ[262] would be quite in contact with the Antrum[263] were it not for a membrane –
The foramen infra orbitarum is the Passage for the Nerve frequently affected with Tic douloureux –[264]
Sometimes a fracture {of the Nose} is rendered compound by the formation of an abscess which renders it extremely tedious of Cure –
The pituitary Membrane of the Nose is expanded on the spongy and contorted surface of the inferior turbonated[265] Bone –
A Probe passed into the ductus ad Nasum goes under the inferior turbanated[266] Bone –
The Lachrymal Sac is lodged on the Os Unguis –
The Os Unguis is situated to the anterior and inferior part of the Orbit.
The Septum of the Nose is formed of three parts 1 Nasal part of the Ethmoid 2 B[y] the Vomer posteriorly 3 By Cartilage anteriorly.

259 Plural of 'Os Malarum': the malar bones.
260 Superior maxillary bone.
261 Nasal duct.
262 Wisdom teeth.
263 The antrum of Highmore of the superior maxillary bones: see *GA*, 42.
264 The infraorbital foramen transmits the superior and inferior maxillary nerves, which are themselves the second and third branches of the trigeminal nerve.
265 Misspelling for 'turbinated'.
266 See n265.

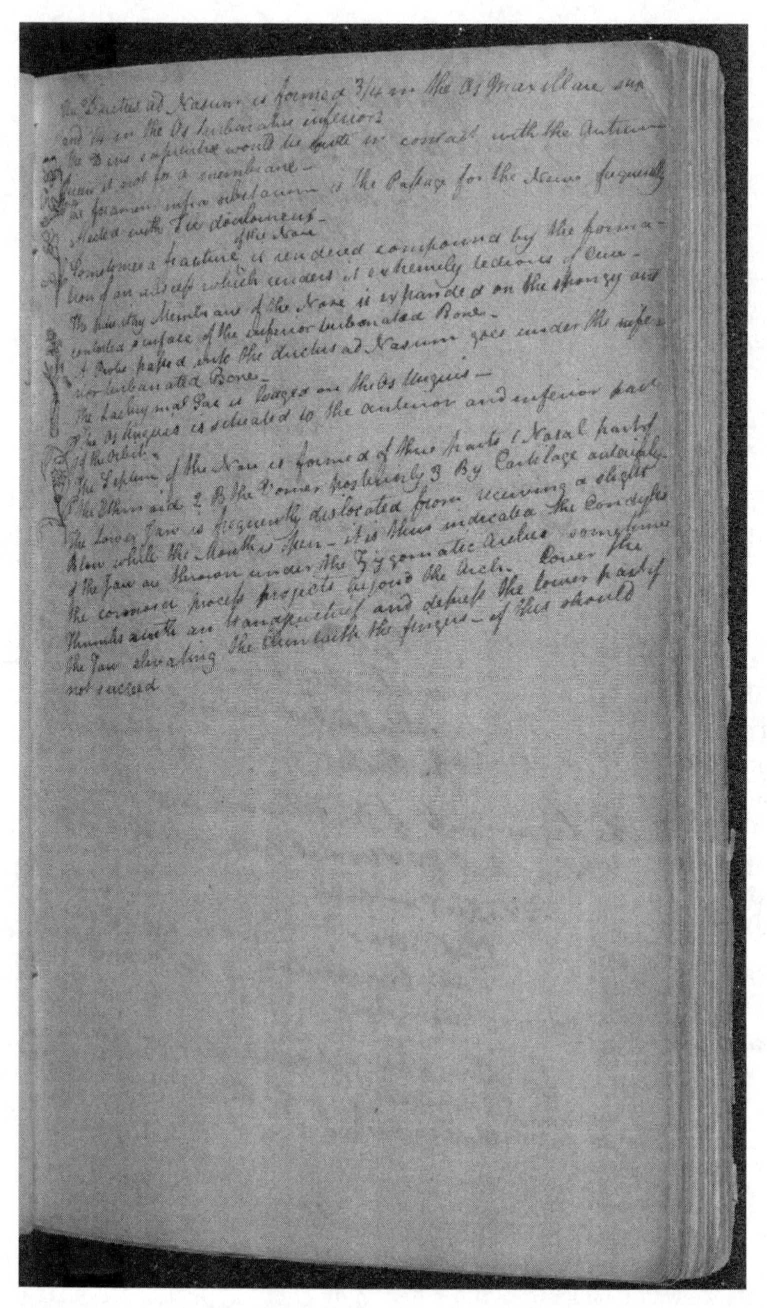

**Figure 6:** Ff19r, showing Keats' marginal sketches of flowers. From 'John Keats' medical Notebook'. Image © City of London, Keats House, Hampstead.

The Lower Jaw is frequently dislocated from receiving a slight Blow while the Mouth is open – it is thus indicated the Condyles of the Jaw are thrown under the Zygomatic Arches sometimes the coronoid process projects beyond the Arch. Cover the Thumbs ~~a~~ with an Handkerchief and depress the lower part of the Jaw elevating the Chin with the fingers – if this should not succeed
[Four flowers are drawn along the inner margin of this page]

–

[Ff19v]

Syndesmology.[267]

The Ligaments of the Spine are
Seven, – The Anterior Vertebral
– – Posterior Vertebral
– Crucial[268]
– Interspinal
– Intertransverse
– Capsular & the Nuchæ.
The Ligaments of the Ribs are
Seven – Capsular of the Head of ye Rib
Capsular of the tubercle of |Do| Rib
Internal Ligament of ye Neck
External – – of ye Neck
Proper Ligaments between ye |Ribs|
Capsular – – between ye Cart|i[l?]|[269]
& Proper – – – of ye last Rib.
The Ligaments of the Clavicle are
Six 3 at the Sternal End and three at the Scapular End.
Capsular
Inter Clavicular
Rhomboid[270]
} At the Sternal End of the Clavicle

267 'That branch of anatomy which treats of the ligaments' (*OED*).
268 Also known as 'cruciform'.
269 Cartilages.
270 Also known as costo-clavicular ligament.

Conoid[271]
Trapezoid } At the Scapular End of y^e Clavicle
Capsular

—

[Ff20r = Blank]

—

[Ff20v]

The Ligaments of the Scapular[272] are
3 The Anterior Ligament thereof
– Superior Costal Ligament[273]
and the third passing from y^e root of y^e Processus Acromion[274]
to y^e edge of y^e glenoid Cavity[275]
The Ligaments of the Elbow Joint
Seven, External Lateral or Brachio Radia|lis|[276]
Internal Lateral or Brachio Cubital|is|
Capsular Ligament of y^e Joint[277]
Coronary Ligament of y^e Radius[278]
Oblique Ligament[279] &
2 other Ligaments called the inner and outer Muscular Ligaments

271 Conoid and trapezoid are together known as the coraco-clavicular ligaments. They help form the shoulder joint.
272 For 'scapula'.
273 There is no costal ligament attaching to the scapula, but the superior transverse ligament attaches to the scapular notch on its costal surface.
274 Labelled 'Acromion process' at *GA*, 159.
275 Located on the lateral angle of the scapula and articulating with the head of the humerus bone.
276 *GA*, 162.
277 Possibly a reference to the joint capsule; the capsular ligament is usually classed as belonging to the shoulder joint.
278 Usually known as the annular or orbicular ligament.
279 *GA*, 161.

The Foramina in y^e interosseous Ligament
2. One at the upper part for the passage of y^e internal interosseal Artery, both Arteries are going to the back of the Wrist.
The Ligaments of the Wrist Joint
The External Transverse
The Internal Transverse &
Capsular, which passes over the Radius and 3 Carpi[280]
The Ligaments of y^e Pelvis
5. Ileo Sacral joining y^e Sacrum to y^e Ilium
Superior Transverse
Inferior Transverse
2 Sacro Sciatic Ligaments viz Ex^t & In^t Obturator[281]
[There is an '&' symbol on the outer margin, aligned with 'Obturator']

—

[Ff21r = Blank]

—

[Ff21v]

by the 2 sacro sciatic Ligaments 2 holes are found the one called the ischiatic notch[282] for y^e passage of the pyriform Muscle, the Sciatic Nerve & the gluteal, ischiatic and pudendal Arteries.

The other[283] for the passage of the obturator internus | | its Tendon, and the pudendal Artery[284]

The Ligaments of y^e Hip Joint
2 Capsular & y^e Ligament-Teres[285]

280 I.e. three bones of the carpus.
281 External and internal obturators.
282 Greater sciatic notch.
283 Lesser sciatic foramen derived from the lesser sciatic notch.
284 The lesser sciatic foramen transmits the pudendal nerve.
285 *GA*, 171.

The Ligaments of y^e^ Knee Joint

10. The Ligament of the Patella[286]
- External lateral
- Internal lateral
- Posterior or oblique popliteal[287]
- Capsular
- Alar
- 2 Crucial Ligt^s^ Ant & Post[288]
- 2 Semilunar of y^e^ Semil. Cartil|age|

Attachments.

The Ligament of y^e^ Patella from the lower part thereof to the Tubercle of y^e^ |+++|[289]

External Lateral from the external condyle of the Os femoris to y^e^ head of y^e^ |Fibula|

Internal Lateral from the internal condyle to the head of y^e^ Tibia

Posterior Lig^t^ from the external condyle to y^e^ head of y^e^ tibia

Capsular surrounds the Joint including Os Femoris, Patella & Tibia

Alar Lig^t^ from the fore part of y^e^ Capsular Lig^t^ to the Lig^t^ of y^e^ Pate|lla|

Crucial Lig^ts^ cross each other the <u>anterior</u> arises from y^e^ depression between the Condyles and passes to the back of the rough ridge at y^e^ top of y^e^ Tibia. The <u>Posterior</u> to y^e^ tubercle between the 2 articulating surfaces at the head of the Tibia.

Semilunar Lig^ts^ unite the Semilunar Cartilages to the edge of y^e^ Head of y^e^ Tibia.

—

[Ff22r = Blank]

—

286 Anterior, or ligamentum patellæ.

287 Posterior, or ligamentum posticum Winslowii.

288 Anterior and posterior.

289 Tibia.

[Ff22v]

The Ligaments of the Ankle Joint.[290]

5 The Deltoid passing from y$^{e}$ Mall.[291] internus to y$^{e}$ os Naviculare and Astralagus
2 The anterior Lig$^{t}$ of the Fibula from the Mall. extern.[292] To y$^{e}$ Astralagus.
The Middle Ligam$^{t}$ of the Fibula from the Malleolus extern to the Os Calcis
The Posterior Lig$^{t}$ of y$^{e}$ Fibula pass from y$^{e}$ Malleolus extern to y$^{e}$ Astralagus
& The Capsular Lig$^{t}$ of the Ankle Joint covering the Tibia Fibula and Astralagus.

—

[Ff23r = Blank]

—

[Ff23v]

Sphlanchnology.[293]

The Contents of the Thorax are
The Pleura, Anterior and posterior Mediastinum the Lungs,[294] Heart,[295] pericardium and Thymus Gland.[296]
Contained within the posterior Mediastinum is
The Thymus Gland.
Cavaties in the Thorax are
3. Two formed by the Pluræ and one by y$^{e}$ Pericard.

290 *GA*, 178 and 179.
291 Malleolus.
292 Malleolus externus.
293 'Splanchnology' is '[t]he scientific study of the viscera' (*OED*).
294 *GA*, 652.
295 *GA*, 630 and 634.
296 The thymus gland is a lymphoid endocrine gland situated in the neck which helps regulate the immune system.

The Heart is placed

Within the Pericardium lying much towards the left side, its apex being about even with y$^{e}$ 4$^{th}$or 5$^{th}$ Ribs

It is kept in this situation by 8 large blood vessels which may be seen within the Pericardium viz

The Superior Cava
Inferior Cava
2 Right pulmonary Veins
2 Left pulmon.—
Aorta &
Pulmonary Artery.

The divisions of the Thymus Gland.

It has been divided into six lobes, it is placed near the under part of the sternal extremity of y$^{e}$ Clavi|cle| before y$^{e}$heart: it then runs up the neck as far as y$^{e}$ Thyroid Gland or Cricoid Cartilage.[297] If an incision be made into it a milky fluid issues, but for what purpose it is intended we are ignorant.

The Lobes of the Lungs are

5 Three to the right & two to the left.[298]

The Trachea[299]

The Trachea or Air Tube commences at y$^{e}$ extremity of y$^{e}$ Larynx, at the bottom of y$^{e}$ Cricoid Cartilage: it passes down the neck anteriorly to the Œsopha|gus|

—

[Ff24r = Blank]

—

[Ff24v]

When it has reached as low as the third dorsal Vertebra it bifurcates into the right & left Bronchiæ of which the right is the large~~st~~{r} but the left longer of the two: these go to the Lungs.

It is composed of numerous portions of Cartilage of the

297 *GA*, 641.
298 *GA*, 654.
299 *GA*, 649.

Horse shoe shape having at its posterior part muscular fibres placed.

The Structure of the Heart.[300]

The Heart is composed of 4 Cavaties surrounded by muscular fibres, two of which are Auricles and 2 ventricles.

The right Auricle has 4 Openings into it viz those from the superior and inferior Cavæ, one into the Ventric|le| and the other into the coronary Vein.

The Right Ventricle has 2 Openings into it:– one from the Auricle the other into the Pulmonary Artery.

The Left Auricle has 5 Openings:– 4 from the Pulmonary Veins and one the ventricular open|ing|

The Left Ventricle has 2 Openings:– one from y^e left Auricle, the other into y^e Aorta.

The Tuberculum Loweri[301] is situated between the openings of the Venæ Cavæ within the Right Auricle.

The Valvular Nobilis Eustachii[302] is placed at y^e commencement of y^e Vena Cava inferior.

The Mouth of the Coronary Vein is protected

By a large Valve of a Semilunar Shape called the Semilunar Valve of the Coronary Vein.

—

300 *GA*, 630 and 634.

301 Tubercle of lower, or intervenous tubercle.

302 Eustachian valve.

CHAPTER ONE

# John Keats' Medical Notebook

## An Overview

The provenance of Keats' medical Notebook is both well known and shrouded in mystery. Currently held by Keats House, Hampstead and the City of London Corporation, it was inherited by them, along with the rest of the 'Dilke Collection', from the Hampstead Public Library, to whom it had in turn been bequeathed by Sir Charles Wentworth Dilke, the grandson of Keats' friend Charles Dilke. The manuscript features the legend '425 in my catalogue Ch. Dilke' inside the front cover, and Sir Charles' bookplate on the inside of the back cover.[1] Keats' first biographer, Richard Monckton Milnes, in his *Life, Letters, and Literary Remains, of John Keats* (1848), mentioned it as '[a] book of very careful annotations, preserved by Mr. Dilke' – by which he meant Keats' friend.[2] Evidently, Sir Charles Wentworth Dilke had inherited Keats' medical Notebook from his grandfather before bequeathing it in turn to the Hampstead Public Library. We have, thus, a clear record for the whereabouts of this manuscript from at least 1848, but it is less clear when Keats' friend Dilke had originally acquired the medical Notebook, for it does not feature in the list of books in Keats' possession drawn up shortly after the poet's death.[3] Perhaps Keats gave it to Dilke before leaving for Italy; Brown would not have known this, as he was in Scotland in the weeks immediately leading up to Keats' departure. When and how Dilke acquired the manuscript remains unclear, but despite this gap there

1 JKMN, inside front cover, inside back cover.

2 Richard Monckton Milnes, *Life, Letters, and Literary Remains, of John Keats.* 2 vols (London: Edward Moxon, 1848), I, 29.

3 *KC*, I, 253–60.

is no doubt that the Notebook belonged to Keats. Scholarship over the twentieth century has established that the notes are undoubtedly in Keats' hand, and the subject and content of these notes can be demonstrated as having derived, for the most part, from lectures he attended as a student at Guy's Hospital, London, from October 1815 to March 1817. This chapter opens with an account of the provenance of the medical Notebook before describing its bibliographic features. A brief consideration of the only previously published edition of the manuscript is followed by a detailed exploration of the perplexing issues relating to its contents, including the source of the notes and the authenticity of the hand that wrote them. The final section discusses accounts of Keats' medical Notebook in the major biographies, news reports, and features in popular journals such as the *Times Literary Supplement*.[4]

## The Earliest Accounts

The first reference to Keats' medical Notebook is to be found – as already noted – in Milnes' *Life, Letters, and Literary Remains, of John Keats* (1848). Writing of the notebook, Milnes observes that it 'attests [Keats'] diligence, although a fellow student, who lodged at the same house, describes him as scribbling doggerel rhymes among the notes, particularly if he got hold of another student's syllabus'.[5] This fellow student was Henry Stephens, who had shared lodgings with Keats at St Thomas' Street and who provided for Milnes (via George Felton Mathew) a long account of his recollections of the poet. These reminiscences are invaluable as the only extant record of Keats at Guy's by someone who knew him *and* hospital life at the time, but allowances must be made for the fact that Stephens was recalling events at least 30 years after the fact (in 1847).[6] About Keats at lectures Stephens wrote: 'Whilst attending lectures, [Keats] would sit & instead of Copying out the lecture, would often scribble some doggrell rhymes, among the Notes of Lecture.'[7] Recalling

4 The excellent counter-factual and fictional works on Keats are unfortunately beyond the scope of this book.

5 Milnes, *Life*, I, 29.

6 For a detailed discussion, see Chapter 2.

7 *KC*, II, 210.

lectures that he and Keats had attended together, Stephens distinctly remembers Keats *not* taking notes during the lecture. This would suggest that Keats wrote up his notes afterwards and, certainly, the overall cleanness of Keats' notes – with no ink blots, stains or drips (bearing in mind that he was writing with a dipping pen) – is surprising, considering the crowded lecture theatres. Stephens' account of Keats' apparent lack of attention is belied, however, by the notice of his imminent elevation to a dresser-ship, as well as by his passing his licentiate examination. If Keats was seemingly inattentive at lectures, it did not hamper his ability to succeed.

The next major Keats biography, by William Michael Rossetti in 1887, makes a passing reference to the medical Notebook's existence: 'Keats attended the usual lectures, and made careful annotations in a book still preserved.'[8] Writing in the same year, Sidney Colvin stated: 'I have before me the MS. book in which he took down his own notes of a course, or at least the beginning of a course, of lectures on anatomy; and they are not those of a lax or inaccurate student.'[9] In the revised, expanded, and updated version of his biography, *John Keats His Life and Poetry His Friends Critics and After-Fame*, published in 1917, Colvin fleshed out the section on Keats' medical career. Referring to the Notebook, he stated in his footnote that it 'is in the collection bequeathed by the late Sir Charles Dilke to the public library at Hampstead':[10]

> we have an actual tangible relic to show how Keats's attention in the lecture room was now fixed and now wandered, in the shape of a notebook in which some other student has begun to put down anatomy notes and Keats has followed. Beginning from both ends, he has made notes of an anatomical and also of a surgical course, which are not those of a lax or inaccurate student, but full and close as far as they go.[11]

Colvin had seen the medical Notebook: in the earlier (1887) version of his biography he mentioned having the manuscript in front of him,

8 William Michael Rossetti, *Life of John Keats* (London: Walter Scott, 1887), 19.
9 Sidney Colvin, *Keats* (1887; Cambridge/New York: Cambridge University Press, 2011), 15.
10 Colvin, *Life*, 30.
11 Colvin, *Life*, 30.

and he was the first to notice the flowers 'squeezed into the margins of one or two pages … sketches, rather prettily touched'.[12] Amy Lowell, writing in the early 1920s, also tracked down the medical Notebook to the Dilke Collection, and noticed the flowers.[13] She wrote:

> [Keats] worked hard, as is shown by a note-book on his courses of anatomy and surgery. The notes are full and explicit. Little drawings appear occasionally among them, a flower or two absent-mindedly jotted down, probably when the lecturer grew dull or diffuse, but there is nothing odd in that.[14]

Lowell is informative on the details of Keats' medical career – her diffuse narrative spans over a hundred pages – but her commentary on the medical Notebook parallels Colvin's: both viewed the drawings of flowers as proving Keats' distraction. None of these Keats biographers, of course, had access to a published edition of the medical Notebook.

Three of Keats' friends and contemporaries had written biographical essays on him. Leigh Hunt, in his chapter on 'Mr Keats' in *Lord Byron and Some of His Contemporaries* (1828), was mainly concerned with Keats' poetry, but sketched in the outlines of his life:

> After receiving the rudiments of a classical education at Mr. Clarke's school at Enfield, [Keats] was bound apprentice to Mr. Hammond, a surgeon, in Church-Street, Edmonton; and his enemies having made a jest even of this, he did not like to be reminded of it; at once disdaining them for their meanness, and he himself for being sick enough to be moved by them.[15]

Hunt made no mention of Keats' Notebook or his time at Guy's, as that was outside the scope of his narrative. Charles Brown – Keats' closest friend in later life, who did not, however, know him while he was a medical student – wrote an incomplete biography of Keats,

12 Colvin, *Life*, 30.
13 Lowell, *Keats*, I, x.
14 Lowell, *Keats*, I, 75.
15 Leigh Hunt, *Byron and Contemporaries*, 247.

which was first read out at the Plymouth Institution in 1836.[16] Whatever Brown wrote about that period of Keats' life, therefore, reflected what he'd heard about it from Keats himself or from others who had known him at that time. Of the poet's medical training he wrote:

> He was educated at the Rev$^{d}$ M$^{r}$ Clarke's school at Enfield, and afterwards apprenticed to M$^{r}$ Hammond, a surgeon, in Church Street, Edmonton. ... After the usual term of years with M$^{r}$ Hammond, he became a student at Guy's Hospital; where he was indefaticable in his application to anatomy, medicine, and natural history.[17]

Brown's account remained unpublished for a century, appearing in print only in 1937. We are indebted to Brown for his description of Keats' recollection of his last operation; there is, however, no mention of Keats' medical Notebook in his essay.[18] Given that Keats was careful to keep his medical books – in May 1818 he wrote to Reynolds that he was 'glad at not having given away my medical Books' – and given that he started lodging with Brown in December of the same year, this may seem a curious omission.[19] Possibly the reason Brown didn't mention the medical Notebook is that he didn't have access to it: the manuscript ended up in Dilke's possession, and he and Brown had quarrelled after Keats' death.[20]

Finally, in 1861, Charles Cowden Clarke, the only one of these three contemporaries whose acquaintance with Keats pre-dated his medical studies, published his 'Recollections of Keats' in the *Atlantic Monthly*.[21] Clarke had known Keats from his schooldays, but when Keats moved to London and Guy's they temporarily lost touch (Clarke mistakenly assigns Keats as a student of St Thomas'). His essay included the famous anecdote about the composition of 'On

16 Charles Armitage Brown, *Life of John Keats*, ed. Dorothy Hyde Bodurtha and Willard Bissell Pope (London: Oxford University Press, 1937), 17.

17 Brown, *Life*, 41.

18 Brown, *Life*, 43. Milnes, who had access to Brown's MS, misquoted his account of Keats' last operation in his biography.

19 *LJK*, I, 277.

20 *NL*, 360.

21 CCC.

First Looking into Chapman's Homer' and this recollection of Keats' account of pursuing a career in medicine:[22]

> In one of our conversations about this period, I alluded to his position at St. Thomas's Hospital, – coasting and reconnoitring, as it were, that I might discover how he got on, and, with the total absorption that had taken place of every other mood of his mind than that of imaginative composition, what was his bias for the future, and what his feeling with regard to the profession that had been *chosen for him*, – a circumstance I did not know at that time. He made no secret, however, that he could not sympathize with the science of anatomy, as a main pursuit in life; for one of the expressions that he used, in describing his unfitness for its mastery, was perfectly characteristic. He said, in illustration of his argument, – 'The other day, for instance, during the lecture, there came a sunbeam into the room, and with it a whole troop of creatures floating in the ray; and I was off with them to Oberon and Fairy-land.' And yet, with all this self-styled unfitness for the pursuit, I was afterwards informed, that at his subsequent examination he displayed an amount of acquirement which surprised his fellow-students, who had scarcely any other association with him than that of a cheerful, crotchety rhymester.[23]

Extrapolating from this account, it seems clear that Clarke is recalling a time before Keats' licentiate examination of 25 July 1816, but after he had taken up his duties as a dresser – a period from which no letters survive, with the earliest extant dating from the summer of 1816. If Clarke's memory is a somewhat unreliable source of information for that period, the Notebook is perhaps a more reliable one. None of these writers had access to any publication that made a serious attempt to investigate the contents of Keats' medical Notebook or establish its provenance. That changed in 1925, when William Hale-White – himself a doctor – published his pioneering essay 'Keats as a Medical Student', which discussed the medical Notebook as a Keats manuscript of interest in its own right.

Hale-White's essay was concerned with Keats' medical Notebook, his career in medicine, and especially the time he spent at Guy's. As a

22 CCC, 90.
23 CCC, 90–91.

result, his interest in the manuscript was principally biographical and he studied it with an eye to medical history. He offered an 'authoritative record of Keats's sojourn at Guy's' – including the 'entries in the books kept in the Medical School Office at Guy's' concerning Keats – and made the first attempt to establish the provenance of the Notebook and the notes in it.[24] He also took steps to ensure that the manuscript was preserved and arranged to have a collotype facsimile made of it.

## The Only Published Edition

Maurice Buxton Forman published an edition of Keats' medical Notebook entitled *John Keats's Anatomical and Physiological Note Book printed from the holograph in the Keats Museum Hampstead* with Oxford University Press in 1934; this had a print run of 350 copies and an American reprint was issued in 1970.[25] Forman's edition produced a full transcription of the manuscript, beginning with a brief 'Prefatory Note' outlining the background of the Notebook and pointing the reader to Hale-White's essay, 'Keats as a Medical Student', for further details.[26] Citing Hale-White as his source, Forman quoted the entries associated with Keats from the Guy's Hospital records, and added from the Minute Book of the Court of Examiners of the Society of Apothecaries: 'John Keats was examined by Mr. Brande and the Court granted him the Certificate for which he had applied.' This entry is dated 25 July 1816 (misprinted by Forman as '1916'): the certificate confirmed Keats as a licentiate of the society and gave him the right to practise outside London.[27] The medical Notebook is then described as a bibliographic object, before Forman briefly summarized its contents prior to delineating his editorial principles. He has attempted, he explained, 'to preserve the character of the Note Book as far as reasonably possible, and to that end I have followed the arrangement of the original with but few exceptions'.[28]

24 Forman, v, quoting Hale-White, 'Keats as a Medical Student', 249–50.
25 Forman, insert between pp. ii and iii.
26 Forman, v.
27 Forman, vi.
28 Forman, vii.

This question of 'arrangement' arises because the notes in the original manuscript, as we have seen, are distinctively ordered. Forman claimed to have retained most of this particularity, but '[t]he principal exception to this scheme is the bringing together of the two sections of Lecture 4 and placing them immediately following Lecture 3. From that point the arrangement of the pages follows the holograph.'[29] As we have seen, Lecture 4 is split between the front and back ends of the Notebook. Forman – though he did not explicitly say so – obviously decided to privilege the reader's ease of comprehension over fidelity to Keats' original arrangement of his notes. Other minor occasions, Forman explained, 'where notes have been drawn from another page in accordance with Keats's reference marks, and where text has been continued in the margins of an opposite page, are indicated individually'.[30] In the manuscript these notes and text are in fact dispersed and continued on and across different pages; the edition brings them together with the matter that properly relates to them. This shifting of text, Forman said, is always individually indicated. Similarly, he advised that when 'it has appeared ... desirable, for the sake of clearness' he has 'insert[ed] words and letters that do not occur in the manuscript ... within conical brackets'.[31] Otherwise, he stated that Keats' slips in writing or errors in spelling are reproduced as they occur in the manuscript.

Given that Keats' medical Notebook is written from both the front and back, the imposition of any kind of conventional sequential order on it departs from the original arrangement: '[e]ach page of manuscript is presented separately', Forman explained, 'the theoretical number of the page in the Note Book being given as a chapter heading, and the pages beginning from the end of the book being distinguished by the addition of an asterisk'.[32] This edition, therefore, is obviously not a facsimile, but nor is it a conventionally transcribed copy. Forman attempted a balancing act, trying to present a printed text as close as 'reasonably possible' to the manuscript, which could also be read continuously in a sequential fashion.[33] However, he didn't offer any annotation to the material

29 Forman, vii.
30 Forman, vii.
31 Forman, vii.
32 Forman, vii.
33 Forman, vii.

in the Notebook: 'It would be worthless for a layman to offer any comment on the anatomical and physiological value of the Notes and Lectures.'[34] In refraining from commenting on the 'anatomical and physiological value', however, he in fact refrained from *all* commentary – even of an explanatory kind – resulting in an edition strangely shorn. The foremost difficulty with Forman's edition stems from this attempt to straddle a scholarly edition and a diplomatic transcription. In trying to compromise between two separate forms meeting disparate needs, it serves neither purpose satisfactorily, with the accuracy of its editorial apparatus open to doubt.

The medical Notebook's importance is twofold. Firstly, the notes were taken by Keats: they represent a tangible material link to the poet and analysing them may shed light on his thought processes and methods of working, as well as for that period in his biography. Secondly, it provides primary evidence of the training offered by the London teaching hospitals, and as such represents the cutting edge of British medical science during the Romantic period. Forman's approach to this promising material is curious: he was uninterested in possible insights into British medical history, seemed unconvinced that it had any significance for Keats' poems, and did not attempt to uncover the document's history in relation to Keats' biography. Even in the early 1930s, the Notebook was over a century old: medical science had developed rapidly in the interim, and some concepts mentioned in the manuscript were outdated, while others had evolved. Medically specific words appearing in the manuscript had changed their meanings, but Forman supplied no commentary to aid the reader in understanding such obsolete or mutated vocabulary. For a scholarly edition this is unusually reticent.

Forman did provide a helpful list of 'Persons referred to in the Lecture Notes', but this was occasionally somewhat short on details.[35] For instance, he listed a 'Dr. Jones', but offered no further information. In fact, this was John Frederick Drake Jones, a member of the Royal College of Surgeons, London, who published *A Treatise on the Process Employed by Nature in Suppressing the Haemorrhage from Divided and Punctured Arteries, and on the Use of Ligature; concluding with Observations on Secondary Haemorrhage* (1805). The *Treatise* explored haemorrhages and the best ways to treat

34 Forman, vii–viii.

35 Forman, ix.

them: Jones conducted experiments on animals and assimilated the existing literature and case histories, and his work contributed to a clearer understanding of bodily reaction in cases of haemorrhage.[36] Other instances where more detail would be helpful and could be supplied easily include the entries for Abernethy, John Hunter, and 'Mr. Huson': Forman gave dates and a clarification that 'Huson' was actually called 'William Hewson', but did not record that all three were eminent surgeons. Similarly, he did not note that William Thomas Brande was from 1813 professor of chemistry to the Apothecaries' Society, or that van Haller (Swiss) and Galvani (Italian) were famous physicians.[37] The outline entry 'Mr. Grosvenor, of Oxford' is a reference to John Grosvenor (1742–1823), surgeon and editor of the *Oxford Journal*.[38]

One page of the Notebook is reproduced as a photograph opposite the edition's title page and captioned as the 'twenty-seventh page of the Note-Book', where Keats discusses the structure of the nose and draws flowers in the margin.[39] Four flowers are drawn in a vertical line next to the gutter – the top-most is a pansy, or possibly a *Viola tricolor*; the third one from the top is stuck in a vase; and the fourth flower has a leaf curling over the top of it (see Figure 6). The ghostly impression of writing on the reverse side of the paper is visible in this photographic facsimile. Forman's caption does not clarify whether this image is of the twenty-seventh page from the front of the Notebook or from the back. Upon reading the whole, of course, we come to know that it is the twenty-seventh from the front – that is, Ff19r. Tipped into Forman's volume at this point is a small slip containing an 'Erratum': 'Page 36, line 7: *For* Sometimes fracture *read* Sometimes a fracture'.[40]

In terms of verbal transcription, Forman is almost always accurate. There are passages that were and sometimes still are illegible, owing either to paper and/or ink decay or to quirks of handwriting: these

36 See Jones, *A Treatise*, 56–57.

37 See L. S. Jacyna, 'Abernethy, John (1764–1831)', Jacob W. Gruber, 'Hunter, John (1728–1793)', J. F. Payne, rev. Michael Bevan, 'Hewson, William (1739–1774)', and Frank A. J. L. James, 'Brande, William Thomas (1788–1866)', *ODNB*; 'Albrecht van Haller' and 'Luigi Galvani', *EB*.

38 Michael Bevan, 'Grosvenor, John (1742–1823)', *ODNB*.

39 Forman, ii.

40 Forman, insert between pp. 36 and 37.

Forman clearly indicates as being so. Occasional phrases have been misread: for example, at Bf4r, we find this sentence: 'The Arteries of the Spinal Marrow are derived from the Vertebrae.'[41] This makes no sense, and it is hard to believe that Astley Cooper would have said or Keats written such a thing. In reality the sentence reads: 'The Arteries of the Spinal Marrow are derived from the Vertebral.' Instances of this kind are rare, however. There are occasional discrepancies between readings suggested by Hale-White and those offered by Forman – in these cases, Forman is almost always (more) accurate. One such discrepancy occurs at a point that has significance for Keats' poetry. In 'Lecture 10' at Bf4v, Hale-White has the 'patient K.' where Forman reads, correctly, 'The Patriot K.' – a reference to the Polish patriot Thaddeus Kosciusko (1746–1817).[42] Although it has long been noted that Kosciusko is mentioned in Keats' medical Notebook and that Keats subsequently wrote a sonnet to him, the full extent of correspondences between notes and sonnet has not been recognized. Here is what Keats wrote in his Notebook at Bf4v:

> ~~Thos~~ The Patriot K. having
> had the Sciatic Nerve divided by a pike wound was a
> long while before his limb recovered its sensibility.

From the form of the entry, it seems that this detail caught Keats' attention at once – he left a space after the 'K', as if he intended to fill in the name once he found out how to spell it (his sonnet 'To Kosciusko' turns on 'thy great name alone' (1)). As a reader of *The Examiner* Keats would certainly have heard of Kosciusko: Hunt's leading article on 3 July 1814, for instance, contains this: 'The very mention of the name of KOSCIUSKO, after having been compelled to ring the changes so often upon the BONAPARTES and the FERDINANDS, – the mighty tyrants and the mean, – is like a new music, coming to us in a summer wind.'[43] Keats' hero of 'high feeling' (2) was, in his medical Notebook, a man who had lost 'sensibility'

41 Forman, 53.

42 Hale-White, 'Keats as a Medical Student', 255; Forman, 55.

43 *The Examiner* (3 July 1814): 429. For how Keats' sonnet to Kosciusko is indebted to Hunt's article, see Thomas McLean, *The Other East and Nineteenth-Century British Literature: Imagining Poland and the Russian Empire* (Basingstoke: Palgrave Macmillan, 2012), 102.

– the ability to feel – because of damage to his sciatic nerve.[44] As the sciatic nerve runs down the leg, an injury that 'divided' it would also affect Kosciusko's ability to walk. In his sonnet Keats looked forward to some 'happy day, / When some good spirit walks upon the earth' (9–10), when the 'new music' of Kosciusko's name would be revered alongside King Alfred and 'the great of yore' (11). These were associations that stayed with Keats: he wrote of Kosciusko again in *Sleep and Poetry*, describing how in 'a poet's house' (354) he had seen the 'cold and sacred busts' (357) of King Alfred and 'Kosciusko worn / By horrid sufferance – mightily forlorn' (387–88). Taken together, this intersection of ideas – including Kosciusko's 'sufferance' – displays intriguing connections with Kosciusko's injury as described in Keats' medical notes. It is this inter-weaving of different aspects of knowledge and imagination that Hale-White compromised by mis-transcription, and which Forman did not comment upon in his own edition.

The distinctive arrangement of Keats' notes requires its editor to take a decision on the manner of presentation, which is bound to affect the experience of reading the notes. An editorial decision such as this also implies a critical stance. Forman did not explain his own editorial decision, but it is clear from his 'Prefatory Note' that he chose to privilege the reader's ease of navigation and comprehension over absolute fidelity to the manuscript. However, he did not follow this decision through to its logical conclusion: the lack of annotation does not help the reader. The edition does not reproduce the notes as arranged in the manuscript, but it also does not always clearly indicate as much, with the result that it occasionally misleads its readers. For example, in a pioneering article comparing Keats' medical notes with those of his fellow student Joshua Waddington, George A. R. Winston's comments suggest that he understood Forman's footnotes to be part of Keats' manuscript. A section of the article, sub-headed 'The Confusion in Keats's Notes', begins thus:

> In Forman's transcription there is a footnote on page 3: 'The fourth page has the continuation of Lecture 2 in the left-hand and bottom

44 For 'sensibility', *OED* lists the following: 'The state or property of being capable of sensation ...; the ability to respond to sensory stimuli; †a specific sensory function (*obsolete rare*). Also, the degree to which someone or something, esp. a sensory organ or tissue, is able to respond to stimuli.'

> margins, See Fifth Page.' On referring to the fifth page (5) this footnote appears, 'The above passage beginning with 'lated in 3¾ hours is written in the margin of the Fourth Page'. The beginning of this sentence is on page five line 17, 'Blood without the access of Air coagulated in 3 ¾ hours and with it in ¼ hour according to Mr. Huson's Experiment'. The word 'coagulated' is the fifth word of line 18 and 'lated is the ending of that word, which proves the haphazard manner in which Keats scattered his notes.[45]

Keats did indeed 'scatter' his notes, but in his manuscript the word 'coagulated' is *not* 'the fifth word of line 18' – it is the last word of the last line of the fifth page from the front: that is, Ff3r. With no room there for the complete word, Keats wrote 'coagu' on that page, and continued with 'lated' on the left-hand margin of the facing page, Ff2v. This may be eccentric, but is not quite as haphazard as Winston believes; he has been misled because the manner of Forman's presentation persuaded him that Forman's footnotes were Keats'. Forman claimed to have 'indicated individually' each instance where he shifted text around to facilitate presentation, comprehension, and navigation, but in point of fact he consistently *omitted* to do so for the marginalia.[46] Nor did he say anything about the order in which Keats' notes were taken, although – given that in places notes are squeezed into the margins around other pre-existing notes, and sometimes written across these – there is clear evidence for a chronology to the note-taking. Admittedly, Forman pointed the reader at the outset to Hale-White's essay, which mentioned as much in passing, but the choice not to address this aspect of the medical Notebook within the body of its publication is rather unusual.[47]

Keats' marginalia – the source of the complexity in his page layouts – comprise three types: continuation of lecture notes (e.g. at Ff2v and Ff3v); additions or insertions (e.g. at Ff11v and Ff12r); and after-thoughts (e.g. at Ff1v and Ff2r). Forman printed Keats' marginalia continuously within the main body of text, where one can conjecture that Keats would ideally have meant them to be. However, he gave no indication that these passages were, in fact, marginalia and not part of the original running text in the manuscript. This attempt

45 *KW*, 107–08.

46 Forman, vii.

47 Hale-White, 'Keats as a Medical Student', 255.

at integration occasionally caused problems, requiring Forman to compromise to prevent his transcription becoming incomprehensible. In turn, however, this editorial compromise changed the form of the notes in unexpected ways so that the final publication bore little resemblance to the original notes. Consequentially it is only by comparing Forman's transcription with the original that one can ascertain the relative status and position of the text printed.

On the first page of the transcription in Forman's edition can be found an example of this confusing treatment of the marginalia. It contains the transcription of Ff2r, which Forman accurately denoted, following his system of assigning page numbers, as 'THIRD PAGE'.[48] In the manuscript, this page has extensive marginal notes, written in the inner margin near the gutter (see Figure 3). There are in total four separate marginal notes, grouped in such a manner on the page that at first sight they appear as a cluster of three. These four marginal notes are related to distinct portions of the main text on the page, and Keats takes care to indicate these relationships by employing a set of symbols – '♦', '◊', 'c', 'x' – linking each marginal note to its appropriate referent. Forman, however, incorporated the notes within the main text with no indication that they were marginalia. He took care to separate them and, as far as possible, inserted them at that point within the main text where Keats' indications suggested they should be. Nevertheless, in that the text does not indicate what material comprised the marginal notes in the manuscript, it is misleading. Moreover, because of the many differences between the original manuscript layout and the layout for the printed transcription, even this attempt to maintain fidelity by inserting the marginalia where Keats' symbols indicated is compromised. The following is a section from Ff2r, which Keats cross-referenced with his marginalia:

> 3[c] Brain Medullæ oblongata and Spinalis, & Nerves
> This system has 4 Function    1 Sensation[x]
>     2 Volition
>     3 Involuntary Motion
>     4 Sympathy.

The superscripts 'c' and 'x' refer to two distinct marginal notes: note 'c' reads 'The Mind has 3 Functions 1 Memory, 2 Judgement 3

48 Forman, 1.

Imagination'; note 'x' reads 'The Organs of Sense are 5 Feeling, Sight, Hearing, Smell, Taste'. Keats' presentation manages simultaneously to convey the relationships these marginal notes bear to the main text without interfering with or obscuring the text itself. His system of annotation – on this page and throughout his medical Notebook – is in fact remarkably similar to the one he later suggested to Reynolds in 1819: 'It may be interesting to you to pick out some lines from Hyperion and put a mark x to the false beauty proceeding from art, and one || to the true voice of feeling.'[49] Keats recommended that Reynolds make use of symbols in the margins to record and link his critical response to lines from the poem *Hyperion*, just as several years earlier, writing in his medical Notebook, he had himself made use of symbols to record and cross-reference his medical notes.

For Forman, this reliance on symbols and marginalia presented a challenge. He evidently realized that if he inserted the marginalia into the text, the passage would read:

> 3 The Mind has 3 Functions 1 Memory, 2 Judgement
> 3 Imagination Brain Medulla oblongata and Spinalis, & Nerves
> This System has 4 Function 1 Sensation The Organs
> of Sense are 5 Feeling, Sight, Hearing, Smell, Taste.
> 2 Volition
> 3 Involuntary Motion
> 4 Sympathy

The difficulties inherent in Forman's method are well illustrated here. He was therefore obliged to present the passage thus:

> 3 Brain Medulla oblongata and Spinalis, & Nerves
> This system has 4 Function 1 Sensation
> 2 Volition
> 3 Involuntary Motion
> 4 Sympathy.
> The Organs of Sense are 5 Feeling, Sight, Hearing, Smell, Taste.
> The Mind has 3 Functions
> 1 Memory, 2 Judgement 3 Imagination[50]

49 *LJK*, II, 167.
50 Forman, 1–2.

This layout is quite different from the original, and while it may be the best solution within Forman's editorial parameters, it does not indicate which passages are marginalia, and Forman did not annotate to clarify.

## Sources of Keats' medical notes

Hale-White used his reading of a sentence in Lecture 4, at Ff1r, to establish which course of lectures Keats' notes derived from. Forman followed Hale-White in this, not noticing that the reading Hale-White cited as evidence was contradicted by Forman's own – minor but significant – variation in transcription (Forman is accurate). Hale-White believed that the notes headed with a lecture number were 'notes of a series of physiological lectures' because the first line on the first page – that is to say, Ff1r – read 'Lectr. 4. Arteries continued from page 3. Physiology'.[51] He stated that 'Keats makes notes of a course of twelve lectures and heads them Physiology, so that these notes were almost certainly taken from Astley Cooper's lectures.'[52] Keats, however, had done no such thing. The sentence in question actually reads – as Forman correctly transcribed it – 'Lect$^{r}$ 4. Arteries continued from page 3. Physyology of Arteries and their diseases'.[53] This undercuts Hale-White's argument in favour of his proposed source in Cooper's lectures.

Because Forman followed Hale-White unquestioningly without noticing that his own transcription contradicted Hale-White's evidence, his attribution of material in the Notebook to lectures by Cooper must also be considered doubtful. It cannot be considered a certainty, when the basis is Hale-White's misreading, that the notes derived from any lectures on 'Physiology' and 'Anatomy'. Indeed, it appears unlikely that Keats studied on any course with the single word 'Physyology' – or even 'Physiology' – in its title, while there is good reason to suppose he attended at least two lecture courses featuring the word 'Anatomy'. His licentiate certificate on a standard printed form reads:

51 Hale-White, 'Keats as a Medical Student', 250.

52 Hale-White, 'Keats as a Medical Student', 254.

53 Forman, 9.

*July 25th* 1816

*189* MR. *John Keats of full age*—CANDIDATE for
a CERTIFICATE to practise as an APOTHECARY in *the Country.*
An APPRENTICE to MR. *Thomas Hammond of Edmonton*
APOTHECARY for *5* Years
TESTIMONIAL from *Mr. Thos. Hammond*—

LECTURES.
*2* COURSES on ANATOMY and PHYSIOLOGY.
*2*—THEORY and PRACTICE of MEDICINE.
*2*—CHEMISTRY.
*1*—MATERIA MEDICA.
HOSPITAL ATTENDANCE.
*6* MONTHS at *Guy's & St. Thomas's.*—
as
MONTHS at
*168 Examined by Mr. Brande & approved*[54]

This document unquestionably suggests that Keats took two courses on 'Anatomy *and* Physiology' (my italics); however, identifying these courses is not a simple matter. The syllabus for courses at the United Hospitals, as advertised in the *London Medical and Physical Journal*, was as follows:

> *Medical School of St. Thomas's and Guy's Hospitals.* – The Autumnal Course of Lectures at these adjoining Hospitals will commence in the beginning of October, viz.
>
> At St. Thomas's – Anatomy and the Operations of Surgery, by Mr. Astley Cooper and Mr. Henry Cline. Principles and Practice of Surgery, by Mr. Astley Cooper.
>
> At Guy's – Practice of Medicine, by Dr. Babington and Dr. Curry. Chemistry, by Dr. Babington, Dr. Marcet, and Mr. Allen. Experimental Philosophy, by Mr. Allen. Theory of Medicine, and Materia Medica, by Dr. Curry and Dr. Cholmeley. Midwifery,

54 Robert Woof and Stephen Hebron, *John Keats* (Grasmere: The Wordsworth Trust, 1995), 60. The 'Testimonial' from Hammond has apparently not survived.

> and Diseases of Women and Children, by Dr. Haighton. Physiology, or Laws of the Animal Œconomy, by Dr. Haighton. Structure and Diseases of the Teeth, by Mr. Fox.[55]

Advertisements in the *Morning Chronicle* through the month of September 1815 confirm this information. On 5 September 1815, readers were told:

> MEDICAL SCHOOL of GUY'S HOSPITAL. – The COURSE of LECTURES will commence the beginning of viz.:—
>
> PRACTICE of MEDICINE, by Dr. BABINGTON and Dr. CURRY – CHEMISTRY by Dr. BABINGTON, Dr. MARCET, and Mr. ALLEN. – EXPERIMENTAL PHILOSOPHY, by Mr. ALLEN – THEORY of MEDICINE, and MATERIA MEDICA, by Dr. CURRY and Dr. CHOLMELEY – MIDWIFERY, and DISEASES of WOMEN and CHILDREN, by Dr. HAIGHTON.—PHYSIOLOGY, or LAWS of the ANIMAL ECONOMY, by Dr. HAIGHTON.—STRUCTURE and DISEASES of the TEETH, by Mr. FOX— N.B. These several Lectures, with those on Anatomy, and on the Principles and Practice of Surgery, given at the Theatre of St. Thomas's Hospital adjoining, are so arranged, that no two of them interfere in the hours of attendance;[56]

On September 11, 1815, they were informed:

> ST. THOMAS's HOSPITAL. – Mr. ASTLEY COOPER and Mr. HENRY CLINE will begin their COURSE of ANATOMICAL and SURGICAL LECTURES on Monday, October 2, at two o'clock.[57]

55 Advertisement, *The London Medical and Physical Journal* 34 (July–December 1815): 259. <https://books.google.gr/books?id=luQEAAAAQAAJ&pg=PA440&dq=london+medical+and+physical+journal+1815&hl=en&sa=X&ved=0ahUKEwj5rLDonfLeAhVFalAKHc4VCLkQ6AEIKTAA#v=onepage&q=Guy's&f=false> (accessed 25 November 2018).

56 Advertisement, *Morning Chronicle* (5 September 1815): 1.

57 Advertisement, *Morning Chronicle* (11 September 1815): 1.

And finally, on 18 September 1815, can be found the following intimation:

> ST. THOMAS and GUY'S HOSPITALS. – Mr. ASTLEY COOPER will begin his LECTURES on SURGERY on Monday the 9th of October.[58]

Taken together, Keats' certificate and these advertisements indicate that the only course of lectures Keats *could* have taken with the word 'Physiology' in the title was Dr Haighton's, on 'Physiology, or the Laws of Animal Œconomy'. Keats may or may not have attended these lectures, but there are no notes from that lecture series in his medical Notebook.[59]

Comparing Keats' notes with the manuscript volumes of notes by Keats' contemporary Joshua Waddington, George Winston argued that both derived from what Waddington called Astley Cooper's 'Lectures On Anatomy; And The Principal Operations Of Surgery' delivered at the Theatre, St Thomas' Hospital.[60] Even this is not as straightforward as it seems. Winston's title – derived from the title Waddington gave his volume of notes – appears an amalgamation of the titles of *two* different lecture courses: the *joint* series by Cooper and Henry Cline Jnr, referred to variously as 'Anatomy, and the Operations of Surgery' or 'Anatomical and Surgical Lectures', and Cooper's separate course on 'Principles and Practice of Surgery', also referred to as 'Lectures on Surgery', both delivered at the Theatre, St Thomas' Hospital. However, Waddington also created an independent manuscript volume entitled 'Lectures On The Principles and Practice, Of Surgery', containing his notes from the lecture series on 'Principles and Practice of Surgery' (or the 'Lectures on Surgery') delivered solely by Cooper.[61] This suggests that Waddington's 'Lectures On Anatomy; And The Principal Operations Of Surgery' meant the lectures on 'Anatomy, and the Operations of Surgery' also

58 Advertisement, *Morning Chronicle* (18 September 1815): 1.

59 *PP*, 27.

60 *KW*, 102.

61 Joshua Waddington, *Lectures On the Principles and Practice, Of Surgery ...* . MS Volume. Papers of Joshua Waddington, King's College London (KCL), GB 0100 G/PP1/62/5; *KW*, 103.

known as the 'Anatomical and Surgical Lectures', delivered jointly by Astley Cooper and Henry Cline Jnr.

The misattribution of Keats' medical notes as 'Physiological' derives, I believe, from Hale-White, who drew upon the following statement from *Memorials of John Flint South* referring to Cooper and Cline Jnr's course on 'Anatomy, and the Operations of Surgery': 'The first twelve lectures given by Astley Cooper we were accustomed to call the physiological lectures – on what, however, has long since been called by the French general anatomy.'[62] This puzzling statement can be decoded by looking at Waddington's notes for 'Lectures On Anatomy; And The Principal Operations Of Surgery'. Waddington has notes for a total of 97 lectures in two volumes, in which he has either skipped lectures 33 and 77, or misnumbered the first as 34 and the second as 78 and continued with the sequence(s) thus established. His Volume 1 contains the lecture notes for which comparative sections can be found in Keats' medical Notebook: it begins with the 'Introductory Lecture' and continues till 'Lecture 55th The Heart (continued)'. (Keats' medical notes end at Ff24v after discussing 'The Structure of the Heart'). Volume 2 contains the conclusion for 'Lecture 55th' and continues until 'Lecture 99th'. The titles of lectures 79–88 in Volume 2 are essentially repetitions of the titles for lectures 3–10 in Volume 1.[63] Thus, at first glance, there appear to be two series of lectures, separated by intervening material, dealing with arteries, veins, absorbents, and nervous system/nerves, but in fact the contents of these lectures are very different. For example, 'Lecture 3rd On the Arteries' in Volume 1 of Waddington's notes discusses the structure, physiological properties, and functions of arteries as an anatomical object, while 'Lecture 79th On the Arteries' in Volume 2 details the positioning of various arteries within the anatomical structure of the human body. A similar distinction in content also holds true for the other lectures sharing titles. This is the reason '[t]he first twelve lectures … [the students] were accustomed to call the physiological': it was to distinguish them from the second run of more anatomically focused lectures bearing the same title towards the end of the course.[64]

62 *Mem*, 33.

63 See Waddington; and Joshua Waddington, *Lectures on Anatomy; And The Principal Operations of Surgery … Vol. 2nd.* MS Volume. KCL, GB 0100 G/PP1/62/4.

64 *Mem*, 33.

This has not been adequately explained, either by Hale-White in his original article, or by Forman in his published edition, resulting in some later commentators misunderstanding the matter and assuming that Keats' notes are from lectures on 'Physiology', despite the fact that there was no such course delivered at Guy's in 1815–16.[65]

## The Question of Hand-writing(s)

Related to the difficulties discussed above is the matter of the handwriting in Keats' Notebook. There has been some doubt as to whether the manuscript features writing in one hand or two. Colvin believed that the notes on anatomy were in a different hand (see Figure 4: Ff4v of the Notebook for an example of this hand), and wrote in his biography that 'some other student has begun to put down anatomy notes and Keats has followed' (see Figure 3: Ff2r for an example of what Colvin considered to be Keats' hand).[66] Hale-White took a different view:

> I came to the conclusion that they were in the same handwriting – that of Keats. For example, the formation of the capitals is the same, the *y*s are similar and the way the letters are run together is alike. To confirm this opinion I called on Mr. Doubleday; we compared these notes with the many letters in the Dilke collection. Mr. Doubleday had no doubt that the two sets of notes were both in Keats' handwriting. Finally I took the notes to Mr. T. J. Wise; he kindly examined them, compared them with specimens of Keats' handwriting of the same date ... and said that, without doubt, all the notes were written by Keats.[67]

Doubleday was Librarian to the Hampstead Public Library and, by the time Hale-White was writing, secretary of the Keats Memorial Association of Hampstead, England.[68] T. J. Wise was a book collector,

65 For instance, *JK*; Andrew Motion, *Keats* (London: Faber & Faber, 1997); and R. S. White, *John Keats: A Literary Life* (Basingstoke: Palgrave Macmillan, 2010).

66 Colvin, *Life*, 33.

67 Hale-White, 'Keats as a Medical Student', 251.

68 Mabel A. E. Steele, 'Three Early Manuscripts of John Keats', *Keats-Shelley Journal* 1 (January 1952): 59; Lowell, *Keats*, I, xii.

forger, and accomplice of Keats' and Shelley's editor Harry Buxton Forman.[69] Buttressed by their support, Hale-White claimed that the Notebook was written entirely by Keats, and in his 'Prefatory Note' Maurice Buxton Forman added his authority to this belief:

> The difference between the two sets of notes led Sir Sidney Colvin to suggest that some student other than Keats was responsible for those on anatomy. This point was closely examined by Sir William Hale-White, Mr. W. E. Doubleday, and Mr. T. J. Wise (see page 251 of Sir William's article), and the conclusion they arrived at, and in which I concur, was that all the notes were written by John Keats.[70]

Since that time, commentators have concurred that the Notebook was written entirely in Keats' hand: on a first reading the two hands look different, but on closer examination they are demonstrably written by a single person.

The proofs that Hale-White adduced in attributing both hands to Keats are limited, and Forman added no further evidence. In 1952 Mabel Steele conducted a more detailed examination of the two hands in the medical Notebook, comparing them to other extant Keats manuscripts from the period.[71] Her work, and my own examination of the handwriting, led me to conclude that Hale-White was correct: the two 'hands' in the medical Notebook are both Keats'. The broadly spaced, large, and sloping hand (e.g. at Ff4v: see Figure 4) – which Colvin thought belonged to some other student – bears comparison with Keats' more deliberate, formal handwriting, as seen in his early letters to John Taylor or his late letter to Percy Bysshe Shelley; while the other, more cramped, hand (e.g. at Ff2r: see Figure 3) is so unmistakeably Keats' that it is unchallenged to date, and bears comparison with the majority of Keats manuscripts.[72] An expert opinion on such a vexed issue was

69 Alan Bell, 'Wise, Thomas James (1859–1937)'; J. F. R. Collins, 'Forman, Henry Buxton [Harry] (1842–1917)', *ODNB*.

70 Forman, vii. The relevant passage from 'page 251 of Sir William's article' is quoted directly above.

71 Steele, 'Three Early Manuscripts', 58–60.

72 See, for instance, 'Letter to John Taylor, 27 February 1818', 'Letter to Percy Bysshe Shelley, 16 August 1820', 'Letter to George and Georgiana Keats,

desirable, however, and I consulted Margaret Webb, an experienced graphologist and a graduate member of the British Institute of Graphologists.[73] She studied and compared images of pages from the Notebook, featuring both the hand that is undoubtedly Keats' and the one about which there has been doubt, and opined that 'all are from the same hand'.[74] In her report she noted that 'some samples of writing are tightly packed and there is more space left between words in others. This depends on the type of available paper, and any slight differences in letter forms are due to environmental or mood changes within the writer, but the overall style remains the same'.[75] She categorically stated that Ff11v and Ff23v, which feature the handwriting that has been doubted, were, in her opinion, 'written by the person who wrote the standard hand (Keats)'.[76]

However, there is in the Notebook yet another hand, which takes up the writing in the middle of 'Lecture 10' (Bf4v: see Figure 2) – 'Physiology of the Nervous System' – and ceases abruptly 19 lines below. After establishing that a sensation is 'an impression made on the Extremities of the Nerves conveyed to the Brain' and outlining the observations that prove this, Keats notes the example of Kosciusko: '~~Thos~~ The Patriot K. having had the Sciatic Nerve divided by a pike wound was a long while before his limb recovered its sensibility.' This sentence ends a little way off the gutter; the very next sentence, which begins on a new line, features a markedly different handwriting. The notes in this new handwriting pick up where Keats left off and go on to discuss how divided nerves reunite and what causes different sorts of sensations in different parts of the body. Then, midway through the last line of the page, Keats' usual

February–May 1819', 'I stood tip-toe upon a little hill'; 'To Autumn', Stephen Hebron, *John Keats: A Poet and His Manuscripts* (London: British Library, 2009), 83–86, 157–60, 123–26, 51–52, 143–44.

73 The British Institute of Graphologists, 'Directory of Graphologists A–Z', web, <www.britishgraphology.org/professional-services/directory-of-graphologists> (accessed 8 November 2018).

74 Margaret Webb examined the images for Bf2v, Bf3r, Bf4v, Ff2r, Ff3v, Ff11v, and Ff23v. The first four have on them examples of the standard Keatsian hand; at Ff3v the standard and comparative hand occur on the same page; and the latter two are examples of the comparative hand. Margaret Webb, email message to Nicholas Roe, 23 September 2013.

75 Webb, email, 23 September 2013.

76 Webb, email, 23 September 2013.

hand resumes: 'A celebrated italian put out the Eyes of a Bat and turned it loose into a Room and found that it did not strike itself against the Parieties'.[77] Nobody to date has mentioned the existence of this 'third' hand and it is hard to be certain that it does belong to Keats. Margaret Webb, however, states that this handwriting, despite its different appearance at first sight, is also Keats'.[78] In the light of her comments on how 'mood changes within the writer' affect handwriting, it is notable that the different hand appears immediately after the anecdote about Kosciusko.[79] Keats had, it seems, been so struck by this observation that it was reflected in his handwriting, until composure was restored and his normal hand resumed.

## Keats' Medical Notebook in Popularly-read Works

Contemporary reviewers of Forman's edition appear to have considered the medical Notebook an interesting piece of 'Keatsiana'. The *Times Literary Supplement* reviewed it on 7 June 1934, stating that '[t]o the reader of poetry the notes are of no direct interest, and even for the biographer of Keats their evidence is only circumstantial'.[80] Allowing the medical Notebook to be significant because it was in Keats' hand, the review recognized that the 'interest of the notes' resided in the medical history it might illuminate but did not expand upon this insight. It also highlighted Keats' unusual choice of words – 'pins and needles' – though this phrase had been in use since the early eighteenth century.[81] Although factually mistaken, it is worth noting that this reviewer attempted to analyse the language of the medical notes taken by the poet. A review in the *British Medical Journal* largely shared these views:

> Every medical lover of Keats's poetry knows that he was a dresser at Guy's Hospital, that he qualified at the Apothecaries' Hall on

77 JKMN, Bf4v–Bf5r.

78 Webb, email, 23 September 2013.

79 Webb, email, 23 September 2013.

80 William R. Le Fanu, 'Keats's Medical Note Book', *Times Literary Supplement* (7 June 1934): 404.

81 *OED* cites first use of this idiom in 1710, offering examples from 1786 and 1813, but does not cite Keats' use of it. 'pin, n.1', *OED*.

> July 25th, 1816, ... Mr. M. N. Forman [*sic*] has done well to print the notes, even though in an edition of only 350 copies. He would have done still better could he have issued the whole book in facsimile, for the single page he reproduces makes one hunger for more.[82]

Both reviews took an interest in the handwriting, and both showed interest in the notes being from lectures by Astley Cooper.[83] This is not surprising, for even in 1940 the Master of the Society of Apothecaries was appealing to 'people with medical ancestries connected with St. Thomas's and Guy's Hospitals', to see whether 'they have manuscripts of notes on Cooper's anatomy lectures', adding that this would be of value to Keats studies.[84] Taken together, Hale-White's original article and Forman's edition galvanized a period of relative interest in Keats' medical career, with contemporary and popular publications including a book review in the *Times Literary Supplement* of a descriptive catalogue of manuscripts in the Library of the Medical Society of London; an article discussing the poem *Isabella; or, The Pot of Basil*; and an article by B. Ifor Evans on the obscure and disputed 'Alexander fragment'.[85]

The first major Keats biography to be published after Forman's edition was Dorothy Hewlett's *Adonais: A Life of John Keats* (1937), followed by a revised and enlarged second edition in 1949 in which Hewlett discussed Keats' medical Notebook at some length, but did not mention Forman's edition. Her description of the manuscript was both effusive and contradictory, but she succeeded in suggesting some of its imaginative potential: 'Amid the serious and scientific entries there is one delightful and human touch that we can imagine Keats writing down with a curl of his wide, humorous mouth: "In diseases medical men guess, if they cannot ascertain a disease they call it nervous."'[86] One year after Hewlett's first edition William

82 Unsigned review, *British Medical Journal* 1 (9 June 1934): 1040.

83 Le Fanu, 'Medical Note Book', 404.

84 'News and Notes', *Times Literary Supplement* (31 August 1940): 417.

85 William R. Le Fanu, 'Medical Manuscripts', *Times Literary Supplement* (22 September 1932): 657; Herbert Gladstone Wright, 'Keats's "Isabella"', *Times Literary Supplement* (17 April 1943): 192; Benjamin Ifor Evans, 'Keats as a Medical Student', *Times Literary Supplement* (31 May 1934): 391.

86 Dorothy Hewlett, *A Life of John Keats* (London: Hurst and Blackett, 1949), 38. The sentence she quotes is from Bf5r of the Notebook; Forman transcribes it correctly on page 57 of his edition.

Hale-White published *Keats as Doctor and Patient*.[87] Rather than a full conventional biography, this book focused on the medical aspects of Keats' life: his training as an apothecary's apprentice, his period at Guy's Hospital, his role as primary care-giver to his brother Tom, and, finally, as a tubercular patient himself. Most of the information Hale-White offered on Keats' medical Notebook was repeated from his 1925 essay; in one instance, however, he deviated from what he wrote there, and this deviation affected Keats biographies for the next half century. Discussing Keats' sketches in his medical Notebook, he wrote: 'Keats apparently found this part of surgery [resetting fractures] dull, for he has drawn pictures of flowers and fruit at the side of these notes.'[88] There are in fact no pictures of fruit in Keats' medical Notebook – a fact Hale-White was well aware of. I believe the 'fruit' entered his book accidentally, as a typographical error perhaps: Keats had drawn a *foot* at Ff11v (see Figure 5). Unfortunately, two of the three major Keats biographies published in the 1960s – Walter Jackson Bate's and Aileen Ward's – reprinted this error, and it has become a commonplace in discussions of the manuscript.

Writing in 1963 in *John Keats: The Making of a Poet*, Aileen Ward cited Forman's edition in her 'Selective Bibliography' and wrote of Keats' medical Notebook:[89]

> Gradually Keats's brown leather-covered notebooks, one of which has survived, filled up with close-packed summaries of lectures with here and there a few drawings of skulls and fruits and flowers in the margins. At times, it appears, Keats found note-taking tedious ... Compared with the careful notes [of] a fellow student, Joshua Waddington, ... Keats's are sketchy and disjointed. This may mean that Keats was quicker-witted and more retentive than Waddington, or simply that his detailed transcription of his lecture notes – which every student was expected to make – has not survived.[90]

87 William Hale-White, *Keats as Doctor and Patient* (London: Oxford University Press, 1938).

88 Hale-White, *Doctor and Patient*, 22.

89 Aileen Ward, *John Keats: The Making of a Poet* (London: Secker and Warburg, 1963), 441.

90 Ward, *Making of a Poet*, 51.

It is by no means certain that Keats possessed medical *notebooks*, though it is not an unreasonable conjecture. Ward's odd conjunction of 'close-packed notes' that are nevertheless 'sketchy and disjointed' suggests that she was relying on secondary sources: the sections of the Notebook that are 'close-packed' contain more detail than 'summaries of lectures' – they represent full records of what Keats heard. The notes written in a more spacious hand are more accurately described as 'summary', with little of the cramping and crowding that 'close-packed' notes display. It is possible that Keats made more thorough transcriptions that have not survived, but the claim that every student was expected to make notes as detailed as Waddington's is difficult to substantiate. Ward mentions as her source Winston's article, and this is the relevant section from it:

> By making these comparisons [between Keats' notes and Waddington's] it may be possible to throw further light on the question whether Keats was a keen and industrious student, … and whether he took sufficient care to write out his notes in fuller detail at his leisure, as was advised by Sir Astley Cooper at the end of his introductory lecture. The words of advice, quoted from Waddington, were, 'take short notes of the Lectures; having dissected generally, go through the different parts particularly; and let me advise you to pay particular attention to Morbid Preparations for be assured there is no other true knowledge of Anatomy than that derived from observations of the Living, and on the Dead; and also by experiments made upon living Animals'.[91]

Waddington's transcription suggests that Cooper laid greater stress on dissection and observation than on note-taking, though he did encourage 'short' notes that would assist the practical, and research-orientated, ends of medicine – and Keats' Notebook shows that he heeded Cooper's advice.

Walter Jackson Bate's hugely influential biography was also published in 1963: he discussed Keats' medical Notebook as follows, citing the Forman edition in his footnotes:

> A small leather notebook survives, containing notes to lectures by the famous Astley Cooper, already at the head of his profession. …

91 *KW*, 102–03.

> At first glance, Keats would seem to have taken his lecture notes on whatever page fell open, and then, when the book filled, to have started to insert further notes between the lines of those made earlier: the inference being that he was either completely indifferent or hopelessly confused. From a comparison of two volumes of careful notes taken by a contemporary at Guy's Hospital, Joshua Waddington, Miss Mabel Steele has explained the apparent lack of order. Keats first neatly copied out a syllabus for the forthcoming lectures. He obviously assumed that the syllabus was the important thing – perhaps all that was really necessary – though he left space here and there throughout it, as well as before and after, in case anything crucial needed to be inserted. Then, showing up at the lectures in the crowded amphitheatre, he finally started to write because he saw others writing. He may even have begun as late as Lecture IV, the notes for which appear on the first page of the notebook, and then afterwards, using the notes of other students, have tried to get something down for the earlier lectures. In time, as the separate pages filled, notes were written in the margins of the syllabus, and others even between the lines of it. Hence the confusion. We can infer that the whole procedure of lectures and note taking puzzled him at first. Later, the fullness of the notes varies according to subject. Lectures on bone setting he seems to have found dull. Next to them he sketched little pictures of flowers and fruits. The notes to the lectures on physiology are more detailed.[92]

This is a very problematic account, the more so because it appears in such an influential work. Keats' notes are certainly distinctively ordered, but they are not 'hopelessly confused'. That there was an order to them had been pointed out by earlier biographers (Colvin, Lowell) and researchers (Hale-White, Forman, Hagelman), all of whom had shown that Keats was not a 'completely indifferent' student. Steele's explanation – which Bate says he quotes from unpublished papers – is also not wholly convincing. What she describes as a 'syllabus' – presumably distinguished from the 'lecture notes' – contains remarkably detailed notes in tabular form: for example, those 'On Osteology' (from the front, folio 4–18 versos only, as well as rectos for folios 7, 12, 13, and 19). Although the subject matter of some of the

92 Walter Jackson Bate, *John Keats* (Cambridge, MA: The Belknap Press of Harvard University Press/London: Oxford University Press, 1963), 46–47.

'lecture notes' (e.g. 'Bone' at Bf8r) overlaps with that of the 'syllabus' ('Osteology'), the material is different: the former discusses the composition of bone while the latter details the skeleton's structure. The argument that 'as separate pages filled, notes were written in the margins ... and others even between the lines' overlooks the reality that Keats was not short of space – there are 'a hundred and eighteen blank pages' by Hale-White's count between the notes written from the front of the Notebook and those from the back.[93] Barring an occasional exception (e.g. at Ff1v), when notes are inserted in margins or between lines the matter inserted has direct bearing on the existing notes (e. g. at Ff11v) or is a continuation of notes on the opposing page (e.g. Ff3v). Bate also reproduces Hale-White's reference to non-existent sketches of 'fruits', and his idea that Keats found lectures on bone-setting 'dull' because he sketched flowers beside them is questionable on two counts. First, the 'lectures on bone-setting' are the ones Bate says – quoting from Steele – that Keats copied as a 'syllabus' in advance: if this was so, Keats could have broken off writing when 'bored' and would have had no reason to waste time doodling. Second, it is possible that Keats' sketches reflect a creative engagement with the material of his notes: the flowers are drawn next to notes on the structure of the nose (at Ff19r), just as a foot is sketched among notes on the bones of the feet (at Ff11v). Other commentators have noted imaginative links between the sketches and adjacent medical notes: Hagelman suggested that Keats may have been revising botanical lessons during a lull in the lecture; while Roe pictures Keats making an imaginative leap from the nose to the perfume of flowers to the 'half-blown flower' of his sonnet 'To Chatterton'.[94] These accounts give a sense of Keats' creative engagement with his medical studies; a possibility Bate overlooked, but one which rings true given Keats' sense of imaginative involvement with the world.[95]

Of the three major biographies published in the 1960s, Robert Gittings' *John Keats* (1968) discussed Keats' medical career and Notebook in greatest detail, but it made no mention of Forman's edition:

93 Hale-White, 'Keats as a Medical Student', 251. In fact, there are 123 blank pages.

94 Hagelman, 'Medical Profession', 130; *NL*, 80.

95 See *LJK*, I, 186, 386–87 for Keats' own accounts of his imaginative engagement with the world.

> [O]ne of [Keats'] notebooks has survived from this period, ... Keats was not altogether a good note-taker; as with his appreciation of character, it was the vivid, the picturesque and the out-of-the-way that attracted him. Cooper ... was full of good phrases which Keats noted in full, perhaps to the exclusion of more weighty matter. His notes on Cooper's tenth lecture, scanty in other respects, record that 'The patriot K(osciusko) having had the Sciatic Nerve divided by a pike wound was a long while before his limb recovered its sensibility'... Keats found that the best way of remembering the many facts of surgery and medicine was to attach them to concrete and striking examples; he himself once explained to Cowden Clarke the workings of the stomach by comparing that organ to a nest full of young birds. It was not an orthodox way of taking notes, but it accorded with his natural temperament and brought him quick success.[96]

It is not altogether clear why Gittings thought Keats' notes 'scanty' and lacking in 'weighty matter' when they stretch to 'the vivid, the picturesque and the out-of-the-way', and were calculated to be in tune with Keats' natural powers of retention. The Notebook, after all, was a working record of information to assist Keats in qualifying as an apothecary, and – as Gittings observed – the notes served their purpose and brought Keats success.

The last major twentieth-century biography of Keats, Andrew Motion's *Keats* (1997), referred to 'his surviving notebook – a small pocket-sized affair, bound in limp brown leather':[97]

> When [Keats'] notes are compared to those made by Joshua Waddington, a contemporary at Guy's, they sometimes seem 'sketchy and disjointed', and show that his concentration lapsed. ... Many of them, though, are full and detailed. Some are written out neatly. Others are notes he would probably have amplified later. The doodles of skulls, fruits and flowers ... are just as likely to be anatomical or botanical subjects as signs of inattention. ... It is the notebook of someone who found certain topics more interesting than others, who may well have supported its information with

96 *JK*, 51.

97 Motion, *Keats*, 79–80.

> work done elsewhere, and who evidently thought he was doing enough to pass his qualifying examinations.[98]

Motion evidently drew on Ward and Bate for this account, for the idea of Keats doodling 'fruits' could not have survived a reading of the manuscript itself; that said, his statement that the Notebook provides evidence of a student who found certain topics more interesting than others rings true.

R. S. White's *John Keats: A Literary Life* (2010), concerned to relate Keats' life story to his poetical works, offered a puzzling account:

> We have Keats's copy of his 'Anatomical and Physiological Note Book', a printed record of Cooper's lectures, interleaved with blank pages often filled with notes taken by Keats in the lectures. Generally speaking, their language is far from that we find later in his poetry ... There are, however, touches of Cooper's famous witty asides: 'In diseases Medical Men guess, if they cannot ascertain a disease they call it nervous ...' (p. 57), which Keats may later parody in describing himself as '*narvus*', but much of the prose is impenetrably technical. Words occur that must have arrested the budding poet: '[Aneurism is] a Pulsating swelling ...' (p. 12); 'The St[r]eam of Blood in a Vein near to an artery has a distinct Pulsation (p. 13).'[99]

White's annotation cited Forman's edition as his source, but it is mystifying that he came to conclude that the medical Notebook was a 'printed record ... interleaved with blank pages often filled with notes taken by Keats'.[100] Keats' use of '*narvus*' almost certainly arose from his medical knowledge, as White suggested, and phrases such as 'pulsating' and 'S[t]ream of Blood' were not without potential for his poetry – as we shall see shortly.

Nicholas Roe's *John Keats: A New Life* (2012) discussed Keats' medical Notebook at some length and connected the material to his poetry, treating the format and layout of the notes as a possible prefiguration of the characteristic turns and returns of Keats' poetic imagination:

98 Motion, *Keats*, 80.
99 White, *Literary Life*, 26–27.
100 White, *Literary Life*, 234.

> Keats kept detailed notes of what Cooper said ... Keats's notebook shows he was struck by Cooper's audacious speculations about whether 'Blood possessed Vitality' and how arteries 'expel Blood in the last Struggles of Life'. He took down an anecdote about the Polish patriot Thaddeus Kosciusko ... Oddities like 'the Behaviour of a Frog after having been guillioteened' caught his attention ... Keats was making notes for his examinations, but there was matter here for poetry too.
>
> Keats's medical notebook survives as an extraordinary document of his mind and it can stand comparison with his poetry manuscripts. ... Keats embellished the later pages with little drawings of flowers; while Cooper was explaining the structure of a human nose Keats was imagining the perfume of flowers and then, perhaps, the 'half-blown flower' of his own sonnet on Thomas Chatterton's untimely death ... From now on, his knowledge of anatomy and physiology would enable him to materialise those experiences in the throbbing life of muscles, nerves, arteries, bone and blood –[101]

This remains the most extensive account of the medical Notebook's possible influence on Keats' poetry offered by a biography of the poet, and it was long overdue. Habits formed in youth often persist over a lifetime, after all, and in Keats' case the means by which he sought to '"get Wisdom – get understanding"' at Guy's – with the medical Notebook being the tangible evidence of that time – carried over to a lifetime of learning.[102] In 2015 Roe announced his discovery of a contemporary newspaper account describing 'Mr. Keats' in action as 'one of the Surgeons belonging to Guy's Hospital' – the only one we know of that describes Keats at work as a doctor.[103]

Keats' medical Notebook is a fascinating manuscript, vital for our understanding of Keats as a poet and our knowledge of early nineteenth-century medical training. This chapter has offered an account of the provenance and features of the medical Notebook; the next will explore some of the poems Keats wrote during his medical training.

101 *NL*, 79–80.

102 *LJK*, I, 271.

103 Nicholas Roe, 'Dressing for Art: Notes from Keats in the Emergency Ward', *Times Literary Supplement* (27 May 2015): 14–15. Quotation from 'London Adjourned Sessions', *Morning Chronicle* (23 April 1816): 3.

CHAPTER TWO

# John Keats' 'Guy's Hospital' Poetry

John Keats' poetic and medical careers overlapped from the start. His earliest surviving poem, 'Imitation of Spenser', dates from 1814, when he was apprenticed to apothecary–surgeon Thomas Hammond at Edmonton.[1] His poetic 'apprenticeship' with Charles Cowden Clarke, begun in his last months at Enfield School, continued during his time with Hammond: Clarke recalled that '[h]e rarely came empty-handed; either he had a book to read, or brought one with him to be exchanged'.[2] Two years later Keats, now a dresser at Guy's Hospital, recalled these afternoons of poetry in his verse epistle 'To Charles Cowden Clarke':

> ... Ah! had I never seen,
> Or known your kindness, what might I have been?
> What my enjoyments in my youthful years,
> Bereft of all that now my life endears?
>
> (72–75)

This chapter explores the relationship between Keats' two callings, poetry and medicine, focusing on the poems he composed while at Guy's Hospital in the years 1815–17. It suggests that Keats' life in the hospital environment was an important stimulus for his imagination: all except five of the poems published in his 1817 collection were composed, and the volume itself put together, while he was still working at Guy's. As we shall see, Keats' patterns of composition reflected his schedule at the hospital as well as the influence of his social life. Somewhat surprisingly, perhaps, hectic full-time

1 *Poems*, 539.
2 *RoW*, 124–25; CCC, 88.

employment at Guy's Hospital seems to have been an enabling factor for his poetic imagination and productivity.

The timing of Keats' removal to London is not known, and has remained a vexed issue for biographers.[3] The administrative records of Guy's Hospital, however, give the date of his formal enrolment as a pupil and chart his progress to a dressership. Records kept at the Medical School Office of Guy's show that on 1 October 1815 Keats registered as a pupil, paying the office fee of £1 2s. Later in the month – probably on 2 October 1815 – he paid the hospital fee of £25 4s., thus completing the formalities for registering as a surgeon's pupil for 12 months. Just four weeks later, on 29 October 1815, £6 6s. was returned to Keats, 'he becoming a dresser'. Finally, under the heading 'Dressers to the Surgeons entered at Guy's Hospital', the record states that on 3 March 1816 John Keats was appointed a dresser under Mr Lucas for a period of 12 months.[4] Thus, Keats spent approximately 18 months – from October 1815 to March 1817 – attached to Guy's. It is likely that the majority, if not all, of the material in his medical Notebook was transcribed during the first six months of his tenure there, when he had not yet undertaken his more time-consuming dresser's duties.

Dressers, distinguished from ordinary pupils by the 'plaister-boxes' they carried as their badge of office, were vital to the hospital.[5]

3 Gittings believed that Keats formally completed the full five years of his apprenticeship with Thomas Hammond and so could have gone to London only in the summer of 1815. However, Roe argued that Keats did *not* in fact complete the full five-year term, based on statements made by George Keats and others, and believed that Keats could have gone up to London earlier. Citing precedent from John Flint South and John Green Crosse, Roe suggested the possibility – in light of his extremely rapid progression to dresser – that Keats informally attended the United Hospitals of Guy's and St Thomas' for some time before formally enrolling there. Dilke, Brown, and Clarke all agree that Keats left his apprenticeship earlier than expected. See *JK*, 31, 47; *PP*, 13, 24; *NL*, 47–48, 56–57.

4 This is the summary offered by *JK*, 47, 49, 51. Based on entries in Guy's Hospital Entry of Physicians and Surgeon's Pupils and Dressers 1814–1827, Surgeon's Pupils of Guy's and St Thomas's Hospitals 1812–1825, and Guy's and St Thomas's Pupils and Dressers 1755–1823 ranged in alphabetical order. MS Volumes. King's College London (KCL), Guy's Hospital Medical School: Records: G/FP3/2, G/FP4/1, and G/FP1/1.

5 *Mem*, 26.

They accompanied the surgeons on their rounds; assisted them in the performance of operations; were chiefly responsible for pre- and post-operative care of surgical patients; and attended to outpatients. Each dresser spent a set number of weeks as the 'duty dresser', living at his own expense in the hospital and in charge on 'taking-in day' (Thursday at St Thomas'; Wednesday at Guy's), when new cases were assessed.[6] John Flint South recalled the dresser's duties on 'taking-in day' thus:

> He took charge of all the surgical cases, which were received at ten o'clock on Thursday, the 'taking-in day', as it was called [Wednesday for Guy's]. He attended to all the accidents and cases of hernia which came in during his week of office, and he dressed hosts of out-patients, drew innumerable teeth, and performed countless venesections, till two or three o'clock, as might be, till the surgery was emptied .... When the surgeon arrived the dresser on duty would show him, among the out-patients, any case about which he needed further help or which he thought advisable to be admitted, as likely to issue in an operation.[7]

The duty dresser was also responsible for attending to emergencies on the wards during his duty week and, if necessary, sending for the surgeon.[8] Senior dressers – described by one contemporary account as those who have 'been long enough in train to lose the trembling hand' – had 'the execution of everything but the great operations, the smaller and most frequent ones he is allowed to perform ... before the end of the year he becomes, as it were, an Assistant Surgeon'.[9] Dressership, thus, was a time-consuming and onerous responsibility envisaged as part of a promising student's practical training.[10]

During this busy period from October 1815 to March 1817, Keats appears to have written just short of 40 poems – although it is not always possible to date all of this early poetry. The verse epistle 'To George Felton Mathew', however, is dated 'November 1815' in *Poems*

6 BT, 207.
7 *Mem*, 25.
8 BT, 208–09.
9 Quoted in BT, 208.
10 BT, 212.

(1817): thus, shortly after Keats' enrolment at Guy's Hospital.[11] 'To Solitude' is usually placed in October or November 1815, though there is no way to date it conclusively;[12] the sonnet 'Oh Chatterton!' is presumed to have been written some time in 1815; and the piece beginning 'Woman! When I behold thee ...' is dated to 1815 or 1816.[13]

In what follows I treat the sonnet 'To Solitude', published in *The Examiner* on 5 May 1816, as the first poem Keats wrote while enrolled at Guy's.[14] It is not known precisely when Keats wrote the sonnet, but a week before its publication on 28 April 1816 Hunt had announced 'J.K., and other Communications, next week'.[15] This meant that he must have received a copy of 'To Solitude' before 27 April at the latest, in time to insert that notice for Sunday's paper on the 28th. John Middleton Murry argued that there are verbal echoes of Keats' sonnet to be found in George Felton Mathew's 'To a Poetical Friend', which drew a response from Keats in the form of the verse epistle 'To George Felton Mathew'.[16] Murry argued that the last stanza of Mathew's poem,

> And let not the spirit of Poesy sleep
> Of Fairies and Genii continue to tell –
> Nor suffer the innocent deer's timid leap
> To fright the wild bee from her flowery bell[17]

alluded to Keats' sonnet with its imagery of 'the deer's swift leap' startling 'the wild bee from the fox-glove bell' (7–8).[18] This would mean that Mathew had to have seen the sonnet 'To Solitude' before composing his own poem, which in turn would suggest that it had been written before Mathew's 'To a Poetical Friend'.[19] Murry further

11 *Texts*, 107.

12 *Texts*, 106–07. I have usually followed the titles given in *Poems*, with the exception of the sonnet 'To Solitude', for which I use the title given to it in its first publication in *The Examiner*.

13 *Texts*, 99, 105.

14 *The Examiner* (5 May 1816): 282.

15 *The Examiner* (28 April 1816): 264.

16 John Middleton Murry, *Studies in Keats* (London: Oxford University Press, 1930), 3–5.

17 Quoted in Murry, *Studies*, 4.

18 Murry, *Studies*, 4.

19 Murry, *Studies*, 4–5.

suggested that Keats' epistle 'To George Felton Mathew' of November 1815 was written in response to Mathew's poem. Hence, he argued, Keats' allusion to his burgeoning medical career – '... far different cares / Beckon me sternly from soft "Lydian airs"' (18–19) – was a response to Mathew's appeal to 'warm thee in Fancy's enlivening rays; / And wash the dark spots of disease from thy soul'.[20] This yielded a sequence of poetry in which the sonnet 'To Solitude' was first written; echoed and responded to by Mathew in 'To A Poetical Friend'; and answered in Keats' 'To George Felton Mathew'.[21] As 'To George Felton Mathew' is dated by Keats November 1815, 'To Solitude' was probably written some time before.[22] But the sonnet also shows the influence of Wordsworth: 'the deer's swift leap / Startles the wild bee from the fox-glove bell' (7–8) clearly echoes Wordsworth's 'Prefatory sonnet' ['Nuns fret not at their Convent's narrow room'] to his *Poems* (1815):

> ... Bees that soar for bloom,
> High as the highest peak of Furness Fells,
> Will murmur by the hour in Foxglove bells:
> (5–7)[23]

In late March 1815 Wordsworth had brought out his first collected edition in two octavo volumes and, according to Robert Gittings, Keats acquired them that autumn.[24] While it is not possible to date 'To Solitude' precisely, evidence pointing to October or November 1815 is sufficiently persuasive to make this his first 'Guy's Hospital' poem.

Identifying the last poem Keats wrote at Guy's is similarly complex. 'On the Sea' was written on the Isle of Wight and included in a letter to Reynolds of 17 and 18 April 1817.[25] While the date of 'On *The Story of Rimini*' is less clearly cut, it was

20 Murry, *Studies*, 4.
21 Murry, *Studies*, 5–6.
22 Roe, while agreeing with the sequence advocated by Murry, suggested a date in November: see *NL*, 71, 77–79.
23 William Wordsworth, *Poems, in Two Volumes, and Other Poems, 1800–1807*, ed. Jared Curtis (Ithaca, NY: Cornell University Press, 1983), 133.
24 *JK*, 52.
25 *Texts*, 137; *LJK*, I, 132.

evidently composed before Keats' letter to Charles Cowden Clarke of 25 March, in which it is mentioned as a recent composition.[26] The exact date that Keats left Guy's is unknown, but it seems logical to suppose that he officially ceased to be a dresser one year after he took up that role – that is, on 3 March 1817.[27] 'On *The Story of Rimini*' is, therefore, cautiously identified as the last poem Keats wrote while at Guy's.

These, then, are the poems Keats wrote while attached to Guy's Hospital, either as pupil or dresser.[28]

## Phase I

*At 28 St Thomas' Street, Southwark (October 1815–July 1816)*
1. 'To Solitude': written 1815 or 1816, probably October or November 1815, while lodging with George Cooper and Frederick Tyrell at St Thomas' Street.
2. [Epistle] 'To George Felton Mathew': written November 1815.
3. 'Had I a man's fair form, then might my sighs': written 1815 or 1816, while with Cooper and Tyrell *or* while sharing with Henry Stephens and George Wilson Mackereth in the same building.[29]
4. 'Hadst thou liv'd in days of old': written on or shortly before 14 February 1816 as a valentine for Mary Frogley, while lodging with Stephens and Mackereth at St Thomas' Street.
5. 'I am as brisk': written probably in 1816 (written on the second page of the extant holograph of 'Hadst thou liv'd in days of old').
6. 'Give me women, wine, and snuff': written towards the end of 1815 or during the first half of 1816.

26 *Texts*, 136–37; *LJK*, I, 127.

27 The entry concerning Keats' dressership in the Guy's records is: '1816, March 3, John Keats under Mr. Lucas. Time 12 mths, from Edmonton, £1.1s'. See Entry ... 1814–1827. KCL, G/FP3/2.

28 The dates/probable dates for composition taken from the 'Textual Notes' of *Poems*, unless stated otherwise. The chronology presented here follows that volume. I have prioritized Stillinger's dating in *Poems*, as this is his more recent work. However, *Texts* presents more detailed accounts on bibliography and textual transmission: therefore, where the dating agrees in both, I reference *Texts* for bibliographical analysis.

29 For more on this shift, see *NL*, 76–77.

7. 'Specimen of an Induction to a Poem': written 1816, probably in spring after the publication (in February) of Hunt's *The Story of Rimini*.
8. 'Calidore: A Fragment': written 1816, probably in the spring.
**'To Solitude' published in *The Examiner*: 5 May 1816**
9. 'To one who has been long in city pent': written June 1816.
10. 'Oh! how I love, on a fair summer's eve': written 1816, possibly in the summer (dated '1816'). This poem cannot be definitively dated before Keats took his licentiate examination, but, erring on the side of caution, I will count it thus in what follows. Therefore, written while living with Stephens and Mackereth at St Thomas' Street.
11. 'To a Friend Who Sent Me Some Roses': written 29 June 1816.
12. 'Happy is England! I could be content': perhaps written 1816. Another poem which cannot definitively dated, and so cannot be said to have been certainly written before Keats took his licentiate examination. I err on the side of caution in counting it as written while living with Stephens and Mackereth in St Thomas' Street.
**Licentiate examination: 25 July 1816**

## Phase II

*At Margate (August–September 1816)*
13. [Sonnet] 'To My Brother George': written August 1816.
14. [Epistle] 'To My Brother George': written August 1816.
15. [Epistle] 'To Charles Cowden Clarke': written September 1816.
All three poems above were written back to London, where the recipients were.

*At 8 Dean Street, Southwark (September 1816–mid-November 1816)*
16. 'How many bards gild the lapses of time': probably written 1816. Not firmly dated, but generally considered as having been written immediately before the 'Chapman's Homer' sonnet and, thus, while living with his brothers George and Tom at 8 Dean Street.
**Introduction to Leigh Hunt: 19 October 1816**
17. 'On First Looking into Chapman's Homer': written October 1816 (dated thus in *The Examiner*).
18. 'Keen, fitful gusts are whisp'ring here and there': written October or November 1816, shortly after meeting Hunt.

19. 'On Leaving Some Friends at an Early Hour': written October or November 1816 shortly after the preceding poem.

*At 76 Cheapside (mid-November 1816–mid-March 1817)*
20. 'To My Brothers': written on 18 November 1816, Tom Keats' birthday, while living with his brothers George and Tom at 76 Cheapside.
21. 'Addressed to Haydon' ['Highmindedness, a jealousy for good']: written 1816, after meeting Haydon in mid-October.
22. 'Addressed to the Same' ['Great spirits now on earth are sojourning']: written 20 November 1816.
**Hunt publishes on 'Young Poets' in *The Examiner*: 1 December 1816**
23. 'To G.A.W.': written December 1816 (dated thus in Tom Keats' transcript).
24. 'To Kosciusko': written December 1816 (dated thus in the *Examiner*).
25. *Sleep and Poetry*: written after Keats met Hunt and before the complete manuscript for *Poems* (1817) was delivered. Stillinger suggests a composition date between October and December 1816, but John Barnard argues that, like the succeeding poem 'I stood tip-toe', the composition and/or fair copying of this poem may have continued well into December, even as the rest of the 1817 volume was already in the press.[30]
26. 'I stood tip-toe upon a little hill': completed December 1816 (dated thus at the end of Keats' draft), and possibly begun several months earlier, in summer 1816. Completed while living with his brothers at 76 Cheapside, but possibly begun while at Dean Street, or even while living with Stephens and Mackereth at 28 St Thomas' Street.
27. 'Written in Disgust of Vulgar Superstition': written perhaps 22 December 1816 (dated 'Sunday Evening Dec[r] 24 1816' in Tom Keats' transcript: the closest Sunday to this in 1816 was 22 December).
28. 'On the Grasshopper and Cricket': written 30 December 1816 in a competition at Hunt's house.
29. 'After dark vapours have oppressed our plains': written 31 January 1817.

30 See *Poems*, 556; and Barnard, 'First Fruits or "First Blights": A New Account of the Publishing History of Keats's *Poems* (1817)', *Romanticism* 12.2 (July 2006): 87.

30. 'To a Young Lady Who Sent Me a Laurel Crown': perhaps written 1816 or 1817.
31. 'On Receiving a Laurel Crown from Leigh Hunt': written at the end of 1816 or early 1817 (Hunt's two sonnets on receiving a crown of ivy from Keats are dated 1 March 1817).
32. 'To the Ladies Who Saw Me Crown'd': written at the end of 1816 or early 1817 (dating the same as for the preceding poem).
33. 'God of the golden bow': written at the end of 1816 or early 1817 (shortly after the preceding poems).
34. 'This pleasant tale is like a little copse': written February 1817.
35. 'To Leigh Hunt, Esq.' [Dedication for the 1817 *Poems*]: written February 1817.
36. 'On Seeing the Elgin Marbles': written 1 or 2 March 1817.
37. 'To Haydon with a Sonnet Written on Seeing the Elgin Marbles': written 1 or 2 March 1817 (same as for the preceding poem).
38. 'On a Leander Which Miss Reynolds, My Kind Friend, Gave Me': probably written March 1817. Possibly while living with his brothers at 76 Cheapside, though it may have been written after the move to 1 Well Walk.

*At 1, Well Walk Hampstead (from mid-March 1817)*
39. 'On *The Story of Rimini*': written March 1817, before the 25th of that month, probably while living with his brothers at 1 Well Walk, though it might possibly have been written at 76 Cheapside.

These 39 poems amount to 1,749 lines in the reading texts in Stillinger's edition of *The Poems of John Keats*, exclusive of variant readings. This is a significant amount of poetry to produce in any 18-month period, and rendered more extraordinary by the fact that Keats was engaged full-time in a demanding post at Guy's.

'To A Friend Who Sent Me Some Roses' is dated Saturday 29 June 1816, well *before* Keats took his licentiate examination; 'Happy is England!' is of uncertain date, probably in 1816; while the sonnet and epistle 'To My Brother George', both written from Margate in August 1816, were definitely penned *after* the examination.[31] We can see, therefore, that in the period of ten months from October 1815 to July 1816 (both months inclusive), Keats wrote at least ten and

31 *Texts*, 113, 114–15.

possibly as many as 12 poems in this first phase of hospital poems. In the second phase between 25 July 1816 and March 1817 – eight months – he wrote at least 26 poems while fulfilling his duties as a dresser.[32] To understand the significance of these two phases of composition at Guy's requires some consideration of their background and context.

Through the summer of 1815 Keats joined the Mathew Circle – a group of minor poets and acquaintances associated with George Felton Mathew, who was fond of long romantic epics such as Wieland's *Oberon* and the *Ossian* poems at that time. Aileen Ward observed that while he may seem an improbable companion for Keats, he offered something Keats needed: 'the admiration of a contemporary and the stimulus of a fellow craftsman'.[33] Keats' verse epistle 'To George Felton Mathew' of November 1815 marks his last interaction with these pre-Guy's poetic friends. In essence, it is a poem of adieu, acknowledging a summer spent together and disengaging himself from his companion poet(s):

> Too partial friend! fain would I follow thee
> Past each horizon of fine poesy;
> Fain would I echo back each pleasant note
> As o'er Sicilian seas, clear anthems float
>
> (11–14)

Keats had already outgrown Mathew's conventional poetic taste and mediocre compositions.[34] 'To George Felton Mathew' identifies a

32 The poems 'Oh! How I love, on a fair summer's eve'; 'Happy is England! I could be content' and 'How many bards gild the lapses of time' cannot be dated definitively. I have followed the conjectures of Keats' editors in placing them in the chronological list. Miriam Allott and Jack Stillinger agree on the placement of 'How many bards gild the lapses of time' and 'Oh! how I love, on a fair summer's eve', and this list reflects their placement of these poems. However, they do not coincide on 'Happy is England! I could be content': Stillinger locates it immediately after 'To a Friend Who Sent Me Some Roses' while stating that there is no certain date, while Allott, admitting the same, suggests that it may date from the winter of 1816 and places it after the sonnet 'To Kosciusko'. See John Keats, *The Poems of John Keats* ed. Miriam Allott (London: Longman, 1970), 59–60, 60–62, 46, 46–47, 100–01; and *Poems*, 63–64, 64, 54, 54–55, 55.

33 Ward, *Making of a Poet*, 42.

34 *JK*, 57–58.

fresh direction, acknowledging the place of poetry in a new life of medicine and hospital duties:

> ... far different cares,
> Beckon me sternly from soft 'Lydian airs,'
> And hold my faculties so long in thrall,
> That I am oft in doubt whether at all
> I shall again see Phoebus in the morning:
>
> (17–21)

In 'thrall' to his studies at Guy's, as these lines suggest, Keats' verse for the next few months was mostly occasional. 'Had I a man's fair form' and 'Hadst thou lived in days of old' are light-hearted, appreciative lyrics addressed to women. 'I am as brisk' is doggerel verse. 'Specimen of an Induction to a Poem' and 'Calidore' are more ambitious pieces – verbal and stylistic echoes suggest that they were conceived and written as a response to Hunt's *The Story of Rimini* (1816), which Keats was reading at this time – but they remained incomplete.[35] 'To one who has been long in city pent' echoes *Paradise Lost*, and shows Keats' increasing control over the sonnet form, as does 'How I love, on a fair summer's eve'. 'To a Friend Who Sent Me Some Roses' was written to thank an old school friend, Charles Wells, who had sent the flowers. 'Give me women, wine and snuff' is the only surviving Keats poem that was apparently written while at a medical lecture at Guy's: he had scribbled it on the inside cover of fellow student Henry Stephens' Chemistry 'Syllabus'.[36] All of these poems, light-hearted and engaging but without much introspective depth, belong to the first phase of hospital poems, written before Keats' licentiate examination of July 1816, at a time when establishing himself in the medical career was apparently his priority.[37]

35 *NL*, 83–85, 88, 89.

36 See *KC*, II, 210 for Stephens' recollection, and Hrileena Ghosh, '"Give me Women Wine and Snuff": A New Account of John Keats's Poem', *Keats-Shelley Review* 30.2 (September 2016): 113–21 for more on the manuscript. There is no record of Keats' note-taking in chemistry classes, and no verses of any kind in his medical Notebook.

37 Keats may also have written a prose fragment, beginning 'Whenne Alexander', at this time. Walter Cooper Dendy, who had enrolled as a student at Guy's in 1813, wrote in *The Philosophy of Mystery* (1841) that he remembered seeing

Henry Stephens, Keats' fellow student and sometime housemate, recalled that Keats 'attended Lectures and went through the usual routine, but he had no desire to excel in that pursuit'.[38] Stephens' recollections provide valuable information, but must be treated with care: writing to George Felton Mathew in 1847 in response to a plea for information for Richard Monckton Milnes' *Life, Letters, and Literary Remains*, his account is confused by the burgeoning myth-making that was already surrounding Keats the poet, as will be described in the next few pages.

*

In the 27 years between his death in Rome on 23 February 1821 and the publication of Milnes' book in 1848, Keats' reputation as a poet had been on a gradual rise – albeit sustained by two mythical versions of him.[39] The first, which made Keats out to be an apothecary–poetaster, dated from August 1818 and 'The Cockney School of Poetry IV' article in *Blackwood's Edinburgh Magazine*.[40] In his survey of Keats' reputation, J. R. MacGillivray observed:

> *Blackwood's* published four articles in 1818 containing scoffing references to Keats, six in 1819, four in 1820, three in 1821, five in 1822, six in 1823, seven in 1824; ... On the average, every second or third month they published more witticisms about 'Johnny Keats', or 'pestle-man Jack', the silly Cockney bard 'who, like Apollo, practices poetry and pharmacy'.[41]

Notice that, by this account, *Blackwood's* 'witticisms' continued for at least three years after Keats' death.

Keats compose this piece while at a lecture delivered by Astley Cooper. I have not placed it within the list for two reasons: first, it is not a poem and second, its date of composition is extremely uncertain, as it is yet to be established that Keats and Dendy ever attended the same lecture series. See Ifor Evans, 'Keats as a Medical Student', 391; Claude Lee Finney, *The Evolution of Keats's Poetry* (New York: Russell and Russell, 1956), 90–91, 276; and *John Keats*, ed. Elizabeth Cook (Oxford: Oxford University Press, 1990) for more on the 'Alexander fragment'.

38 *KC*, II, 208.

39 MacGillivray, *Bibliography*, xii–xiii.

40 MacGillivray, *Bibliography*, xxiii–xxv.

41 MacGillivray, *Bibliography*, xxv.

The second myth, which portrayed Keats as a delicate genius harried to his grave by harsh criticism, was in place within a year of his death, following publication of Shelley's elegy *Adonais* in which Keats is likened to 'a pale flower by some sad maiden cherished' (48).[42] This idea of Keats as a sensitive poet done to death was elaborated in private accounts and publications by Keats' admirers and detractors (John Wilson Croker's review of *Endymion* in the *Quarterly*, September 1818, was identified as the culprit, rather than *Blackwood's* more scurrilous 'Cockney School of Poetry' articles). More than two years after Keats' death, *Blackwood's* was still promoting the idea of a vulnerable apothecary–poetaster:

> Round the ring we sat, the stiff stuff tipsily quaffing.
> [Thanks be to thee, Jack Keats; our thanks for the dactyl and spondee;
> Pestleman Jack, whom, according to Shelley, the Quarterly murdered
> With a critique as fell as one of his own patent medicines]

The passage is annotated as follows:

> *Tipsily quaffing.* – From a poem about Bacchus, written by poor Jack Keats, a man for whom I had a particular esteem. I never can read the Quarterly of late, on account of the barbarous murder it committed on that promising young man.[43]

This kind of thing became routine in *Blackwood's* after the fourth 'Cockney School' essay of October 1818; more curious is the fact that the myth of a poor, vulnerable Keats was also promoted by his friends.

John Hamilton Reynolds, in his 'Advertisement' for *The Garden of Florence; and Other Poems* (1821), mentions the plan that he and Keats had formulated to write poems from stories in Boccaccio:[44]

> – but illness on his part, and distracting engagements on mine,

42 Wolfson, 'Keats enters history', 18.

43 Quoted in MacGillivray, *Bibliography*, xxvi.

44 Keats referred to this plan in a letter to Reynolds dated 27 April 1818: see *LJK*, I, 274.

> prevented us from accomplishing our plan at the time; and Death now, to my deep sorrow, has frustrated it for ever!
>
> He, who is gone, was one of the very kindest friends I possessed, and yet he was not kinder perhaps to me, than to others. His intense mind and powerful feeling would, I truly believe, have done the world some service, had his life been spared – but he was of too sensitive a nature – and thus he was destroyed! One story he completed, and that is to me now the most pathetic poem in existence![45]

Reynolds does not mention Keats by name, but the allusion to a 'friend' who was also a poet 'of too sensitive a nature', which led him to be 'destroyed', would have been clear to readers. Meanwhile, in 1822, Charles Brown, one of the executors of Keats' will, had the epitaph that Keats had selected for himself – 'Here lies one whose name was writ in water' – prefaced by a text stating that Keats 'on his Death Bed, in the Bitterness of his Heart at the Malicious Power of his Enemies, Desired these Words to be engraven on his Tomb Stone'.[46]

William Hazlitt also contributed to the evolving Keats myth in his *Table-Talk*. In the essay 'On Living to One's-Self' he wrote of the remarks made in the *Quarterly* and *Blackwood's* and their supposed effects:

> This epithet [Cockney School] proved too much for one of the writers in question, and stuck like a barbed arrow in his heart. Poor Keats! What was sport to the town, was death to him. Young, sensitive, delicate, he was ... unable to endure the miscreant cry and idiot laugh, [and] withdrew to sigh his last breath in foreign climes.[47]

In an essay 'On Effeminacy of Character', Hazlitt observed: 'I cannot help thinking that the fault of Mr. Keats's poetry was a deficiency in masculine energy of style. He had beauty, tenderness, delicacy, in an

45 John Hamilton [Reynolds], *The Garden of Florence; and Other Poems* (London: John Warren, 1821), xii.

46 *JK*, 435.

47 William Hazlitt, *Table-Talk: Essays on Men and Manners* (1821–22; London/Edinburgh: Henry Frowde, 1901; reprint 1905), 131–32.

uncommon degree, but there was a want of strength and substance.'[48] Later, he summarized Keats: 'He gave the greatest promise of genius of any poet of his day. He displayed extreme tenderness, beauty, originality, and delicacy of fancy; all he wanted was manly strength and fortitude to reject the temptations of singularity in sentiment and expression.'[49] This 'gendering' of Keats – depicting him as having qualities and attributes that were traditionally 'feminine' (extreme tenderness, sensitivity, delicacy, beauty) – was an adjunct to the myth that he was killed off by a critique: it was also implicit in Shelley's 'Preface' to *Adonais* quoted below:[50]

> The genius of the lamented person to whose memory I have dedicated these unworthy verses, was not less delicate and fragile than it was beautiful; and where cankerworms abound, what wonder, if its young flower was blighted in the bud? The savage criticism on his *Endymion*, which appeared in the *Quarterly Review*, produced the most violent effect on his susceptible mind; the agitation thus originated ended in the rupture of a blood-vessel in the lungs; a rapid consumption ensued, and the succeeding acknowledgements from more candid critics, of the true greatness of his powers, were ineffectual to heal the wound thus wantonly inflicted. ... I am given to understand that the wound which his sensitive spirit had received from the criticism of *Endymion*, was exasperated by the bitter sense of unrequited benefits; the poor fellow seems to have been hooted from the stage of life ...

In the final instalment of his 'Memoir for Shelley' in the *Athenaeum* (1832), Thomas Medwin invoked the figure of a helpless, 'feminine' Keats to show off the 'masculine' strength of Shelley, girded for battle in defence of the weak: 'that Shelley could wield a lash of bronze for others, he proved in Adonais'.[51]

Doubtful of this death-by-criticism myth, Leigh Hunt noted that he had told Byron 'he was mistaken in attributing Mr. Keats's

48 Hazlitt, *Table-Talk*, 346.

49 Quoted in *CH*, 248, from William Hazlitt, 'Critical List of Authors' to his volume on *Select British Poets, or New Elegant Extracts from Chaucer to the Present Time, with Critical Remarks* (1824).

50 Wolfson, 'Keats enters history', 18–19, 24–25.

51 Quoted in Wolfson, 'Keats enters history', 25.

death to the critics'.[52] Nevertheless, Hunt furthered the myth by reviewing and quoting from *Adonais* in *The Examiner* (7 July 1822) and by dwelling on Keats' suffering and misery in *Lord Byron and Some of His Contemporaries* (1828). Byron himself, by inserting a stanza into *Don Juan* bemoaning 'John Keats, who was killed off by one critique', also helped to promote the story.[53] (Being Byron, however, he was inclined to scepticism, and converted the pathos of the original myth to a very *Don Juan*-esque bathos: ''Tis strange the mind, that very fiery particle, / Should let itself be snuffed out by an Article').[54] The longevity of this myth was such that Dorothy Hewlett's 1937 biography was titled *Adonais: A Life of John Keats*.[55]

While British periodicals squabbled about Keats, Europe and the New World were discovering his poetry for themselves. In 1829 the French publishers Galignani pirated and produced in Paris an edition of selected poems by Coleridge, Shelley, and Keats, which included an anonymous memoir of Keats written by Cyrus Redding:

> [Keats] had but just completed his twenty-fourth year when he was snatched away from the world, and an end put forever to a genius of a lofty and novel order. Certain party critics, who made it their object to lacerate the feelings, and endeavour to put down by vituperation and misplaced ridicule every effort which emanated not from their own servile dependents or followers, furiously attacked the writings of Keats on their appearance. ... The unmerited abuse poured upon Keats by this periodical work is supposed to have hastened his end, which was slowly approaching when the criticism before mentioned appeared.[56]

The Galignani edition with this account of Keats' 'hastened end' was promptly taken over and reissued by American publishers.[57]

52 Hunt, *Byron and Contemporaries*, 266.

53 See *Don Juan* XI, stanza 60 in Lord Byron, *The Complete Poetical Works*, ed. Jerome J. McGann. 7 vols (Oxford: Clarendon Press, 1980–93), V, 483.

54 *Don Joan* XI, stanza 60 in Byron, *Poetical Works*, V, 483.

55 Dorothy Hewlett, *Adonais: A Life of John Keats* (London: Hurst and Blackett, 1937). For an account of Keats' afterlives see Holmes, 'Keats the Well-Beloved', in *This Long Pursuit*, 219–41.

56 *CH*, 261–62.

57 MacGillivray, *Bibliography*, xlviii.

MacGillivray noted how in Philadelphia in 1831 J. Howe 'set-up and stereotyped a volume ... which followed page-for-page the text of the Galignani edition, included the same memoirs only slightly altered, was of the same general format, and had a frontispiece, with portraits, which was a very close copy of the original'.[58] He traced 17 variants of this twice-pirated 'American-Galignani edition' apparently published between 1831 and 1853.[59]

Meanwhile, protracted disputes prevented the publication of a biography.[60] John Taylor was considering one as early as 19 February 1821, stating '[Keats'] life is a Subject of public Interest, and it will be written.'[61] In June of that year, this appeared in the *Morning Chronicle*:

> Speedily will be published, with a Portrait,
> MEMOIRS and REMAINS of JOHN KEATS,
> Printed for Taylor and Hessey, Fleet-Street. Of whom may be had,
> ENDYMION, a Poetic Romance, by John Keats, 8vo. 9s.
> LAMIA, ISABELLA, and other Poems, by John Keats, 7s. 6d.[62]

*Blackwood's* also carried a similar notice.[63] This projected biography quickly stalled: Charles Brown felt it unseemly to rush into publication, and was unconvinced that Taylor was a suitable author. He wished to check and correct the memoir before publication, and refused access to any papers unless Taylor agreed.[64] Severn had sent his account of Keats' last days to Brown, and to write a biography without this source was impossible, so Taylor shelved the plan. Furthermore, Brown and Taylor were at odds with Keats' only surviving brother, George – who possessed many of Keats' letters as well as more information about his early life than anyone else. George himself suggested that Reynolds should write

58 MacGillivray, *Bibliography*, xlviii.
59 MacGillivray, *Bibliography*, xlviii – xlix, 8–11.
60 MacGillivray, *Bibliography*, xxxvii – xxxviii.
61 Edmund Blunden, *Keats's Publisher: A Memoir of John Taylor* (London: Jonathan Cape, 1936), 85–86.
62 Advertisement, *Morning Chronicle* (4 June 1821): 2.
63 MacGillivray, *Bibliography*, xxxviii.
64 MacGillivray, *Bibliography*, xxxviii.

a biography.[65] While these disputes raged, Taylor happened to meet Richard Abbey at a dinner in 1827 – some six years after Keats' death – and heard from him an account of Keats' early days that led him to conclude '[t]hese are not Materials for a Life of our poor Friend which it will do to communicate to the World'.[66]

In 1828 Hunt published his essay 'Mr. Keats' in *Lord Byron and Some of His Contemporaries*. Not the least significant aspect of this was that it goaded Brown into action: he started collecting materials, spurred on by an inquiry from Galignani, who was publishing the 1829 volume.[67] To supplement the papers he had in his possession, Brown applied to Severn and Fanny Brawne, both of whom agreed to help.[68] In Florence in 1832 Brown told Richard Woodhouse that the biography would be completed by the next winter.[69] However, in 1834 Severn reproached him for delay – ''Tis an injustice to withhold these two works [the memoir and *Otho the Great*] any longer. I remember you said "the public should never have the tragedy until they have done justice to Keats's other works". *The time has come, and* I FEAR THE TIME WILL PASS'.[70] Brown's memoir was eventually read at the Plymouth Institution on 27 December 1836.[71] However, Brown and Dilke had quarrelled over the Keats brothers' finances after John's death, and now Dilke threatened Brown with an injunction should he publish his memoir without George's permission. In 1841 George withdrew his objection, but by this point Brown had decided to emigrate for New Zealand.[72] Before he left he gave his draft memoir, all the Keats papers in his possession, and the right to publish them to Richard Monckton Milnes: as Brown put it, Milnes was 'a poet himself, an admirer of Keats, and in my mind, better able to sit in judgment on a selection for publication than any other man I know'.[73]

65 MacGillivray, *Bibliography*, xxxviii. Reynolds did, in due course, contribute to Milnes' *Life*.

66 *JK*, 3–4.

67 MacGillivray, *Bibliography*, xl.

68 MacGillivray, *Bibliography*, xxxix–xl.

69 MacGillivray, *Bibliography*, xxxix–xl.

70 Quoted in MacGillivray, *Bibliography*, xli.

71 Brown, *Life*, 17.

72 MacGillivray, *Bibliography*, xli.

73 MacGillivray, *Bibliography*, xli–xlii.

Meanwhile, in 1825, Taylor and Hessey, who held the copyright for the majority of Keats' poems, had been bankrupted.[74] Thereafter John Taylor hesitated to print more editions of Keats' poems: in 1835 he told John Clare that he feared 'even 250 copies would not sell'.[75] Nevertheless, with the rise of a new generation of poets – Tennyson, Arthur Hallam, Elizabeth Barrett, and others – who appreciated Keats' verse and ignored the politics of a previous generation, Keats' reputation steadily grew.[76] Finally, in 1840 Taylor permitted the publication of a 'Smith's Standard Library' volume of selected poems by Keats; this was quickly followed by a second volume in 1841.[77]

*

Henry Stephens' recollections of Keats at Guy's were penned in 1847 and should be read against this background of the poet's developing reputation, particularly as a poet so sensitive that he could be undone by a harsh critique. As Susan Wolfson observes, 'Shelley's myth proved so potent that Keats's actual history reorganized itself around it.'[78] I believe that this tendency to 'reorganize' can also be seen in Stephens' recollections. Keats almost certainly showed a preference for poetry at Guy's, and may have said that he wished to be as famous as Byron. This did not mean he had already resolved to abandon medicine – indeed, that he was at Guy's at all oversets such a claim. Moreover, Stephens came to know Keats only when they started sharing lodgings, and this was after George Cooper and Frederick Tyrell left Guy's at Christmas 1815.[79] So Stephens knew Keats only when he was already into his second term at Guy's and aware of his imminent elevation as a dresser. That this was after the Christmas vacation may also be pertinent, for John Flint South noted that 'this vacation always did mischief, for the work done after it was never as

74 Barry Symonds, 'Taylor, John (1781–1864)', *ODNB*.

75 Blunden, *Publisher*, 199.

76 MacGillivray, *Bibliography*, xliv–xlvi.

77 MacGillivray, *Bibliography*, xlix–l.

78 Wolfson, 'Keats enters history', 27.

79 *KC*, II, 207–08; William S. Pierpoint, *The Unparallel Lives of Three Medical Students: John Keats, Henry Stephens and George Wilson Mackereth* (London: The Stephens Collection, 2010), 3. Roe states that Cooper and Tyrell left Guy's 'early in 1816': see *NL*, 76.

active as previously'.[80] Some biographers have suggested that Keats could not choose to leave Guy's until he turned 21 on 31 October 1816 and was no longer subject to Abbey's guardianship.[81] Such a scenario is contradicted by Keats' evident aptitude for study; the numerous pages of lecture-notes in his Notebook; his rapid progression to dresser; *and* his taking up that post on the allotted date. None of this suggests a wayward student or one who was only marking time, as Stephens' reminiscence implies. It *does* indicate that throughout Keats' attendance there he was genuinely interested in medicine and intended to succeed in that profession. Even Stephens conceded that 'when [Keats] condescended to talk upon other subjects he was agreeable & intelligent, He was quick & apt at learning, when he chose to give his attention to any subject.'[82]

Keats appeared at Apothecaries' Hall on 25 July 1816 to be examined for his licence, and passed apparently without difficulty.[83] That this was not a mere formality can be seen from the statistics: in 1816 the Apothecaries' Act had been in place for a year. In that year, one candidate out of every nine had been turned down for a licence – a failure rate of approximately 12 per cent.[84] Evidently this was a rigorous qualification: Keats' fellow student George Mackereth did not pass the examination, while Stephens, who had postponed his attempt because he feared not passing, still required two tries and passed only on his second attempt.[85] Stephens recalled how Keats 'surprise{d} many of us by his passing', but conceded that 'he was very quick in acquiring any thing'.[86] '[I]t was the examination in Latin which the student[s] most feared', Stephens recalled – that is, translations from Latin originals in the *Pharmacopoeia Londoniensis* and from physicians' prescriptions that constituted one part of the licensing examination.[87] Keats had translated the *Aeneid* as a schoolboy and his proficiency in Latin stood him in good stead – strikingly, if somewhat oddly, poetry ensured Keats' success in medicine.

80 *Mem*, 38.
81 Bate, *Keats*, 59, 110, 118; *JK*, 85.
82 *KC*, II, 210.
83 Woof and Hebron, *John Keats*, 60.
84 *JK*, 72.
85 *JK*, 72.
86 *KC*, II, 211.
87 *KC*, II, 211; *NL*, 92.

Immediately after his licentiate examination Keats took a holiday at Margate, where he wrote the sonnet and epistle 'To My Brother George'.[88] These two poems express a change of mood in the second phase of his hospital poems. Though still, in some sense, occasional pieces, these are more introspective, pensive, ambitious, and thought-provoking works than much of his earlier light verse, and there are clear indications that Keats was considering his future. The 'wonders' seen in the sonnet to George compel him to 'think on what will be, and what has been' (8), while the epistle addresses his poetic ambitions for the first time since 'To George Felton Mathew', written nine months earlier as he commenced at Guy's. Perhaps, however, the most significant piece in this respect is the poem he wrote immediately after the ones to George: 'To Charles Cowden Clarke'.

The Keats brothers had lost touch with Clarke for almost a year, even though Clarke was also in London, staying with his sister Isabella Towers and her husband at Clerkenwell. When George discovered his whereabouts, he informed his brothers.[89] Before returning to London from Margate, Keats set about re-establishing contact through a verse epistle in couplets, like the poem he had recently written to George.[90]

This verse epistle 'To Charles Cowden Clarke' marks a turning point in Keats' poetic biography. It was the first time Keats acknowledged Clarke's formative role in his development as a poet, and it is an emphatic avowal of indebtedness. Clarke already knew that Keats was writing poetry – in February 1815 he had been given 'Written on the Day Mr Leigh Hunt Left Prison' – but here Keats explicitly acknowledged Clarke's influence.[91] In doing so he placed Clarke in a position of implicit interest in his success, for the poem was a calculated appeal for further help in his poetic enterprise:

88 *Poems*, 551; *JK*, 74; White, *Literary Life*, 48–49.

89 *LJK*, I, 104.

90 John Barnard questions whether Keats spent two months on holiday at Margate, citing Keats' duties at Guy's Hospital and the dresser's rota there. See BT, 212; *Poems*, 60–63, 552.

91 Leigh Hunt was released from prison on 2 February 1815, but Clarke's account does not make it clear whether Keats handed over his sonnet on the subject to Clarke that same day. CCC, 89; *NL*, 65.

> ... you first taught me all the sweets of song:
> The grand, the sweet, the terse, the free, the fine;
> What swell'd with pathos, and what right divine:
>
> (53–55)

The appeal worked. Clarke was soon in touch with his old pupil, and did what he had earlier failed to do: he introduced Keats to the 'wrong'd Libertas' – the editor of *The Examiner*, Leigh Hunt, now recovered from his prison sentence and in a position and frame of mind to mentor Keats. That Hunt had already published 'To Solitude' may have made him more receptive to Clarke's recommendation – yet, without Clarke's introduction, Keats could not have hoped to meet Hunt with the rapidity that ensued. Further friendships arising from their renewed intimacy helped to fix Keats' determination to pursue poetry.[92] Clarke gave Keats an introduction to Benjamin Robert Haydon, through whom he met John Hamilton Reynolds and William Wordsworth, and went to see the Elgin Marbles.[93] It is also possible that Clarke introduced Keats to Hazlitt, and there is no doubt that that introduction was the result of Clarke introducing Keats to the Hunt Circle.

Joining Hunt's Circle in autumn 1816 lent impetus to Keats' determination to leave his medical training and focus on poetry. Unlike the mocking reception his poems received from students at Guy's, in Hunt, Haydon, Reynolds, and the rest he found established artists and writers who appreciated his verse and saw its promise.[94] This must have been gratifying for an ambitious young poet, and provided the encouragement needed to make a final break on completing his year as a dresser. All of Keats' letters from the latter part of 1816 discuss his social life to the exclusion of hospital duties and, immediately after the epistle 'To Charles Cowden Clarke', there is an increase in occasional verse directly traceable to the influence

92 Ronald Sharp's essay, 'Keats and Friendship' in *The Persistence of Poetry*, ed. Ryan and Sharp, 66–81 addresses Keats' general conception of friendship; here, I am interested in how specific friendships with members of the Hunt Circle influenced Keats' poetry between October 1816 and March 1817.

93 *NL*, 110, 123, 150; *JK*, 89, 99, 116.

94 See *KC*, II, 208–09. According to Henry Stephens, whenever Keats showed his poems to a fellow medical student – 'Newmarsh or Newmarch' – from St Bartholomew's Hospital, 'it was sure to be ridiculed, and severely handled'.

of the Hunt Circle. The sheer quantity of poetry written also went up. In the ten months between October 1815 and his examination on 25 July 1816 (both months inclusive) he wrote 485 lines of poetry; in the eight months from August 1816 to March 1817 (both months inclusive) he wrote 1,264 lines.[95]

The reacquaintance with Clarke and the promise of Hunt's patronage thus had an immediate effect on Keats' poetic productivity. His excitement at the prospect of meeting Hunt is the subject of Keats' earliest surviving letter, written to Clarke on 9 October 1816: 'I can now devote any time you may mention to the pleasure of seeing M$^{r}$ Hunt— 't will be an Era in my existence.'[96] This momentous introduction took place on 19 October 1816, and soon afterwards Keats wrote his most accomplished poem to date: the sonnet 'On First Looking into Chapman's Homer'.[97] This sonnet dated from Keats' and Clarke's talks on poetry after their reacquaintance in London: Clarke termed it their first 'symposium' and recollected it as being 'a memorable night ... in my life's career'.[98] They met at Clerkenwell and talked through the night, poring over a folio edition of Chapman's Homer lent by Hunt, who had earlier described it as 'a fine rough old wine' in *The Examiner*.[99] Thus, if Clarke was the immediate influence, Hunt's interest was also at work in the circumstances leading to the sonnet's composition: as Ward observes, 'the poem as a whole expresses [Keats'] rising excitement of the previous weeks, from the moment Clarke promised to introduce him to Hunt.'[100] Hunt, when he saw the sonnet, was impressed: he praised it to Hazlitt and Godwin, and chose it as the poem with which to conclude his 'Young Poets' article in *The Examiner* that December.[101] Certainly it concentrates ambition, imaginative scope, and formal control more powerfully than any of Keats' writing hitherto.

95 These figures are arrived at from the reading text of the poems presented in *Poems*; variants and alternate versions would be higher than the figures given here.

96 *LJK*, I, 113.

97 *NL*, 102–03.

98 CCC, 89.

99 Leigh Hunt, 'Harry Brown's Letter to His Friends: Letter VII', *The Examiner* (25 August 1816): 536–37.

100 Ward, *Making of a Poet*, 76.

101 Ward, *Making of a Poet*, 77; Leigh Hunt, 'Young Poets', *The Examiner* (1 December 1816): 759.

From this point onwards the theme of sociality dominates Keats' poetry to a degree not seen since his days with the Mathew Circle. 'On First Looking into Chapman's Homer' shows the influence of Keats' acquaintances acting obliquely; the next two sonnets he wrote take their subject matter more directly from his social activities. Clarke recalled that 'Keen, fitful gusts are whisp'ring here and there' was written '[v]ery shortly after [Keats'] installation at [Leigh Hunt's] cottage', and 'On Leaving Some Friends at an Early Hour' was written 'shortly after' the preceding poem.[102] The warmth and company invoked in 'Keen, fitful gusts' was a recollection of Hunt's house, where the talk ranged in all directions during 'evenings joco-serio-musico-pictorio-poetical'; while the friends he was forced to leave early – probably because of his duties at Guy's – were members of the Hunt Circle.[103] At the same time there was an increase in letters from Keats, all discussing social engagements. The following is a list of all the extant letters written by Keats (either singly or co-authored with his brothers) up to the end of March 1817:[104]

1. November 1815: To George Felton Mathew (verse epistle)
2. 13 June 1816: The Keats Brothers to Richard Abbey
3. August 1816: To George Keats (verse epistle)
4. September 1816: To Charles Cowden Clarke (verse epistle)
5. 9 October 1816: To Charles Cowden Clarke
6. 31 October 1816: To Charles Cowden Clarke
7. 1 November 1816: To Joseph Severn
8. 8 or 11 November 1816: To Charles Cowden Clarke
9. 20 November 1816: To B. R. Haydon
10. 21 November 1816: To B. R. Haydon
11. 17 December 1816: To Charles Cowden Clarke
12. 9 March 1817: To J. H. Reynolds

102 *RoW*, 134, 135.

103 Quoted in Ward, *Making of a Poet*, 79.

104 My source for this list is *LJK*. Rollins notes that 'Keats wrote "three words" on the lost cover enclosing' the epistle 'To George Keats' (August 1816) and that there may be missing letters to George Keats from the spring of 1817: see *LJK*, I, 9. Since some of Keats' earliest letters are verse epistles, there is some overlap between his letters and poems; in such cases I have indicated as much in parentheses. When a letter was written jointly by all three Keats brothers I specify the writers as being 'the Keats brothers'.

13. 17 March 1817: To J. H. Reynolds
14. 25 March 1817: To Charles Cowden Clarke

Most of these letters are addressed to members of the Hunt Circle, with Clarke figuring as a particularly frequent correspondent (six letters). From the first letter – his verse epistle of 'farewell' to Mathew at the start of his Guy's career – this list reveals how Keats' social horizons gradually expanded. Keats starts corresponding more frequently from August 1816 onwards, after his licentiate examination in July, but for the next three months his letters are solely addressed either to his brother George or to Clarke. It is only from November – shortly after the 'era' of his introduction to Hunt – that his circle of correspondents widens to include others such as Severn, Haydon, and Reynolds. This expansion in his social engagement is mirrored in his poetry, which is, more and more as the year wears on, inspired by his convivial activities.

Considered in this light, the sonnet 'To My Brothers' represents a movement increasingly visible in Keats' verse and life at this point: to engage with company congenial to him. In pursuing a medical career he had placed himself in new surroundings, at a distance from his family and, after his split from the Mathew Circle, from poetic companionship. From the summer of 1816 there is a turn back towards his brothers, a reach out to Clarke, and then an entry into the Hunt Circle. When he travelled to Margate he did not go alone: his brother Tom was with him; once there, he wrote poems to his other brother, George.[105] Except for the epistle 'To George Felton Mathew' and a note of business co-authored with his brothers, the earliest letters extant from Keats date from Margate – his verse epistles to George and to Clarke.[106] It is almost as if, having secured a qualification that would allow him to pursue his medical career and earn a living, Keats decided to reconsider his life and take stock. An immediate effect of this is apparently an urge to reconnect with the familiar: his family and his oldest friend Clarke. Another, as seen from the sonnet 'To My Brother George' as well as the verse epistles 'To My Brother George' and 'To Charles Cowden Clarke', is a reconsideration of his future, and what place poetry might play in it. From his writings in Margate, as well as from his subsequent actions, it does not seem that

105 White, *Literary Life*, 48, 49.
106 *LJK*, I, 105–13.

he reached any firm decision. That came later: after the introduction to Hunt, and possibly after Hunt's article 'Young Poets' in *The Examiner*.[107] Nevertheless, it was during the time in Margate that, by reaching back towards his past, Keats set in motion the sequence of events and introductions that would define his future.

With Keats shuttling between London and Margate, and from place to place within London, analysis of his poems by location of composition indicates additional patterns in his poetic output. The sharp increase in Keats' rate of composition after his July 1816 licentiate examination has already been noted, but is it also possible that where he was living – and with whom – influenced his poetic productivity. Considering his poetic output in terms of location, by far the greatest concentration of poetic composition took place while Keats was living with his brothers at Cheapside. It is, perhaps, significant that the first poem that can be dated confidently to Cheapside is the sonnet 'To My Brothers', written on Tom's birthday and evoking a scene of domestic harmony reigning in the 'fraternal' (4) household.[108] As Stephens's recollections show, Keats' poetic ambitions exposed him to the mockery of his fellow medical students:

> [Keats] had no idea of Fame, or Greatness, but as it was connected with the pursuits of Poetry ... The greatest men in the world were the Poets, and to rank among them was the chief object of his ambition. – It may readily be imagined that this feeling was accompanied with a good deal of Pride ... [which] had exposed him, as may be readily imagined, to occasional ridicule, & some mortification.[109]

Unlike the medical students, Keats' brothers supported his poetic endeavours. As already noted, the composition of 'On First Looking into Chapman's Homer' was influenced, in important ways, by the Hunt Circle; however, equally significant was the circumstance that, after spending all night reading with Clarke, Keats came home to a place where he could continue that imaginative engagement with Chapman's Homer. Living with his brothers, at Dean Street and later

107 *KC*, II, 211.
108 *Texts*, 118.
109 *KC*, II, 208–09.

at Cheapside, Keats could apply himself to poetry without fear of 'mortification'.

This congenial domestic atmosphere contributed to the significant increase in Keats' poetic production after moving to Cheapside in November 1816, as did the influence and encouragement of the Hunt Circle. Both factors combined to encourage his decision to publish *Poems* (1817). It was in Cheapside that, as Clarke recalled, this volume 'was determined upon, in great part written, and sent forth to the world'.[110] Tom Keats fair-copied some of the poems, and George was possibly involved in negotiating the publication arrangement with the Ollier brothers, whom Keats met through the Hunt Circle, and who had set up as publishers with Hunt's support.[111]

John Barnard has shown that Keats could not have considered publishing with the Olliers until the winter of 1816 because the Olliers had only just set up as publishers at the beginning of December that year: Keats' collection was one of the first books they published.[112] Stephens had claimed that it was the appearance of 'Young Poets' in *The Examiner* (1 December 1816) that absolutely determined Keats' turn to a poetic career.[113] Thereafter Hunt was preoccupied with Shelley, who was in the throes of a family crisis following his first wife Harriet's suicide in mid-December. The Christmas holiday of 1816/17 may have seen a slowing of the hospital schedule, though as a dresser Keats was unlikely to receive the full vacation that students enjoyed. All of these factors combined to ensure that, in addition to composing poetry, by the close of the year Keats was also spending a considerable amount of his time at Cheapside preparing copy for the press. The Keats household thus became a workshop for the creation of *Poems* (1817). Perhaps it is not surprising, then, that there are no surviving letters from Keats for almost 12 weeks from 17 December 1816 to 9 March 1817. He was living with his brothers, with Clarke a frequent caller; Haydon was occupied with his paintings or visiting the Elgin

110 *RoW*, 137.

111 George Keats wrote to the Olliers complaining of their failure to sell copies of *Poems* (1817) in April 1817, suggesting that his interest in the volume was more than just that of a passive well-wisher. Keats recalled in 1819 how George 'always stood between me and any dealings with the world' (*LJK*, II, 113). See Barnard, 'First Fruits', 83, 74.

112 Barnard, 'First Fruits', 83, 74.

113 *KC*, II, 211.

Marbles; and Hunt was busy with Shelley – so Keats may simply not have had occasion to write. However, his preoccupation with preparing his poems for the press and the resumption of the full load of dresser's duties after the holidays may also have been contributing factors for this period of silence: Keats was probably duty dresser at Guy's at least once during this January (either 1–15 January or 22–29 January: it is impossible to be more precise).[114] His correspondence resumes on 9 March 1817, after the conclusion of his dressership and on the day that Reynolds's review of *Poems* (1817) appeared.[115]

It was also at Cheapside that Keats completed the two long poems that opened and closed *Poems* (1817). 'I stood tip-toe upon a little hill', was composed over several months, and finished in December 1816.[116] This was Keats' first attempt at a long poem after 'Calidore: A Fragment', which, having grown to 162 lines, had been abandoned. Fraternal company at Cheapside may have been crucial to ensuring that 'I stood tip-toe' did not suffer a similar fate, by allowing Keats to sustain composition to its closing question: 'Was there a Poet born?' (241). That Keats was able to compose *and* complete long poems at this time is evident from *Sleep and Poetry*: its 404 lines round off *Poems* (1817).[117] Though it is not clear exactly when he started writing it, it was 'sometime during October–December 1816': that is, after his introduction to Hunt and before the completed manuscript for *Poems* (1817) had been delivered to the printer.[118] Clarke recalled that

> [i]t was in the library at Hunt's cottage, where an extemporary bed had been made up for him on the sofa, that he composed the framework and many lines of the poem on 'Sleep and Poetry,' – the last sixty or seventy being an inventory of the art-garniture of the room.[119]

It is in these lines, a homage to 'art-garniture' in 'a poet's house' (354), that Keats sees the 'cold and sacred busts' (357) of King Alfred

114 BT, 210.
115 See *LJK*, I, 123; *CH*, 45–49.
116 *Texts*, 122–23; and Barnard, 'First Fruits', 87.
117 Aileen Ward sees this as Keats' 'poem of dedication', pledging himself to a poetry. See Ward, *Making of a Poet*, 90.
118 Ward, *Making of a Poet*, 121.
119 CCC, 91.

and Kosciusko 'worn / By horrid sufferance – mightily forlorn' (387–88).[120] No longer a specimen of nerve damage in a medical lecture, in Hunt's house Kosciusko was transformed into one of Keats' 'mighty dead': the geographical move from Cheapside to the Vale of Health had given Keats a fresh sense of poetic possibility that would shortly propel him away from the fraternal and social circles of the city. Nevertheless, it was the stability and supportive atmosphere of the households at Dean Street and Cheapside that helped him bring this most ambitious poem to a conclusion, and with none of the personal crises that would accompany the composition of *Endymion* in the following year.[121]

Keats' preoccupations – with medicine, his future and the role of poetry in it – are reflected in these longer poems. Precisely when Keats started writing 'I stood tip-toe' is unknown, but it was certainly while he was fulfilling his dresser's duties at Guy's. Leigh Hunt recalled that the poem was 'suggested to [Keats] by a delightful summer-day, as he stood beside the gate that leads from the Battery on Hampstead Heath into a field by Caen Wood'.[122] Hunt cannot have been recollecting from personal observation, since he met Keats only in October 1816.[123] He must, therefore, be recounting this information from some other source. Stillinger cites the possibility that Hunt may have inferred 'beautiful summer day' from the poem itself: this may be so, but it does not explain how Hunt came up with the other details.[124] The most likely source of information for Hunt was, of course, Keats himself, during one of their evenings at the Vale of Health. The poem certainly displays the most direct echoes of his hospital experiences at the time he was dresser:

> The breezes were ethereal, and pure,
> And crept through half closed lattices to cure
> The languid sick; it cool'd their fever'd sleep,
> And soothed them into slumbers full and deep.
> Soon they awoke clear-eyed: nor burnt with thirsting,

120 Kosciusko makes an appearance in JKMN, Bf4v.

121 See John Barnard, 'Keats's "Forebodings": Margate, Spring 1817, and After', *Romanticism* 21.1 (April 2015): 1–13.

122 Hunt, *Byron and Contemporaries*, 249.

123 *NL*, 102–03.

124 *Texts*, 122.

> Nor with hot fingers, nor with temples bursting:
> And springing up, they met the wond'ring sight
> Of their dear friends, nigh foolish with delight
> (221–28)

Keats' medical opinion on the effects of 'air quality' can be seen from his letter of 5 September 1819, admonishing John Taylor that to recover his health 'it must be proper country air'.[125] Astley Cooper noted how 'low degrees of heat diminish the quickness of the Pulse', in a lecture on 'Arteries' that Keats heard.[126] The inner city 'breezes' off the Thames at Guy's may have 'cool'd' fevered patients as Cooper claimed, but could not possibly be considered in any way 'ethereal, and pure'. The section quoted above appears in the middle of Keats' recounting of Endymion and Diana's story – invoking the figure of a 'Poet, sure a lover too' (193) who 'gave meek Cynthia her Endymion' (204) – and it is surely significant that as the 'languid sick' recover 'their tongues were loos'd in poesy' (235). Keats' breezes, therefore, seem to amalgamate the medical with the poetic: while fresh air in the Guy's Hospital wards may have offered limited relief to patients, 'breezes ethereal, and pure' stirred only in the poet's imagination, bringing the soothing melody of 'soft numbers' (237). It is now known that stimulating the brain by conversation can have beneficial effects, even for patients in a coma; in the nineteenth century, too, efforts were made to keep patients' minds occupied. One way in which this was achieved was by reading to them: the Guy's Hospital rules stated that all 'Patients as are able must every morning on the Ringing of the Chapel-Bell, attend Divine Service there' and that 'On Sunday Evening ... some sober Person in each Ward ... shall, at the Desk, with an audible Voice, Distinctly read two Chapters, one in the Old Testament and one in the New (and every Evening some Person shall, at the Desk, read the Prayers appointed)'.[127] The intention behind the Bible-reading was certainly religious, but the nineteenth century believed that good morals were a prerequisite for good health: in his medical Notebook, Keats noted that '[t]he Young who lead a life of Intemperance are subject to ossification'; while

125 *LJK*, II, 155.

126 Waddington, 39.

127 H. C. Cameron, *Mr Guy's Hospital 1726–1948* (London: Longmans, Green and Co.: 1954), 74–75.

Leigh Hunt, on seeing a child 'all over sores, and encased in steel', could not help wondering about paternal 'irregularities'.[128]

The 'ethereal' breezes of poetry can be thought of as a pagan version of what daily prayers might effect: soothing the sick. 'I stood tip-toe' is a pastoral poem, in which every turn towards tragedy is thwarted and all ends well. However, Keats' poetic ambitions were growing, as his reflections in *Sleep and Poetry* show. He wishes for 'ten years, that I may overwhelm / Myself in poesy' (96–97), and sketches out a plan for poetic compositions following the classical progression from pastoral subjects through to tragedy and epic. Likewise, Keats' desire to engage imaginatively with 'a nobler life, / ... the agonies, the strife / Of human hearts' (123–25) may be read as an expression of his wish to write in the tragic and epic genres, classically held in highest esteem. However, as a dresser he was also familiar with the range of physical 'agony' that a 'human heart', an organ of the body having '4 Cavaties surrounded by muscular fibres', could be subjected to.[129] In his mature poetry Keats would bring his anatomical knowledge into play to sharpen poetic sense and impact, and his phrase about 'the strife / Of human hearts' offers a first intimation of the physician-poet for whom 'axioms in philosophy [were] not axioms until they are proved upon our pulses'.[130]

Keats' formal medical training concluded in March 1817, and in April he took ship for the Isle of Wight, leaping 'headlong into the Sea' of poetry that became *Endymion*.[131] He had chosen to focus his energies on attempting to 'gain [his] Living' through the practice of poetry rather than medicine, yet the poem he wrote is suffused with medical imagery and derives much of its vitality from its physiological depictions of human passion.[132] This quality was to infuse his mature poetry as well, contributing greatly to its enduring appeal. The close association of the two careers of medicine and poetry in his formative period of 1815–17 thus set the pattern for the years – and poems – to come.

128 JKMN, Ff1r; Nicholas Roe, *Fiery Heart: The First Life of Leigh Hunt* (London: Random House, 2005), 88.

129 JKMN, Ff24v.

130 *LJK*, I, 279.

131 *LJK*, I, 374.

132 *KC*, I, 307; for detailed analysis of *Endymion* see Chapter 5.

CHAPTER THREE

# Keats' Medical Milieu

John Keats was writing poetry throughout his tenure at Guy's Hospital while also working full-time at his medical studies – so what did Guy's offer in terms of professional training and opportunity? This chapter considers the perplexing issue of the source from which Keats' medical notes derived, showing that – though they are indeed from Astley Cooper and Henry Cline Jnr's joint lecture course on 'Anatomy, and the Operations of Surgery' – the course itself was subject to rescheduling and restructuring in the year 1815/16. This affected the form and, especially, the content of Keats' medical Notebook. The chapter also reveals, that as a medical student at an elite London teaching hospital, Keats had privileged access to intellectual capital that would influence his life and, in time, his poetry. Keats' time at Guy's brought him face-to-face with the more macabre aspects of early nineteenth-century surgical training – practising dissection on freshly exhumed corpses, for instance – and trained him as a competent surgeon in his own right. I have not offered exhaustive detail of the experiences Keats *might* have had, choosing to focus instead only on those events that certainly affected him, and made him more alive to the 'light and shade' of life and the world.[1] Ultimately, Keats' ability to hold in view multiple perspectives would find triumphant expression in the great odes, with their focus on the vitality found in the shadow of non-being; in a fleeting bird-song, with its power to make a listener forget his own troubled self while also expanding his imaginative vision into the world; in the '[s]eason of mists' ('To Autumn', 1), balanced finely between the warm fecundity of summer and the chill sterility of winter; in 'Beauty that must die' ('Ode on Melancholy', 21).

1 *LJK*, I, 387.

## The Source for Keats' Lecture Notes

The source from which Keats derived his medical notes has always been something of a puzzle. In 1825 Hale-White conjectured that it was Cooper and Cline's *joint* lectures on 'Anatomy, and the Operations of Surgery', but as we saw in the first chapter the proofs he adduced for this conclusion were less than convincing. A possible resolution may, however, lie in the preserved notebooks of Keats' fellow students. In 1943 George Winston identified one such set of notes, taken by Joshua Waddington, Keats' contemporary at Guy's.

Waddington's manuscript notebooks, currently preserved in the archives of King's College London, are a set of six volumes containing fair copies of lecture notes taken in 1815/16 by Joshua Waddington, a medical student at the United Hospitals of Guy's and St Thomas'. Records kept by the medical school office at Guy's show that Waddington registered as a pupil on 6 October 1815 – that is, five days after Keats had done so.[2] Although he was older than Keats (born 1793 or 1794), Waddington attended at Guy's for at least some of the time that Keats did, and they went to the same lectures. Thus, there exists among the six volumes of Waddington's notebooks a second set of notes for the lectures represented in Keats' medical Notebook.

The collection of Waddington's notebooks, bequeathed in 1899 to 'the Library of Guy's Hospital, by H. W., A Son of Joshua Waddington, F. R. C. S.', includes one volume of notes from lecture courses by John Haighton on 'Midwifery'; a volume from William Babington and James Curry on the 'Practice of Medicine'; three volumes from lectures delivered by Astley Cooper; and one that comprises Waddington's own case notes.[3] Each of his six notebooks has a title page specifying the lecture course, lecturer, date, and place where the course was delivered and, where required, a volume number. It is the three volumes containing notes from lectures by Cooper that are of interest here.

One of these three is a single volume of notes, described on the title page as taken from 'Lectures On The Principles and Practice, Of Surgery; Delivered at the Theatre S$^{t}$ Thomas's Hospital, between the 1$^{st}$ of October 1815, and the 1$^{st}$ of June 1816; By Astley Cooper

2 *KW*, 102. Based on entries in Pupils and Dressers 1755–1823 and Entry ... 1814–1827. King's College London (KCL), G/FP1/1 and G/FP3/2.

3 Waddington, bookplate on inside cover.

Esq.'[4] The two other volumes contain notes from a different lecture series, usually delivered jointly by Cooper and Henry Cline Jnr; each of these has on its title page: 'Lectures On Anatomy; And The Principal Operations Of Surgery; Delivered at the Theatre, S^t. Thomas's Hospital; between the 1^st of January, and the 1^st of June 1816; By Astley Cooper Esq^re', followed by the volume number (i.e. 1^st and 2^nd, respectively).[5] The first of these two volumes on 'Lectures On Anatomy; And The Principal Operations Of Surgery' contains notes comparable with the contents of Keats' medical Notebook: that is, a series of lectures starting with 'Lecture 1. Introductory Lecture' and concluding with 'Lecture 55 – The Heart (continued)'. The notebook actually contains notes for just 54 lectures, since there is no 'Lecture 33' in it (see Chapter 1).[6] Winston concluded that these notes were taken from the same lecture series as that from which Keats took the notes in his medical Notebook, but this identification raises two perplexing questions.

Waddington's notebooks indicate that the 'Lectures On Anatomy' were delivered solely 'By Astley Cooper Esq^re', at the Theatre, St. Thomas', 'between the 1^st of January, and the 1^st of June 1816'.[7] However, the 'Lectures On Anatomy' were usually delivered *jointly* by Astley Cooper and Henry Cline Jnr.[8] Waddington never mentions Cline Jnr, even though notes for the lectures that were usually delivered by him on the muscles are included in the volume.[9] It seems curious that Waddington, who took the trouble to write up his notes in fair copy, would omit to mention a change in lecturer. Perhaps he thought it unimportant, or simply forgot, though there is evidence that other students who attended the same course were more scrupulous; in 1813, for instance, Alderman Partridge had noted beside the twenty-fifth lecture: 'Lectures delivered by Henry Cline Esq^r'.[10]

4 Waddington, *Lectures On … Surgery*. KCL, GB 0100 G/PP1/62/5.

5 Waddington; and Waddington, *Lectures on Anatomy … Vol. 2nd*. KCL, GB 0100 G/PP1/62/4.

6 *KW*, 105.

7 Waddington, title page.

8 Advertisements, *The London Medical and Physical Journal* 34, 259 and *Morning Chronicle* (11 September 1815).

9 *Mem*, 34–35.

10 Alderman Partridge, *An Epitome of the Anatomical Lectures delivered by Astley P. Cooper and Hen^y Cline Esq^rs at St Thomas's Hospital Borough*. MS Volume. KCL, GB 0100 G/PP1/43.

Partridge's surviving notebook is an intriguing mix of rough notes and fair copy; in appearance, in fact, it seems to fall somewhere between Keats' and Waddington's notes. Partridge appears to have taken his notes in pencil originally, then rewritten – or on occasion, over-written – them in ink, tidying and clarifying as he wrote. There is no evidence that Keats took his original notes in pencil, but his marginalia and cross-referencing reveal that he certainly went back over them. Waddington's notebooks are clearly fair copies. Partridge's notes correspond so exactly with the contents of Waddington's – and indeed Keats' – that they are undoubtedly from the same series of 'Lectures On Anatomy', albeit from a different year. This difference of year is important, for it may help shed light on the puzzle presented by Waddington's dating of his notes.

Most contemporary accounts, as well as newspaper advertisements for the session 1815/16, indicate that Cooper and Cline Jnr's joint course of 'Lectures On Anatomy' routinely commenced in October. That would suggest that the 'Lectures On Anatomy' attended by Waddington and Keats should have started in *October 1815* and not January 1816, as stated by Waddington.[11] Given that Waddington's notes start with 'Lecture 1. Introductory Lecture' there is no reason to suppose that he missed the first few lectures, especially since he registered on 6 October 1815.[12] The fact that Waddington has an entirely separate notebook of material culled from Astley Cooper's single-handed 'Lectures On The Principles and Practice, Of Surgery', dated as they were in fact delivered 'between the 1st of October 1815, and the 1st of June 1816', complicates things further. It confirms that Waddington's notes on 'Lectures On Anatomy; And The Principal Operations of Surgery' were indeed from the joint series delivered by Cooper and Cline Jnr on 'Anatomy, and the Operations of Surgery', but does not explain why, if Cooper's course on the 'Principles and

11 Advertisement, *Morning Chronicle* (11 September 1815): 1; *The London Medical and Physical Journal* 34, 259 and *The London Medical and Physical Journal* 35 (January – June 1816): 165. Web. <https://books.google.gr/books?id=_kICAAAAYAAJ&printsec=frontcover&dq=london+medical+and+physical+journal+1816&hl=en&sa=X&ved=0ahUKEwivg9y0tPTeAhWLZVAKHVZqBnQQ6AEIKTAA#v=onepage&q=london%20medical%20and%20physical%20journal%201816&f=false> (accessed 8 November 2018).

12 *KW*, 102; Pupils and Dressers 1755–1823 and Entry … 1814–1827. KCL, G/FP1/1 and G/FP3/2.

Practice of Surgery' commenced as normal and as advertised, Cooper and Cline Jnr's course should apparently have been delayed by three months so that they commenced in January 1816.[13] If Waddington's dating is accurate – and there seems no reason to doubt this – this would appear to suggest a last-minute change in schedule.

There was, in fact, a significant precedent for this. Partridge, in his notes from the same lecture series delivered two years earlier, clearly states that the lectures commenced on 'Jan^y^ 20^th^ 1813' and concluded on 'April 22, 1813'.[14] Advertisements in October 1812 for 'The WINTER COURSE of LECTURES' had significantly omitted to mention Cooper, Cline Jnr, or their courses, while, on 18 January 1813, *The Morning Post* carried this notice:[15]

> ST. THOMAS's HOSPITAL. —Mr. ASTLEY COOPER and Mr. HENRY CLINE will begin their Course of ANATOMICAL and SURGICAL LECTURES, on WEDNESDAY, 20th inst. at Two o'clock.[16]

It is certain that 'begin' in this instance does not mean 'begin again after the winter break', given that two days earlier, on 16 January 1813, *The Morning Post* had advertised:

> ST. THOMAS's and GUY'S HOSPITAL. – Mr. ASTLEY COOPER will RE-COMMENCE his LECTURES on SURGERY on MONDAY, the 25th of January, at Eight o'clock in the Evening.[17]

Partridge's dates, clearly, are accurate: for whatever reason, Cooper and Cline Jnr's 'Lectures on Anatomy', which usually commenced in October, were postponed to January and advertised accordingly.

13 A notice in the *Morning Chronicle* reads: 'ST. THOMAS AND GUY'S HOSPITALS. – Mr. ASTLEY COOPER will begin his LECTURES on SURGERY on Monday the 9th of October'. See *Morning Chronicle* (18 September 1815): 1.

14 Partridge, *Epitome*, KCL, GB 0100 G/PP1/43.

15 *Morning Chronicle* (7 September 1812): 1; repeated *Morning Chronicle* (21 September 1812): 1.

16 *Morning Post* (18 January 1813): 1.

17 *Morning Post* (16 January 1813): 1.

What is odd about the year 1815/16 is that the 'Lectures on Anatomy' were widely advertised as beginning (as usual) in October 1815 and then silently rescheduled to January 1816, when, as Waddington shows us, they were delivered by Astley Cooper alone. Where was Cline Jnr and why this apparently unforeseen change in the lecturing schedule?

The Minutes book of the Physical Society of Guy's Hospital states that in May 1815 both Cooper and Cline Jnr were elected presidents of the Physical Society for the coming year.[18] However, an entry of the 'Private Minutes of the 8$^{th}$ Meeting', dated 25 November 1815, reads: 'M$^{r}$ Saumarez was elected a President *vice* H. Cline Jun$^{r}$ Esq$^{re}$ absent from illness'.[19] The 'Private Minutes' for the next meeting, on 2 December 1815, note that '[a] Letter was received from M$^{r}$ Saumarez announcing his acceptance of the Office of President'.[20] Thereafter, Richard Saumarez (a surgeon at the Magdalen Hospital, Streatham) served as one of the presidents until 9 March 1816, when he 'resigned his seat as President & M$^{r}$ Green was elected in his stead'.[21] Joseph Henry Green's increasing involvement is noted in the minute books, and Henry Cline Jnr's name never reappears. It seems likely that illness absented him from the Physical Society from autumn 1815 until his death from pulmonary tuberculosis ('consumption') in 1820.[22]

If Cline Jnr was too ill in autumn 1815 to attend the Physical Society it is likely that he was also unable to deliver his 'Lectures on Anatomy'. The fact that he was elected president of the Physical Society in May 1815 suggests that his illness was a sudden and unexpected malaise – possibly early symptoms of the disease that

18 'Private Minutes of the 31$^{st}$ & last Meeting / May 6 1815', Minutes Book of the Physical Society of Guy's Hospital 1813–1820. MS Volume. Guy's Hospital: Physical Society, KCL, GB 0100 G/S4/M9.

19 'Private Minutes of the 8$^{th}$ Meeting / Nov$^{r}$ 25 1815', Minutes Book of the Physical Society of Guy's Hospital 1813–1820, KCL, GB 0100 G/S4/M9; Nick Hervey, 'Saumarez, Richard (1764–1835)', *ODNB*.

20 'Private Minutes of the 9$^{th}$ Meeting / Dec$^{r}$ 2 1815', Minutes Book of the Physical Society of Guy's Hospital 1813–1820, KCL, GB 0100 G/S4/M9.

21 'Private Minutes of the 23$^{rd}$ Meeting / Mar 9 1816', Minutes Book of the Physical Society of Guy's Hospital 1813–1820, KCL, GB 0100 G/S4/M9.

22 Michael Bevan, 'Cline, Henry (1750–1827)', *ODNB*; Susan C. Lawrence, *Charitable Knowledge: Hospital Pupils and Practitioners in Eighteenth-Century London* (Cambridge: Cambridge University Press, 1996), 344.

would kill him (pulmonary tuberculosis can take years to progress, with periods of latency interspersed by points of crisis). If he was taken ill just before the 'Lectures on Anatomy' were due to commence in October, the practical decision would be to postpone the course until he recovered. This might explain the decision to delay for three months until January 1816 and (Cline not recovering sufficiently) Cooper having to deliver lectures – such as those 'On the Muscles' – that would normally have been Cline Jnr's. Waddington's and Partridge's notes allow us to establish the source of Keats' notes with certainty – they were derived, as Hale-White conjectured, from Cooper and Cline's *joint* 'Lectures on Anatomy', but with the entire course apparently commencing in January 1816 rather than in October, as had been advertised, and with Cooper as sole lecturer.[23]

This rescheduling may also explain why Keats apparently stopped keeping notes halfway through the lecture course, with his last entry corresponding to some of the content in Waddington's 'Lecture 54th On the Heart'.[24] On 3 March 1816 Keats took up his duties as a dresser.[25] From this point on he may not have had time to attend every lecture, or he may have been called upon during the lectures to assist with dissections or demonstrations. At all events, he had less time than hitherto to write up his notes – and there is reason to suppose that at least some of the notes in Keats' Notebook were written up after lectures rather than at them, as we shall see in the next chapter.

## The London Teaching Hospitals

Waddington's notes – especially for the first half of the course – offer a starting point for considering the medical knowledge available to Keats from his lectures. Another starting point is the reputation for excellence that the London teaching hospitals enjoyed in the early nineteenth century, both in Britain and on the continent. Goellnicht recounts how the French doctor Philibert Joseph Roux, on a visit to London in 1814 to compare the hospitals with those in Paris,

23 Hale-White, 'Keats as a Medical Student', 254.

24 Waddington, 543–55.

25 Pupils ... 1812–1825 and Pupils and Dressers 1755–1823. KCL, G/FP4/1 and G/FP1/1.

'was struck by the high quality of the surgery', which he correctly attributed to the influence of John Hunter. Roux concluded that the London hospitals were better than the French ones.[26] The Italian medical historian, A. Flajani, agreed with him, writing in 1807 that 'In England the hospitals have attained a degree of perfection rarely attained in other countries.'[27] Over the course of the eighteenth century the London charitable hospitals had transformed themselves into institutions of training as well as of treatment;[28] as Hermione de Almeida says, the *Plan de constitution pour la medicine en France*, which became the charter for the Paris medical schools, 'described the English teaching hospitals as specific models for future French teaching institutions of medicine and surgery'.[29] Flajani noted with interest the practical lessons in medicine and surgery that were given in the wards of hospitals such as St Bartholomew's, St Thomas', and Guy's, and recognized the breadth of clinical experience offered by the medical school of the United Hospitals of Guy's and St Thomas', with its 700 patient beds. He also singled out Drs Babington, Curry, and Marcet of Guy's Hospital for the quality of their instruction.[30] William Babington taught Keats Chemistry and the Practice of Medicine, and was a physician whose primary interests lay in chemistry and minerology.[31] He was acquainted with Humphry Davy, the internationally renowned chemist who was also a poet-friend of Coleridge, Southey, and Wordsworth, having helped see the second edition of *Lyrical Ballads* through the press, and organized Coleridge's 1808 lecture series on 'Poetry and the Imagination' at the Royal Institution.[32] Alexander Marcet, who jointly offered the courses on Chemistry with Babington, was an experimental chemist of high repute: his identification of xanthic

26 *PP*, 24.

27 Quoted in *RMJK*, 26.

28 For the rise of the London teaching hospitals, see Lawrence, *Charitable Knowledge*.

29 *RMJK*, 27.

30 *RMJK*, 27.

31 *PP*, 23–24, 30; J. F. Payne, rev. John C. Thackray, 'Babington, William (1756–1833)', *ODNB*.

32 Holmes, *Age of Wonder*, 275, 299–300. Davy was, like Keats, a good example of how closely the intellectual circles of the arts and sciences could be interwoven in the Romantic period.

oxide led to the discovery of xanthines, and he collaborated with the Swedish chemist J. J. Brezelius, whose animal chemistry he helped popularize in England.[33] Keats' medical Notebook contains no notes from his lectures on Chemistry, but its contents reflect the international outlook of the Guy's teaching staff: the notes name the French surgeon Julien Jean César Gallois and the Swiss physician Albrecht van Haller, and detail experiments by the Italian Luigi Galvani and observations on the pulse rate by the German physician Johann Blumenbach.[34] This internationalism was also reflected by the library of the Guy's Hospital Physical Society, whose books were proposed by the members and bought with money contributed by them, making it unlikely that they would buy books they had no interest in reading.[35]

The Guy's Hospital Physical Society was founded in 1769 or 1771 and rapidly established itself as a respected body, devoted to the discussion of medical and scientific issues. In the 1780s and 1790s, when interested laymen such as Gilbert Wakefield, John Thelwall, and Henry Fuseli could attend meetings, the Physical Society 'was "a society of literary men ... composed of surgeons, physicians, and men of science in general" which met regularly to hear scientific papers and embraced radical ideas'.[36] By 1815 it also allowed medical students into its ranks as members, and Keats' fellow lodger George Cooper became a member in October 1815.[37] Other students known to Keats also joined: Stephens and Mackereth in November 1815, Waddington in October 1816.[38] The society met every week during term and discussed matters of medical interest, which by 1815 consisted largely of case histories.[39] While many of these emerged from the wards of London hospitals, some were received as correspondence, including

33 *PP*, 23–24, 30; N. G. Coley, 'Marcet, Alexander John Gaspard (1770–1822)', *ODNB*.

34 JKMN, Bf5r, Bf8v, Bf5v, Ff1r.

35 *RMJK*, 29–31.

36 Roe, *Dissent*, 174; John Barnard, 'Keats, Andrew Motion's Dr Cake, and Charles Turner Thackrah', *Romanticism* 10.1 (April 2004): 5.

37 BT, 214.

38 'Private Minutes of the 6th Meeting/ Novr 11 1815', 'Private Minutes of the 7th Meeting/ Novr 18 1815', 'Private Minutes of the 1st Meeting/ October 5 1816', and 'Private Minutes of the 2nd Meeting / Oct 12 1816', Minutes Book of the Physical Society of Guy's Hospital 1813–1820, KCL, GB 0100 G/S4/M9.

39 Barnard, 'Thackrah', 5.

from the Royal Infirmary at Edinburgh that of 'Robert Fraser a soldier of 49', who apparently died of liver disease, and from Dublin 'Mariann Clarke', who survived an attack of puerperal fever.[40] Mr Saumarez offered a case history sent from Banda Mira in the colonies,[41] while in April 1815 Mr Warcup read out a case that must have been sobering for them all: 'a student at Edinburgh who in dissecting a woman … wounded with the scalpel the back part of the forefinger … he died in 40 hours'.[42] In addition to discussing medical issues the Physical Society also funded – as already noted – a specialist library, and in the early years of the nineteenth century made a concerted effort to catalogue and preserve their holdings and increase their collection. In 1811 they resolved to keep a salaried librarian to oversee lending and preservation of the books, and from 1816 the collection was insured.[43] New acquisitions were proposed by the committee every week, and the range of suggestions and purchases tells us, as Hermione de Almeida observes, 'much about the quality of … instruction and the intellectual tenor of the Guy's community during Keats's time':[44]

> Davy, Priestley, John Brown, Erasmus Darwin, James Gregory, Brodie, Prichard, William Lawrence, William Brande, Abernethy, John Murray, Munro, John Barclay, Hutton, Duncan, Elliotson, Fowler, Fordyce, Ferriar, Baillie, Playfair, Saumarez, Heberden, Young, John and Charles Bell, Percival, Adams, Home, and Walker, were some of the contemporary authors in medicine and science represented in the cabinets of the library … along with the collected works of major medical figures like Hunter, Haller, and Cullen, and a full complement of textbooks published by current

40 Robert Fraser's autopsy was inconclusive, but found his liver enlarged and 'tuberculated'. 'Public Minutes at the 27th Meeting / April 10 1813' and 'Public Minutes at the 27th Meeting / Jan. 27 1816', Minutes Book of the Physical Society of Guy's Hospital 1813–1820, KCL, GB 0100 G/S4/M9.

41 'Public Minutes at the 19th Meeting/ Feb 4th 1815', Minutes Book of the Physical Society of Guy's Hospital 1813–1820, KCL, GB 0100 G/S4/M9. Saumarez's friend worked for the East India Company, so 'Banda Mira' is more likely to be a reference to an area in western India than to the Banda Islands of Indonesia, which were held by the Royal Navy from 1810 to 1817.

42 'Public Minutes at the 30th Meeting/ April 29 1815', Minutes Book of the Physical Society of Guy's Hospital 1813–1820, KCL, GB 0100 G/S4/M9.

43 *RMJK*, 29.

44 *RMJK*, 30.

> and recent members of Guy's Hospital. Nor were the books confined to recent English studies, for one could also find editions (usually in translation) of European physicians and scientists like Orfila, Broussais, Landrè-Beauvais, Blumenbach, Bichât, Laënnac, Alexander von Humboldt, Bayle, Gall, Spurzheim, Lavatar, Bischoff, Sauvages, Cuvier, and Lamarck. Seminal medical texts from previous centuries were also available ... Pharmacopoeias of the major hospitals and infirmaries, dictionaries like *Quincy's Lexicon-Medicum*, and encyclopedias ... provided a range of knowledge for library users, and these were further supplemented by philosophical works by authors as diverse as Paley, Newton, Thomas Brown, and Herder. In addition, the Guy's Physical Society Library by 1816 held subscriptions to an unusual variety of periodicals ... .[45]

The library of the Physical Society was well set to cater to the expectations outlined by contemporary accounts of what medical students and professionals should read. One such was *The Hospital Pupil's Guide, being Oracular Communications, addressed to Students of the Medical Profession*, first published in 1816 with a second edition in 1818: R. S. White has described it as 'falling into the genre of "prolegomena" to medical studies, offering inspiration, advice and some instruction (such as footnoted 'further reading' in each branch of the medical studies ...)'.[46] *Oracular Communications* listed upwards of 130 monographs, in addition to dictionaries, encyclopaedias, dissectors, pharmacopoeias, and journals, as material for further reading. Its pseudonymous author 'Æsculapius' advised that 'unwearied diligence in the pursuit of every branch of knowledge' was an 'indispensable qualification' for a career in medicine:[47]

> The acquisition of increasing information, a pursuit which knows no limit, must be the grand object of your life; not only during the

45 *RMKJ*, 30.

46 White, '"Like Esculapius of Old"', 17–18. The first publication in 1816 bore the title *Oracular Communications, addressed to Students of the Medical Profession*.

47 Æsculapius, *The Hospital Pupil's Guide, being Oracular Communications, addressed to Students of the Medical Profession* ... (1816; 2nd ed.: London: E. Cox and son, 1818), 18.

> period allotted to an acquaintance with the elementary principles of your profession, but also from the dry details of monotonous practice. … Knowledge is readily to be obtained; but it must be sought after: … this diligence must be uninterrupted: it must not be occasional only, and guided by a blind attachment to *any part* of the study; but it must arise from a determination to obtain all the information that can be acquired … .[48]

Moreover, medical students should possess a 'competent knowledge of the Latin, Greek and French languages', and the author stresses that they should already have acquired this competence before taking their places at the London teaching hospitals.[49]

Standards of professional behaviour expected from successful medical students at the London teaching hospitals were high. 'Æsculapius' noted that the move to London, especially, came with many potential pitfalls for aspiring students, and took pains to warn them to be on their guard against the 'amusements of the metropolis':[50]

> The candidate for medical honours comes to London *to study*, and he will find *abundant recreation in professional pursuits*. Let him therefore relinquish the amusements of the theatre: since it is a fact that those who are seen flitting about the lobby of Covent Garden, or Drury Lane … *will frequently not reach home till the following morning*; while their time will be lost, their health ruined, and their funds shamefully squandered. … It will be injustice to you … were I to omit one word of caution on the subject of *billiards*. … The amusement in itself may be harmless … but the society to which it leads, and its easy introduction to *gaming* … demonstrate its pernicious tendency … if there be any other prominent method of *murdering talent*, it will present itself to the mind of my readers. The ground on which I inveigh against them, is not on the *nature* of the amusement itself … but on the circumstances with which it is connected, and its entire unfitness for medical students.[51]

48 Æsculapius, *Oracular Communications*, 18–20.

49 Æsculapius, *Oracular Communications*, 20, 24.

50 Æsculapius, *Oracular Communications*, 48.

51 Æsculapius, *Oracular Communications*, 49–50.

Evidently, instructors and well-wishers alike worried about how the city and its pleasures might distract medical students from their studies and attendance at hospital. Keats was fond of the theatre, certainly, and not above occasional gambling; he also visited the pleasure gardens at Vauxhall, where he conceived a passion for a woman he witnessed ungloving her hand.[52] He wrote two poems addressed to her: 'Fill for me a brimming bowl' immediately after his glimpse of her and 'Time's sea hath been five years at its slow ebb' in 1818.

Despite these distractions, his situation in London was an important factor for Keats' intellectual development, for it was an unrivalled centre of intellectual activity. London was a cultural hub, and its scientific circles maintained close communication with peers on the European continent. The city regularly hosted a variety of public lectures and debates and was the stage for important scientific announcements. We know that Keats possessed a ticket for William Allen's lectures on Experimental Philosophy of 'perpetual' validity; but he was also on the spot for the announcement of the invention of the Davy Safety Lamp in January 1816 and for the so-called Vitalism Debates, which unfolded at the Royal College of Surgeons.[53]

## The Vitalism Debates

The Vitalism Debates started innocuously. In February 1814 John Abernethy – a former student of John Hunter and senior surgeon at St Bartholomew's – delivered a series of lectures at the Royal College of Surgeons as part of his duties as professor of anatomy at that institution. His topic, 'An Enquiry into the Probability of Mr. Hunter's Theory of Life', derived from Hunter's theory that blood possessed vitality, as outlined in his *Treatise on the Blood, Inflammation and Gun-Shot Wounds ...* (1794).[54] Hunter's research had shown that blood sustained life by uniting with surrounding parts, responding to external stimuli through coagulation, and maintaining its temperature in the extremities of the body and despite changes in ambient temperature. Additionally, blood flow

52 *NL*, 60.

53 *NL*, 75.

54 Holmes, *Age of Wonder*, 308.

was necessary to the body parts to support life, and death often took place when the blood lost its ability to coagulate. Hunter observed:

> When the blood is circulating, it is subject to certain laws to which it is not subject when not circulating. It has the power of preserving its fluidity ... the living principle in the body has the power of preserving it in this state. This is not produced by motion alone .... If the blood had not the living principle, it would be, in respect of the body, as an extraneous substance. Blood is not only alive itself, but is the support of life in every part of the body .... Life, then is preserved by the compound of the two [blood and nerves], and an animal is not perfect without the blood: ... the motion of the blood may be reckoned, in some degree, a first moving power, and not only is the blood alive in itself, but seems to carry life everywhere .... Here then would appear to be three parts, viz. body, blood and motion, which latter preserves the living union between the other two, or the life in both. These three make up a complete body, out of which arises a principle of self-motion .... [55]

He concluded that 'the living principle first begins in the blood'.[56]

Hunter's theory was not new when Keats studied at Guy's – Hunter wrote that he 'had held the opinion for above thirty years, and ... taught it for near twenty of that time'.[57] Among his students was Astley Cooper, Keats' instructor at Guy's. In Keats' marginal notes for 'Lect^r 2^nd On the Blood' he wrote about

> M^r Hunter who thought | | Blood possessed Vitality thought it underwent a change like the contraction of Muscular Fibres at the time of death The Muscles do not relax and the Blood does not coagulate in an Animal killed by lightening. M^r C's opinion is the Blood is prevented from coagulating by nervous energy.[58]

55 John Hunter, *A Treatise on the Blood, Inflammation and Gun-Shot Wounds, to Which is Affixed, A Short Account of the Author's Life, by his Brother-in-Law, Everard Home* (London: G. Nicol, 1794), 85–86.

56 Hunter, *Treatise*, 91.

57 Hunter, *Treatise*, 77.

58 JKMN, Ff3r, Ff2v.

As Hermione de Almeida has noticed, this is almost 'verbatim Hunter' and Keats' notes show 'full familiarity with those essentials that gave rise to Hunter's first declarations on the nature of life'.[59] These 'declarations' and the ideas that underpinned them unexpectedly flared into controversial life during Keats' tenure at Guy's, eventually reaching an audience far beyond the medical professionals they had been originally intended for.

Hunter had stated that blood was 'the most simple body we know of, endowed with the principle of life'; Abernethy insisted that blood itself could not explain life, but might carry it in the form of a vital fluid.[60] Drawing on the intellectual and experimental authority of Humphry Davy's Bakerian Lectures at the Royal Society, he suggested that this vital fluid might be akin to electricity:

> The experiments of Sir Humphry Davy seem to me to form an important link in the connexion of our knowledge of dead and living matter ... [they] lead us to believe, that it is electricity, extricated and accumulated in ways not clearly understood, which causes those sudden and powerful motions in masses of inert matter, which we occasionally witness with wonder and dismay.[61]

He proposed that if vitality was a 'subtle, mobile, invisible substance, superadded to the evident structure', then there would be 'equal reason to believe that mind might be superadded to life as life is to structure'.[62] Abernethy's argument, therefore, was not simply physiological – it also had metaphysical and religious significance: he was arguing that there was scientific evidence for the theological notion of the soul. His lectures aroused much interest in medical and scientific circles, which only increased in 1816 when Abernethy's former protégé, William Lawrence, attacked this conception of some mysterious vital fluid in his first series of lectures to the Royal College of Surgeons:

59 *RMJK*, 87.

60 Hunter, *Treatise*, 77.

61 John Abernethy, *An Enquiry into the Probability and Rationality of Mr Hunter's Theory of Life; Being the Subject of the First Two Anatomical Lectures delivered before the Royal College of Surgeons, of London* (London: Longman, Hurst, Rees, Orme, and Brown, 1814), 48–50.

62 Abernethy, *Enquiry*, 39, 94.

> this vital principle is compared to magnetism, to electricity, and to galvanism; or it is roundly stated to be oxygen. 'Tis like a camel, or like a whale, or like what you please. You have only to grant that the phenomena of the sciences just alluded to depend on extremely fine and invisible fluids, superadded to the matters in which they are exhibited; and to allow further that life and magnetic, galvanic and electric phenomena, correspond perfectly: the existence of a subtle matter of life will then be a very probable inference. On this illustration you will naturally remark, that the existence of the magnetic, electric, and galvanic fluids, which is offered as a proof of the existence of a vital fluid, is as much a matter of doubt, as that of the vital fluid itself. … Electricity illustrates life no more than life illustrates electricity.[63]

Lawrence was scathing in his criticism of the metaphysical and religious aspects of Abernethy's propositions, which he denounced as deeply unscientific:

> It seems to me that this hypothesis or fiction of a subtle invisible matter, animating the visible textures of animal bodies, and directing their motions, is only an example of that propensity of the human mind, which has led men at all times to account for those phenomena, of which the causes are not obvious, by the mysterious aid of higher and imaginary beings.[64]

Abernethy responded acerbically to Lawrence's comments in his own lectures to the college in 1817, denouncing 'Modern Sceptics' who espoused French materialism without regard for the effects such ideas might have on social stability. Predictably, this drew from Lawrence a stinging rebuke, and the controversy rumbled on until 1819, with each party amassing groups of supporters and the principals exchanging increasingly caustic views in their Royal College lectures. These Vitalism Debates captured the public imagination, and the exchanges were closely followed and reported by widely read literary

63 William Lawrence, *An Introduction to Comparative Anatomy and Physiology; being the Two Introductory Lectures Delivered at the Royal College of Surgeons, On the 21st and 25th of March, 1816* (London: J. Callow, 1816), 169–71.

64 Lawrence, *Introduction*, 174.

journals such as the *Edinburgh Review* and the *Quarterly Review*. The issue, which started as a scientific argument, quickly became at the hands of the popular press a theological debate on whether a vital fluid, 'super-added' to the body, could or should be conceived of as the soul.[65] Finally, in 1819, Lawrence – under increasing pressure from the Royal College of Surgeons and a number of medical institutions – withdrew his *Lectures on Physiology, Zoology, and the Natural History of Man* (1819), though he continued to champion scientific freedom and in 1822 allowed the radical publisher Richard Carlile to issue a pirated edition of his book. The standoff continued until 1829, when Lawrence, who stood for election to the council of the Royal College of Surgeons, retracted his radical and 'materialist' views and was reconciled with his old mentor Abernethy.

## The Brunonian Hypothesis

The subject of vitality – of life – whether in the blood or otherwise, had been of interest in medical circles at least since the 1780s. Even such interested laymen as the radical reformer John Thelwall weighed in: on 26 January 1793 he read out his essay on 'Vitality' at the meeting of the Physical Society of Guy's Hospital. It sparked much discussion, with five subsequent meetings being devoted to debating its contents.[66] Thelwall took Hunter's ideas of the vitality of blood as his starting point, but ended by defining life as 'that state of action (induced by specific stimuli on matter specifically organized), by which the animal functions, or any of them, are carried on'.[67] Other major theories in the 1790s also considered life to reside in a form of action, though Thelwall's ideas differed in some details and

65 The Vitalism debates inspired Coleridge, a former patient of Abernethy's, to co-author a paper with his doctor James Gillman: their 'Notes Towards a New Theory of Life' attempted to steer a middle path between the more extreme positions. They also informed Mary Shelley's *Frankenstein; or, A Modern Prometheus* (1818), in which an electric spark is used to impart life to the collection of dead animal parts that Victor Frankenstein had pieced together to create his Creature.

66 For the text of Thelwall's essay see Nicholas Roe, *The Politics of Nature: William Wordsworth and Some Contemporaries*, 2nd ed. (Basingstoke: Palgrave, 2002), 89.

67 Quoted in Roe, *Politics of Nature*, 118.

in its political bias. If Thelwall's view was one that provoked debate but not consensus, another contemporary theory of life that became influential in British Romantic medical circles was proposed by the Scottish physician John Brown.

In his *Elementia Medicinae* (1780), Brown drew upon the works of Albrecht van Haller and the Scottish physicians Robert Whytt and William Cullen to suggest that 'life is a ... forced state, ... the tendency of animals every moment is to dissolution'.[68] Haller had showed that sensibility was a specific property of nerves, which Whytt disputed even while agreeing that the nervous system was responsible for most of the processes of health and disease.[69] For Whytt, the muscle tissue was a part of the nervous system, and possessed sensibility.[70] Building on this base, Cullen theorized that sensibility might arise from an immaterial fluid-like substance in the nervous system, which he termed 'excitement'. Cullen believed, therefore, that excitability was the source of vitality.[71] Brown borrowed Cullen's term 'excitability', but applied it differently: in his work, 'excitability' meant the capacity of a creature to use and respond to stimuli, or 'exciting powers'. For Brown, every creature was born with a fixed quantity of 'excitability' stored in the nerves and muscles, and life was sustained by constantly expending it. The process of living, therefore, depleted an animal's reserves of 'excitability', but some amount of it could be recovered during sleep. Health depended on 'excitability' being maintained in an even supply in the body; withdrawal or over-expression of 'excitability' caused disease. Most diseases were manifestations of 'direct debility' – by which Brown meant insufficient 'excitability' being manifested by the body – and could be cured by exposure to external stimuli, the most powerful of which were wine and opium. However, illness also occurred if too many 'exciting powers' acted upon the body and too much 'excitability' was expended – this was termed 'indirect debility'

68 John Brown, *The Elements of Medicine; or, A Translation of the Elementa Medicinæ Brunonis. With Large Notes, Illustrations and Comments. By the Author of the Original Work. In Two Volumes* (London: J. Johnson, 1788), I, 59.

69 'Albrecht von Haller', *EB*; Neil Vickers, *Coleridge and the Doctors: 1795–1806* (Oxford: Oxford University Press, 2004), 26–28, 44.

70 Vickers, *Coleridge and the Doctors*, 26–28, 44.

71 Vickers, *Coleridge and the Doctors*, 44.

and in such cases patients were advised to avoid all stimulants. Vitality in Brown's view thus depended on two conditions: the body must possess a sufficient quantity of 'excitability', and it must be exposed to a sufficient – but not excessive – degree of stimulation by 'exciting powers'. As Neil Vickers observes, 'Life and death along with all the states of health and disease are merely the consequences of the interaction of these two quantities.'[72]

While Brown's theory was accepted in British and continental medical circles, there were also reservations about it. In Brunonian physiology all diseases were systemic, since health depended on a level of 'excitability' that was consistent in all parts of the body at any given moment. Local interventions, therefore, were pointless – and this threatened to leave surgeons without a job: surgical operations are, by definition, local interventions, although they may have systemic implications.[73] One anti-Brunonian was Richard Saumarez, who we have encountered already in the Physical Society. Well known in London medical circles, Saumarez worked for many years as a surgeon at the Magdalen Hospital, becoming an honorary governor in 1805. While there, he had published in 1798 a controversial *New System of Physiology*, in which he opposed Brunonian physiology and argued that doctors should concentrate on understanding the interdependency of various organs in the body, and treat the body as a whole system composed of distinct but interlinked parts.[74] Keats, as we have seen, never became a member of the Guy's Hospital Physical Society, but many of his fellow students were, as were his instructors: Saumarez's fellow office bearers at the Physical Society in 1815 included Astley Cooper; and when he stepped down he was replaced by Keats' 'Demonstrator at Guy's' Joseph Henry Green.[75] It is likely that, as a surgeon's pupil and dresser at Guy's Hospital in 1815–17,

72 Vickers, *Coleridge and the Doctors*, 45.

73 For an account of the different professional duties undertaken by Physicians, Surgeons and Apothecaries, see R. Campbell, *The London Tradesman …* , 3rd ed. (London: T. Gardner, 1758), 42–53, 63–66.

74 Hervey, 'Saumarez', *ODNB*.

75 Hervey, 'Saumarez', *ODNB*; 'Private Minutes of the 31st & last Meeting / May 6 1815', and 'Private Minutes of the 23rd Meeting / Mar 9 1816', Minutes Book of the Physical Society of Guy's Hospital 1813–1820, KCL, GB 0100 G/S4/M9; *LJK*, II, 88. For more on Keats and the Physical Society, see John Barnard, 'John Keats in the Context of the Physical Society, Guy's Hospital, 1815–1816', in *Medical Imagination*, ed. Roe, 73–90.

Keats would have been well aware of the criticisms of Brunonian physiology that were current in his circles. Additionally, as someone who routinely performed surgical operations, it seems unlikely that he could have found Brown's ideas completely convincing. His treatment of Jane Hull's gunshot wound in March 1816 shows, at the very least, that he was unwilling to depend on the Brunonian hypothesis when faced with a patient he thought he could help surgically.[76]

## Keats as a Surgeon: Jane Hull, Dissection, and 'Resurrection'

On the morning of 25 March 1816 Jane Hull was brought into Guy's Hospital bleeding profusely from a wound in her head. Keats was one of the dressers in charge and later testified that '[s]he had received a severe wound in the back part of her head with a pistol ball; the ball had pierced the lobe of her ear, taken a direction along the occiput, and lodged in the neck, from whence [he had] extracted it.'[77] This, the first account discovered of Keats in action as a surgeon, gives us insight into why Keats was offered a dressership within a month of enrolling at Guy's: his testimony marks him out to have been calm and methodical under pressure. In the absence of equipment to suction away blood from the wound or produce an internal image of the injury, Keats had to depend on his knowledge of anatomy to project the trajectory of the pistol ball. He knew, as his medical notes reveal, that '[t]he Os Occipitis is but rarely broken' – therefore, the ball must have taken a path 'along the occiput'.[78] That Keats was right was proved by his success in extracting the ball from her neck where he'd looked for it, as well as from the fact that Jane Hull survived her ordeal.[79]

Keats was evidently well-trained in surgery by the time he took up his dressership; equally, his training was not limited to observing and working with patients. His 'Certificate to Practice as an Apothecary' states that he attended two lecture courses on 'Anatomy and Physiology'; his notes from one of these, 'On

76 See Roe, 'Mr. Keats'.

77 *Morning Chronicle* (23 April 1816): 3.

78 JKMN, Ff13r.

79 Roe, 'Mr Keats', 280.

Anatomy, and the Operations of Surgery', usually delivered jointly by Cooper and Cline Jnr, survive in his medical Notebook.[80] Astley Cooper was adamant that the best – indeed the only – way to truly learn anatomy was through dissection: 'Dissection alone affords a good practical kno[w]ledge of anatomy.'[81] *The London Dissector* – one of the recommended textbooks – instructed students to practise 'every little operation' during dissection 'which can give the dexterity of hand so essential to the surgeon':[82]

> The grand object of the surgical student is to acquire a knowledge of the relative situation of parts. This should be kept in view in all his anatomical labours. ... This species of knowledge will afford him the most essential assistance in his future operations on the living subject; in which indeed it is so necessary, that we are perfectly astonished to see persons rash enough to use the knife without possessing this information ... .[83]

'Æsculapius' agreed with this stress on dissections: the *Oracular Communications* states that, of the various ways of acquiring knowledge of anatomy, 'dissection is certainly the most important', and insists that '[t]he inestimable value of this pursuit demands every hour which can possibly be spared for it.'[84] Joseph Henry Green, as demonstrator of anatomy at the United Hospitals, was responsible for overseeing student dissections and had published his *Outlines of a Course of Dissections* in 1815. This book was recommended by Cooper and in circulation at Guy's before Green published an enlarged version of it as *The Dissector's Manual* in 1820. Medical students had scheduled hours for dissections five days a week, and conscientious students were expected to spend as much time as they could spare, in addition to these scheduled slots, in dissecting.

There was clear agreement that dissections were a vital part of anatomical training, but securing cadavers before the passage of the 1832 Anatomy Act was not easily done. Unable to acquire

80 Hughes and Hughes, 'Keats Memorial Lecture', 139.

81 [Anon.], *The Lectures of Astley P. Cooper Esq$^{r}$ on Surgery given at St Tho$^{s}$ Hospital Vol. 1$^{st}$*. MS Volume, 9. KCL, GB 0100 G/PP2/10.

82 *LD*, 2.

83 *LD*, 2–3.

84 Æsculapius, *Oracular Communications*, 34.

this essential for their trade by legal means, the London teaching hospitals were forced to rely on grave-robbers or 'resurrection men'. Guy's and St Thomas' were supplied by a gang of four men: Ben Crouch, Bill Butler, Jack Harnett, and Bill Harnett.[85] Deliveries of freshly exhumed corpses were made by night and medical students were drafted in to clean the deliveries; in 1814 a price of four shillings was paid 'to the dissecting-room man for cleansing, and a pound more if it were injected with wax'.[86] Contemporary accounts suggest that medical students sometimes accompanied the 'resurrection men' on their rounds. With the medical profession depending on the activities of these 'resurrection men', self-interest induced the medical community to aid them in their macabre profession: John Flint South describes how

> there was a sort of tacit or positive understanding that if the men *got into trouble* the teachers should do all they could, with or without legal assistance, to get the men off at the police examination; and, if they did not succeed, to find them bail for the appearance at sessions; and in case of conviction to give them and their families pecuniary assistance.[87]

On at least one occasion Keats' landlord – a tallow chandler named Markham – took delivery of a body for Keats' former fellow lodger, George Cooper. Cooper, who had completed his dressership and moved to Brentford, was keen to keep up his anatomical studies and enlisted his former landlord's aid in acquiring a skeleton for private study. Markham, perhaps with help from some of his medical lodgers, had waxed a corpse, packed it in a hamper, and dispatched it to Cooper by boat.[88] Clandestine activities involving illegally acquired corpses were an inescapable fact of a medical life, and Keats could not have avoided knowledge of the work done by the 'resurrection men' even if he'd tried. He may not have tried very hard: in 'Give me women, wine and snuff' – the only poem he wrote in a lecture theatre – Keats irreverently jokes about the 'day of resurrection' (4).[89] For all

85 *Mem*, 93.
86 *Mem*, 96–97.
87 *Mem*, 101.
88 *Mem*, 81–82.
89 *KC*, II, 210.

his flippancy, however, the dissection room was to leave its mark on Keats: his poetry is replete with anatomically specific details, and *Isabella* contains a 'resurrection' scene.[90] 'The thing was vile with green and livid spot' (475), he wrote of Lorenzo's exhumed head in that poem, with 'wild hair' (403) and 'sepulchral cells' (405) instead of eyes – a reminder that the poet was all too familiar with the ghoulish aspect of decaying human flesh.

This chapter has focused on some features of Keats' life and experiences during his tenure at Guy's Hospital. The intellectual ferment that characterized London was the constant backdrop to Keats' medical career and provides the biographical and intellectual context for Keats' 'Guy's Hospital' poems and the notes in his medical Notebook. The next chapter focuses on the notes themselves and what they reveal about Keats as a medical student and poet.

90 For a detailed analysis of the relationship between Keats' medical education and the 'resurrection' scene in *Isabella* see Hagelman, 'Medical Profession', 210–66.

CHAPTER FOUR

# John Keats at Guy's

## Scholar and Poet

John Keats' medical Notebook was most in use between January and June 1816, while he was surgeon's pupil and dresser at Guy's Hospital. Taken at the same time and from the lecture series Keats attended – Cooper and Cline Jnr's joint course on 'Anatomy, and the Operations of Surgery', probably delivered by Cooper alone – were Joshua Waddington's notes. In Waddington's notebook, therefore, we have a comparative for Keats' notes, and studying the two together makes it possible to see what was distinctive about Keats' note-taking and methods of working. The first part of this chapter accordingly compares the two sets of notes, establishes that they are from the same lecture series, and shows that, although Keats has essentially the same information as Waddington, his habits of concision, reorganization, and cross-referencing mean they are presented in a different – indeed, a distinctive – form. Keats' notes are characterized by verbal compression, a stress on the natural rhythms and cadences of the English language, and the use of imagery to render its contents memorable. This chapter relates these uniquely Keatsian features to his poetic compositions in the years after he left Guy's and analyses how his medical notes prefigure the distinctive patterns of his poetry.

### Existing Comparisons of Keats' and Waddington's Notes

George Winston, who first drew attention to Waddington's lecture notes, observed: 'Compared with Waddington … it has been possible to trace almost all of [Keats' notes]. There are a few lines in Keats which cannot be traced in Waddington and definitely assigned to a particular lecture … '.[1] Like Winston, most commentators so far have adopted an impressionistic approach in comparing Waddington's notes with Keats'. Donald Goellnicht mentions Waddington's notes only in passing to state that Dorothy Hewlett compared them with Keats'.[2] Hewlett, considering the two sets of notes, concluded baldly that 'compared with Waddington's laborious work Keats's notes are sketchy and intermittent'.[3] Winston is more thorough, but hampered by reading Waddington's manuscript alongside Forman's 1934 edition rather than the original holograph: his dependence on Forman's annotations for the layout of Keats' notes tended to confuse rather than clarify.[4] Moreover, he did not compare the complete set of Waddington's notes against Keats', nor was he concerned with the full contents of Keats' medical Notebook. When he found that material in Waddington appeared to be missing in Keats, he did not make a thorough check of *all* Keats' notes.

There are many difficulties entailed in comparing these two sets of notes. A text that might serve as an objective 'control' does not exist: Cooper and Cline Jnr's lectures on 'Anatomy, and the Operations of Surgery' were never published. Parts of what Cooper said during this course overlapped with his evening lectures on 'Principles and Practice of Surgery', later published in an authorized edition by Cooper's former apprentice and Keats' fellow lodger Frederick Tyrell.[5] There are similarities between these published volumes and Keats' and Waddington's notes describing surgical procedures, but they are insufficient for Tyrell's edition to serve as a 'control' text (and it is an edition of an entirely separate lecture series – Cooper was reusing material in different lecture courses). Winston appears to treat Waddington's notes as a 'control' for judging Keats', but there is no obvious reason for this decision: we would need Cooper's original lecture script for the purpose, and this does not appear to have survived.

1 *KW*, 104.

2 *PP*, 34.

3 Hewlett, *Life*, 38.

4 *KW*, 101, 107–08.

5 Astley Cooper, *The Lectures of Sir Astley Cooper, Bart., F.R.S., Surgeon to the King, &c. &c. on the Principles and Practice of Surgery; with Additional Notes and Cases*, ed. Frederick Tyrell. 3 vols (London: Thomas and George Underwood; Simpkin and Marshall, 1824–1827).

Waddington's notes, clearly a fair copy written up after the lecture, were presumably worked up from rough or short-hand notes taken at the lecture.[6] By contrast, Keats' notes do not appear fair copied. He added information in later marginal notes, and tended to group his material together by topic, as shown by his decision to write along the margins and his system of cross-referencing. Evidently Keats treated his medical Notebook as a working document – a dynamic repository of information that could be augmented and updated as needed – whereas Waddington seems to have aimed at an elegant script for future consultation. This divergence suggests that Waddington's notes cannot serve as a satisfactory 'control' text against which to assess Keats' and may explain why no one has attempted a systematic comparison. Winston relied upon impressions and made no attempt to quantify, even in basic terms, the similarities that led him to conclude they shared a single origin. Nor did he detail the divergences that justified his sweeping conclusion that '[c]ompared with Waddington many passages in Keats's notes are most confusing.'[7] While not denying the value of close reading and readerly impression, I suggest that a quantitative framework may also yield valuable information about Keats' methods of working. Accordingly, a basic statistical analysis follows.

## Current Comparison: Methodology and Observations

In the statistical analysis that follows, I focus on two lectures. The choice of lectures was dictated by the fact that, as the lecture series progressed, Keats' notes become briefer, eventually becoming little more than lists of points. It was necessary to focus on the earlier lectures to have sufficient material for the kind of quantitative comparison I proposed. Additionally, the confusion caused by Keats misnumbering Lecture 7 as 'Lect[r] 6' and continuing this misnumbered sequence until he reached Lecture 10 induced me to avoid Lectures 6–9. I finally chose to focus on Lectures 4 and 10: the former is early in the series; the latter after the misnumbered sequence but before Keats abandoned numbering his lectures at Lecture 12. Lecture 4

6 Hewlett claims that 'it was the custom then to repeat each statement three times' but does not cite any source for this detail. See Hewlett, *Life*, 38.

7 *KW*, 104.

discusses the arteries: in Keats' medical Notebook it commences at Ff1r and is titled 'Lect$^{r}$. 4. Arteries continued from page 3', while Waddington gives it the heading 'Lecture 4$^{th}$ On Arteries and Veins'.[8] Lecture 10 is concerned with the nervous system: Keats' notes start at Bf4v under the heading 'Lect$^{r}$ 10. Physiology of the Nervous System', while Waddington's title is 'Lecture 10$^{th}$ The Nervous System (concluded)'.[9]

In comparing these lecture notes, I used a combination of approaches. I first transcribed the notes for the same lecture side-by-side, hoping that this would offer visual or verbal confirmation of the extent of similarity – the sense shared by all commentators that these two sets of notes *must* be from the same lecture series. In these juxtaposed notes, I proceeded to identify elements of similarity and difference that might help give cohesion to a comparative reading. I identified many passages (sentences or paragraphs) with a high degree of similarity. I also identified contradictory claims. Certain sentences stood out as unique to Keats' notes, and some of them struck me as being in some way uniquely 'Keatsian'. There were words or phrases that exactly matched in both sets of notes, suggesting they originated – in most cases – from the lecturer. In some striking instances, the words were an exact match, but reversed in order: for example, Keats writes 'Arteries are either in a state of Systole or Dyastole', where Waddington has 'Arteries are always either in a state of Diastole, or Systole'.[10] For the statistical portion of my analysis I have treated these cases of identical but reversed text as identical, though later in the critical commentary I treat them as distinct and significant. Since Keats' notes are usually more compact than Waddington's, the word count for passages that match but do not use identical words yield two different numerical values; I have taken the mean (i.e. average) of the two as most suitable for conducting this basic comparison.

Keats' notes for 'Lect$^{r}$. 4. Arteries' are just under two-thirds the length of Waddington's, at 1,111 words to 1,775 words.[11] The two have 133 words that are identical, often occurring as phrases, which makes the possibility of this being a coincidence less likely. This high proportion of identical words suggests that both sets of notes

8 JKMN, Ff1r; Waddington, 35.
9 JKMN, Bf4v; Waddington, 101.
10 JKMN, Ff1r; Waddington, 35.
11 JKMN, Ff1r, Bf1r; Waddington, 35–49.

almost certainly derive from the same lecture. Almost 57 per cent of the content of Keats' notes bear so much similarity to the contents (approximately 41 per cent) of Waddington's that, even when the words used are not identical, the sense is. The fact that both sets of notes progress in the same order and with the same organization of ideas and sequencing of facts further strengthens the impression that they are drawn from the same lecture – and that the organization and sequencing derived therefore from the lecturer, Astley Cooper.

Similarly, my comparison of the two sets of notes for Lecture 10 on the nervous system also reveals that, at 905 words, Keats' notes are just over half the length of Waddington's, at 1,712 words;[12] and 419 words from Keats broadly match 474 words from Waddington, which means that – taking their average – 447 words broadly match. Those 447 words represent approximately 49 per cent of the total content of Keats' lecture notes and approximately 26 per cent of the total content of Waddington's notes. The two sets of notes have 112 words identically in common: a proportion of approximately 12 per cent of the total for Keats and approximately 7 per cent of the total for Waddington. Once again, the two sets of notes share the same order, sequence, and underlying organization, making it likely that these factors derived from Cooper's original lecture delivery. And, once again, Keats' notes are significantly more compact than Waddington's. Why are Keats' notes so much shorter?

## Characteristics of Keats' Note-taking

Keats' notes do not contain significantly less information than Waddington's; Waddington usually writes at greater length. Some of the detail that he includes, and Keats omits, could be regarded as superfluous for a competent medical student: for instance, Waddington explicitly mentions that the aorta distributes 'branches which go to all parts of the body' while Keats does not.[13] An informed medical student would know that the aorta branches into smaller arteries which carry the blood to various parts of the body. Another similar instance is where Keats notes that 'Pulsation does not take place exactly at the same time at y$^{e}$ Extremities and

12 JKMN, Bf4v – Bf5v; Waddington, 101–15.

13 Waddington, 35.

at the Heart'.[14] Keats stops there; Waddington goes on to detail how this is to be inferred: by taking the pulse 'upon' the carotid artery (carrying blood to the head and neck) and the radial (at the wrist) at the same time.[15] While this information is helpful to a lay reader, only an unusually incompetent doctor would not know that the pulse in arteries closer to the heart matches the cardiac rhythm more closely. The difference in pulsation between carotid and radial arteries is still used as a diagnostic tool, and is basic information that a competent medical student would be expected to remember. Keats and Waddington had both served medical apprenticeships and would certainly have known such fundamentals. What distinguishes the detail in their notes, then, is their respective approaches: Waddington, writing a complete fair copy of notes for preservation, aimed for a completeness not practically necessary; while Keats, who treated his Notebook as a repository of practical information, omitted what he considered unnecessary, resulting in a less detailed but no less useful document for a medical student facing a licentiate examination.

## Keats and Risk: Operating to Succeed

On occasion, Keats and Waddington contradict each other. In notes about aneurism, Keats states that 'Mr. C. knows 10 cases … ', while Waddington – who writes his notes apparently verbatim and in the first person – has 'I have known two instances … '.[16] Here one of them probably misheard, but other instances of divergence are more mystifying. Keats writes 'If there be in a Fever a determination of Blood to the Head the Pulse will increase', where Waddington has 'Sometimes in Fever the Pulse is slower, this generally when there is a great determination of Blood to the Head'.[17] These two statements are bafflingly opposed: Cooper could not possibly have said both things; therefore one of them must have got it wrong. Generally, the raised metabolic demands during a fever cause the pulse rate to increase: the higher the fever the higher the pulse rate. However,

14 JKMN, Ff1r.
15 Waddington, 35.
16 JKMN, Bf1r; Waddington, 45–47.
17 JKMN, Ff1r; Waddington, 39.

certain fevers – such as typhoid – are characterized by a medical condition known as relative bradycardia. This means that, unlike in other fevers, the pulse rate does not rise in direct proportion to body temperature, and the blood pressure is also lower than expected.

Occasionally, discrepancies occur in matters of detail: where Keats has '2 or 3 Months' required for the repair of 'small nerves', Waddington has 'from 6, to 8 months'.[18] This is a considerable disparity difficult to explain as the result of mishearing or misunderstanding. Keats' 'small' is vague and may indicate that he was thinking of smaller nerves than the ones Waddington thought of as 'small'; it is also possible that Waddington meant nerves that would *probably* unite in '2 or 3 Months' would *certainly* have reunited by '6, to 8 Months'. Moreover, their apprentice experiences may have suggested different time frames: Waddington allowed for a longer period to be certain of healing while Keats was content to risk a shorter period of convalescence that might fit many – but not all – cases. The implications of this subjective disparity are worth exploring.

Keats' decision to give up medicine for poetry after investing time and money in training at Guy's suggests a willingness to take risks. He threw up his medical apprenticeship, took a chance with *Endymion*, and hazarded the Scottish Highlands seemingly without a second thought. And so in his poetry: lop-sided rhymes, open run-on couplets, and experiments with sonnet forms all suggest how he would risk a line for a 'happy lot' ('Ode to a Nightingale', 5). In medicine, however, the contrary could also be the case. The last operation Keats performed was an arteriotomy, which was 'done by making an oblique incision over the Artery and puncturing its Coats'.[19] Brown recollected Keats describing his

> overwrought apprehension of every possible chance of doing evil in the wrong direction of the instrument. 'My last operation', he told me, 'was the opening of a man's temporal artery. I did it with the utmost nicety; but, reflecting on what passed through my mind at the time, my dexterity seemed a miracle, and I never took up the lancet again.'[20]

18 JKMN, Bf4v; Waddington, 101.
19 JKMN, Ff1r.
20 Brown, *Life*, 43.

A capacity for risk – 'every possible chance' – is by no means a bad quality in a doctor. Keats had in front of him Astley Cooper, a surgeon at the head of his field who was willing to take chances in pursuing success. With Cooper to look up to, Keats may often have felt encouraged to confront doubt with 'dexterity' and hope for the best. He would have known that Cooper was a pioneer of surgical techniques for ligatures on arteries: a risky operation (like opening a temporal artery), since one mistake would result in the patient bleeding to death. Cooper took chances because, without surgical intervention, a patient with an arterial aneurism would certainly die. In June 1817 (shortly after Keats left Guy's) Cooper became the first person to place a ligature on the aorta successfully.[21] His patient was a porter named Charles Hutson who came into Guy's in April 1817 with an aneurism fed by the aorta.[22] He was admitted, and, with the surgeons aware of the extreme risk of attempting an arterial ligature, kept under observation and palliative care.[23] Hutson continued gradually to fade, but a crisis brought about the decision to operate: he started bleeding profusely from his abdomen. The duty dresser Daniel Gossett, together with Cooper's apprentice Charles Aston Key, managed to staunch the haemorrhage, but felt it necessary to summon Cooper himself.[24] Gossett later recounted in a letter to Bransby Cooper – Astley's nephew, heir, and biographer – that, the evening before he operated, Cooper spent hours in the dissecting room with cadavers.[25] Edward Osler, then a medical student at Guy's, wrote that Cooper's original intention had been to tie the iliac artery (which feeds into the aorta) and that this was what he practised on the cadavers. However, when he operated, he found the iliac so ulcerated that he was forced to staunch the wound from the aorta – and thus he came to perform an aortic ligature.[26] Whether this was a premeditated decision or a moment's brilliant improvisation,

21 Burch, *Digging up the Dead*, 208–10; Bransby Blake Cooper, *The Life of Sir Astley Cooper, Bart., interspersed with Sketches from his Note-books of Distinguished Contemporary Characters*. 2 vols (London: J.W. Parker, 1843), II, 202–06.

22 Cooper, *Life*, II, 202–03.

23 Cooper, *Life*, II, 203.

24 Cooper, *Life*, II, 203–04; Burch, *Digging Up the Dead*, 208.

25 Cooper, *Life*, II, 204–05.

26 Edward Osler, [Letter]. MS. KCL, GB 0100 G/PP1/39.

on 25 June 1817 Cooper successfully completed an aortal ligature on Hutson; 'unable to see what his hands were doing ... [he] proceeded by feel' and as if by what Keats would later call 'half-knowledge'.[27] This was not the first time that Cooper had interested himself in dangerous ligatures: in 1805 he had placed a ligature on the carotid artery of Mary Edwards, an operation in which additional difficulties are presented by the involved and delicate structure of the neck.[28] Keats' willingness to confront doubtful outcomes could have been an asset in a surgical career, even as 'possible chances' also impelled him towards the risky business of operating in 'half-knowledge' as a poet.

Having served apprenticeships, Waddington and Keats already had considerable medical experience. Indeed, early nineteenth-century medical practice depended almost as much on empirical experience as it did on scientific knowledge. For instance, while Cooper thought that mercury was dangerous because it lowered a patient's resistance, and therefore prescribed it only in small doses and never for gonorrhoea (for which he believed it was ineffectual), Solomon Sawrey, Tom Keats' doctor, *would* prescribe mercury for gonorrhoea, but only because he believed it to be the first stage of syphilis. However, Cooper's colleague James Curry considered mercury one of the most efficacious drugs of the age, and prescribed it for maladies far less dangerous than syphilis.[29] Another manifestation of such widely divergent medical opinion can be found in the extraordinary range of diagnoses offered for Keats' illness in his last year: from the initial self-diagnosis of pulmonary tuberculosis, through a nervous complaint, followed by another diagnosis of tuberculosis, to Dr Clark's statement at Rome that Keats' complaint was in the stomach.[30] Advanced tuberculosis such as Keats' eventually results in systemic failure: one by one all organs start malfunctioning. Keats

27 Cooper, *Life*, II, 205; Burch, *Digging Up the Dead*, 209–11; *LJK*, I, 194.

28 Burch, *Digging Up the Dead*, 180–81. The carotid nestles among many other vital structures – blood vessels, nerves, trachea, œsophagus – that would be catastrophic to disturb or disrupt. However, in operating upon the carotid, Cooper had the advantage of being able to see what he was doing. For the aortal ligature he was entirely reliant on his sense of touch and knowledge of anatomy to guide his actions.

29 *PP*, 202; *JK*, 448–49.

30 Brown, *Life*, 64; *NL*, 361, 363–64, 370, 389; *LJK*, II, 261, 262, 273–75, 288–89, 305, 306, 327; *KC*, I, 172.

was easily agitated, he suffered palpitations, his digestion was out of order – but these were all symptoms of a single disease. Doctors knew that chronic ailments such as 'consumption' could manifest in many forms, but before the advent of the electron microscope and sophisticated methods of body imaging it was much harder to know when a specific symptom heralded a new disease and when it was part of the spectrum that lingering terminal complaints, such as tuberculosis and cancer, can present. Therefore, they were forced to rely on precedent; and, since each doctor had a unique subset of experiences and empirical knowledge, this was more likely to affect their judgement. Something similar was probably at work when Keats and Waddington, while broadly agreeing that it took several months for a small nerve to heal, varied so much on the number of months. In other cases, differences between the two sets of notes are matters of degree: for example, Keats' 'animal may li[v]e' lacks the certainty of 'animal will survive' (Waddington).[31] In some cases, one of them adds information not recorded by the other: both note that ganglia were thought to give 'power to nerves', but only Waddington sets down that this opinion 'is now believed to be fallacious'.[32]

More intriguing is the single instance where Keats originally writes the same as Waddington, then crosses it out and rewrites so that the sentence takes on an opposite meaning. This occurs in a discussion of veins. Waddington writes '[veins] have 3 coats, the 1st is highly elastic'.[33] Keats had originally written 'The elastic coat of a Vein is of much greater strength than that of an Artery', only to cut out 'greater' and set down 'less' instead.[34] It is true, of course, that to say that a vein's elastic coat is less strong than an artery's does not contradict the general statement that the first coat of veins is highly elastic; nevertheless, that Keats changed 'greater' to 'less' implies that his understanding did not fully coincide with Waddington's.

There are also passages in Keats' notes that have no corresponding sections in Waddington's, and vice versa. Sometimes this is the result of detailing different experiments. Thus, while Waddington sets out the opinion 'that there was another sense which was of use, when that of sight was destroyed ... which gained very little credit', Keats

31 JKMN, Bf4v; Waddington, 103.
32 JKMN, Bf5v; Waddington, 115.
33 Waddington, 49.
34 JKMN, Bf1r.

writes of a 'celebrated Italian' who 'put out the Eyes of a Bat'.[35] Keats notes the experiments of 'Le Gallois' (the French surgeon Julien Le Gallois) on the spinal marrow and galvanism; Waddington does not.[36] In his notes to this lecture Keats names 'The Patriot K.', whose sciatic nerve was cut in battle; Waddington does not, though both discuss injuries to the sciatic nerve.[37]

It is not surprising that Astley Cooper spoke of Kosciusko in his lecture, since he was much in the news in 1816, and his injuries were referred to widely in English newspapers. *The York Herald and General Advertiser* offered a history of Kosciusko's military campaigns in January 1815, noting that 'Kosciusko fell, and with him fell the liberties of Poland.'[38] *The Morning Post* and *Caledonian Mercury* reported on his movements in 1815; several newspapers, among them *The Morning Post* and *The Examiner*, carried Helen Maria Williams's account of Kosciusko's arrival in Paris.[39] On 19 November 1815 *The Examiner* included Hunt's sonnet 'To Kosciusko', which Keats almost certainly read – and Cooper too, for he was a liberal.[40] Moreover, in the published version of Cooper's surgical lectures (not the same lecture course as Keats' notes, but with some overlap in content) Cooper *does* cite the case history of 'Koschiusko [*sic*], the Polish General' who 'had his sciatic nerve injured by a pike'.[41] Cooper apparently felt that Kosciusko, as a liberal hero afflicted with medically significant injuries, would add colour to his lecture and, at least as far as Keats was concerned, he judged rightly.[42]

Most differences in content can be put down to mishearing, or mistakes made in transcribing; differences in style reflect

35 Waddington, 105; JKMN, Bf4v – Bf5r.

36 JKMN, Bf5r – Bf5v.

37 JKMN, Bf4v.

38 *The York Herald, and General Advertiser* (14 January 1815): 2.

39 *Morning Post* (8 July 1815): 3; *Caledonian Mercury* (7 August 1815): 4; Helen Maria Williams, 'Kosciusko', *Morning Post* (10 November 1815): 4; and *The Examiner* (12 November 1815): 734. See also Williams, 'Kosciusko', Letter to the Editor, *Morning Chronicle* (10 November 1815): 3; and 'Kosciusko', *Liverpool Mercury* (17 November 1815): 6.

40 Leigh Hunt, 'To Kosciusko', *The Examiner* (19 November 1815): 746.

41 Further on in this lecture Cooper also cites Nelson's amputation as a case history of the after-effects of tying a nerve along with the blood vessel when performing a ligature. See *Lectures of … Cooper*, III, 262, 264.

42 *Texts*, 121.

contrasting personalities and intentions of the note-takers. As the course developed Keats' notes became shorter and his tendency to condense and combine material, sometimes from several lectures together, became more marked. However, even when reorganized in this way, the information content of his notes continued to match Waddington's, until his medical Notebook stopped abruptly with 'The Structure of the Heart'.[43]

## Keats on the Bones of the Skull: A Balancing Act

Keats took up his duties as dresser on 3 March 1816. As discussed earlier, for the year 1815/16 the course on 'Anatomy; And The Principal Operations Of Surgery' – as Waddington calls it – apparently started in January 1816. We do not know why Keats stopped taking notes, but it is certain that, as this lecture course progressed, he got busier. Simultaneously, his notes also started displaying radical reorganization, excising repetitive matter by resequencing and collating similar information. In tandem with this revisionist tendency, Keats increasingly wrote his notes on the versos only, leaving the rectos blank except for occasional instances.

A comparison of Keats' notes with Waddington's later in the lecture series reveals that his tendency to compression increased markedly as the course progressed. Using the same methodology as for the earlier lectures, I juxtaposed Keats' notes on the bones of the skull against Waddington's. Keats had stopped numbering lectures individually by this time: his discussion of the bones in the body is titled 'Of Osteology'; within this section, Ff12v–Ff17v discuss the bones of the skull. In Waddington, these lectures are numbered 25–28. In comparing these notes, my intention was to analyse the degree to which Keats was rearranging the material in the lectures. I found that, at this later stage in the series, Keats resequenced and distilled material significantly to avoid repetition and concentrate his resources. He left out surgically and diagnostically irrelevant details, such as Cooper's disquisition on differences between skulls of different races. He also reorganized the form and order of presentation. At this stage in the lecture course Keats' notes most often take the form of lists; on the rare occasions he used paragraphs, he made careful use of indentation

43 JKMN, Ff24v.

and spacing to group related elements together and distance unrelated ones. Occasionally he added annotations – for instance at Ff14v, where he added a footnote to record information he had inadvertently left out of a discussion on the relationship between the ethmoid bone and the nasal plate.[44] The extent of difference between Keats' organization and Waddington's is shown in the table below. The column on the right displays the lecture number, as presented in Waddington's notes, in bold; against it, on the left, we see the page numbers for the corresponding sections in Keats' notes (thus, material from Waddington's notes for Lecture 26 appear throughout versos 12 to 16 in Keats' notes). In this left column presenting the page numbers for Keats' notes, Ff13r is highlighted in bold font to draw attention to the fact that material drawn from three different lectures in Waddington (25, 27, and 28) appear on this one page in Keats' notes:

| Keats' notes | Waddington's notes |
|---|---|
| Ff12v | **25** |
| **Ff13r** | |
| Ff12v | |
| Ff12v | **26** |
| Ff13v | |
| Ff14v | |
| Ff15v | |
| Ff16v | |
| **Ff13r** | **27** |
| Ff15v | **28** |
| **Ff13r** | |
| Ff15v | |
| Ff13r | |
| Ff16v | (no corresponding section) |
| Ff17v | |

44 JKMN, Ff14v.

As this table indicates, Keats made significant adjustment to the organization of the material compared with its order in Waddington's notes. Since Waddington's notes are narrated in the first person and read as a commentary to a demonstration ('I have shown you …'), they also contain much repetition. Keats' rearrangement allows him to avoid this by moving subjects and topics around to suit *his* purposes. A striking example of this is at Ff13r of Keats' medical Notebook: the entire page is devoted to notes on surgical procedures, which – according to Waddington – are drawn from across three lectures: 25, 27, and 28.

That Keats could thus resequence and reorganize his notes without drastically compromising their information content makes it virtually certain he did not take all of them at the same time, or in a lecture theatre. It is possible that he limited himself during the lectures to taking selective notes, writing only on the versos. Perhaps anticipating that he might need to flesh out his notes, or reorder them, he left the rectos blank, to be filled in later with appropriate information. The fact that the vast majority of notes for all the lectures that Keats heads 'Of Osteology' are written on the versos seems to support this scenario. Moreover, the material noted in the versos is similar in style, presentation, and handwriting: well-spaced pages in a large, clear hand, organized by indentations and into lists. The rectos, when they contain notes, exhibit a more hurried and cramped hand, as if the writer is unsure how much material he will be able to fit into a limited space of paper – which would only be the case if the verso behind the recto had already been filled.

Ff13r of Keats' medical Notebook is instructive in understanding his methods of resequencing material. This page consolidates practical information on surgery, scattered across lectures 25, 27, and 28 in Waddington. The order in which this information is arranged by Keats does not fit Waddington's sequencing; moreover, other material from these lectures appears in different pages of Keats' Notebook, as shown by the table above. This means that Keats selected the information on Ff13r based on the topic it addressed: advice on how to diagnose and treat fractures. Because the page features information from lectures 27 and 28 in addition to lecture 25, this means Keats must have been aware not only of the contents of these three lectures 25, 27, and 28, when he made his notes, but also of lecture 26, since Cooper would have delivered his lectures in order. Keats therefore collected information delivered across *four* lectures and concentrated them onto a *single* page, selecting only matter relevant to his chosen topic. Therefore, when Keats set down these notes he was already aware of the contents of *all four lectures*, and consciously chose to reorganize the material as he felt best suited his purpose. In a word: he synthesized his notes on the diagnosis and treatment of fractures from multiple source lectures delivered by Cooper.

Keats' capacity for synthesis, evident in his medical Notebook, also appears in correspondence addressing a variety of recipients on several subjects during the same period. During the weeks that Keats composed his journal-letter to George and Georgiana Keats, February–May 1819, he also wrote to Haydon and Fanny Keats multiple times, engaging the former on the thorny issue of financial assistance while advising Fanny on the catechism.[45] He also corresponded with Severn, and he was simultaneously writing poetry: the journal-letter contains drafts or transcriptions of 'Why did I laugh tonight? No voice will tell', 'When they were come unto the Faery's Court', 'Character of C.B.', 'As Hermes once took to his feathers light', 'La Belle Dame sans Merci', 'Song of Four Fairies', two sonnets 'On Fame', the sonnet 'To Sleep', and 'Ode to Psyche'. Additionally, he drafted a review of Reynolds' *Peter Bell* for *The Examiner* in this letter.[46] Keats' facility in switching from subject to subject, correspondent to correspondent, chimes with his self-description as a 'camelion Poet', and the Keats who could, as a correspondent, simultaneously engage various interests resembles the medical student who could synthesize and assemble notes on multiple topics from apparently diverse lecture sources.[47] Equally, Keats' poetic interests need not have compromised his focus on his

45 John Barnard's edition of Keats' *Selected Letters* presents the letters in the order in which they were written, dividing the longer letters (such as the one to the George Keatses, February – May 1819) into the sections as they were written chronologically, and allowing other correspondence written in between these sections to take their place in the middle. This makes evident how quickly and frequently Keats engaged simultaneously in correspondence with different parties on different subjects, apparently without much difficulty. Keats advises Fanny of the catechism in a letter dated 31 March 1819: *LJK*, II, 49–51.

46 *LJK*, II, 58–109.

47 *LJK*, I, 387.

medical studies: in their brevity and selectivity, his notes reveal a student who was pressed for time yet able to sustain his medical/ intellectual pursuits alongside the imaginative work of his poetry.

## 'Keatsian' Notes, Burgeoning Poetry

As I have pointed out, sometimes Waddington writes a sentence for which Keats gives a different, contrary or otherwise modified word order. These instances show that Keats' sense of verbal rhythm emerges even in his medical notes. In Lecture 4, for example, the sentence 'Arteries are either in a state of Systole or Dyastole' has a sense of sibilant balance that Waddington's counterpart ('The arteries are always in a state of Diastole, or Systole') lacks: Keats' choice – whether conscious or not – to use a 'y' in 'Dyastole' instead of the more usual (and now standard) 'i' neatly places the two words in a symmetrical albeit oppositional relationship.[48] The words thus embody the pulsating action of the beating heart and are reminiscent of what Christopher Ricks referred to as the 'possible suggestivenesses' of Keatsian (mis)spellings.[49] The cumulative force of Keats' sentence emphasizes the sibilent connection of 'state ... Systole ... Dyastole' far more than Waddington's version, even though the words in it are exactly the same. Similarly, and also from Lecture 4, Keats' choice to order the veins of the body as 'Superficial and deep seated' shows a pleasing sense of moving inwards – in keeping with the discussion of the coats of the veins shortly afterwards, where both Keats and Waddington start with the topmost coat and move to deeper layers. Generally, throughout this lecture, Cooper's tendency was to describe the outermost elements first before moving inwards, layer by layer – this organization was almost certainly Cooper's, since it informs both sets of notes – but it may be revealing that Keats was apparently committed to maintaining that balance. Later, he would adopt the same pattern in his 'Ode to a Nightingale': the poem moves gradually inwards and downwards, into and through darkness, exploring ever deeper layers of the imagination as if anatomizing creativity in process.

48 JKMN, Ff1r; Waddington, 37.

49 Christopher Ricks, *Keats and Embarrassment* (1974; Oxford: Oxford University Press, 1976), 71.

Though it opens with an acknowledgement of suffering that is miserably personal and located firmly in the present –

> My heart aches, and a drowsy numbness pains
> My sense, as though of hemlock I had drunk,
> Or emptied some dull opiate to the drains
> One minute past, and Lethe-wards had sunk:
> (1–4)

– the poem expands its scope almost immediately to take account of more general, historically persistent miseries. Is it fanciful to detect a systolic/diastolic pattern here? Barbara Everett argued that the turn from an engagement wholly selfish (in the sense of utterly invested in the self) to one that starts looking towards the wider perspectives of unjust suffering comes as early as the second line of the poem, with Keats' use of the word 'hemlock'. The pattern of contraction and expansion is clear. Hemlock is inextricably associated in the western cultural imagination with the death of Socrates, and Keats' use of the word immediately brings to the poem a tacit acknowledgement of historical injustice, further generalized and expanded upon in stanza 3 with its description of the 'weariness, the fever, and the fret' (23), before the wretched and dispossessed through the ages are portrayed in stanza 7, where 'misery … writes itself a history'.[50] Alongside this acknowledgement of woe is the constant attempt to escape it in an imagined world of vernal blooms and sensual luxuries. The focus for this escapist move is the figure of the bird ('light-winged' (7) and so not earth-bound) and its song – an audible manifestation of the imagination's capacity to bring into existence a rare and transient beauty, rendered the more special for its impermanence. The bird-song has power: it brings the poet to the verge of sensual immolation, provoking in him 'such an ecstasy' (58) that he is threatened with a loss of self. Pulled back from the brink of annihilation, accounts of misery give way to a vision of 'Charm'd magic casements, opening on the foam / Of perilous seas, in faery lands forlorn' (69–70). The vision pulls poet and poem back to the present, and the movement of this stanza reproduces in miniature an

50 Barbara Everett, 'Keats: Somebody Reading', in *Poets in Their Time: Essays on English Poetry from Donne to Larkin* (London: Faber & Faber, 1986), 142–43, 144.

imaginative truth represented in the cyclical movement of the poem as a whole: that the human mind and the imagination can attain an inalienable state of happiness and freedom, regardless of external circumstances. Everett noted that the poem's

> logic works by rejection and a kind of attrition: but a sumptuous and benign rejection and an attrition ('I cannot see what flowers are at my feet') that brings the searching imagination to its true end in sympathy. Poetic happiness finds out where it belongs, which is, oddly but naturally, with unhappiness, in the company with those who are sad or deprived, who resemble the poet only in the fact that they too gave attention to the bird's song'.[51]

In 'Ode to a Nightingale', the imagination is shown to better hemlock, opiates, or alcohol in escaping suffering, but its dangers are also acknowledged: reaching the highest intensity of imaginative insight risks not only sensual deprivation ('I cannot see what flowers are at my feet' (41)), but also, ultimately, self-annihilation ('To thy high requiem become a sod' (60)). Perhaps, here, one can recall Astley Cooper, feeling his way inwards 'in a mist' of blood and living flesh to tie an aortic aneurism, without being able to see what he was doing – between hope and doubt, and at every moment aware of mortal danger, yet reaching further inwards, knowing this was the only way to save a life. Without plumbing the deepest, most inward recesses of imaginative life, one can never arrive at open casements with their vital, promising possibilities. To reach that depth of imagination, however, one must 'anatomize' the self, starting at the surface, and reaching deeper, and still deeper, interrupted by the press of reality on all sides – much as one cannot start dissecting a cadaver inside-out, but must start by peeling back the skin to expose the muscles, and so downwards and inwards until one reaches the skeleton, which forms the base of the entire structure.

Returning to the notes for Lecture 4: it is intriguing to see that Keats preferred the more modern word 'Sanguineous' to Waddington's archaic 'Sanguiferous'.[52] That this is immediately followed by one of Keats' cross-references – 'See Page 1' – may perhaps be the reason: by 'Page 1' Keats appears to mean Ff1v of his

51 Everett, 'Keats', 144.
52 JKMN, Bf1r; Waddington, 49.

Notebook, which lists major veins and offers information on their origins.[53] His attempt to link related information through cross-referencing shows how Keats thought of his medical Notebook as a 'database' to be continually added to. In this instance, it allows him to use the more general word, meaning 'of or pertaining to blood', rather than Waddington's specific 'Sanguiferous' ('bearing or conveying blood'), because his cross-reference links to a page where he has already noted that veins originate in arteries and that the two 'original arteries' (the aorta and the pulmonary arteries) terminate in veins.[54] Through his network of cross-references and marginalia, Keats appears to be constructing an ontological structure that in some ways anticipates his image of the 'wreath'd trellis of a working brain' (60) in 'Ode to Psyche'. Alan Richardson has shown how that image is evocative of Gall and Spurzheim's descriptions of the fibrous, interwoven texture of the brain's white matter: '[the] description of how the "fibres" of the medullary pyramids "cross or decussate each other" ... especially brings trellis work to mind.'[55] Cooper himself mentioned these characteristics of the medullary substance, as shown by Keats' lecture notes on 'The Nervous System':

> The Medullary substance seems tobe [*sic*] composed of fibres ... Nerves are composed of numerous Cords this is still the case in the smallest. They take a serpentine direction. They arise by numerous branches from the Substance of y^e^ Brain – there is however a contrary opinion extant. The Dura Mater does not accompany the Nerves to any distance – they are hoever [*sic*] covered with Pia Mater. The Nerves frequently meet and form a Plexus: Nerves also form Ganglions ... .[56]

Whether he was conscious of the similarity or not, Keats' system of note-taking, with its marginal intersections and cross-references, resulted in a comparably intricate, interwoven 'plexus' resembling the nervous structure of the brain, as explained in Cooper's lectures. These two aspects merge in 'Ode to Psyche' where Keats imagines

53 JKMN, Bf1r.
54 'sanguinous, adj.', 'sanguiferous, adj.', *OED*.
55 Richardson, *Science of the Mind*, 124–25.
56 JKMN, Bf4r.

a mental landscape that is simultaneously created by and located within 'the wreath'd trellis of [his] working brain' (60).

Some of Keats' notes have no counterpart in Waddington's. These can be divided into two categories. The first are details that appear to have struck Keats more than Waddington: for instance, in Lecture 4, Keats chooses to name 'Dr. Jones' and his observations on inflammation sealing an artery; Waddington has the same information without the surgeon's name.[57] The opposite also occurs: Waddington, describing how the pulse varies at different ages, names Johann Blumenbach; Keats quotes the same information but omits the name.[58] Elsewhere there are instances where Keats has information that appears, at first sight, to be wholly missing in Waddington, but which, on closer examination, proves to be linked with information that Waddington has recorded. In these cases, the emphasis, mode of expression, and selected details quoted are unique to Keats. It may be significant that these passages discuss material which interested Keats, independently from his medical studies. For example, although both Keats and Waddington wrote about arteries drained of blood after death, only Keats described their 'power of expelling the Blood in the last Struggles of Life'.[59] This dramatic expression lingered in Keats' imagination, to be summoned at the close of *Hyperion*, where 'wild commotions shook' (III. 124) Apollo's frame:

> Most like the struggle at the gate of death;
> Or liker still to one who should take leave
> Of pale immortal death, and with a pang
> As hot as death's is chill, with *fierce convulse*
> Die into life; so young Apollo anguish'd:
> (III. 126–30; my italics)

Keats' use of 'convulse' is medically precise: the verb carries with it the pathological sense of '[t]o affect with a succession of violent involuntary contractions of the muscles, so as to produce agitation of the limbs or whole body; to throw into convulsions'.[60] Poised on the verge of divinity, Apollo's convulsions resemble those that – as

57 JKMN, Ff1r; Waddington, 41.
58 JKMN, Ff1r, Waddington, 37.
59 JKMN, Ff1r.
60 'convulse, v.', *OED*.

Keats' lecturer told him, and as his own experience with patients confirmed – 'expelled the Blood' and presaged death. Using the word 'die' to describe Apollo's metamorphosis into full divinity highlights the similarities of the experience.[61] And yet, of course, Apollo's experience of 'dying into life' is one that no human can undergo: mortals cease to live when they die, but Apollo's agony is vivifying, transforming him into the god of medicine, music, and prophecy. Keats uses a medically precise vocabulary to create a powerfully concentrated acknowledgement of the differences separating Apollo from his human readers, while also indicating the subtle similarities that connect them. Likewise, in *The Fall of Hyperion*, the poet–narrator, attempting to approach Moneta, feels 'a palsied chill / … / … ascending quick to put cold grasp / Upon those streams that pulse beside the throat' (I. 122–25). These 'streams' are the carotid arteries (the jugular vein is also located beside the throat, but Keats knew a vein has a weaker pulse). Moneta informs the poet–narrator that he 'hast felt / What 'tis to die and live again before / Thy fated hour' (I. 141–43). Once again, death-throes are imagined as arteries 'grasped', contracted, with the blood forcibly expelled. That Keats equated life with oxygen-rich arterial blood flowing through the circulatory system is obvious from his reported reaction to his first pulmonary haemorrhage: 'I know the colour of that blood; – it is arterial blood.'[62] His late fragment 'This living hand' imagines blood wishfully ebbed out of the reader to flow into the poet, reanimating him: 'thou would wish thine own heart dry of blood, / So in my veins red life might stream again' (5–6).

Keats' notes for Lecture 4 describe circulation within the heart: 'Where the Blood meets in the right auricle the force of the {two streams of} Blood from the ascending and descending Cavae oppose each other and {respectively} drive back a po[r]tion of Blood in to y[e] Vessels'. He then observes, in a comment absent from Waddington's notes, that this 'made the Ancients suppose that the Blood ebbed and flowed'.[63] That Keats was intrigued by the 'history' of the heart is perhaps unsurprising: by 'the Ancients' he appears to have meant the collective Graeco-Roman foundation of western medical thought, traditionally considered to be summarized in

61 JKMN, Ff1r.
62 Brown, *Life*, 64.
63 JKMN, Bf1r.

the writings of Galen (Galenus Claudius, the famous physician based in Rome during the second century AD). Keats would have known from Lemprière's *Classical Dictionary* that Galen and Hippocrates (to whom Galen confessed himself 'greatly indebted') were 'two celebrated physicians' to whose 'diligence, application and experiments' modern medicine owed 'many useful discoveries', but also that 'often their opinions are ill-grounded, their conclusions hasty, and their reasoning false'.[64]

Galen's work helped define the structure of the spinal cord, the processes of respiration, and the working of the cardiovascular system. However, having only limited access to human cadavers, he was forced to rely on comparative anatomy, basing his ideas on observations of animal vivisections.[65] This caused errors: for instance, describing the cardiovascular system, Galen posited two different types of blood. In the Galenic system, blood originated in the liver and flowed through veins. This venous blood, rich in animal spirits composed in the brain and routed through the nerves, nourished the body as well as carried away wastes. Arterial blood, by contrast, originated in the heart and carried *pneuma*, spirituous air necessary for life, to all parts of the body. The Galenic system accounted for pulsation by modifying its Aristotelian heritage: Aristotle thought pulsation was a result of the innate heat of the heart, but Galen argued that it derived from an innate faculty in the arteries themselves. This pulsative arterial motion caused the blood to flow into the heart when it was dilated (diastole), and to ebb out again, causing the heart to tighten (systole). The active agent, therefore, was not the heart, but rather the pulsing arterial blood. For Galen, arterial blood was created when a small quantity of venous blood in the right ventricle of the heart flowed into the left ventricle through minute pores in an intraventricular septum. In the left ventricle it combined with air from the lungs to form the requisite vital spirits,

64 John Lemprière, *A Classical Dictionary; containing a copious account of all the proper names mentioned in ancient authors; with the value of coins, weights, and measures, used among the Greeks and Romans; and a Chronological Table* (1788; Seventh Edition. London: T. Cadell & W. Davies, 1809) [unpaginated].

65 The Graeco-Roman emphasis on the inviolate dignity of the human body meant that dissecting a corpse was sacrilegious: see Roy Porter, *The Greatest Benefit To Mankind: A Medical History of Humanity from Antiquity to the Present* (London: Harper Collins, 1997; Fontana Press, 1999), 56, 74–76.

to be distributed by the arteries.[66] The entire system depended on the intraventricular pores – which do not exist in humans. Once this lack of pores was established, the Galenic cardiovascular system had to be reconsidered.

It is likely that Astley Cooper mentioned these classical ideas of cardio-vascular circulation to stress the importance of dissection. Most mistakes in understanding human anatomy resulted from the inability to conduct human dissections, and dissection remained controversial in Keats' time. Cooper's remark about 'the Ancients' evidently registered with Keats, recalling his reading in Lemprière and suggesting, perhaps, thoughts of a 'grand march of intellect' or progressive narrative of scientific history.[67] Certainly, the reasons Oceanus offers for the fall of the Titans in *Hyperion* are of a progressive, almost evolutionary cast, where every entity is naturally succeeded by one that is better: 'So on our heels a fresh perfection treads' (II. 212). This is not to suggest that Keats believed so, but there is no doubt that he was sufficiently interested to note down 'ancient' views of blood – however 'ill-grounded'.[68] Galen is not mentioned in Keats' letters or poems, but 'the Ancients' are well represented: historical figures such as Socrates, Cleopatra, Brutus, and 'great Caesar' (*The Jealousies*, 496) appear alongside mythical beings such as Psyche, Saturn, Endymion, and Apollo.[69]

Convulsed in vivifying agony at the close of *Hyperion*, Apollo shows Keats' imagination transmuting medical knowledge into poetry. The 'expulsive' power of the arteries in death-throes is reimagined by Keats in light of the 'ancient' belief that 'the Blood ebbed and flowed'.[70] If blood in the arteries naturally ebbed and flowed, then, in certain circumstances – Apollo's convulsions on the threshold of divinity – blood could be visualized flowing *back* into the arteries: where the ebbing expulsion of blood from arteries

66 Allen G. Debus, *Man and Nature in the Renaissance* (Cambridge: Cambridge University Press, 1978), 57; Porter, *Greatest Benefit*, 211.

67 *LJK*, I, 282.

68 Lempriere.

69 David Pollard. *A Key-Word-in-Context Concordance to the Hyder E. Rollins Edition of the Complete Letters of John Keats* (Hove: Geraldson Imprints, 1989); *A Concordance to the Poems of John Keats*, ed. Michael G. Becker, Robert J. Dilligan, and Todd K. Bender (New York: Garland Publishing, 1981).

70 JKMN, Ff1r, Bf1r.

signified death, blood resuming its flow could signal a return 'into life'. The close of *Hyperion* hints at this poetic merging of ancient medical belief with contemporary medical knowledge, and it is made more explicit later, in 'This living hand'. Keats knew that, in physiological terms, 'the Ancients' were wrong about blood 'ebbing and flowing', but in his imaginary physiology medical myth and knowledge were transformed into poetic truths: Apollo convulsed and died into life as a god, while the poet imagined for himself a vampiric transfusion, draining the reader of life '[s]o in my veins red life might stream again' ('This living hand', 6).

## 'Well-condensed' Notes and 'Poetical Concentrations'

Keats preferred compression to elaboration. Waddington described what happens in a sneeze in his notes for Lecture 10: 'Sneezing, … is … remarkable, for here some substances applied to the nose, occasion an act of the abdominal muscles, and a valve to be opened in the Throat, in order to admit of the discharge of air.'[71] Keats wrote a single sentence: 'Sneezing is an instance of complicated sympathy.'[72] Practically speaking, Keats' compact statement offers as much information as Waddington's more prolix description – provided one understands what 'sympathy' means. 'Sympathy' was believed to be a non-conscious or involuntary function mediated by the nerves; the word still carries a physiological sense of 'relation between two bodily organs or parts (or between two persons) such that disorder, or any condition, of the one induces a corresponding condition in the other'.[73] The action of the sympathetic faculty of the body is either simple or complex, depending on how directly the stimulus engages the part(s) concerned, how many parts are involved, and how complex the process that results from this 'sympathetic activity'. As Waddington's description makes clear, sneezing is an instance of complex sympathy because stimulus to the nose excites muscles in various parts of the body (face, chest, diaphragm, abdomen) which then act in concert without conscious decision or desire to do so on the part of the person sneezing. Keats, having earlier defined

71 Waddington, 111–13.
72 JKMN, Bf5r.
73 'sympathy, n', *OED*.

'sympathy', omitted to elaborate what almost anyone can describe. One finds similar patterns repeating throughout both sets of notes, with Keats' ability to condense and focus his medical notes anticipating some characteristics of his mature poetry.

Occasionally, Keats concentrates a long description in Waddington's notes into a single image, as when he writes: 'Volition … does not reside entirely in the Brain but partly in y^e^ spinal Marrow which is seen in the Behaviour of a Frog after having been guillioteened.'[74] This ability to condense and distil later emerged in Keats' poetry, with Leigh Hunt observing that his works were characterized by 'poetical concentrations'.[75] In his *Examiner* review of *Poems* (1817) Hunt recalled the incident that led to his first acquaintance with Keats: an occasion when Horace Smith – one of the foremost parodists of the age – heard Keats' line '*That distance of recognizance bereaves*' and remarked 'What a well-condensed expression for a youth so young!'[76] This line is structured so that the verb 'bereaves' closes the predicate, with the subject appearing in the previous line ('With solemn sound – and thousand others more'). It has no pronouns but uses two prepositions: a significant proportion considering that it is composed of five words. The verb choice is unusual: Keats' sense that sounds cannot be identified because of distance would not normally suggest 'bereaves', which brings a sense of loss that works powerfully with the noun 'recognizance'. His choice to use this rather than the more obvious 'recognition' lends his poem the legal, emblematic, and heraldic associations of 'recognizance' while affirming the verbal mastery of the poet himself. The phrase 'recognizance bereaves' is far from the medical register of the language in Keats' Notebook, but the lyrical style Horace Smith detected in that poem was also apparent in Keats' habit of condensing notes at Guy's. That Keats was still working at Guy's when he wrote 'How many bards gild the lapses of time' makes the link all the stronger.

Of course, the purpose of notes preparatory to an examination is not poetic. Nevertheless, good poems are frequently memorable, and it is in a student's interest that notes should be so too. Keats, with his poet's instinct for verbal music, may have found it easier to remember

74 JKMN, Bf5r.
75 Hunt, *Byron and Contemporaries*, 266.
76 Hunt, *Byron and Contemporaries*, 55–63; *RoW*, 132–33.

cadenced word patterns: this might explain those instances in his notes, discussed above, where he used the same words as Waddington but reversed the order, or retained the sequence of veins 'Superficial and deep seated' throughout Lecture 4, thus maintaining a sense of moving inwards through the whole.[77] He need not have been conscious that he was emphasizing and rearranging words: if he naturally responded to rhymes, as there is reason to suppose, he may well have done so without being aware of it.[78] It is also easier to remember compact, carefully arranged material, hence Keats' combination of judicious transcription, tight phrasing, and a network of marginalia and cross-references. It is these elements of rhythm and verbal selection in his medical notes that suggestively foreshadow Keats' lyrical genius in condensing intricate webs of suggestive words, ideas, images, and associations. A few examples will show how these qualities of writing, found in his prose medical notes, also informed his later poetry.

Writing about 'Ode to a Nightingale', Thomas McFarland noticed 'the intense compression of "a beaker full of the warm South"', and observed that this expression encapsulates 'a logical progression running from beaker, to the idea of the wine in the beaker, to the recognition that grapes grow in the south of France and that wine is then made from them, to the understanding that the atmospheric condition necessary to grapes is warmth'.[79] McFarland's word 'compression' may be used figuratively 'of thought, language, or writing' to describe 'the condensation of thought or language'.[80] In psychoanalytic study, however, the word 'condensation' describes 'the process by which images characterized by a common affect are grouped ... to form a single composite or a new image'.[81] This

77 JKMN, Bf1r.

78 Haydon recounted how an old Mrs. Grafty, who used to be neighbour to the Keats family, recalled for George how John, when he had just learnt to speak, would, instead of answering questions put to him, make a rhyme on the last word of what he was asked in response. See Benjamin Robert Haydon, *The Diary of Benjamin Robert Haydon*, ed. W. B. Pope. 5 vols (Cambridge, MA: Harvard University Press, 1960), II, 107.

79 Thomas McFarland, *The Masks of Keats: The Endeavour of a Poet* (Oxford: Oxford University Press, 2000), 208.

80 'compression, n.', *OED*.

81 'condensation, n.', *OED*.

affective sense is also applicable here, for the entire sequence of ideas outlined by McFarland coalesces in the line into a single image: that of a vessel filled with wine. The line, thus, while suggesting a complete set of associations and ideas, also encapsulates them all within the single image of a wine-filled container. It is possible, similarly, to expand Keats' statement in his notes that 'the Behaviour of a Frog after having been guillioteened' shows the power of 'volition' to be influenced by the spinal marrow.[82] Such expansion would resemble more closely Waddington's detailed account:

> Volition does not reside altogether in the Brain but in part in the Spinal Marrow; this is proved by taking off the Head of an Animal, & placing it upon its back, when it will be found to turn upon its Belly; but if you carry a wire down the Spinal Marrow, the animal will cease to have the power of turning itself ... .[83]

However, such elaboration is unnecessary. Keats' compact image of a guillotined frog allows us to comprehend just as much as Waddington's detailed explanation. This ability, to capture an entire sequence of logical progression in a single phrase, is a hallmark of Keats' most striking poetry and a manifestation of his genius already evident in his medical notes. That Keats occasionally incorporates images or ideas from his Guy's Hospital experiences in his poems makes this continuity even more obvious, as we will see.

In the first book of *Hyperion* Saturn sits 'Upon the sodden ground / His old right hand lay nerveless, listless, dead, / Unsceptered; and his realmless eyes were closed' (I. 17–19). These lines are a masterpiece of compression, and they operate on several levels. Keats knew that a hand or limb with nerves incapacitated (so, 'nerveless') is incapable of voluntary motion (rendering it 'listless') and thus devoid of use, action, or feeling (therefore, 'dead').[84] However, 'nerveless' has multiple meanings: in anatomical terms it means 'not provided or supplied with nerves', but it can also mean 'lacking energy, weak, listless, limp' – and both senses of the word are applicable here.[85] Acknowledging this to be an instance of

82 JKMN, Bf5r.

83 Waddington, 107–9.

84 JKMN: see Lecture 10 at Bf4v – Bf5v.

85 'nerveless, adj.', *OED*.

synecdoche, the word can also be thought to refer to the figure of Saturn himself, as 'lacking courage or resolve; weak, incapable of effort'.[86] Saturn is dejected and despondent because dispossessed of his realm: Keats attaches the word 'Unsceptered' to the list of adjectives describing Saturn's hand to remind us of this fact – but he does so after the line break, thus ensuring that the difference between the previous anatomical adjectives and *this* political one is acknowledged. The juxtaposition also hints that, when Saturn was king of the gods, having a sceptre in his hand was as natural as nerves are in a human hand. The earlier adjectives all described Saturn's hand in physical terms; 'Unsceptered' relates that physical state to his current plight and, in so doing, opens the way to an appreciation of his psychological crisis, which in turn is reflected in and by his physical condition. This is the measure of Saturn's loss: the ability to enforce his will on the universe and to perceive its reactions – precisely the mediating function that nerves perform between the brain and the extremities in a human body. Keats suggests, through the progression of adjectives, that though the original cause of Saturn's powerlessness was psychological – a devastating change in his circumstances – it now also manifests as a physiological reality; the effects of being 'disanointed' as a god is embodied as physical infirmity. This multifaceted and nuanced understanding of what it might mean, in emotional and physiological terms, for a god to lose his divinity, is made possible by Keats' precise knowledge of anatomy and his genius for verbal compression. This is further borne out by the unusual word Keats chose to describe Saturn's eyes: as McFarland observes, although 'realmless' – a rare word meaning 'deprived of a realm' – would not ordinarily be considered a modifier for 'eyes' (except in the world of *King Lear*), the conjunction of the two 'exactly compresses still further the compression noted above'.[87] Saturn's eyes are 'realmless', just as he is himself: this underscores the account of his plight imaged by his 'unsceptered' hand. Keats' words 'unsceptered' and 'realmless' implicitly invite the reader to consider a 'sceptered' Saturn possessing a 'realm'. That all-powerful Saturn is not shown in the poem, but, by allowing readers to imagine the extent of

86 'nerveless, adj.', *OED*.

87 'realmless, adj.', *OED*; McFarland, *Masks of Keats*, 138.

his fall, Keats heightens the pathetic affect of this dispossession, rendering it more memorable for being unspoken.

*Hyperion* ceases with Apollo on the threshold of godhead; at the end of *The Eve of St. Agnes* the lovers disappear into the storm of legend. In 'Ode to a Nightingale' the bird is both one of Keats' '[t]hings real' and a symbol, and the poem brings the poet to the threshold of death, only to leave him hovering between sleep and wakefulness.[88] 'To Autumn' is a poem dedicated to a season of 'mists and mellow fruitfulness' (1) – a season of transience, in which the warm fecundity of summer gradually shades into the chill sterility of winter. These are just a few of the more famous of Keats' poems containing instances of his tendency to 'concentrate' and contrast. It is perhaps no accident that all of them are concerned with thresholds – with the uncertain, in-between regions that straddle past and present, humanity and divinity, life and death, health and sickness, dreaming and waking. Thresholds are liminal spaces, characterized by mutability and transience, and Keats' poetry is especially alive to the vitality of the threatened. He may or may not have known (there is no record of this in his medical Notebook) that physicians had a term – *spes phthisica* – for the extraordinary vitality exhibited by many tuberculosis patients.[89] Whether Keats himself experienced *spes phthisica* or not, his poetry illuminates precisely the vitality that can be found in the midst of debility, and it does so through the contrasts set up by the poet's masterful use of compression. Typically, anything subject to change is also subject to time, and Keats frequently employs compression to manipulate the effects of temporality. Saturn, defeated, with his 'realmless eyes' (*Hyperion*, I. 19) is imagined as still as a statue while time moves on; Hyperion, unvanquished, 'flared' (*Hyperion*, I. 217) into the poem in a blaze of movement charted in relation to the progress of time. The 'gathering swallows' (33) of 'To Autumn' communicate, with the lightest of touches, the sense of time's encroachment, rescuing the poem from the possibility of a final closure and keeping it true to the transient beauty of its subject.

88 *LJK*, I, 243.

89 'Spes' means hope in Latin; 'phthisis' is the name for tuberculosis and was usually used to describe pulmonary TB. 'Spes Phthisica', therefore, roughly translates to 'hope of/from pulmonary tuberculosis', and refers to a euphoric state of vitality often experienced by sufferers of pulmonary tuberculosis. Goellnicht states in *PP*, 203, that he believes Keats experienced the condition.

Compression allows Keats to highlight such contrasts and focus attention on the life and beauty that exists in the shadow of death.

Keats' medical notes show, in early form, some of these features that characterized his mature poetry. Compared with Waddington, he paid greater attention to the cadences of words and wrote more balanced and finely tuned prose. Some of the subjects covered in his medical Notebook feed directly into Keats' poetry, others do so more obliquely – yet it is surely suggestive that his notes on strictly medical subjects draw in the Classics and the world of liberal politics. Perhaps most significantly, his ability to concentrate ideas in a sentence or embody them in an image is as evident in his medical notes as it would later be in 'Ode to a Nightingale' or *Hyperion*. Indeed, some of the most distinctive and recognizable lines in Keats' poems flowed from the imaginative potential of his notes taken at Guy's Hospital. He would have been a different poet had he not trained in medicine, and his knowledge of anatomy and physiology – as judged from the contents of his medical Notebook – reappears constantly in his imaginative life. When Keats wrote of a poet being 'physician to all men' (*The Fall of Hyperion*, I. 190) he was being more literal in his description than has perhaps been noted or realized.

CHAPTER FIVE

# *Endymion* and the Physiology of Passion

*Endymion: A Poetic Romance* was written by John Keats immediately following his Guy's Hospital tenure. It was the longest poem he ever wrote, and one he conceived as 'a test, a trial of my Powers of Imagination and chiefly of my invention'.[1] Its importance, therefore, is threefold: it was Keats' longest work; it was written immediately after the period of his association with Guy's and is accordingly most likely to show the influence of his hospital career; and it was a poem that he himself considered 'a test' of his abilities as a poet. In this chapter I offer a close reading of the poem and of the biographical circumstances surrounding its composition. Reading *Endymion* through the contents of Keats' medical Notebook allows a fresh perspective on the physiology that underlies and informs the poem's depictions of passion. The chapter further shows how critical responses to the poem – whether benign or hostile – realize and respond to this element of it. I conclude with an exploration of Keats' knowledge of Romantic medical ethics, and how this informs his delineation of figures of healers in *Endymion*, whose actions and emotional responses are carefully calibrated in keeping with contemporary advice on appropriate medical conduct. The physiological treatment of passion in *Endymion* gives the work its distempered life, and the poem showcases Keats' extraordinary ability to convey extreme emotions through anatomical description and medical vocabulary – a characteristic feature of his best works that imparts to them their enduring vitality.

1 *LJK*, I, 169–70.

## The Beginnings of *Endymion*

*Endymion* had been planned for quite some time before it was committed to paper. Keats referred to 'I stood tip-toe' – dating from summer or early autumn of 1816 – as 'Endymion' throughout its composition, and the poem includes a passage on Endymion and Cynthia (193–240).[2] At some later point, perhaps as he was finishing it in a last 'attack', the idea of *Endymion* as a separate long poem occurred to Keats, although Henry Stephens dated its first line earlier than this (see below). In this section I consider the beginnings of *Endymion*, which – as I will show – had a long gestation overlapping with Keats' career at Guy's Hospital.

Keats probably finished his contracted year as a dresser at Guy's on 3 March 1817. However, he did not immediately settle down to write a long poem. Two weeks later, on 17 March, he wrote telling Reynolds:

> [m]y Brothers are anxious that I sho$^{d}$ go by myself into the country ... and now that Haydon has pointed out how necessary it is that I sho$^{d}$ be alone to improve myself, they give up the temporary pleasure of<t> living with me continually for a great good which I hope will follow – So I shall soon be out of Town.[3]

It took him some time to act upon these intentions.

Between 17 March and 25 March 1817 the Keats brothers moved from 76 Cheapside to 1 Well Walk, Hampstead, much closer to Hunt at the Vale of Health. This was a decisive move away from the City of London, with its associations of business and the oppressive proximity of his former guardian and custodian of the Keats family wealth, Richard Abbey. For Keats personally the inner city also had obvious associations with his career at Guy's; by moving to Hampstead and Hunt, he was consciously settling in a location associated with poetry and his current poetic hero (disillusionment with Hunt was to come later). Indeed, his first poem after quitting Guy's was a sonnet 'On *The Story of Rimini*':

> Who loves to linger with that brightest one
> Of heaven, Hesperus – let him lowly speak

2 *Texts*, 122.
3 *LJK*, I, 125.

These numbers to the night and starlight meek,
Or moon, if that her hunting be begun …
(5–8)

The 'moon … hunting' is a reminder of the celestial huntress Diana, and of the long poem Keats was planning. The sonnet must have been written around the time of the move, since Keats implied that it had been recently composed in the first letter he wrote from Well Walk (to Charles Cowden Clarke on 25 March 1817).[4] Why he wrote a sonnet on *The Story of Rimini* more than a year after its publication is unclear: possibly it was an attempt to re-engage Hunt's attention, recently distracted by Shelley, who was in a state of crisis after the suicide of his wife Harriet and a Chancery case for the custody of their children. Keats' own ambiguous feelings towards Shelley, hospital duties, and awareness of the disastrous Chancery case in his own family history all encouraged him to keep away from Hunt. Once the Shelleys had left, writing a sonnet on Hunt's most important poem would help revive their friendship. Keats' phrase 'a region of his own' ('On *The Story of Rimini*', 11) echoes his early sonnet 'Written on the Day That Mr. Leigh Hunt Left Prison', with its vision of Hunt's 'genius' taking flight to 'regions of his own' (12). Moving to Hampstead was a comparable attempt to take control of his future (even if this brought him into conflict with Abbey) and carve out poetic 'regions of his own' – and Hunt was apparently a major influence on these life decisions.

Keats eventually left London on 14 April 1817, six weeks after he left Guy's and four weeks after he resolved to 'be alone'. He caught the evening stagecoach to Southampton, arrived next morning, and took a boat to the Isle of Wight later that day. On 16 April he walked to Shanklin, and the following day moved into lodgings at Carisbrooke, writing to Reynolds that he was 'about to become settled'.[5] He enclosed his sonnet 'On the Sea' in this letter; *Endymion* he would 'forthwith begin'.[6] These announcements, designed to reassure his friend that he was doing what he had set out to do, were marked by a curious temporal elision. Keats uses the future tense: he is 'about to become settled', which is not the same as being settled

4 *LJK*, I, 127.
5 *LJK*, I, 130.
6 *LJK*, I, 134.

just now; he will begin his poem 'forthwith', but has not yet started. His statements indicate a pattern of delay, in which, however, he casts himself as already in the process of creation: it is almost as if *not* working on *Endymion* was somehow significant to its composition.

Keats' next letter, written at Margate on 10 May, told Hunt he had begun his 'Poem about a Fortnight since and have done some every day except travelling ones'.[7] This is vague, but suggests that he had commenced *Endymion* around 27 April. John Barnard has argued that this letter uses rhetorical strategies to disguise the crisis of confidence that overtook Keats on the Isle of Wight and sent him rushing to Margate and Tom.[8] He also shows that Haydon's letter to Keats of 8 May echoes the language and imagery of the opening lines of *Endymion*, and therefore Haydon must have read a draft of them.[9] In his reply to Haydon on 10 May Keats wrote: 'The Trumpet of Fame is as a tower of Strength the ambitious bloweth it and is safe.'[10] This, as Barnard notes, is a direct response to Haydon's of 8 May, which praises a 'delicious poem' and states, 'You have taken up the great trumpet of nature and made it sound with a voice of your own.'[11] Although the 'delicious poem' is usually said to be 'On the Sea', the 'great trumpet of nature' comes from the first book of *Endymion*:[12]

> And now at once, adventuresome, I send
> My herald thought into a wilderness:
> There let its trumpet blow, and quickly dress
> My uncertain path with green, that I may speed
> Easily onward, thorough flowers and weed.
>
> (I. 58–62)

All of this indicates that *Endymion* was underway when Keats left the Isle of Wight and that, while he was en route for Margate, Haydon – in London – had apparently read the opening lines at least as far as line 60.

7 *LJK*, I, 139.
8 See Barnard, '"Forebodings"'.
9 Barnard, '"Forebodings"', 4.
10 *LJK*, I, 141.
11 Barnard, '"Forebodings"', 4; *LJK*, I, 136.
12 Barnard, '"Forebodings"', 4.

There is, however, one account of *Endymion*'s opening lines that challenges this chronology. Keats' fellow student at Guy's, Henry Stephens, claimed, in conversations late in life with Sir Benjamin Ward Richardson, that he was present when Keats composed the opening line of *Endymion*. Richardson knew both Stephens and George Wilson Mackereth, although he was more familiar with the former. In conversations 'from 1856 to his death in 1864', Stephens 'was never weary in telling [Richardson] about Keats'.[13] It was during these talks that he recalled Keats composing the first lines of *Endymion*:

> In a room, Mr. Stephens told me, he was always at the window peering into space, so that the window-seat was spoken of by his comrades as 'Keats's place'. Here his inspiration seemed to come most freely. Here, one evening in the twilight, the two students sitting together, Stephens at his medical studies, Keats at his dreaming, Keats broke out to Stephens that he had composed a new line: –
>
> 'A thing of beauty is a constant joy.'
> 'What think you of that, Stephens?'
> 'That it will live for ever.'[14]

Stephens' recollection drafts the first line in their shared lodgings at 28 St Thomas' Street, Southwark. Since Keats left St Thomas' Street after his July 1816 licentiate examination, this suggests that he 'broke out' the first line of *Endymion* before the examination, when he was beginning as a dresser at Guy's, and that the idea of *Endymion* was fermenting for most of his dressership.

The accuracy of Stephens' recollection may be open to doubt, since he forgot to mention it in his reminiscences of 1847; yet, if true, it offers further evidence that *Endymion* had a very long evolution.[15] Furthermore, this account appears to suggest that Keats arrived at one of the most famous lines in his œuvre – 'A thing of beauty is

13 Benjamin Ward Richardson, 'An Esculapian Poet – John Keats', in *The Asclepiad: A Book of Original Research and Observation in the Science, Art and Literature of Medicine, Preventive and Curative.* 11 vols (London: Longmans, Green and Co., 1884–1897), I, 138–39.

14 Richardson, 'An Esculapian Poet', 148–49.

15 *KC*, II, 206–14.

a joy for ever' (*Endymion*, I. 1) – with his medical friend Stephens' help.[16] There is also the curious overlap of an earlier poem and a later one represented by 'I stood tip-toe' and *Endymion*. This is not a singular instance: *Hyperion* and its reincarnation *The Fall of Hyperion*; the two sonnets on the Elgin Marbles; the poems on the crowning with laurel (and the subsequent apology and rededication to Apollo composed a few weeks later); and even *The Eve of St Agnes* and the unfinished *The Eve of St Mark* can be thought of as Keatsian 'revisitings' of themes and imagery. When he wrote to Reynolds in May 1818 that 'Every department of knowledge we see excellent and calculated towards a great whole ... An extensive knowledge is needful to thinking people', perhaps he was commenting more directly on his process of creation as a 'gradual' calculation than has hitherto been realized.[17] Growing out of his Guy's experience and 'I stood tip-toe', it is not surprising that *Endymion* is saturated with evidence of Keats' medical knowledge and training, deployed in poetry and imagined into a pastoral arcadia. That evidence is the subject of my next section.

## *Endymion*'s Debilities

*Endymion* is the story of a love affair between the goddess of the moon, Diana (or Cynthia) and the shepherd king Endymion. Keats described its plot to his sister Fanny:

> Many Years ago there was a handsome Shepherd who fed his flocks on a Mountain's Side called Latmus – he was a very contemplative sort of Person and lived solitry ... little thinking – that such a beautiful Creature as the Moon was growing mad in Love with him – However so it was; and when he was asleep on the Grass, she used to come down from heaven and admire him excessively

16 Hale-White offers a slightly different account of this event but neglects to mention his source: 'We are told that to Stephens he pronounced the line "A thing of beauty Is a constant joy". Stephens said he thought it wanted something. Keats pondered and then burst out with "I have it, 'A thing of beauty is a joy forever'". It is likely therefore that this famous line had its birth in the St Thomas's Street lodgings': see Hale-White, *Doctor and Patient*, 35.

17 *LJK*, I, 277, 281.

> from a long time; and at last could not refrain from carrying him away in her arms to the top of that high Mountain Latmus while he was dreaming –[18]

Keats' summary makes no mention of the numerous characters that flit in and out of his poem, in which – as Byron testily observed – lovers meet only to talk of desire. In lieu of passionate consummation, the poem turns upon love-sickness, and Keats is careful to describe its physiological symptoms.[19] Endymion swoons (I. 398, 637; II. 193–283, 868; IV. 999), suffers palpitations (II. 355–57), is distracted and restless (I. 653; II. 47–55, 137–39, 218), is impervious to temperature changes (II. 53–55), and spends much of the poem claiming to be either dizzy (I. 565; II. 183–87; III. 1006–09), feverish (II. 319; III. 105–07), or both. Recalling his first meeting with Diana causes Endymion discomfort, and everyone he encounters can tell that he is unwell. Diana, as a goddess, is less severely afflicted, but Venus can identify symptoms of malady: 'an idle tongue / A humid eye, and steps luxurious' (III. 909–10).

When Endymion first appears in Book I the entire congregation at the festival of Pan is aware that all is not well:

> … hourly had he striven
> To hide the cankering venom, that had riven
> His fainting recollections. Now indeed
> His senses had swoon'd off: he did not heed
> The sudden silence, or the whispers low,
> Or the old eyes dissolving at his woe,
> Or anxious calls, or close of trembling palms,
> Or maiden's sigh, that grief itself embalms:
> But in the self-same fixed trance he kept,
> Like one who on earth had never stept –
> Aye, even as dead-still as a marble man,
> Frozen in that old tale Arabian.
>
> (I. 395–406)

18 *LJK*, I, 154.

19 Richard Marggraf Turley discusses how *Endymion*, even as it apparently moves towards closure, can be seen to be 'folding back in on itself' (p. 17), and relates this to Keats' anxieties about having 'not a right feeling towards Women' (*LJK*, I, 341): Turley, *Boyish Imagination*, 15–19.

Endymion is here in a 'fixed trance', oblivious to the concerned gaze of fellow shepherds and their families. He has 'striven' to overcome a 'cankering venom' induced, it is later revealed, by his dream-vision. 'Venom', in addition to referring specifically to the 'poisonous fluid ... secreted by certain snakes and other animals', also more generally refers to any 'poison ... any poisonous or noxious substance, preparation, or property', and can be used figuratively to indicate 'something comparable to or having the effect of poison; any baleful, malign, or noxious influence or quality'.[20] In this instance, the figurative meaning carries the most weight, especially when modified by the adjective 'cankering': 'that cankers (in various senses); corroding, corrupting; spreading harmfully and insidiously'.[21] The after-effects of his dream-vision leave Endymion forgetful, absent-minded, with 'fainting recollection': this phrase suggests that his ability to recollect, as well as his recollections, were affected, and both were 'faint' – not only did he not remember, but, when he did so, his recollection was imprecise. He is also deeply distracted: the line 'His senses had swoon'd off' suggests that, though Endymion is not (yet) in a full 'swoon', he is as unaware of his surroundings as he would be if actually in a 'swoon'. Although the primary meaning of the verb 'to swoon' is 'to faint', it can also indicate a sinking '*to* or *into* a less active condition or a state of rest'.[22] As a noun, 'swoon' refers to 'the action of swooning or the condition of one who has swooned', as well as to 'a fainting-fit'; a rare, obsolete sense of the word, used by Spenser, is 'a (deep or sound) sleep'.[23] Keats uses 'swoon' in all of these senses in *Endymion*. He also co-opts the word into descriptions of natural phenomena: the *Oxford English Dictionary* credits *Endymion* with first use of the word in this figurative sense, citing the lines 'Strange ministrant of undescribed sounds, / That came a swooning over hollow grounds' (I. 285–86).[24] In his 'trance', Endymion is unaware – as if his senses have fallen asleep, although he is awake. Only his sister can rouse him from this state: she leads him to a secluded spot and Endymion finally reveals his encounter (he does not yet know it was with Diana)

20 'venom, n. and adj.', *OED*.
21 'cankering, adj.', *OED*.
22 'swoon, v.', *OED*.
23 'swoon, n.', *OED*.
24 'swoon, v.', *OED*.

and its effect on him. Keats likens Endymion, in his 'fixed trance', to the young king of the Black Islands from *The Arabian Nights*, the 'marble-man', and it is instructive to trace this allusion to its source. In *The Arabian Nights* this young king was married to his cousin, an enchantress, but she did not love him and preferred a slave. The king, overhearing maids gossiping about this, followed his wife one night and attempted to kill her beloved, but succeeded only in wounding him. The lady went into mourning and spent her days tending to her injured lover, until the king lost his temper and struck her. Enraged, she cursed him, changing his lower half into marble, so that he was unable to move and sexually 'frozen'.[25] The 'marble man' allusion points to love as a possible cause of Endymion's malady and it can be read as a warning that obsessive passion endangers health, peace of mind, and sexual fulfilment. It also serves to heighten suspense: the king of the Black Isles was unloved by his cousin–wife, and she was directly responsible for his plight, much as Diana bears responsibility for Endymion's 'fixed trance' and sexual frustration. Will Diana return Endymion's love, and 'unfreeze' him?

Even recollecting his encounter causes Endymion discomfort: 'a conflicting of shame and ruth / Was in his plaited brow' (I. 761–62). Keats would have been aware of the psychological effects of trauma from personal experience (he hid under the schoolmaster's desk after receiving news of his mother's death in 1810) and also from encounters with survivors of surgery at Guy's. One of the more articulate survivors of an early nineteenth-century operation – conducted without anaesthesia, which was yet to be discovered – was Fanny D'Arblay (née Burney), who underwent a mastectomy at her home in Paris on 30 September 1811.[26] She recounted the operation

25 Edward William Lane, trans., *The Thousand and One Nights: The Arabian Nights' Entertainments*, ed. Stanley Lane-Poole. 4 vols (London: George Bell and Sons, 1906), I, 47–54.

26 Fanny Burney was fortunate to be attended by a team that included some of the most skilled surgeons and physicians in France – and indeed, Europe – at the time. Dominique-Jean Larrey (1766–1842), who performed the mastectomy, gained renown as an army surgeon during the Napoleonic Wars: the best known of his almost heroic feats of battlefield surgery are the 200 amputations he performed within 24 hours after the Battle of Borodino. He was assisted by Antoine Dubois (1756–1837), the leading French obstetrician of the day and the inventor of the Dubois forceps; and François Ribes (1765–1845) and

in a letter to her sister Esther, written over several months (March – June 1812):

> not for days, not for Weeks, but for Months I could not speak of this terrible business without nearly again going through it! I could not *think* of it with impunity! I was sick, I was disordered by a single question – even now, 9 months after it is over, I have a headache from going on with the account! & this miserable account, which I began 3 Months ago, at least, I dare not revise, nor read, the recollection is still so painful.[27]

Recalling the physical sensation of a lancet cutting into flesh generated symptoms of psychological trauma: she 'could not speak ... could not *think* ... sick ... disordered'. Endymion had not undergone surgery, yet Keats suggests his 'disorder' is a 'conflicting' of similar intensity.

More details of Endymion's condition follow. He spends days 'wandering in uncertain ways' (II. 48): 'Now he is sitting by a shady spring, / And elbow-deep with feverous fingering / Stems the upbursting cold' (II. 53–55). In this passage, his distraction is such that he is impervious to the water's cold, yet, oddly, his 'fingering' of it is 'feverous'. The choice of word is felicitous: 'feverous' means '[i]ll of a fever; affected by fever', as well as '[a]pt to cause fever', and also carries two senses otherwise ascribed to the word 'feverish': '[o]f, pertaining to, of the nature of, or characteristic of a fever' and the more figurative '[e]xcited, fitful, restless, now hot now cold', which could also be considered an accurate description of fever symptoms.[28] The conflicting sensations of fever and 'upbursting cold' in *Endymion* resemble the mingled pleasures that Keats imagined for minnows in 'I stood tip-toe',

> Staying their wavy bodies 'gainst the streams,
> To taste the luxury of sunny beams

Philippe-Eléanor-Godefroy Aumond (1775–1825), both of whom won acclaim as battlefield surgeons.

27 Fanny Burney (Madame D'Arblay), *The Journals and Letters of Fanny Burney: Vol. 6: France 1803–1812*, ed. Joyce Hemlow et al. (Oxford: Clarendon Press, 1975), 613.

28 'feverous, adj.', 'feverish, adj.', *OED*.

> Temper'd with coolness. How they ever wrestle
> With their own sweet delight ...
>
> (73–76)

The minnows take pleasure from the combination of cool water and hot sun; the 'luxury of sunny beams' depends on their being supplemented and complemented by the cool 'streams'. Keats shared this idea of the pleasure of mingled sensations with Leigh Hunt, an advocate of such 'doubled pleasures': in a memorandum addressed to his son Thornton, written while imprisoned at Horsemonger Lane, Hunt described 'the complicated luxury of resting limbs, a cooling air, a fanciful passage' using the same word as Keats ('luxury') to describe combined, opposed yet complementary sensations and the emotion they aroused.[29] Keats was much in Hunt's company during the final stages of writing 'I stood tip-toe', but, long before meeting Hunt, he had read contrastive passages such as this from *The Story of Rimini*:

> Sorrow, to him who has a true touched ear,
> Is but the discord of a warbling sphere,
> A lurking contrast, which though harsh it be,
> Distils the next note more deliciously.
>
> (IV. 17–20)[30]

Keats' first published poem, 'To Solitude', spoke of the 'doubled pleasure' of accompanied solitude and later poems continued to dwell on the 'luxury' of opposing sensations. The sonnet 'To Homer', written in 1818, shows his sense of how contrary effects might lead to pleasure of a sort otherwise unavailable:

> Aye on the shores of darkness there is light,
> And precipices show untrodden green,
> There is a budding morrow in midnight,
> There is a triple sight in blindness keen;
>
> (9–12)

29 Quoted in Roe, *Fiery Heart*, 186.

30 Leigh Hunt, *The Selected Writings of Leigh Hunt: Vol. 5: Poetical Works, 1801–21*, ed. John Strachan (London: Pickering and Chatto, 2003), 195.

Later poems show the same sensual appreciation, in the drama of warmth and chill that permeates *The Eve of St Agnes*; in the contrast between Saturn's stillness and Hyperion's blazing movement in *Hyperion*; in the sense, in 'Ode to a Nightingale', that loss of vision ('I cannot see what flowers are at my feet' (41)) does not detract from, but rather heightens, the pleasure to be derived from the bird's song; in the fine balance struck between 'living' and 'dying' in the final stanza of 'To Autumn'. When Astley Cooper informed his auditors, as Keats noted, that 'If there be in Fever a determination of Blood to the Head the Pulse will increase. Heat readily increases the Pulse – the warm bath will elevate the Pulse to 120. Cold on the contrary will diminish soon reduce it … [*sic*]', he was effectively diagnosing the physiology of Huntian 'doubled pleasures' or Keatsian 'luxuries'.[31] The sensations evoked on applying Cooper's medical advice – cool water on hot skin, or warm water on cold skin – are of a piece with the 'luxury' Keats' minnows experience, in a cold stream with the sun shining on them. Cooper's immediate point of reference for his comments may well have been the work of his late instructor John Hunter, who, in his influential *A Treatise on the Blood, Inflammation and Gun-Shot Wounds* (1794), had outlined the role blood played in the regulation of body temperature. Hunter also believed, as Keats wrote in his medical Notebook, that 'Blood possessed Vitality'.[32] As we saw in Chapter 3, Keats was well aware of the many competing ideas for the source of vitality prevalent in early nineteenth-century medicine, including the Brunonian theory that considered life to be 'a forced state', with an organism dependent on an adequate supply of contrastive stimuli to stay alive.[33] In this view, Keats' minnows – experiencing the 'luxury of sunny beams / Temper'd with coolness' ('I stood tip-toe', 74–75) from the water they are in – are exposed to the perfect combination of stimuli for sustaining life. Thus, not only did Keats anticipate, through his negatively capable identification with poetic subjects, some of the physiological explanations that Romantic medicine proffered to explain life, but in turn his imaginative and sensual instincts also received affirmation from his medical knowledge and the training he underwent at Guy's Hospital.

31 JKMN, Ff1r.

32 JKMN, Ff2v.

33 Brown, *Elements*, 59.

Hunt, it seems, showed Keats the possibilities for imagining contrary physiological experiences as a 'luxurious' equilibrium between warmth and chill that could be felt on the pulse, an insight that appeared to be confirmed by Cooper in his medical lectures. Endymion's actions, however, are distempered and 'feverish': he is restless and fitful, apparently susceptible to temperature changes even though there is no alteration of ambient atmospheric temperature. His 'feverous fingering' suggests the agitated movement of fingers as he absent-mindedly plays with water, impervious to its cold. Feverish symptoms appear repeatedly in the poem:

> Poor Cynthia greeted him, and sooth'd her light
> Against his pallid face: he felt the charm
> To breathlessness, and suddenly a warm
> Of his heart's blood
>
> (III. 104–07)

Endymion is pale, breathless, and feels a sudden 'warm': again, the effects of love seem to parallel those of a fever. 'Feverous' is a word Keats uses elsewhere in his poetry, and always with precision: in *Isabella* the heroine's old nurse wonders at her demeanour when they are on their way to the forest and Lorenzo's grave – 'What feverous hectic flame / Burns in thee, child?' (348–49); while in *The Eve of St Agnes* Porphyro's heart is described as 'Love's fev'rous citadel' (84). Both Isabella and Porphyro are possessed by passion, like a 'citadel' or stronghold that is afflicted by fever and thus besieged from within its walls. In *Hyperion* the fallen Titans likewise experience a kind of dreadful quarantine, 'Dungeon'd in opaque element' (II. 23), and 'Without a motion, save of their big hearts / ... horribly convuls'd / With sanguine feverous boiling gurge of pulse' (II. 26–28).[34] Deposed and vanquished, these Titans are imprisoned in close confinement, implying feverish conditions of heat. External conditions, such as extreme heat, can affect physiology, as Keats knew: Cooper had informed him that 'Heat readily increases the Pulse – the warm bath will elevate the Pulse to 120' – an observation powerfully amplified in Keats' 'boiling gurge of pulse'.[35]

34 A 'gurge' is a whirlpool, with the verb 'to gurge' meaning 'to make a whirlpool'. 'Gurging' is the adjectival form. See 'gurge, v.', *OED*.

35 JKMN, Ff1r.

Endymion's debility is also revealed by passages where he appears so deeply transported by emotion that his senses fail. A vision sends him into a frenzy – 'At this with madden'd stare, / And lifted hands, and trembling lips he stood' (II. 195–96) – following which he apparently faints, only regaining consciousness after almost a hundred lines of poetry (at II. 282–83). Immediately thereafter, interspersed within a long soliloquy, Endymion describes his symptoms: 'Within my breast there lives a choking flame' (II. 317); 'A homeward fever parches up my tongue' (II. 319); 'Upon my ear a noisy nothing rings' (II. 321); and 'Before mine eyes thick films and shadows float' (II. 323). In his medical Notebook, Keats had noted down in his marginalia for 'Lect^r. 1^st': 'The Organs of Sense are 5 Feeling, Sight, Hearing, Smell, Taste'.[36] Endymion's self-diagnosis suggests that all his senses, except for smell, are affected. He is unable to see properly, his hearing is deranged, his mouth is hot and dry: these too are feverish symptoms. The phrase 'Upon my ears a noisy nothing rings' is particularly intriguing: Endymion hears 'nothing', yet his ear is 'noisy' and 'rings'. Cooper's lecture had supplied an explanation: 'If there be in Fever a determination of Blood to the Head', what Keats called the 'gurge' of increased pulsation in blood vessels will generate a ringing sensation in the ears.[37]

Endymion's pulse is registered elsewhere in the poem, as Diana notices:

> 'Endymion! dearest! Ah, unhappy me!
> His soul will 'scape us – O felicity!
> How he does love me! His poor temples beat
> To the very tune of love – how sweet, sweet, sweet.
> Revive, dear youth, or I shall faint and die …'
> (II. 762–66)

Diana notes the pulsation of arteries across Endymion's temples: either the frontal branch of the superficial temporal artery (at the side of the temples), or the supraorbital artery, or the supratrochlear artery (both of which traverse the forehead). All three are sufficiently large to provide a pulse point, and sufficiently close to the skin to be visible. That she says his 'poor temples beat' suggests, however, that

36 JKMN, Ff2r.
37 JKMN, Ff1r.

she is looking at the superficial temporal artery, since that is at the temple. From Cooper's lectures, Keats knew that 'Arteriotomy is principally performed on the temporal Artery. It is done by making an oblique incision over the Artery and puncturing its Coats.'[38] Keats' last operation – he told Charles Brown – 'was the opening of a man's temporal artery'.[39] He assured Brown that 'the muse had no influence over him in his determination [to quit medicine], he being compelled, by conscientious motives alone, to quit the profession, upon discovering that he was unfit to perform a surgical operation.'[40] Keats' conscientious motives for laying down his lancet may reflect his awareness that to identify too closely with his patients or their injuries – 'the ball had pierced the lobe of her ear, taken a direction along the occiput, and lodged in the neck' – may not be in his patients' best interests, or his own: excessive sympathy may interfere with rational judgement, and in the doctor–patient relationship that can have fatal consequences.[41]

Once again, it is Astley Cooper's medical lectures, through the notes in Keats' medical Notebook, that allows us to understand the symptoms and physiology of Endymion's passion. Diana suggests that, if he does not revive, she – though a goddess, and more than human – will succumb in the same way. Thus there is an intriguing suggestion of reciprocity or mutual sympathizing in their disorder. 'Sympathy. By this the Vital Principle is chiefly supported. The function of breathing is a sympathetic action.'[42] Keats' notes concern the operation of sympathy within a single living organism, where a number of muscles, arteries, nerves, and other physiological structures work to concert a single action, such as breathing; what Diana suggests is a sort of reciprocal sympathy – or conspiracy – between two beings, so that the ill-health of one threatens to affect the other physically, to make her feel she must 'faint and die' if he does not revive.[43] John Hunter had documented cases where the

38 JKMN, Ff1r.

39 Brown, *Life*, 43.

40 Brown, *Life*, 43.

41 *Morning Chronicle* (23 April 1816): 3.

42 JKMN, Bf5r.

43 'conspiracy, n.', *OED*. The word 'conspiracy' derives from Latin 'conspirare': 'to breathe together'. *OED* lists 'Union or combination (of persons or things) for one end or purpose; harmonious action or effort … (In a good or neutral

patients believed their own thoughts and sensations were those of bystanders, and James Curry, who taught Keats at Guy's, noted that 'in extreme cases, patients feel "sympathy between different persons"'.[44] Something of this nature appears to be afflicting Diana, for her discomfort is caused not by physiological disorder but by what Keats and Cooper describe as 'nervous', and what would now, following Coleridge, be called 'psychosomatic'.[45] Sufficiently revived by Diana to reciprocate her 'Entranced vows and tears' (II. 827), Endymion falls asleep, from which he awakes alone, having 'swoon'd / Drunken from pleasure's nipple' (II. 868–69), thus confirming the impression that Endymion is overcome by his passion to the point where he loses his senses. As Christopher Ricks observed, 'swoon'd' is particularly apt in this passage because 'a baby *does* swoon from the nipple, its eyelids waver and then it is received into a full intoxication.'[46] The immediate association of 'swoon'd / ... from ... nipple' with a helpless babe at the breast adds to the sense of Endymion's debility: it is as if he has regressed to a state of passive infant dependency. Even in the final scene of the poem, Endymion is found kneeling 'Before his goddess, in a blissful swoon' (IV. 999). Diana appears to have the ability to reduce her beloved to a state where his ability to stay awake, aware, and conscious is as fragile as a new-born infant's. In this regression, perhaps the poem's hero reflects a quality that Keats acknowledged in his 'Preface' to the 'youngster' *Endymion*: 'there is a space of life between, in which the soul is in a ferment, the character undecided, the way of life uncertain, the ambition thick-sighted: thence proceeds mawkishness, and all the thousand bitters which ... [one] must necessarily taste in going over the following pages'.[47] By this account, *Endymion* is an immature poem, in terms of both its author's skill and its narrative: it is 'a feverish attempt, rather than a

sense)' as one of its possible meanings, though it notes that this sense is now obsolete or archaic.

44 *PP*, 155.

45 JKMN, Bf5r: 'In diseases Medical Men guess, if they cannot ascertain a disease they call it nervous'; 'psychosomatic, adj.', *OED*. One meaning listed for 'psychosomatic' is 'involving or depending on both the mind and body': *OED* credits S. T. Coleridge with first usage '*a*1834'.

46 Ricks, *Embarrassment*, 106.

47 *Poems*, 102–03.

deed accomplished'.[48] The poem's critics also picked up the terms Keats himself used to register the 'feverish' ineffectuality of the poem.

The 'space of life' to which Keats refers is usually taken to mean adolescence, although the 'ferment' might also describe Keats' fraught attempts to get the poem underway:

> I went to the Isle of Wight – thought so much about Poetry so long together that I could not get to sleep at night – and moreover, I know not how it was, I could not get wholesome food – By this means in a Week or so I became not over capable in my upper Stories, and set off pell mell for Margate, at least 150 Miles.[49]

Despite its comic tone, this passage describes a crisis, a situation in which Keats was unable to sleep or eat, resulting in him becoming 'not over capable'. Presumably, Keats meant that his thinking was muddled and irrational; but is it also possible that he was referring to a more physiological symptom? Could Keats, who was not eating enough (it is not clear that he was eating at all), have been feeling dizzy or faint during this period when he lacked rest and food? Fainting – episodes of which are referred to as 'syncope' in medical terminology – is a non-specific symptom caused by any number of factors and bodily mechanisms, but is ultimately the result of the brain either briefly losing, or believing that it has lost, adequate blood supply. Prolonged lack of food, resulting in abnormally low blood sugar levels, is one of the triggers that can trick the body into believing the brain has lost vascular supply, setting in motion a sequence of physiological responses that result in a fainting fit. Whether or not Keats suffered episodes of fainting in the Isle of Wight, lack of food would have made him feel weak, probably dizzy. He also could not sleep, because he thought too much about 'Poetry'. The shepherd–hero of *Endymion* is also a young man 'not over capable' who – though he can fall asleep – can get no restful sleep. This is not to suggest that Diana in the poem is some simple representation of Keats' fixation with 'Poetry', or that *Endymion* grew solely or wholly out of Keats' distress on the Isle of Wight; but it is not impossible that Keats' debility, experienced at first hand, allowed him imaginative access to Endymion's.

48 *Poems*, 102.
49 *LJK*, I, 138.

Keats' medical Notebook does not specifically mention fainting or loss of consciousness. He does note during a discussion of arteries: 'In some parts they take a tortuous course as in the lips, the Brain. The principal use of this is to slacken the force of the Circulation which especially in the brain necessary – which is farther guarded against by their passing through foramina'.[50] Modern medicine agrees that one of the reasons for the peculiar vascular structure in the brain is the necessity of having extensive penetration of an oxygen-rich supply of blood into the soft tissue, because brain cells suffer more and die faster from hypoxia than other body cells with a lower metabolic rate, as well as to slow and control blood flow in that area.[51] This means, however, that the brain is particularly susceptible to changes in blood pressure, the symptoms of which include fainting or, when less severe, dizziness.[52] When Endymion is not swooning, he is dizzy. His first dream-vision is heralded by a fit of dizziness – 'Thus on I thought, / Until my head was dizzy and distraught' (I. 564–65) – and culminates in a swoon after his encounter with Diana. The same pattern is followed in his second encounter with her: 'I do think the bars / That kept my spirit in are burst – that I / Am sailing with thee through the dizzy sky!' (II. 185–87). If the sky is perceived by Endymion to be 'dizzy', the implication is that Endymion is feeling dizzy, and transferring this physiological sensation to the sky. This fit of dizziness leads into a swoon (II. 195–200), and when he regains consciousness he is once again alone (II. 282–83) – thus replicating the sequence of his first meeting with the moon goddess. He also becomes dizzy at Neptune's palace and faints 'At Neptune's feet' (III. 1013). Keats did not read *The Anatomy of Melancholy* until

50 JKMN, Ff4r. 'Foramina' is the plural of 'foramen': an opening or orifice, usually in bone and allowing passage.

51 John E. Hall, 'Chapter 62: Cerebral Blood Flow, Cerebrospinal Fluid, and Brain Metabolism', *Guyton and Hall Textbook of Medical Physiology*, 13th ed. (Philadelphia, PA: Elsevier, 2016).

52 Change in blood pressure does not directly affect cerebral blood flow: cerebral blood flow is always maintained at a constant *despite* fluctuation in blood pressure. However, in cases of extreme fluctuation of pressure, the sympathetic nervous system (which controls the body's involuntary, acute stress response) intervenes to control blood flow, either by constricting or dilating the arteries and capillaries in the brain. These actions of the sympathetic nervous system render the brain peculiarly sensitive to fluctuations in blood pressure. See Hall, 'Chapter 62', for more.

after the publication of *Endymion*, but when he did so he would find Burton closely interested in the physiology of 'love-melancholy'.[53] Symptoms of 'love-melancholy', according to Burton, include altered pulse (it speeds up when the beloved is near), palpitations, and an inability to sleep.[54] Writing specifically of Venus and Adonis and 'the Moon with Endymion', he cites their inability to stop kissing: 'They cannot, I say, contain themselves, they will be still not only joining hands, kissing, but embracing, treading on their toes, etc., diving into their bosoms, and that *libenter, et cum delectatione*.'[55] Moreover, they 'cannot look off from whom they love, they will *impregnare eam ipsis oculis*, deflower her with their eyes, be still gazing, staring, stealing faces, smiling, glancing at her, as … the Moon on her Endymion'.[56] Keats' Endymion and Diana do spend a lot of the poem kissing, looking, and dreaming – and, as Byron grumpily observed, not doing much else.[57] Burton concluded 'there is no end of love's symptoms, 'tis a bottomless pit'.[58]

Nor is Endymion the only character in the poem to suffer some form of 'love-melancholy'. Both Peona and the Indian Maid (a human incarnation of Diana) are rendered dizzy with shock when Endymion sends them away, planning to spend his life as a hermit: 'Whereat those maidens, with wild stare, / Walk'd dizzily away' (IV. 903–04). And divine Diana, as Burton pointed out, is affected too: Venus claims to discern subtle signs that she is not at ease: 'an idle tongue, / A humid eye, and steps luxurious, / Where these are

53 Gittings believes Keats started reading Burton during winter 1818/19, but Ward argues for a date in June 1819. Janice Sinson, in an essay surveying Burton's influence upon Keats, posits April 1819 for Keats' first reading. See *JK*, 269–70; Ward, *Making of a Poet*, 289; and Janice Sinson, *John Keats and The Anatomy of Melancholy* (London: Published by the Keats-Shelley Memorial Association, 1971).

54 Robert Burton, *The Anatomy of Melancholy, What it is: With all the Kinds, Causes, Symptomes, Prognostickes, and Several Cures of It. In Three Maine Partitions with their several Sections, Members, and Subsections. Philosophically, Medicinally, Historically, Opened and Cut Up*, ed. Holbrook Jackson (1621; London: J. M. Dent and Sons, 1978), Part III, Sect. 2, Mem. 3: 135–36.

55 Burton, *Anatomy of Melancholy*, Part III, Sect. 2, Mem. 3: 138.

56 Burton, *Anatomy of Melancholy*, Part III, Sect. 2, Mem. 3: 138–39.

57 Byron complained in a letter to John Murray dated 9 September 1820 that Keats' writing 'is a sort of mental masturbation'. See *CH*, 129.

58 Burton, *Anatomy of Melancholy*, Part III, Sect. 2, Mem. 3: 184.

new and strange, are ominous' (III. 909–11). Diana's symptoms resemble Endymion's, but are less severe and better hidden: she, too, is restless and absent-minded; her 'humid eye' suggests she is more emotional than is usual for her. Although the emotional and psychological pressures do not manifest in physiological symptoms of the same order as Endymion's, she is not unaffected either.

Even the poet–narrator is not immune, and in the proem to Book III the sight of the moon is enough to cause 'palpitations': 'O Moon! The oldest shades 'mong oldest trees / Feel palpitations when thou lookest in' (III. 52–53). Lemprière's entry on Diana noted that, although 'she was the patroness of chastity, yet she forgot her dignity to enjoy the company of Endymion, and the very familiar favors which, according to mythology, she granted to Pan and Orion are well known.'[59] Keats need not have relied on medical training to know that sexual excitement causes the heart to race. Nevertheless, the word 'palpitations' *is* medically specific: it refers to the 'throbbing, quivering, or contraction' of a body part, and specifically to 'perceptibly fast, strong, or irregular beating of the heart' or an 'instance' of the same.[60]

## Critics' Diagnoses

This ambience of fever and feverishness permeates *Endymion* so thoroughly, and at so many semantic levels, that Peter George Patmore, in an insightful review of the poem published in the *London Magazine* in 1820, described it as 'not a *poem* at all. It is an ecstatic dream of poetry – a flush – a fever – a burning light – .'[61] In describing the poem thus he echoes and elucidates Keats' own description, in the published 'Preface', of *Endymion* as 'a feverish attempt'; other criticism of the work also responded to this issue.[62] John Wilson Croker, in *The Quarterly Review*, noted that 'Mr. Keats ... deprecates criticism on this "immature and feverish work" in terms which are themselves sufficiently feverish.'[63] In the fourth

59 Lemprière, *Classical Dictionary* [unpaginated].
60 'palpitation, n.', *OED*.
61 *CH*, 136.
62 *Poems*, 102.
63 *CH*, 112.

essay on the 'Cockney School of Poetry' John Gibson Lockhart played maliciously but cleverly on the fact that Keats had qualified as an apothecary. Lockhart's criticism was more focused on class and politics than literary merit, and the review is riddled with medical references, intended to point to the poet's middle-class origins and remind readers (and Keats himself) that 'It is a better and a wiser thing to be a starved apothecary than a starved poet.'[64] Of *Endymion*, Lockhart writes:

> The old story of the moon falling in love with a shepherd, so prettily told by a Roman Classic, and so exquisitely enlarged and adorned by one of the most elegant of German poets, has been seized upon by Mr. John Keats, to be done with as might seem good unto the sickly fancy of one who never read a single line either of Ovid or of Wieland. ... His Endymion is not a Greek shepherd, loved by a Grecian goddess; he is merely a young Cockney rhymester, dreaming a phantastic dream at the full of the moon.[65]

It is 'sickly fancy' that links Keats as 'starved apothecary' with Keats the 'starved poet' and projects the 'Cockney rhymester' as a swooning 'Greek shepherd'. Meanwhile, in 1820, Lord Byron wrote privately to John Murray about Keats 'viciously soliciting his own ideas into a state, which is neither poetry nor any thing else but a Bedlam vision produced by raw pork and opium'.[66] Except for Patmore, all these writers are hostile to Keats, yet their insights are not worthless. All respond to what Byron termed 'Bedlam vision' and an uneasy sense that the poem itself is overwrought and 'viciously solicited'.

In addition to complaining about the 'feverishness' of Keats' poem, Croker in the *Quarterly* was also discomfited by a sense that it was driven forward by an apparently uncontrolled proliferation of rhyme:

> [The poet] seems to us to write a line at random, and then he follows not the thought excited by this line, but that suggested by the *rhyme* with which it concludes. There is hardly a complete

64 Lockhart, 'Cockney ... IV', 524.

65 Lockhart, 'Cockney ... IV', 521–22.

66 *CH*, 129.

> couplet inclosing a complete idea in the whole book. He wanders from one subject to another, from the association, not of ideas but of sounds.[67]

Francis Jeffrey, reviewing *Endymion* and Keats' 1820 volume in *The Edinburgh Review* in August 1820, echoed this criticism, showing that Keats' rhymes were a genuine source of puzzlement and unease for contemporary reviewers, irrespective of their political views:

> It seems as if the author had ventured everything that occurred to him in the shape of a glittering image or striking expression – taken the first word that presented itself to make up a rhyme, and then made that word the germ of a new cluster of images – a hint for a new excursion of fancy – and so wandered on, equally forgetful whence he came, and heedless whither he was going, till he had covered his pages with an interminable arabesque of connected and incongruous figures, that multiplied as they extended, and were only harmonized by the brightness of their tints, and the graces of their forms.[68]

Jeffrey's word 'germ' is suggestive. The *Oxford English Dictionary* notes that the word has many meanings. Relevant here are the senses: 'an initial stage or state from which something may develop; a source, a beginning'; 'a seed'; 'the primordium of a part of the body'; as well as 'the causative agent or source of a disease' – a meaning that has been traced back to 1700.[69] Almost all of *Endymion*'s early readers recorded their distress at the poem's seemingly rampant rhymes. Shelley, for example, ruefully noted: 'much praise is due to me for having read, the Authors [*sic*] intention appearing to be that no person should possibly get to the end of it.'[70] Keats' intention to provide readers with 'a little Region [of poetry] to wander in' had been subverted by his rhymes; the poem's self-proliferation overwhelmed its narrative form.[71] *Endymion*'s expanse of loose heroic couplets contributed to the almost universal impression that

67 *CH*, 112.
68 *CH*, 203.
69 'germ, n.', *OED*.
70 *CH*, 123.
71 *LJK*, I, 170.

the poem was 'feverish' and 'overwrought' – literally and figuratively dis-eased – an opinion apparently shared by Keats, judging by his description of the work as a 'feverish attempt', the product of a 'soul in ferment'.

## 'Perfectly Interfused': Embodying Emotion

Keats' skill in conveying his characters' emotional states through anatomically precise descriptions of their physical frame is on display throughout *Endymion*. A few examples will demonstrate how this applies as much to minor characters – including those imported via allusion and metaphor – as it does to the lovers. Immediately after the 'Hymn to Pan' in Book I, Keats describes Niobe:

> Perhaps, the trembling knee
> And frantic gape of lonely Niobe,
> Poor, lonely Niobe! when her lovely young
> Were dead and gone, and her caressing tongue
> Lay a lost thing upon her paly lip,
> And very, very deadliness did nip
> Her motherly cheeks.
>
> (I. 337–43)

Christopher Ricks cited this description as an instance where the physicality of Keats' poetry renders it rich with embarrassment; I propose to focus on the physicality of the poetry and how its effects are achieved.[72] The similarities between the physical manifestations of Niobe's sorrow and Keats' description of the fallen Titans in *Hyperion* – 'still upon the flint / He ground severe his skull, with open mouth / And eyes at horrid working' (II. 50–52) – suggests that Keats was drawing upon a common source for these images of deranged grief. It has been suggested that Cottus may recall childhood glimpses of Caius Cibber's statue of 'Melancholy Madness' outside Bedlam; the same may also apply to Niobe and, thus, explain Byron's knowing aside about a 'Bedlam vision'.[73] However, Keats' medical career

72 Ricks, *Embarrassment*, 8–10.

73 Richard Marggraf Turley, *Bright Stars: John Keats, 'Barry Cornwall' and Romantic Literary Culture* (Liverpool: Liverpool University Press, 2009), 145.

would also have afforded opportunities to observe 'mad' people: Guy's had a ward dedicated to patients with mental problems and/ or terminal illnesses.[74] These patients would have been under Keats' care during the weeks when he was duty dresser. Niobe's helpless despair is depicted with diagnostic precision: her knee 'trembles'; her lip is 'paly'; her cheeks are colourless ('deadliness did nip'). Her mouth is open in 'frantic gape', indicating that her mouth is not just limply open but working – opening and shutting a little, almost of its own volition – as she grieves; while her tongue lies like 'a lost thing' against her lips, suggesting an absolute absence of volition, self-possession, or speech. Her reaction, in fact, suggests extreme shock, a state in which all self-possession has been lost: the control of her facial muscles abandoned in her paroxysms of grief. In his medical Notebook, in a discussion of the nervous system, Keats noted how nerves conveyed 'Sensation' from 'the Extremities ... to the Brain', and also controlled muscle movement, termed 'volition', which could be voluntary or involuntary; the latter class includes, in Keats' terms, 'sympathy'.[75] However, these involuntary 'sympathetic' actions could often be 'disordered in function', although 'anatomy cannot discover a corresponding breach of Structure'.[76] This is the case with Niobe: her facial expression suggests derangement, yet she has no disease or physical deformity. Keats notes a case study of 'a Gentleman who had lost sensation and yet had powers of Volition', of whom 'it was observed that he could grasp and hold a substance while his whole attention was directed thereto, but on his turning to a fresh occupation the substance dropped'.[77] Niobe's extreme grief has so far distanced her from normal physiological and psychological functioning that – like the gentleman who could only grasp objects while wholly focused – she has lost control over her musculature. *Endymion* demonstrates Keats' extraordinary ability to indicate extreme mental, psychological, or emotional distress through anatomical descriptions and proves James Russell Lowell's observation that 'in [Keats] the moral seems to have so perfectly interfused the physical man, that you might almost say he could feel sorrow with his hands.'[78]

74 Cameron, *Mr. Guy's Hospital*, 40–48.
75 JKMN, Bf4v, Bf5r.
76 JKMN, Bf4v, Bf5r.
77 JKMN, Bf4v, Bf5r.
78 *CH*, 360.

The depiction of Niobe is an early example of the skill in conveying emotion through precise anatomical description that informs Keats' mature poetry.

Sometimes Keats uses precise anatomical descriptions to reflect the observer's emotional state and involvement. The serried ranks of the comatose lovers in Glaucus' Cave are precisely pictured:

> So in that crystal palace, in silent rows,
> Poor lovers lay at rest from joys and woes. –
> The stranger from the mountains, breathless, trac'd
> Such thousands of shut eyes in order place'd:
> Such ranges of white feet, and patient lips
> All ruddy, – for here death no blossom nips.
> He mark'd their brows and foreheads; saw their hair
> Put sleekly to one side with nicest care;
> And each one's gentle wrist, with reverence,
> Put cross-wise to its heart.
>
> (III. 735–44)

Endymion's observation is finely poised between sympathetic involvement and detached inspection: though the lovers look dead, he notes that their colouring indicates that they are still alive. There is also the awareness, carefully conveyed, that the lovers have been 'plac'd' in position, much as one would place a dead body. Their eyes have been closed, their hair brushed back from their faces, their wrists carefully arranged upon their chests: rows of bodies, laid out with care as they would be in a mortuary, but with one important difference – these are not dead bodies. The language used brings this out: the wrists, though 'put cross-wise to [the] heart' in a posture mimicking the dead, are 'gentle', not stiffened by rigor mortis but soft as is live (sleeping) flesh. As Nicholas Roe observed, '"Gentle wrists" is the choice of a poet who knew how to feel for a patient's pulse.'[79] Endymion cannot lay claim to clinical detachment, but Keats knew that even trained medical professionals could struggle with that: Brown recollected Keats describing his 'overwrought apprehension of every possible chance of doing evil' while performing his 'last operation'.[80]

79 Roe, *Dissent*, 194.
80 Brown, *Life*, 43.

## 'Physician to all men': The Ethics of Healing

Romantic practitioners of medicine were deeply concerned with the ethics of their profession, as shown by the sudden proliferation of a variety of texts – studies dealing specifically with the subject; conduct treatises by well-known practitioners; handbooks aimed at prospective medical students; and pamphlets on staff manners published by the teaching hospitals – discussing the issue. John Gregory's *Observations on the Duties and Offices of a Physician and on the Method of Prosecuting Enquiries in Philosophy*, published in 1770 and issued in a revised edition entitled *Lectures on the Duties and Qualifications of a Physician* two years later, was made required reading in many of the major British teaching hospitals, alongside Thomas Percival's *Medical Ethics: or A Code of Institutes and Precepts Adapted to the Professional Conduct of Physicians and Surgeons* (1803).[81] The numerous reprints these works enjoyed over the next few decades offers a sense of the seriousness with which the subject was taken in the early nineteenth century.

Gregory, whose book has been described as 'the first philosophical, secular medical ethics in the English language', exemplified and shared in the consensus opinion that stressed the personal responsibility of the medical practitioner and his comprehensive knowledge of all branches of medicine as the foundational basis of ethical practice.[82] He wrote that

> The chief of [the moral qualities] is humanity; that sensibility of heart which makes us feel for the distresses of our fellow-creatures, and which of consequence incites us in the most powerful manner to relieve them. ... Sympathy naturally engages the affection and confidence of a patient, which in many cases is of the utmost consequence in his recovery.[83]

81 *RMJK*, 36.

82 Paul Lawrence, 'Gregory [Gregorie], John (1724–1773)', *ODNB*; Lawrence B. McCullough, *John Gregory and the Invention of Professional Medical Ethics and the Profession of Medicine* (Dordrecht: Kluwer Academic Publishers, 1998), 6.

83 John Gregory, *Lectures on the Duties and Qualifications of a Physician* (London: W. Strahan and T. Cadell, 1772), 19.

A bedside manner that reflected a sympathetic recognition of the trials and tribulations of ill health and consequent suffering – Gregory borrowed from Shakespeare in describing it as possessing 'the milk of human kindness' – was considered an essential attribute.[84] According to Gregory, 'besides the qualifications of a proper education', a physician required 'a penetrating genius, and a clear solid judgement' as well as 'a quickness of apprehension' to succeed in his chosen profession; and he also noted that '[i]t is a physician's duty to do every thing that is not criminal, to save the life of his patient, and to search for remedies from every source, and from every hand, however mean and contemptible.'[85] Distinguishing between physicians and surgeons, Gregory noted that '[t]he separation of physic from surgery in modern times, has been productive of the worst consequences':[86]

> In Great Britain, surgery is a liberal profession. In many parts of it, surgeons and apothecaries are the physicians in ordinary to most families, for which trust they are often well qualified by their education and knowledge; and a physician is only called where a case is difficult, or attended with danger. There are certain limits, however, between the two professions, which ought to be attended to, as they are established by the customs of the country, and the rules of their several societies.[87]

Keats, of course, qualified as an apothecary and undertook training that would have enabled him to sit the examination for membership of the Royal College of Surgeons (a step he never got around to taking).[88] It is likely, therefore, that in addition to such standard set texts as Gregory's *Duties* and Percival's *Ethics*, he would also have been aware of ethical and conduct advice aimed specifically at surgeon's pupils. First published in August 1816, when Keats was still associated with Guy's, with a second edition appearing in 1818, *Oracular Communications* can help us gauge the ethical and conduct

84 Gregory, *Lectures*, 19.
85 Gregory, *Lectures*, 16, 39.
86 Gregory, *Lectures*, 44.
87 Gregory, *Lectures*, 50.
88 Campbell, *London Tradesman*, 65–66 describes how, already in the eighteenth century, apothecaries were increasingly taking on duties traditionally ascribed to surgeons or physicians.

advice being offered specifically to surgical students. We can't be certain that Keats knew this book, but – as R. S. White notes – 'the likelihood is high. The most cautious statement we can make is that it gives no more and no less than an unrivalled glimpse of the kind of life, ethos and ideas which Keats would certainly have encountered at Guy's.'[89] This publication, therefore, may help us reconstruct the *kind* of things that Keats, in his specific subject-position as a surgeon's pupil and dresser at Guy's Hospital, was told about medical ethics and expected conduct. Considered in this light, how does it compare to Gregory's *Duties*?

*Oracular Communications* states, unequivocally, that 'no ordinary character is adequate to an office so important' as that of a medical practitioner, and defines 'rectitude of principle, benevolence of disposition and unwearied diligence' as the 'necessary properties of the professional character'.[90] It points out the advantages of gaining the confidence of the patient and suggests this should be attempted by the exercise of 'sympathy, and by that conduct which is prompted by the recollection, that [the] patient is a rational being in a state of suffering'.[91] Particular stress is laid on the importance of extensive medical knowledge: 'All knowledge will be of use to him: and he should not despise any acquisition which will render him at all more fitted for the practice of his profession.'[92] At all times, the paramount consideration governing medical treatment should be the welfare of the patient: '*To do good* is the object you have in view' (italics in original).[93] To this end, '[t]he value of the two sciences [of surgery and internal medicine] must be estimated ... by the positive alleviation afforded.'[94] Thus we see that, in essentials, the advice offered by *Oracular Communications* to surgical pupils at Guy's in well in line with Gregory's *Duties ... of a Physician*.

In Book I of *Endymion*, Peona alone can comfort and succour her ailing brother:

89 White, 'Like Esculapius of Old', 17.

90 Æsculapius, *Oracular Communications*, 11, 12.

91 Æsculapius, *Oracular Communications*, 75.

92 Æsculapius, *Oracular Communications*, 23. Additionally fluency in Greek, Latin, and the modern European languages (particularly French and German) is recommended.

93 Æsculapius, *Oracular Communications*, 78.

94 Æsculapius, *Oracular Communications*, 6.

She led him, like some midnight spirit nurse
Of happy changes in emphatic dreams,
Along a path between two little streams, –
Guarding his forehead, with her round elbow,
From low-grown branches, and his footsteps slow
From stumbling over stumps and hillocks small;
(I. 413–18)

Much has been made of Peona's skill in ministering to her brother – of her ability if not to heal then at least to mitigate the symptoms of his distemper. It is evident that Peona, in her role as 'midnight spirit nurse', conducts herself in a manner that would meet the approval of Romantic texts dealing with medical ethics: she exerts herself in the care of her patient and tries to enter sympathetically into his distress. Determining that the best course of action is to let her brother rest, she accordingly leads him away from the hubbub of the festival to 'her favourite bower's quiet shade' (I. 437), taking care he not hurt himself in the walk there, and persuades him to sleep. However, as Goellnicht noted, in the original draft 'Keats made Peona's procedures in curing Endymion even more medically specific':[95]

When last the Harvesters rich armfuls took.
She tied a little bucket to a Crook,
Ran some swift paces to a dark wells side,
And in a sighing time return'd, supplied
With spar cold water; in which she did squeeze
A snowy napkin, and upon her Knees
Began to cherish her poor Brother's face;
Damping refreshfully his forehead's space,
His eyes, his Lips: then in a cupped shell
She brought him ruby wine; then let him smell,
Time after time, a precious amulet,
Which seldom took she from its cabinet.[96]

In this, first, version, after leading him to rest in the bower, Peona felt Endymion's temperature, left him, and returned with a cloth

95 *PP*, 179.
96 *Poems*, 115: Stillinger notes that 'the passage [was] marked for deletion first by Taylor in pencil and then by Keats in ink'. See also *Texts*, 149.

soaked in cold water and a cup of wine; she used the cloth to cool his forehead and made him drink the wine.[97] Her actions were in keeping with what Keats would have learnt about acceptable bedside conduct, both from standard texts such as Gregory's *Duties* and practical guidebooks such as *Oracular Communications*, but they were also informed by the practical medical knowledge he had acquired while on duty at Guy's. Keats knew that cold water will reduce a fever and lower pulse rate, and that wine is a stimulant: 'If ... a Man ... have an quick unhealthy irritable pulse, the cold bath will sooth the Pulse lowering it with respect to quickness ... Wine although stimulant gives to the Body great additional Strengt[h].'[98]

Thus, we find Keats' hospital experiences and medical lectures suffusing *Endymion*, perhaps more than he himself realized. His 'test' of whether he could 'gain [his] Living' as a poet shows how, even in this endeavour, Keats found himself reaching back towards the knowledge and training he had acquired in the pursuit of his *other* career, medicine.[99] This long poem derives much of its enduring vitality from its precise description of the physiology of passion – its medical foundations impart to it its peculiar potency. Given the intriguing possibility that *Endymion* may have taken months to mature before its actual composition, and given Keats' tendency to rework images and ideas in his poetry, perhaps it is not surprising that his next, and most famous, publication would also be replete with imagery and ideas drawn from medicine. *Lamia, Isabella, The Eve of St. Agnes, and other Poems* was published in 1820, but the poems it contained were composed through the years 1818 and 1819. In the autumn of 1818 Keats watched his brother Tom die of consumption; in 1819, casting about desperately for some means to earn money, he considered returning to medicine: to 'go to Edinburgh & study for a physician', become 'Surgeon to an I[n]diaman', or 'try what [he could] do in the Apothecary line'.[100] Even while he was writing his greatest poems, medicine was never far from Keats' mind, and his last published collection bears the marks of that preoccupation, as my final chapter will show.

97 *PP*, 179–80.
98 JKMN, Ff1r.
99 *LJK*, I, 169; *KC*, I, 307.
100 *LJK*, II, 70, 114, 298.

CHAPTER SIX

# 'The Only State for the Best Sort of Poetry'

We do not know the date on which Keats' most famous collection of poems, the 1820 volume *Lamia, Isabella, The Eve of St. Agnes, and other Poems*, was published. The publishers' 'Advertisement' in the book is dated 'June 26, 1820' – a Monday – when the *Morning Chronicle* also carried an announcement: 'Printed for Taylor and Hessey, 93, Fleet-street; of whom may be had just published, LAMIA, ISABELLA, the EVE OF ST. AGNES, and other Poems. By John Keats, Author of "Endymion."'[1] This appeared again in the *Morning Chronicle* on 30 June and 10 July, with the volume advertised as 'just published'.[2] Meanwhile, on 24 June, John Taylor had written to his father that 'Next week Keats's new Volume of Poems will be published.'[3] Reviews began to appear in July. The conjunction of advertisements, Taylor's assertion, and the reviews makes a strong case for publication in the last week of June 1820, at a time when the author was already gravely ill. However, it was not just the publication of the 1820 volume but also its composition that was dogged by the spectre of ill health: the poems were principally composed during the years 1818–19, when concerns over health and disease, the efficacy of medical intervention, and the possibility of a return to medical practice to 'gain [his] Living' were never far from Keats' mind.[4]

The first part of this chapter discusses the circumstances in

1 Advertisement, *Morning Chronicle* (16 June 1820): 2.

2 Advertisements, *Morning Chronicle* (30 June 1820): 2; and *Morning Chronicle* (10 July 1820): 2.

3 *JK*, 401.

4 *KC*, I, 307.

which Keats composed the poems that made up his 1820 volume, showing how, at every turn, questions related to health, disease, medicine, and death forced themselves upon his attention. My aim has been recuperative, revealing how the lived experiences of biography fundamentally influenced the poetry that came out of it and evaluating the extent to which these infiltrations were consciously allowed. To this end, I also analyse the publication history of the 1820 volume, the appearance of which owed much to extra-literary circumstances. In its concluding part, this chapter reads poems from the 1820 volume through the lens of contemporary medical knowledge and developments, showing how these works function as knowing interventions in current medical debates.

## Part One: The Biographical Angle

Most of the poems in the 1820 volume were composed between February 1818 and September 1819 – overlapping to a large extent with the period Robert Gittings influentially characterized as Keats' 'living year' – but for much of that time, even as he wrote his poems, Keats had no intention of publishing them. I have listed the contents of the 1820 volume by date of composition below; the poems with titles underlined were written while Keats was, fitfully, working on *Hyperion* as well, while those in italics can be dated only to the year of composition. *Lamia* appears three times, because each part was composed individually and then the whole poem revised extensively in early 1820.

Robin Hood (completed by 3 February 1818)
Lines on the Mermaid Tavern (completed by 3 February 1818)
Isabella (February–April 1818)
Hyperion, a Fragment (perhaps begun by 27 October, certainly begun by 18 December 1818; abandoned April 1819)
Fancy (completed by end 1818)
Ode ['Bards of passion'] (completed by end 1818)
The Eve of St. Agnes (January–early February 1819)
Ode to Psyche (completed by 30 April 1819)
Ode to a Nightingale (May? 1819)
*Ode on a Grecian Urn* (1819)
*Ode on Melancholy* (1819)

Lamia (Part I, completed by 11 July 1819)
Lamia (Part II, August–5 September 1819)
To Autumn (19 September 1819)
Lamia (extensively revised in March 1820)

The most striking thing, when these poems are listed by date of composition, is how very distracted Keats was when he wrote them. At no point was he settled, as when he started work on *Endymion*; they were all written while his focus was elsewhere. 'Robin Hood', 'Lines on the Mermaid Tavern', and *Isabella* were composed before *Endymion* appeared, when Keats' attention was still focused on the publication of that poem; *Hyperion* was begun as relief from nursing Tom; and the other poems were written when his own ill health, the state of his finances, and the need to 'gain a Living' (as a surgeon, journalist, or dramatist – but *not* as a poet) dominated Keats' thoughts, as we shall see below.[5]

*'Poor Tom': Illness in the Family*

For much of 1818 Keats was simply distracted. Tom Keats' illness worried his elder brothers, enough that much of their activity in the first half of the year was dictated by what would be best for him. Nor was Tom the only person in Keats' circle whose health was a source of concern: on 21 February Keats wrote to inform his brothers, who were in Teignmouth for Tom's health, that 'Reynolds has been very ill for some time – confined to the house – and had Leeches applied to the chest.'[6] Within a month he wrote to Bailey explaining why he too was now at Teignmouth: 'I had a Letter from Tom saying how much better he had got, and thinking he had better stop – I went down to prevent his coming up.'[7] The next day Keats wrote to the ill Reynolds, insisting that 'sickness' be 'cut'.[8] In his letters from Teignmouth he continually refers to Tom's health: 'Tom has been much worse: but is now getting better'; 'Tom, after a Night without a Wink of sleep, and overburdened with fever, has got up after a refreshing day sleep and is better than he has been for a long

5 *KC*, I, 307.
6 *LJK*, I, 236.
7 *LJK*, I, 241.
8 *LJK*, I, 245.

time.'[9] Though Keats himself was well while at Teignmouth, people he cared about – most importantly Tom, but also Rice and Reynolds – were not; and his exasperated diatribe in a letter to Reynolds of March 1818 reflects his preoccupation with ill health:

> I intend to cut all sick people if they do not make up their minds to cut sickness – a fellow to whom I have a complete aversion, and who strange to say is harboured and countenanced in several houses where I visit – he is sitting now quite impudent between me and Tom – He insults me at poor Jem Rice's – and you have seated him before now between us at the Theatre – where I thought he look'd with a longing eye at poor Kean. I shall say, once for all, to my friends generally and severally, cut that fellow, or I cut you.[10]

Keats personifies 'sickness', describing him as an unwanted 'fellow' who interferes in the normal intercourse he used to enjoy with his brother and friends. He complains that this character is always in the way, and recommends friends should 'cut that fellow', threatening to 'cut' his friends is they do not do so. In this context, the obvious sense of 'cutting' is the colloquial, social one: '[t]he act of "cutting" or refusing to recognise an acquaintance'.[11] For a former dresser, though, another sense of 'cutting' is also applicable in this passage: surgeons 'cut' for gall-stones and tumours, which is 'sickness' presenting itself as a physical growth within the body. Cutting for the stone was, wishfully and sometimes actually, to effect a cure; Keats, therefore, also recommends that his friends 'cut' sickness as a surgeon would 'cut' into a sick body in the operating theatre, in a quest for health.

The anxiety that amusingly marked Keats' letter quoted above also spilled over into his poetry: *Isabella*, begun while Keats was still in Hampstead but completed at Teignmouth, reveals how his circumstantial preoccupations influenced his poetic vocabulary.[12] In its opening stanzas we are told how Isabella and Lorenzo cannot 'in the self-same mansion dwell / Without some stir of heart, some malady' (3–4). Lorenzo spends his nights in 'sick longing' (23), and 'their cheeks ... [become] paler' (26). While Isabella 'Fell sick' (34),

9 *LJK*, I, 251, 276.
10 *LJK*, I, 245.
11 'cut, n.2', *OED*.
12 *Poems*, 601.

'Fell thin' (35), and 'ill' (37), Lorenzo's 'heart beat awfully against his side' (42) and he was 'Fever'd' (46) and 'very pale and dead' (53). Occasionally, even the rhymes seem to betray a preoccupation with illness: in stanza 2, the *b* rhymes for the *ottava rima* are 'still' (10), 'fill' (12), and 'rill' (14) – all three words rhyme on 'ill'. Keats wrote the poem while uncomfortably aware – and attempting to deny his awareness – that Tom's pallor, feverishness, cough, and blood spitting were symptoms of active pulmonary tuberculosis.[13] Even as he attempted to bolster Tom's spirits and his own with hopeful pronouncements from Tom's doctor, Solomon Sawrey, in his poem – perhaps without quite realizing it – the vocabulary of the sick room found expression. A comparable infiltration of 'circumstance' is also apparent in Keats' verse epistle 'Dear Reynolds', written around the same time. Keats attempted to write a cheering tale for his suffering friend, but every turn towards lightness and comedy in that poem is undercut by his sense of dread, that he has seen 'too distinct into the core / Of an eternal fierce destruction' (96–97).[14] Perhaps it is not surprising that the 'evolutionary' argument voiced by Oceanus in *Hyperion* is similar, although framed positively as a natural and inevitable progression. Keats is unlikely to have drawn consciously on 'Dear Reynolds' in writing *Hyperion*; nevertheless, such echoes of themes or ideas, reworked in different poems over a period of time, suggest the continuing tenor of his preoccupations. 'Dear Reynolds' was addressed to an ill friend, written while Keats himself was busy nursing Tom; *Hyperion* was written to distract himself while he was otherwise busy nursing Tom: the juxtaposition of these two moments of composition indicates how pervasive ill health and medicine were in Keats' life during the year 1818, and how his unhappy awareness of the transience of life and health bled into his poetry.

By May 1818 Tom wanted to return to town, and Keats himself needed to do so as he had planned to go on a walking tour to northern England and Scotland with Charles Brown. The brothers left Teignmouth on 4 May and Keats was able to send a good account from Honiton: 'My Brother has borne his Journey thus far

13 *Texts*, 182. Stillinger notes: '"the first few stanzas" [written] before Keats departed for Teignmouth on 4 March, and the rest probably late in March, after finishing work on *Endymion*, and in April; completed by 27 April'.

14 *Poems*, 600.

remarkably well' – but this did not last.[15] When Tom haemorrhaged again they were obliged to stop at Bridport, and it took them a week to get back to Well Walk on 10 May: 'Lord what a Journey I had and what a relief at the end of it – I'm sure I could not have stood it many more days.'[16] The upshot was that Keats himself felt unwell: some two weeks before he was due to leave town he wrote to Severn on 6 June: 'The Doctor says I mustn't go out.'[17] Four days later he told Bailey: 'I am not certain whether I shall be able to go my Journey on account of my Brother Tom and a little indisposition of my own.'[18] From this time onwards, with short periods of respite, Keats' own health would be a matter of continual concern.

*Medical Crises: Keats' Walking Tour and its Aftermath*

In the event, Keats did leave Hampstead on 22 June: he travelled to Liverpool with Brown and the newly married George and Georgiana Keats. At Redbourn he briefly met his fellow lodger from Guy's, Henry Stephens – now a respectable country practitioner and perhaps a reminder to Keats of the career path that he had turned his back on the previous year. Arrived in Liverpool the next day, Keats bid farewell to his brother and sister-in-law, who were emigrating to America, before taking coach for Lancaster, where the walking tour began.[19] Though Keats' letters suggest that he started the tour in good spirits and found genuine enjoyment in both the new sights and – at least initially – the physical exertion, his pleasure was coloured by his awareness that Tom had been left alone at Well Walk, and eventually overtaken by his own toothache, exhaustion, sore throat, and violent cold. Indeed, the tour finished in a doctor's surgery at Inverness, when Keats was ordered back to England because he was too ill to continue: he had literally walked himself 600 miles back into the sick room.

Keats returned to London on 17 August 1818, surprising everyone by his presence and shocking them with his appearance – 'as brown and shabby as you can imagine' – only to find himself immediately

15 *LJK*, I, 283.
16 *LJK*, I, 290.
17 *LJK*, I, 291.
18 *LJK*, I, 293.
19 *NL*, 234–36.

caught up in a medical crisis: Tom was dying.[20] With George now in America, Keats' world contracted almost entirely to the rooms in Well Walk where Tom spent his last days. He was unwell himself, and Sawrey – now treating both brothers – ordered him to stay indoors. Richard Abbey allowed Fanny Keats to visit, and she came several times through September 1818, but thereafter permission was withdrawn. His return also coincided with the appearance of the August issue of *Blackwood's Edinburgh Magazine*, containing the fourth 'Cockney School' essay about the 'Muses' son of Promise': John Keats.[21] An ingenious fabrication combining factual details about Keats with doses of political animosity, the essay mingles outright slander with genuine critical bafflement, and was apparently intended to destroy Keats' poetic career. It did not succeed – adverse reviews actually increased sales of *Endymion* – but it was unsettling for Keats at a time of great personal stress and a source for concern for his publishers.

*'The Cockney School of Poetry, No. IV'*

The main thrust of this fourth 'Cockney School' essay was to attack Keats' social class and educational background: it cited Keats' training as an apothecary as evidence that he was insufficiently educated to write poetry and developed this theme by casting its criticism in medical terms. The opening sentence of the essay set the tone: 'Of all the manias of this mad age, the most incurable, as well as the most common, seems to be no other than the *Metromanie*.'[22] 'Metromanie' is defined as '[a] mania for writing poetry', and the *Oxford English Dictionary* credits William Gifford, in *The Baviad* (1791), with first usage:

> now this pernicious pest,
> This metromania, creeps thro' every breast;
> Now fools and children void their brains by loads,
> And itching grandams spawl lascivious odes;
> (309–12).[23]

20 Quoted in *NL*, 263.
21 Lockhart, 'Cockney ... IV', 519.
22 Lockhart, 'Cockney ... IV', 519.
23 '† metromania, n.1', *OED*; William Gifford, *The Baviad, A Paraphrastic Imitation of the First Satire of Persius* (London: R. Faulder, 1791), 45.

Metromania's 'voiding' and 'spawling' of poetry is appropriately emetic in its effects. In launching his attack with this term, 'Z' signalled Keats' lack of cultural capital, aligning him with 'fools', 'children' and 'grandams'.[24] Writing poetry is represented as a disease, and the figure of the poet – Keats – as an incurable.

In casting poetry as a 'mania', 'Z' was playing on the various senses of the word: while the obvious sense in context was 'a personal obsession, compulsion, or obsessive need; excessive excitement or enthusiasm; a collective enthusiasm, usually short-lived, a "craze" or "rage"', the idea of 'mania' as 'madness, particularly of a kind characterized by uncontrollable, excited or aggressive behaviour', is also available.[25] However, 'Z' – John Gibson Lockhart, who, unlike Keats, *was* classically educated (he attended Edinburgh University and Balliol College) – knew that the word derived from classical Greek: 'mania' is madness, and, for the Greeks, it could be divinely inspired. The best-known classical treatment of 'mania' is Plato's dialogue *Phaedrus*, in which Socrates cites four kinds of sacred 'mania': the madness of prophecy, a gift of Apollo; the madness of poetry, inspired by the Muses; the madness of mysticism, sacred to Dionysus; and the madness of love, consecrated to Aphrodite and her son Eros. The stereotype of the 'mad' poet had long entered popular consciousness, as Keats knew from reading Shakespeare and Milton, and recent instances of 'mad poets' included Collins, Cowper, Chatterton, and – some said – Lord Byron, while William Blake had recently been noticed as 'an unfortunate lunatic' in *The Examiner*.[26] In describing Keats' poetry as symptomatic of a 'malady', 'Z' combines the idea of contagion (poetry as an infection) with insanity: poetry is an infectious disease that manifests as a modern, secular 'mania' – a 'spawling' effusion with no trace of divine inspiration.

24 The term is Pierre Bourdieu's: John Guillory applied it to the processes of canon-formation in *Cultural Capital: The Problem of Literary Canon Formation* (Chicago, IL/London: University of Chicago Press, 1993). Marjorie Levinson did not use the term, but in *Life of Allegory* she interprets Keats' career in terms of his lack of cultural capital.

25 'mania, n.', *OED*.

26 See Plato, *Symposium and Phaedrus*, trans. Tom Griffith (New York/London: Alfred A. Knopf, 2000), 143 (ff.259b–d), 118 (ff.244b). Keats would have known about Plato and Platonic thought from Lemprière, who has a long entry on the philosopher: see *Classical Dictionary* [unpaginated]. For Blake, see *The Examiner* (17 September 1809): 605.

'Z' then utilizes his knowledge of Keats' life history to turn this notion on its head: while John Keats *the poet* is diseased, a different course of life had been open to him:

> His friends, we understand, destined him to the career of medicine; and he was bound apprentice some years ago to a worthy apothecary in town. But all has been undone by a sudden attack of the malady to which we have alluded. Whether Mr John had been sent home with a diuretic or composing draught to some patient far gone in the poetical mania, we have not heard. This much is certain, that he has caught the infection, and that thoroughly. For some time we were in hopes, that he might get off with a violent fit or two; but of late the symptoms are terrible.[27]

'Z' thus casts himself as a kind of Keatsian double – a sympathetic but alarmed observer whose medical understanding of 'malady' should rightly have been Keats'. The essay surveys Keats' supposed lack of education, political sympathies, friendship with Hunt and Haydon, and poetic style, before closing with this advice:

> It is a better and wiser thing to be a starved apothecary than a starved poet; so back to the shop Mr John, back to 'plasters, pills, and ointment boxes,' &c. But, for Heaven's sake, young Sangrado, be a little more sparing of extenuatives and soporifics in your practice than you have been in your poetry.[28]

The slighting reference to 'Mr. John' is typical of the essay's tone: its objective was to question Keats' right to compose poetry, presenting his efforts in terms of contagion and madness. Keats' social background was the principal drawback: he was of the middling classes and, instead of being classically educated, had trained as an apothecary. Apparently, too, he was not alone in his literary aspirations: *Oracular Communications* described medical practitioners as 'the … *literati* of the age'.[29] To 'Z''s dismay, the 'Muses' son of Promise' was one of many: Henry Stephens had literary inclinations; Robert Southey had studied anatomy; and so had Percy

27 Lockhart, 'Cockney … IV', 519.
28 Lockhart, 'Cockney … IV', 524.
29 Æsculapius, *Oracular Communications*, 10.

Bysshe Shelley.[30] Published after this and other attacks in the press, the 1820 volume challenges 'Z''s claims, and, as I shall argue, some of its poems deliberately cast back to the time when 'Mr. John' had been at Guy's Hospital, and knowingly reflect on matters of contemporary medical debate.

*Besieged by Circumstances: September–December 1818*

James Hessey, concerned about Keats' reaction to the *Blackwood's* essay, hosted a dinner party on 14 September where, in addition to Keats, Hazlitt and Richard Woodhouse were present.[31] Keats was apparently in good humour, and Hessey wrote to reassure Taylor:

> Keats was in good spirits ... He does not seem to care at all about Blackwood, he thinks it so poorly done, and as he does not mean to publish any thing more at present he says it affects him less. – He is studying closely, recovering his Latin, going to learn Greek, and seems altogether more rational than usual – but he is such a man of fits and starts he is not much to be depended upon. Still he thinks of nothing but poetry as his being's end and aim, and sometime or other he will I doubt not, do something valuable.[32]

Note that at this point, in September 1818, Keats has made known to his publishers that he does not intend to publish anything.

Keats left Tom's sickroom again a few days later to call on the Reynolds family, where he met their cousin Jane Cox. She made an impression – her shape and voice 'haunted' him – but this distraction soon passed.[33] Back at Well Walk, he wrote to tell Dilke on 21 September that his 'throat has become worse after getting well, and I am determined to stop at home till I am quite well'.[34] Stopping at home, however, proved not to be an option:

30 In his 1847 letter to George Felton Mathew, Stephens stated that he had 'a taste & liking for Poetry' himself. He recollected: 'Sometimes I ventured to show [Keats] some lines which I had written, but I always had the mortification, of hearing them—condemned'. See *KC*, II, 209.

31 *LJK*, I, 368, 380.

32 Blunden, *Publisher*, 56.

33 *LJK*, I, 370.

34 *LJK*, I, 368.

> [Tom's] identity presses upon me so all day that I am obliged to go out – and although I intended to have given some time to study alone I am obliged to write, and plunge into abstract images to ease myself of his countenance his voice and feebleness – so that I live now in a continual fever – it must be poisonous to life although I feel well. Imagine 'the hateful siege of contraries' – if I think of fame of poetry it seems a crime to me, and yet I must do so or suffer – I am sorry to give you pain – I am almost resolv'd to burn this – but I really have not self possession and magninimity enough to manage the thing othe[r]wise – after all it may be a nervousness proceeding from the Mercury.[35]

This letter reveals several things: first, that Keats was writing poetry again (for all that he'd just told his publisher he had no intention to publish); second, that he understood his confinement with a tubercular patient and 'living in a continual fever' was dangerous; third, that he was dosing himself with mercury, presumably for his sore throat; finally, that he was aware his letter revealed how unsettled and 'nervous' he was.[36] He felt besieged by the contrary demands of his circumstances and his temperament: his own health and Tom's should have encouraged him to stay home, but the only way he could avoid feeling overwhelmed was by going out, or writing poetry – though even this came at a price, for he felt guilty for needing distraction. Keats copied 'a free translation' of a sonnet by Ronsard into a letter to Reynolds and may have started work on *Hyperion*.[37] Such were the 'abstract images' he told Dilke that he was 'obliged to write, and plunge into' in order to 'ease [him]self'.[38]

Poetic composition amid stressful circumstances was not new to Keats: his dressership at Guy's Hospital did not diminish his poetic output; in fact – as discussed – he wrote *more* poems as a dresser than he had earlier, or for several months thereafter. Contrariwise, on the Isle of Wight to begin *Endymion* without distractions, he found himself 'not over capable' and left 'pell mell for Margate' and Tom's

35 *LJK*, I, 369.

36 Chronic stress compromises the efficiency of the immune system, and tuberculosis is a contagious disease. The combination placed Keats at high risk for infection.

37 *LJK*, I, 371.

38 *LJK*, I, 369.

steadying presence.[39] For Keats, human company or circumstantial distractions were paradoxical enablers for poetic composition. Equally, poetic composition may have facilitated his career as a dresser, enabling him to withstand the hospital environment and the suffering encountered there. Nursing Tom, Keats knew that he needed the relief of poetic composition to keep functioning: 'Imagine "the hateful siege of contraries" – if I think of fame of poetry it seems a crime to me, and yet I must do so or suffer.'[40] That he was caring for a dying brother (rather than strangers on the ward) accounts for his feelings of guilt about needing distraction, and of course Keats himself was poorly. In this context, it is significant that the quotation illustrating his predicament comes from *Paradise Lost* – the poem to which *Hyperion* is most obviously indebted. In that poem, Satan infiltrates Eden as a 'rising mist' (*PL*.IX.75) and searches for a serpent with intent to possess it and tempt humanity in that guise, soliloquizing the while 'from inward grief' (*PL*.IX.97). Satan is aware of the pleasure he might once have found in the beauty of Paradise, but in his fallen state beauty only increases his torment, 'as from the hateful siege / Of contraries; all good to me becomes / Bane' (*PL*.IX.121–23). Keats feels similarly besieged by his situation: if he goes out, or writes, he feels guilty – 'if I think of fame of poetry it seems a crime to me' – yet it is his only relief from the strain of nursing Tom and coping with his own ill health: he 'must do so or suffer'. And, as Satan was subsequently 'disarmed / Of guile, of hate, of envy, of revenge' (*PL*.IX.465–66) by the sight of Eve amidst her roses, so too Keats, tormented by the conflicting demands of his circumstances and temperament, finds some respite in poetry.[41]

At around the same time, in mid-September 1818, John Wilson Croker's review of *Endymion* appeared in the *Quarterly Review*. This was a different order of criticism than 'Z''s, despite being harsh, unsparing, and lazy (Croker had not finished reading the poem). Croker contended that Keats' poetry was incomprehensible: it was

39 *LJK*, I, 138–39.

40 *LJK*, I, 369.

41 Keats certainly knew this, for the line from *Paradise Lost* that he echoed and refashioned in his sonnet 'To one who has been long in city pent' is part of the simile describing how Satan is affected by the sight of Eve surrounded by flowers.

'more unintelligible, almost as rugged, twice as diffuse, and ten times more tiresome and absurd than his prototype' Hunt's.[42] Keats seemed to 'write a line at random, and then he [followed] not the thought excited by this line, but that suggested by the *rhyme* with which it concludes'.[43] Croker did not allude to Keats' educational background or social class, and if his writing reflected a political bias this was to be expected. Nevertheless, it was this review, rather than 'Z''s more pernicious article, that was identified by Keats' friends and later admirers as the mischief-mongering piece (see Chapter 2). Its immediate effect, however, was to push up sales, with Hessey telling Taylor on 23 October, 'Endymion begins to move at last – 6 Copies have just been ordered by Simpkin & Marshall & one or two have been sold singly in the Shop – there is nothing like making a Stir for it – the papers have said so much about it many persons will doubtless be curious to see what it does contain.'[44] Still, Hessey worried about Keats' possible reaction, and sent him an article in defence of *Endymion*, signed 'J. S.', from the *Morning Chronicle* of 3 October. Keats replied: 'Praise or blame has but a momentary effect .... My own domestic criticism has given me pain without comparison beyond what Blackwood or the <Edinburgh> Quarterly could possibly inflict.'[45] The tone of Keats' letters to close friends suggests otherwise, and the 'plaguy sore throat' and doses of mercury would have contributed to the unease and dis-ease that pervaded his letters during this time.[46]

Richard Woodhouse was no less concerned: on 21 October he wrote to Keats having 'met with that malicious, but weak & silly article on Endymion in the last Quarterly Review'.[47] He discussed and dismissed Croker's review in his letter, before turning to 'our late conversation at Hessey's, <to> on which I have often since reflected'.[48]

42 Theodore Redpath, *The Young Romantics and Critical Opinion 1807–1824: Poetry of Byron, Shelley, and Keats as seen by their contemporary critics* (London: George Harrap and Co., 1973), 473.

43 Redpath, *Younger Romantics*, 474.

44 *KC*, I, 52–53.

45 *LJK*, I, 373–74.

46 See *LJK*, I, 367–69, 370–71, 391–405, II, 31. Symptoms of mercury poisoning include nervousness, mood swings, and irritability.

47 *LJK*, I, 378.

48 *LJK*, I, 380.

Allowing that he may have 'misconceived', Woodhouse states that he 'understood [Keats] to say, [he] thought there was now nothing original to be written in poetry ... That [he] should, consequently, write no more'.[49] The rest of the letter is a long, careful argument against this conclusion. Perhaps Keats tried to shrug off his negative reaction to adverse reviews, but Woodhouse had detected 'dismay' at 'the envious, the malignant [and] the undiscerning' and urged him to fresh resolve.[50] In short, there is reason to suppose that 'Z''s attack, followed by Croker's, heightened Keats' 'nervousness' and intensified feelings of debility and illness. Woodhouse's letter, alongside Charles Cowden Clarke's recollections from this period – until recently overlooked – suggests that this was the case.

On 27 July 1821 the *Morning Chronicle* published a letter, signed 'Y', by someone who claimed to be a 'School-fellow and Friend' of Keats', and to have been present at his first meeting with Hunt and Haydon.[51] Drawing on these details, J. R. MacGillivray postulated that 'Y' was Charles Cowden Clarke. MacGillivray also published a short extract from the letter:

> If it will be any gratification to Mr. Gifford to know how much he contributed to the discomfort of a generous mind, I can as far satisfy it by informing him, that Keats has been awake through the whole night talking with sensative [*sic*] bitterness of the unfair treatment he had experienced; and with becoming scorn of the information which was afterwards suggested to him; 'That as it was considered that he had been rather roughly handled, his *future* productions should be received with less harshness.' So much for the integrity and impartiality of criticism![52]

Clarke included the sleepless night episode in his 'Recollections of Keats', as published in the *Atlantic Monthly* in 1861:

> To say that these disgusting misrepresentations [by *Blackwood's* and the *Quarterly*] did not affect the consciousness and self-respect

49 *LJK*, I, 380.
50 *LJK*, I, 381.
51 Quoted in John Barnard, 'Keats's Sleepless Night: Cowden Clarke's Letter of 1821', *Romanticism* 16.3 (October 2010): 268–69.
52 MacGillivray, *Bibliography*, 101.

> of Keats would be to underrate the sensitiveness of his nature. He felt the insult, but more the injustice of the treatment he had received; he told me so, as we lay awake one night, when I slept in his brother's bed.[53]

John Barnard observes that the only time Clarke could have 'slept in his brother's bed' was autumn 1818, after George had emigrated to America and before Tom's death on 1 December. Moreover, 'Y' specifically mentions Gifford, the editor of the *Quarterly*, to whom Croker's review was mistakenly attributed. Barnard therefore suggests that the 'most probable date [for this incident] is early in October, shortly after the appearance of Croker's review ... at the end of September 1818'.[54] Taken together, Woodhouse's concern and Clarke's supporting presence suggest that Keats was not as carefree as he wished his publishers to believe. With Tom ill and George in America, Clarke was his closest confidante: he had known Keats longest, had been his teacher, and Keats' introduction to poetry owed much to Clarke's instruction. Most significantly, Clarke remembered the young boy who, on hearing of his mother's death, hid under the master's desk; he had seen Keats at his most vulnerable in the past, and supported him through such experiences.[55] The 'sleepless night' was a similarly dark moment, as the strain of nursing Tom, his persistent sore throat, and harsh reviews induced in Keats a heightened sense of injustice – 'talking with sensative [*sic*] bitterness of the unfair treatment he had experienced'.[56] This was the grim backdrop to the composition of some of the most light-hearted poems in the 1820 collection.

Keats told Woodhouse on 27 October that he was 'cogitating on the Characters of saturn and Ops': *Hyperion* was in his thoughts.[57] At around this time he composed two shorter poems: 'Fancy' and 'Bards of passion'. 'Fancy' explores the imagination's freedom to rove at will, untethered by tiresome realities such as sore throats, dying brothers, and bad reviews.

53 CCC, 96.
54 Barnard, 'Sleepless Night', 273.
55 *JK*, 29.
56 MacGillivray, *Bibliography*, 101.
57 *LJK*, I, 387.

Sit thee there, and send abroad,
With a mind self-overaw'd,
Fancy, high-commission'd: – send her!
She has vassals to attend her:
She will bring, in spite of frost,
Beauties that the earth hath lost;

(25–30)

'That which is creative must create itself', Keats had told Hessey; in his poem, it is the ever-roving 'fancy' that is pictured as endlessly vital and creative.[58] 'Bards of passion' is likewise concerned with the posthumous life of poets; recent discussions about poetic reputation and poetry's value may have led Keats to consider the continuing influence of the great poets of the past. 'Pleasure never is at home' ('Fancy', 2): in composing these poems, Keats also escaped the sickly confines of his everyday life, and in so doing was developing and deepening his understanding of poetry and the poetic imagination. Improbably, once again the productive pattern he had established at Guy's, where poetic composition found an enabling element in the strain of his dressership, was recurring: the strain of coping with ill health was pushing Keats towards new poetic frontiers.

Tom was 'no better, but much worse', Keats reported to George and Georgiana Keats; and his journal-letter, composed 14–31 October 1818, once again opened by recounting the ill health of various acquaintances: Dilke, Mrs. Dilke, and Severn are all ill; Haydon's eyes are troubling him; Haslam has been kind to the ailing Tom.[59] 'I think I shall be among the English Poets after my death', Keats wrote, adding that 'I have too many interruptions to a train of feeling to be able to w[r]ite Poetry.'[60] However, he still transcribed a recent composition: ''Tis the witching time of night' alludes to Hamlet's soliloquy about 'the very witching time of night / When churchyards yawn and hell itself breaks out / Contagion to this world' (*Hamlet*, 3.2. 377–78). Hamlet's lines spoke directly to Keats' own 'contagious' situation, and the idea of graves yawning open and the dead rising

58 *LJK*, I, 374.
59 *LJK*, I, 391.
60 *LJK*, I, 394, 401.

again is a grisly pendant to his thoughts of a posthumous life 'among the English Poets'.[61]

Tom died on 1 December and Keats moved into Brown's half of Wentworth Place.[62] In his bereavement, his friends worked hard to keep him occupied – and, in any case, Keats still intended to 'wait a few years before I publish any minor poems – and then I hope to have a volume of some worth', as he announced in January 1819.[63] By the end of 1818 Keats had already written five of the poems that would be published in the 1820 volume – 'Robin Hood', 'Lines on the Mermaid Tavern', *Isabella*, 'Fancy', and 'Bards of passion' – as well as significant sections of *Hyperion*.[64] Since he wished 'to avoid publishing', however, he needed to find a way to 'gain a Living'; a situation complicated by the persistent sore throat which was beginning to hamper his daily life and freedom of movement.[65]

*Debility, Distraction, and Decision: The Making of the 1820 Volume*

It is impossible to say with certainty when Keats first showed signs of tuberculosis, but one can speculate that it was late in 1818, and that this sore throat that plagued him off and on for months after his walking tour was a symptom of his ailment.[66] What started as a simple sore throat brought on by exhaustion and exposure to constant damp in Scotland may, over months, have evolved into an ulcerated tubercular sore throat, as Keats' tuberculosis infection moved into an active stage. Tuberculosis is an opportunistic disease: a primary infection does not automatically translate into an active one. People can live out their lives unaffected by a primary, dormant infection of tuberculosis, contained and kept in check by their immune systems: Joseph Severn, who nursed Keats on his death bed and so was undoubtedly exposed to the disease at its most

61 William Shakespeare, *The Complete Works*, ed. Stanley Wells, Gary Taylor, John Jowett, and William Montgomery (Oxford: Clarendon Press, 1986; 2nd ed. 2005; reprint 2006), 702; *LJK*, I, 394.

62 *NL*, 280.

63 *NL*, 284; *LJK*, II, 26.

64 Keats would make fitful attempts with *Hyperion* into 1819, giving up only in April, but his intensive work seems dwindled after Tom's death.

65 *LJK*, I, 415; *KC*, I, 307.

66 Hillas Smith, 'The Strange Case of Mr Keats's Tuberculosis', *Clinical Infectious Diseases* 38.7 (April 2004): 991–93.

contagious, never exhibited any symptoms and died of unrelated causes in 1879; George Keats, who was also exposed to tubercular contagion from Tom, survived until 1841.[67] In autumn 1818, however, Keats, already exhausted from his Scottish sojourn and weakened by his sore throat, was more susceptible – and as Tom grew worse the risk of infection grew. If Keats was dosing himself with mercury the risk intensified, for mercury is an immunosuppressant, reducing the body's ability to fight infections.[68] From spring 1819 there were warning signs that an infection had taken hold: frenetic activity interspersed by bouts of listlessness; the sore throat that would not heal; increasing concerns over health and unwillingness to 'risk' night air.[69] On 11 February 1819 Keats told his sister that he was 'obliged' to take care of himself, 'and am now in hopes that by this care I shall get rid of a sore throat which has haunted me', suggesting that this sore throat had persisted for some time – perhaps even from his Scottish tour.[70] In early August 1819 he told Fanny Brawne, 'I am quite well', but towards the end of that month a letter to Reynolds preoccupied with health and poetry suggests otherwise:[71]

> I think if I had a free and healthy and lasting organisation of heart and Lungs – as strong as an ox<e>'s – so as to be able [to bear] unhurt the shock of extreme thought and sensation without weariness, I could pass my Life very nearly alone ... But I feel my Body too weak to support me to the height; I am obliged continually to check myself and strive to be nothing. It would be vain for me to endeavour after a more reasonable manner of writing to you: I have nothing to speak of but myself – and what can I say but what I feel? If you should have any reason to regret this state of excitement in me, I will turn the tide of your feelings in the right channel by mentioning that it is the only state for the best sort of Poetry – that is all I care for, all I live for.[72]

67 David Kaloustian, 'Severn, Joseph (1793 –1879)', *ODNB*; Denise Gigante, *The Keats Brothers: The Life of John and George* (Cambridge, MA/London: The Belknap Press of Harvard University Press, 2011), 402–03.

68 *NL*, 275; *JK*, 231–32; White, *Literary Life*, 126; *LJK*, I, 369.

69 See *LJK*, II, 237, 238.

70 *LJK*, II, 38.

71 *LJK*, II, 138.

72 *LJK*, II, 146–47.

The subjunctive that opens this passage is revealing: Keats does not feel himself to have 'a free and healthy and lasting organisation of heart and Lungs' – there is some latent discomfort. It is impossible to tell what Keats himself suspected at this point, but he clearly did not consider himself to be in robust health. He identifies his physical weakness – his need to 'check [himself] and strive to be nothing' – while in the throes of poetic composition requiring 'extreme thought and sensation' as a paradoxical good: it is a 'state of excitement ... that ... is the only state for the best sort of Poetry'. Mental ambition 'to the height' and bodily 'checks' on its fulfilment made up his personality as a poet.[73] Throughout the autumn of 1819 this poetically enabling conflict between his mental ambitions and his physical failings continued: he told Taylor that he had 'been improving in health', and George and Georgiana that he had 'got rid of [his] haunting sore throat'.[74] By winter, however, he was complaining to Fanny Keats: 'You would have seen me if I had been quite well'; 'I am sorry to say I have been and continue rather unwell'.[75] One month later a note to Fanny Brawne said he was 'confined' after a lung haemorrhage.[76] Thus, throughout 1819, Keats' correspondence suggests the grip of a slow-moving but active infection: it did not incapacitate him but was nevertheless debilitating and adversely affected the quality of his life. Perhaps it is no coincidence that the majority of the poems in *Lamia, Isabella, The Eve of St Agnes, and other Poems* – Keats' masterpiece – were composed during this period, when his body and mind combined to leave him, by his own admission, in 'the only state for the best sort of Poetry'.

While principally preoccupied with his health, Keats was also grappling with the difficult issue of finances. In mid-April 1819 he proposed 'to look round at my resources and means – and see what I can do without poetry – To that end I shall live in Westminster.'[77] Over the next few months he thought of going as 'Surgeon to an I[n]diaman', but by 9 June had 'given up the Idea'; a week later, on 17 June, he was 'prepa[r]ing to enqu[i]re for a Situation with an

73 *LJK*, II, 146–47.
74 *LJK*, II, 156, 200.
75 *LJK*, II, 236, 238.
76 *LJK*, II, 250.
77 *LJK*, II, 84.

Apothecary' when Brown intervened and persuaded him 'to try the press once more'.[78] He apparently considered moving to South America.[79] Despite Brown's suggestion, and though he was still writing poetry, he was reluctant to publish, telling Fanny Brawne in mid-July 'I cannot say when I shall get a volume ready.'[80] This did not mean that his publishers were unaware he was writing poetry: Taylor knew of *Isabella* by 9 March 1819 and received a transcript of the complete poem by August.[81] Keats himself sent Taylor an extract from *Lamia* on 5 September.[82] Woodhouse's letter to Taylor of 19–20 September, complaining of Keats' proposed changes to *The Eve of St Agnes*, assumes his familiarity with its original version, so he evidently knew of that poem too.[83] If his publishers were content to wait upon their young author, this is probably because their author kept writing, despite his insistence that he did not want to publish. Indeed, it was news of George's financial crisis, arriving in September 1819, that finally convinced Keats he should try the press again, and then he acted on impulse – rushing to London with manuscripts of *The Eve of St. Agnes* and *Lamia*, as Woodhouse recounted to Taylor:[84]

> Keats was in Town the day before I left. He came <in> into 93 unexpectedly … . He wanted I believe to publish the Eve of $S^t$ Agnes and Lamia *immediately*: but Hessey told him it could not answer to do so now. I wondered why he said nothing of Isabella: & assured him it would please more {than} the Eve of $S^t$ Agnes – He said he could not bear the former now.[85]

Thwarted in his plan to publish for money, Keats next proposed moving to Westminster and writing for periodicals, but by 10 October was back in Hampstead, having abandoned that plan.[86] On

78 *LJK*, II, 114, 117, 121.
79 *LJK*, II, 114.
80 *LJK*, II, 130.
81 *KC*, I, 75, 78–79.
82 *LJK*, II, 155–59.
83 *KC*, I, 89–95; *LJK*, II, 161–65.
84 *LJK*, II, 160.
85 *LJK*, II, 162.
86 *LJK*, II, 218.

17 November Taylor again heard that he had 'come to a determination not to publish any thing I have now ready written'.[87] In the event, the publication of the 1820 volume owed more to the collapse of Keats' health than to any monetary considerations, though publication was agreed upon during a crisis that encompassed both Keats' health and his finances.

George arrived from America in January 1820 to secure his inheritance and settle his financial affairs, and whether by accident or design this settlement left Keats with less money than anticipated.[88] The decision to publish the 1820 volume was taken amid the fallout from this visit, between George's departure on 28 January and 6 March. The only development in that interval that could have influenced this decision was Keats' haemorrhage of 3 February; although his doctors said it was not consumption, he was clearly very ill.[89] On 9 February Woodhouse wrote to Taylor: 'I ought to have read & sent you this before ... *Skim* it over first for the sake of the plot.'[90] What 'this' was is not clear: Rollins conjectured that it was 'one of the poems ("Lamia"?) later published in the 1820 volume'.[91] Thereafter, on 8 March, Brown wrote to Taylor that 'Keats will be unable to prepare his Poems for the Press for a long time. He was taken on Monday evening with violent palpitations of the heart.'[92] A few days later – Rollins conjectures the 13th, but admits the 'date is a guess' – Brown advised Taylor that Keats 'wishes his Poems to be published as soon as convenient ... the volume to commence with St Agnes' Eve'.[93] This was the first time the volume was mentioned as being in prospect, and the timing – immediately after an alarming episode of ill health – was no coincidence. After dithering for a year, Keats and his publishers were finally in agreement. If the protracted collapse of the poet's health enabled his greatest poetic productions,

87 *LJK*, II, 234.
88 *JK*, 377–79.
89 *NL*, 361; White, *Literary Life*, 207–08. See also *LJK*, II, 250–52, and Brown, *Life*, 64–65.
90 *KC*, I, 102.
91 In a footnote to the letter from Richard Woodhouse to John Taylor, 9 February 1820: *KC*, I, 102.
92 *KC*, I, 103.
93 *LJK*, II, 276.

it was the violent onset of terminal disease that clinched the decision to publish them as a collection.

## Part Two: Poetic Reflections On Medical Interventions

The poems in the 1820 collection could hardly be free of the circumstances in which they were composed, but I suggest that some of them are also knowing reflections – albeit in a poetic idiom – on topics of contemporary medical interest, which Keats knew from his time at Guy's Hospital and the reading he undertook. 'Every department of knowledge … [is] calculated towards a great whole', held Keats, and his poems embody this principle in practice, combining his hard-earned medical knowledge with his innate skill as a poet to compose works which 'surprise by a fine excess, and not by Singularity'.[94]

Isabella, *or, A Study in Pathological Love-Melancholy*

Alan Richardson has discussed how Keats' poetry is indebted to contemporary findings about the brain, but here I want to focus on the one poem in Keats' 1820 volume to give primacy to the skull itself.[95] *Isabella* was written between February and April 1818, shortly before Keats observed to Reynolds on 3 May 1818 that he was 'glad at not having given away my medical Books' – in which category must number his surviving medical Notebook, with its sketch of skulls, one whole, one missing the lower jaw and nasal aperture (see Figure 1).[96] Both Richardson and Charles Hagelman argue that *Isabella* draws heavily on Keats' experiences at Guy's, with the former foregrounding the debt to Cooper's lectures revealed in Keats' depiction of Lorenzo's physiological symptoms of love, and the latter arguing that his awareness of the 'resurrection men' – grave-robbers who supplied Guy's with cadavers – contributed to the poem's 'resurrection' scene.[97] Keats' portrayal of Lorenzo's 'fast mouldering head' (430) – his skull – similarly reflects his experience walking the wards.

94 *LJK*, I, 277, 238.
95 Richardson, *Science of the Mind*, 118–28, 141–42, 146–50.
96 *LJK*, I, 277; JKMN, inside back cover.
97 Richardson, *Science of the Mind*, 133; Hagelman, 'Medical Profession', 210–66.

Isabella detaches her lover's head from his corpse and takes it home, caring for it in a macabre imitation of a lover's caress: 'She calm'd its wild hair with a golden comb, / And all around each eye's sepulchral cell / Pointed each fringed lash' (403–05). This is a precise account of the way a human corpse putrefies: Lorenzo no longer has eyes but retains eyelashes, since hair takes longer to decay than flesh, and he has some remnants of eyelids – which take longer to 'moulder' than eyeballs but less time than hair – to which these eyelashes are attached. Keats' particularity in describing Lorenzo's head betrays his intimate knowledge of the stages of bodily disintegration, surely derived from his days dissecting corpses at Guy's. He also acknowledges that putrefying bodies smell: it is no accident that the 'silken scarf' (409) in which Isabella wrapped the head was 'sweet with the dews / Of precious flowers pluck'd in Araby, / And divine liquids come with odorous ooze' (409–11). This is tacit acknowledgement that the stench of Lorenzo's 'mouldering head' needed to be disguised until the sweet basil – with what Culpeper called its 'strong healthy scent' – had time to grow.[98]

The recovery of Lorenzo's head initiates the denouement to the poem and Isabella's final descent into madness. Earlier in the poem Isabella, then pining for Lorenzo's return – 'So sweet Isabel / By gradual decay from beauty fell' (255–56) – was revived by a dream-vision explicitly compared to 'a fierce potion, drunk by chance, / Which saves a sick man from the feather'd pall' (267–68). The 'fierce potion' refers to an 'active' medicine of the sort that Keats as a dresser had experience administering.[99] Keats' medical Notebook demonstrates his awareness of the unpleasant effects of 'active' medicines and makes it clear that it was *because* of these effects that they were prescribed. Discussing absorbents in his notes, Keats wrote: 'All Medicines producing Nausea promote Absorbtion [*sic*] as Digitalis, Antimony &c'; while, in a section on 'The Use of Glands', he observed: 'The means of increasing secretion is by Stimuli as Snuff to y<sup>e</sup> Nose, Purgatives to y<sup>e</sup> intestines.'[100] Before he was at Guy's Keats may have administered such powerful medicines to his mother during her last illness, and it is possible he did so for Tom while writing *Isabella*. Roused by her dream-vision of Lorenzo,

98 *KC*, I, 75.
99 For a different reading of the 'fierce potion' see *RMJK*, 157.
100 JKMN, Bf7r, Bf3r.

Isabella acts with more decision than hitherto, leading the aged nurse to wonder: '"What feverous hectic flame / Burns in thee, child? – What good can thee betide, / That thou should'st smile again?"' (348–50). Keats knew that 'Stimulus when applied where there is gre|at| |d|ebility is a Tonic': 'active' medicines were prescribed to the dying to shock the system back into operation.[101] Isabella reacts to the shock of Lorenzo's ghostly visitation exactly as patients would to 'a fierce potion' – with apathy dispelled and strength renewed. Once assured of Lorenzo's death and in possession of his skull, Isabella's frenzied strength fades and her tearful attention is focused solely on the basil:

> She had no knowledge when the day was done,
> And the new morn she saw not: but in peace
> Hung over her sweet basil evermore,
> And moisten'd it with tears unto the core.
>
> (421–24)

'The Passions of y^e Mind have great influence on the secretions ... Sorrow increases Tears', observed Keats in his medical notes, and his poem faithfully depicts this fact even as it reveals how excessive passion can cause derangement: Isabella's tears nourish Lorenzo's eyeless skull, even as that skull becomes Isabella's reason for living.[102] Without the skull, Isabella dies, 'forlorn' (497).[103]

*Madeline's Distraction and 'the Operation of Attention'*

If *Isabella* is one Keatsian treatment on the theme of passionate love-melancholy, *The Eve of St Agnes* is another.[104] Keats had not read Burton when he composed the former poem, but he had done so by the time he came to compose the second, and both Madeline's distraction and 'vague, regardless eyes' (64) and Porphyro's 'heart on fire' (75) are symptoms of love discussed by Burton. However,

101 JKMN, Ff1r.

102 JKMN, Bf7r.

103 R. S. White reads *Isabella* as a narrative account of loss leading to pathological mourning and melancholia, in 'Keats, Mourning and Melancholia', in *Medical Imagination*, ed. Roe, 129–52.

104 White, 'Mourning', in *Medical Imagination*, ed. Roe, 135–40 discusses Keats' familiarity with 'melancholy' as a cultural concept.

it is Keats' sudden decision, in mid-September 1819, to modify his verses and render Porphyro's actions towards Madeline at the end of the poem more explicit that has caused the most debate. Woodhouse complained to Taylor at the time: 'as it is now altered, as soon as M. has confessed her love, P. <instead> winds by degrees his arm round her, presses breast to breast, and acts all the acts of a bonâ fide husband, while she fancies she is only playing the part of a Wife in a dream.'[105] The publisher insisted that the original version – which could be marketed as suitable for the ladies who comprised most of the poetry-reading public – be reinstated. Yet in both versions one thing remained the same: Madeline, despite being awake and conscious, was not apparently fully aware of what was happening. Her confusion was increased by the fact that her waking reality mimicked her dream so closely that she found it impossible to distinguish between them. In some ways, her predicament was the reverse of a 'waking dream' or reverie, a subject of much discussion in medical circles in the early nineteenth century. In his well-known discussion of 'the operation of attention' Charles Bell explained:[106]

> ... the vividness of the perception or idea, is always proportionate to the degree of undistracted attention which the mind is able to bestow on the object of sensation or of memory. In solitude and darkness, the strength of the memory in the contemplation of past events is encreased, because there is no intrusion in the objects of the outward senses; and the deaf or blind receive some compensation for their loss in the encreased powers which are acquired by a more frequent and undisturbed use of the senses which remain, and a keener attention to the sensations which they present. On the other hand, when we are under the enchantments of a waking dream or reverie, our attention is wholly detached from the present object of the senses; and in this state we may continue to read without understanding.[107]

105 *LJK*, II, 163. Turley offers a psychoanalytic reading of Keats' insecurities as revealed by these revisions in *Boyish Imagination*, 112–15.

106 John and Charles Bell, *The Anatomy and Physiology of the Human Body ...* . 3 vols (1802–1804; 4th ed. London: Longman, Hurst, Rees, Orme and Brown, and T. Cadell and W. Davies, 1816), III, 4.

107 Bell and Bell, *Anatomy*, III, 4–5.

Madeline, emerging from a dream-filled sleep, still believed her 'attention [was] wholly detached from the present object of the senses' because – seeing Porphyro at her bedside – she thought she was asleep, when she was in fact awake and had full awareness of the input of her senses, which told her that Porphyro was at her bedside.[108] *The Eve of St Agnes* depicted a reverie turned on its head, but it was another poem in the 1820 volume that featured Keats' most famous description of a reverie – and became one of the most celebrated accounts of the phenomenon in nineteenth-century poetry.

### *'Guess each sweet': Reverie Explored*

At the end of 'Ode to a Nightingale' the poet startles into awareness – 'Was it a vision, or a waking dream?' (79). The poet's 'drowsy' (1) desire to escape from suffering predominates at the opening of the ode; to suspend what Bell referred to as 'the operation of attention' the effects of poison, opiates, and alcohol, and then 'the viewless wings of Poesy' (33), are invoked: the bird's song serves as a catalyst and guide for this imaginative flight.[109] Early in the poem the poet's physical existence intrudes, but once having freed himself from the trammels of actuality, 'in solitude and darkness' he is better able to concentrate 'keener attention' on sense impressions to arrive at an engagement with and appreciation of the beauty of his surroundings:[110]

> I cannot see what flowers are at my feet,
> Nor what soft incense hangs upon the boughs,
> But, in embalmed darkness, guess each sweet
> Wherewith the seasonable month endows
> The grass, the thicket, and the fruit-tree wild;
> (41–45)

108 Bell and Bell, *Anatomy*, III, 5. Stuart Curran explores the poetic effects of Keats' interest in mental states of 'suspended animation', including sleep, in '"The Feel of Not to Feel It": The Life of Non-sensation in Keats', in *Medical Imagination*, ed. Roe, 153–72.

109 Bell and Bell, *Anatomy*, III, 4.

110 Bell and Bell, *Anatomy*, III, 4. For a reading of 'Ode to a Nightingale' as a contemplation on Keats' 'sense of continual loss, mourning and melancholy', see White, 'Mourning', *Medical Imagination*, 134.

The loss of sight is important, for it is *because* he 'cannot see' that the poet strains his other senses to 'guess each sweet', and, in doing so – in focusing his attention so completely – he arrives at the escape from self that he has been seeking. He has, at this point in the poem, attained a state of reverie. That the 'enchantments of a waking dream or reverie' could be dangerous was noted by Bell: 'it may become disease; for health of mind consists in the due correspondence betwixt the excitement on the outward sense and the operation of the mind thus roused by the external sense.'[111] The poet, in his reverie, finds himself identifying so deeply with the nightingale's song that he is in danger of self-annihilation:

> Now more than ever seems it rich to die,
> To cease upon the midnight with no pain,
> While thou art pouring forth thy soul abroad
> In such an ecstasy!
>
> (55–58)

Recalled by the reminder that physical existence is necessary to his sense impressions ('Still wouldst thou sing, and I have ears in vain —' (59)), the poet is nevertheless still enmeshed in reverie: his imagination spans space and time and others who have heard the bird's song, until the associations of a single word – 'forlorn' (70) – recapture his attention and bring it back to his 'sole self' (72). Waking from the reverie is a disorientating experience, leaving him in a state of uncertainty: 'Fled is that music: – Do I wake or sleep?' (80).

The last words of 'Ode to a Nightingale' encapsulate Madeline's sense in *The Eve of St. Agnes* that she was still asleep when 'Into her dream [Porphyro] melted, as the rose / Blendeth its odour with the violet' (320–31). Both poems explore what Bell termed 'the operation of attention' and its relationship to the imaginative process. Underpinning their explorations of the shadowy regions of thought is an awareness of contemporary medical discussions of the human mind and its functioning. Keats' poetic interventions reveal that any straightforward division of mental states – into dream, reverie, and waking awareness – is simplistic: only by allowing for the tempering influence of the imagination can one hope to account for the range of human thought and how the 'operation

111 Bell and Bell, *Anatomy*, III, 5.

of the attention' relates to the 'object of sensation'.[112] 'What the Imagination seizes as Beauty must be truth', he wrote elsewhere, hinting at this complex relationship between reality and perception and signalling the importance of the mediating powers of the mind to the process of determining 'truth'.[113]

*A Poetic Pharmacy: Poisons and 'Ode on Melancholy'*

If 'Ode to a Nightingale' investigated one phenomenon affecting perception – reverie – 'Ode on Melancholy' explores another. Unlike reverie, which compromises one's awareness of the external world, melancholy – as Keats defines it in his ode – *heightens* perception of reality. In one important way, though, these disparate perceptual conditions are similar: neither can be attained by the ingestion of chemical substances. While opiates and the poison hemlock were presented as agents to loosen ties to external reality in 'Ode to a Nightingale', they were unsuccessful, and it was only when the poet concentrated his attention – 'But, in embalmed darkness, guess each sweet' (43) – that he achieved reverie. In the opening stanza of 'Ode on Melancholy', also, a number of poisons are named – 'Wolf's-bane' (2); 'nightshade' (4); 'yew-berries' (5) – but the poem opens with an injunction *against* their use: 'No, no' (1).

Keats' choice of poisons requires consideration, even as it is clear that he gave them careful attention: the manuscript of 'Ode on Melancholy' reveals that he started writing 'Henbane' before changing his mind and putting 'Wolf's-bane'.[114] As a qualified apothecary, he was sure to have been well-versed in the medicinal properties of plants and the recognition of plant species: the *Oracular Communications* advised that 'knowledge of botany is now become an important consideration to the medical student'.[115] Another contemporary students' guide suggested that former apprentices need not take materia medica as a separate course as '[t]he Apothecaries Company in their examination in this branch, require nothing more than what every apprentice must have learned, and what every course of pharmaceutical chemistry

112 Bell and Bell, *Anatomy*, III, 4.

113 *LJK*, I, 184.

114 Hebron, *Poet and His Manuscripts*, 133.

115 Æsculapius, *Oracular Communications*, 71–72.

could contain.'[116] And, indeed, 'twist / Wolf's-bane, tight-rooted' (1–2) is a precise instruction: William Salisbury, who was associated with the Physick Garden at Chelsea and in 1815 became the botany instructor for Guy's, observed in his *Botanist's Companion* (1816) that the poison of wolf's-bane root was 'most powerful', and that the 'inspissated juice' prepared from it 'should be first administered in small doses'.[117] He noted that 'every part of the fresh plant [*Aconitum napellus*, wolf's-bane] is strongly poisonous, but the root is unquestionably the most powerful'.[118] This was folk knowledge given currency in medical circles by Salisbury: wolf's-bane was listed as 'Aconitum' in Ebenezer Sibly's revised and enlarged edition of *Culpeper's English Physician and Complete Herbal ...* (1789), and readers were told of its 'Government and Danger: These plants are hot and dry in the fourth degree, of a martial venomous quality; if it be inwardly taken, it inflameth the heart, burneth the inward parts, and killeth the body.'[119] Keats combines instruction with an image of desperation: wringing 'poisonous wine' out of the 'tight-rooted' plant is both medically specific and powerfully affective.[120] Henbane, dropped from the poem, was listed by Culpeper in his 1653 translation of the *Pharmacopœia Londinensis* as one of the 'simples' among the class of 'Improper Anodines, or *Narcoticks*'; other plants featured in this list included mandrakes, poppies, opium, and nightshade.[121] Salisbury noted that 'Henbane is a strong

116 'Advice to Medical Students on their Arrival in London', *The London Medical and Physical Journal* 36 (July–December 1816): 193.

117 William Salisbury, *The Botanist's Companion, or an Introduction to the Knowledge of Practical Botany ...* . 2 vols (London: Longman, Hurst, Rees, Orme, and Brown, 1816), II, 44. For an account of how the vocabulary and style of Keats' 1817 volume was influenced by *Botanist's Companion*, see Nikki Hessell, 'John Keats, the Botanist's Companion', in *Medical Imagination*, ed. Roe, 91–107.

118 Salisbury, *Botanist's Companion*, II, 44.

119 Nicholas Culpeper, *Culpeper's English Physician; and Complete Herbal. To which are now first added, Upwards of One Hundred additional Herbs ...*, ed. E. Sibly (London: Green and Co., 1789), Part I, 71.

120 See Gareth Evans, 'Poison Wine – John Keats and the Botanical Pharmacy', *Keats-Shelley Review* 16 (2002): 52. Also see *RMJK*, 168 for some mythological associations of wolf's-bane.

121 Nicholas Culpeper, *Pharmacopœia Londinensis: or the London Dispensatory ...* (London: Peter Cole, 1653), 152.

narcotic poison, and many instances of its deleterious effects are recorded', but also that it was 'much employed ... as an anodyne'.[122] Perhaps the substitution of 'Wolf's-bane' for 'Henbane' was more for reasons of poetry than the qualities of the plants: both are powerful poisons with important medical uses, but 'Wolf's-bane' arguably makes a more dramatic impression.[123]

The next poison is more unspecific: 'nightshades' is the name for a family of plants (Solanaceae), and the singular form of the name is commonly used for three different plant species within the family. This ambiguity on Keats' part must have been deliberate – as a recently trained doctor he could not have been unaware that lack of specificity in identifying possibly toxic plants was a major problem faced by the medical profession. The consequences of misidentification while administering plant-based medication was one that haunted doctors and botanists alike. Salisbury pointedly stated that it was 'high time that those persons who are engaged in the business of pharmacy should be obliged to become so far acquainted with plants, as to be able to distinguish at sight all such as are useful in diet or medicine, or more particularly such as are of poisonous qualities'.[124] Sibly, in his edition of *Culpeper's English Physician; and Complete Herbal*, listed three variants of nightshade: common, deadly, and woody.[125] Common nightshade, he observed, 'is wholly used to cool hot inflammations, either inwardly or outwardly, being in no ways dangerous'.[126] Another edition of *Culpeper's Complete Herbal*, published in 1815 – the year Keats enrolled at Guy's – warned its readers: 'Have a care you mistake not the Deadly Nightshade for [common nightshade]; if you know it not, you may let them both alone, and take no harm.'[127] Apart from the considerable danger of accidental poisoning, the importance of accurately

122 Salisbury, *Botanist's Companion*, II, 60.

123 De Almeida cites wolf's-bane's potency as a nerve poison as reason for its inclusion over the simply narcotic henbane: see *RMJK*, 168–70.

124 Salisbury, *Botanist's Companion*, II, 43.

125 Culpeper, *Culpeper's English Physician*, I, 268–69.

126 Culpeper, *Culpeper's English Physician*, I, 268. De Almeida notes that 'Babington and Curry of Guy's Hospital recommended hellebore, as well as nightshade and wolfsbane, as recorded cures for insanity': *RMJK*, 166.

127 *Culpeper's Complete Herbal ... to which is also added Upwards of Fifty Choice Receipts, Selected from the Author's last Legacy to his Wife* (London: Richard Evans, 1815), 123.

identifying and preparing plant extracts was of topical interest in London medical circles for another reason: in the late eighteenth century the Viennese doctor Anton Störck had published case histories asserting that he had cured cancer with hemlock, but when his treatments were attempted in London they were not successful. The reasons posited for this failure were a variation in the species of hemlock, as well as in the nature and strength of the extract prepared.[128] Thus, it was vitally important to identify medical plants accurately: failure to do so might result in ineffective medication or accidental poisoning.[129]

Writing poetry, Keats chose not to give nightshade the specificity he could have, using the generic name instead. However, his instruction of what to do was again precise: do not 'suffer thy pale forehead to be kiss'd / By nightshade' (3–4), which he identifies with the 'ruby grape of Proserpine' (4). Gareth Evans has suggested that Keats had in mind woody nightshade, also known by the common names amara dulcis, or dulcamara, or bittersweet. This plant takes its last common name from its characteristic of changing from bitter to sweet (or vice versa) when eaten.[130] For Evans, this links to the ambivalence of the ode's final stanza, where 'in the very temple of Delight / Veil'd Melancholy has her sovran shrine' (25–26).[131] Bittersweet certainly has red berries – but so does deadly nightshade, or belladonna – and only this latter can be associated with the Graeco-Roman goddess Proserpine. Keats read in Lemprière that, 'As queen of hell, and wife of Pluto, Proserpine presided over the death of mankind, and according to the opinion of the ancients, no one could die, if the goddess herself, or Atropos her minister, did not cut off one of the hairs from the head.'[132] Atropos is one of the Fates in Greek mythology: Lemprière says that 'she is inexorable,

128 See Evans, 'Poison Wine', 40–45 for Dr Störck's treatments and the reaction in London medical circles, as well as Keats' exposure to these ideas. See *RMJK*, 169 for an account of how one of Keats' instructors reacted to the new medicines proposed by Dr Störck.

129 Both Culpeper and Salisbury have cautionary tales of the dreadful consequences of such mistakes. See, for instance, Culpeper, *Culpeper's English Physician*, I, 201, 269; and Salisbury, *Botanist's Companion*, II, 133–44.

130 Evans, 'Poison Wine', 53; Culpeper, *Complete Herbal*, 1.

131 Evans, 'Poison Wine', 53–54.

132 Lemprière, *Classical Dictionary* [unpaginated].

and inflexible, and her duty among the three sisters is to cut the thread of life'.[133] Deadly nightshade bears the scientific name *Atropa belladonna*; 'atropa' derives from Atropos, recognizing the plant's toxic nature, and Proserpine is the goddess of death. Bittersweet has no such a link with her.[134] Moreover, bittersweet is not sufficiently toxic if touched rather than ingested, but belladonna can kill: Sibly, in his edition of Culpeper, warned that it 'should not be suffered to grow in any places where children resort, for it is a strong poison'.[135] Keats, however, might have been drawn to the ambiguity of the generic term 'nightshade'; left thus unqualified, its 'ruby grape' might be relatively harmless (common nightshade), require careful handling (woody nightshade/bittersweet), or be fatally toxic (deadly nightshade) – alternatives that anticipate the ambivalent status of melancholy, which cannot be sought but must 'fall / Sudden from heaven like a weeping cloud' (11–12).

The 'yew-berries' next invoked are similarly equivocal, for they are the only part of the yew non-toxic to humans.[136] It is possible to consume a yew berry, or to use a rosary made of them – as Keats would *not* do in 'Ode on Melancholy' – and continue unaffected. However, the berries contain seeds that are poisonous. The yew tree has long been associated with magic, poison, death, and the underworld;[137] and Erasmus Darwin invoked its presence in *The Botanic Garden* – a work Keats knew – to describe a graveyard 'where sheds the sickly yew / O'er many a mouldering bone its nightly dew' (2.III.19–20).[138] This description occurs early in the third canto of 'The Loves of Plants'(the second part of *The Botanic Garden*); a few pages later, in a long footnote to 'Macinella' (line 188), Darwin remarks: 'Variety of noxious plants abound in all countries, in our own the deadly nightshade, henbane, hounds-tongue, and many others are seen in

133 Lemprière, *Classical Dictionary* [unpaginated].

134 De Almeida suggests that Keats' 'ruby grapes' links the red berries of deadly nightshade to the rosy seeds of Proserpine's pomegranate: *RMJK*, 170.

135 Culpeper, *Culpeper's English Physician*, I, 269.

136 'English yew', *EB*.

137 For instance, in Virgil's *Georgics*, or Pliny's *Natural History*. De Almeida suggests that mistaking the red berries of the yew for those of nightshade links these, too, to Proserpine. She also finds a link to Apollo: the yew's toxin, Prussic acid, is found in laurel: see *RMJK*, 170–71.

138 Erasmus Darwin, *The Botanic Garden; A Poem, in Two Parts ... With Philosophical Notes* (London: J. Johnson, 1791), Part 2, 91.

almost every high-road untouched by animals.'[139] Earlier, in his first footnote to this third canto, he had described the medical use of the 'dried root of Peony'.[140] Thus, in the space of a few pages and some 200 lines of verse, Darwin had named three plants found in 'Ode on Melancholy': yew, nightshade, and peonies, as well as henbane, which was Keats' original thought before he replaced it with wolf's-bane. This intriguing conjunction suggests that Keats may have read or recalled *The Botanic Garden* in 1819 – indeed, perhaps he inserted wolf's-bane for its fatally vulpine associations, and to cover a debt to Darwin's book.

In addition to featuring in 'The Loves of Plants', 'globed peonies' (17) also feature significantly in herbals:

> The roots of the Male Peony, fresh-gathered, have been found by experience to cure the falling sickness [epilepsy]; ... The root is also effectual for women that are not sufficiently cleansed after child-birth, and such as are troubled with the mother; ... The black seed ... is very effectual for such as in their sleep are troubled with the disease called Ephialtes, or Incubus, but we do commonly call it the Night-mare:[141]

The other flower named in the ode is a rose; and in the herbals roses are presented as a panacea, used to treat headaches; eye, ear, throat or gum pain; inflammations of the heart; St Anthony's fire (Erysipelas); menstrual problems; spitting blood; stomach and liver diseases; leprosy; and 'faintings, swoonings, weakness'; as well as to 'strengthen ... the retentive faculty'.[142] However, for Keats, the importance of roses – scattered throughout the 1820 volume and generally in his poetry, either as a noun or in the adjectival form 'rosy' – is literary and cultural rather than medical.[143] More than any other flower, roses recalled Paradise and the pre-lapsarian world: Milton had ensured that when in *Paradise Lost* he described how, in the Garden of Eden, were 'Flowers of all hue, and without

139 Darwin, *Botanic Garden*, 2,102.

140 Darwin, *Botanic Garden*, 2, 90.

141 Culpeper, *Complete Herbal*, 137–38.

142 Culpeper, *Culpeper's English Physician*, I, 319–22. Quoted from p. 320.

143 See 'rose', 'roses', and 'rosy' in *Concordance to Poems*, ed. Becker, Dilligan, and Bender, 437, 438.

thorn the rose' (*PL*.IV.256). Given Keats' awareness of Milton, his phrase 'morning rose' – indistinguishable aurally from 'mourning rose' – might suggest both pre- and post-lapsarian worlds: beauty, and 'Beauty that must die' ('Ode on Melancholy', 21). All the plants named in 'Ode on Melancholy', thus, had significant medical value, and, except for the rose, are toxic substances. The ambiguity inherent in the fact that deadly poisons can be beneficial, even curative, in small doses, aligns with Keats' views on melancholy: in order to experience the full richness of the melancholy temper one must embrace the 'melancholy fit' (11) and 'burst Joy's grape against [the] palate' (28), much as the hope of recovering health forced patients to ingest remedies that they knew could be fatally poisonous.[144]

The first word of 'Ode on Melancholy', as published, is 'No', and the catalogue of substances and activities that immediately follows are forbidden at every turn. In fact, the first stanza of the ode is a prescription: both in the medical sense as '[a] doctor's instruction, … any treatment ordered by a medical practitioner'; and in its primary legal meaning 'Restriction; limitation; circumscription'.[145] This latter meaning was already archaic in the early nineteenth century, but, since Milton frequently used the word in this sense in both prose and poetry, Keats could not have been unaware of it. Furthermore, though we are accustomed to think of medical prescriptions as positive incentives to action (usually in the form of consuming some medicinal substance), they can also take the form of a negative set of injunctions against certain kinds of action (avoiding some activity or food substance in case of injuries or allergies, for instance). The first stanza of 'Ode on Melancholy' closes – like any medical prescription – with a prognosis of consequences arising from disregarding its advice: 'shade to shade will come too drowsily, / And drown the wakeful anguish of the soul' (9–10). Opening with a stern admonition against a certain course of action, 'Ode on Melancholy' is negatively capable in the sense that, while it cannot offer advice on how to attain

144 De Almeida suggests that it is the peony's 'ambiguous multiplicity' as a poison with 'legendary connections with poetry, with the healing hymn and the stirring paean' in addition to its medical uses that leads Keats to name it as the only poison that could be a medium for true melancholy: see *RMJK*, 171–72.

145 'prescription, n.1', *OED*.

true melancholy, it does provide certain directives on how it cannot be achieved.

Keatsian melancholy cannot be actively sought but will 'fall / Sudden from heaven' (11–12). It is a transient experience, partaking particularly of the transience of experience: its vitality is dependent upon the appreciation of its impermanence. The second stanza of the ode suggests some possible ways of gleaning the 'melancholy fit' (11) to its fullest:

> Then glut thy sorrow on a morning rose,
> Or on the rainbow of the salt sand-wave,
> Or on the wealth of globed peonies;
> Or if thy mistress some rich anger shows,
> Emprison her soft hand, and let her rave …
>
> (15–19)

Nothing mentioned here can be permanent: roses and peonies wilt; rainbows fade; and no one can 'rave' in anger forever. Just as a tiny dose of the toxins named in the first stanza may prove beneficial but any additional drop will kill, so too continual exposure to the 'melancholy fit' will cause the experience to pall. This is made explicit in the third stanza: 'She dwells with Beauty – Beauty that must die' (21). Melancholy, then, is a mental state that is not easily achieved, is by nature transient, and heightens aesthetic appreciation by allowing for a total immersion in the beauty of experience: 'And feed deep, deep upon her peerless eyes' (20). The poem, thus, can be read as an extraordinary confession of triumphant powerlessness: melancholy cannot be sought, and when the fit falls it can only be undergone, with no escape or cure possible. However, acceptance of this lack of willed power – what in a physiological context Keats called 'volition' in his medical Notebook – allows for a fullness of experience unlike any other, and is perhaps a supreme achievement of '*Negative Capability*, that is when man is capable of being in uncertainties, Mysteries, doubts, without any irritable reaching after fact & reason'.[146] 'Ode on Melancholy' ends on a note as disconcerting as it is enabling: 'His soul shall taste the sadness of her might, / And be among her cloudy trophies hung' (29–30). This unnerving image balances the powerlessness embodied in being 'hung' against

146 JKMN, Bf5r, Ff2r; *LJK*, I, 193.

the exaltation inherent in 'trophies' and merges the two in the dissolution implicit in 'cloudy'. It is an image and an ending that perfectly encapsulates Keats' sense, expressed in August 1819, that the weakness of his body 'to support [him] to the height' was 'the only state for the best sort of Poetry'.[147]

147 *LJK*, II, 147.

# Conclusion

In the early nineteenth century students of surgery in the London teaching hospitals were well acquainted with *The London Dissector*. This standard textbook offers four 'General Rules for Dissection' before guiding the reader through the muscular fabric that makes up a human body.[1] The first rule reads:

> The position of the hand in dissecting should be the same, as in writing or drawing; and the knife, held, like the pen or pencil, by the thumb and the first two fingers, should be moved by means of them only; while the hand rests firmly on the two fingers bent inwards as in writing, and on the wrist. The instrument can be guided with much more steadiness and precision in this way.[2]

Keats was thus instructed to hold his surgeon's lancet exactly as he held his poet's pen while composing verse. Throughout this book, I have sought to recover the various ways in which Keats' creativity found expression in his two careers of medicine and poetry, mutually enabling and enriching his success in both. By focusing on his Guy's Hospital Notebook, we have seen how its medical and anatomical contents strikingly prefigure various aspects of his mature poetry.

It has long been noted that the period between Keats' return from Scotland in August 1818 and his composition of 'To Autumn' in September 1819 represented an extraordinarily intense and concentrated period of poetic achievement. It is also fairly generally believed that Keats' rapid development as a poet occurred, for the most part, out of sight, and that his early poetry does not give much indication

1 *LD*, 1.
2 *LD*, 1.

of the genius that was later revealed.[3] Throughout this book I have argued instead that many characteristics of Keats' greatest poetry – the imaginative turns of his poems and plots, the 'concentrations' of his imagery, the precise delineation of extreme emotional states through physical descriptions – can all be found in his earlier poems and in his medical Notebook. If Keats' innate genius flowered most fully during his 'living year', the inherent qualities which enabled him to write his best poems are seen, as it were, in an unvarnished state in his medical notes, and their gradual adaption and deployment in poetry is visible as early as the Margate summer of 1816.

For Keats, the combination of high-pressure hospital commitments and the composition of poetry was a paradoxically enabling situation, with the continual interaction between these two aspects of his life – the medical and the poetic – sustaining and ensuring his ability to write 'verses fit to live'.[4] The American poet James Russell Lowell once observed that Keats was a poet of whom 'you might almost say that he could feel sorrow with his hands' – a statement that was more astute than has been realized.[5] As a surgeon, Keats had literally felt sorrow with his hands – in diagnosing broken bones and assisting with breech-births, in performing surgical operations, and in dissecting cadavers with a knife held as precisely as the pen with which he made entries in his Notebook and composed his poems. More than anything else, it was Keats' visceral, hands-on experiences at Guy's Hospital that made him a 'mighty Poet of the human heart'.[6]

3 See, for instance, Jack Stillinger, *Romantic Complexity: Keats, Coleridge and Wordsworth* (Urbana/Chicago, IL: University of Illinois Press, 2006) and Helen Vendler, *The Odes of John Keats* (Cambridge, MA/London: The Belknap Press of the Harvard University Press, 1983).

4 *Poems*, 102.

5 *CH*, 360.

6 *LJK*, II, 115.

# Bibliography

## Manuscript Sources

***At the London Metropolitan Archives/Keats House, Hampstead***

Keats, John. John Keats' Medical Notebook. K/MS/01/002

***At King's College London***

A. Collection: Guy's Hospital Medical School: Records

1. Student Records

Guy's and St. Thomas's Pupils and Dressers 1755–1823 ranged in alphabetical order. G/FP1/1

Guy's Hospital Entry of Physicians and Surgeon's Pupils and Dressers 1814–1827. G/FP3/2

Surgeon's Pupils of Guy's and St. Thomas's Hospitals 1812–1825. G/FP4/1

2. Personal Papers

Osler, Edward. [Letter]. GB 0100 G/PP1/39 oversized

Partridge, Alderman. *An Epitome of the Anatomical Lectures delivered by Astley P. Cooper and Hen$^{y}$ Cline Esq$^{rs}$ at St Thomas's Hospital Borough.* GB 0100 G/PP1/43

Waddington, Joshua. *Lectures On Anatomy; And The Principal Operations of Surgery: Delivered at the Theatre, St. Thomas's Hospital; between the 1$^{st}$ of January, and the 1$^{st}$ of June 1816; By Astley Cooper Esq$^{re}$. Vol. 1$^{st}$*. GB 0100 G/PP1/62/3

—. *Lectures On Anatomy; And The Principal Operations of Surgery; Delivered at the Theatre, St. Thomas's Hospital; between the 1$^{st}$ of January, and the 1$^{st}$ of June 1816; By Astley Cooper Esq$^{re}$. Vol. 2$^{nd}$*. GB 0100 G/PP1/62/4

—. *Lectures On the Principles and Practice, Of Surgery; Delivered at the Theatre St. Thomas's Hospital, between the 1$^{st}$ of October 1815, and the 1$^{st}$ of June 1816; By Astley Cooper Esq.* GB 0100 G/PP1/62/5

[Anon.], *The Lectures of Astley P. Cooper Esq$^{r}$ on Surgery given at St Tho$^{s}$ Hospital Vol. 1$^{st}$*. GB 0100 G/PP2/10

B. Collection: Guy's Hospital: Physical Society
Minutes Book of the Physical Society of Guy's Hospital 1813–1820. GB 0100 G/S4/M9

### *At Trinity College Cambridge*

Autograph Collection of George Gery Milner-Gibson-Cullum (1857–1921)
Keats, John. Holograph of 'Give me women, wine and snuff'. Cullum/N83/2
Milner-Gibson-Cullum, George Gery. Letter accompanying Keats's holograph of 'Give me women, wine and snuff'. Cullum/N83/1

## Printed sources

Abernethy, John. *An Enquiry into the Probability and Rationality of Mr Hunter's Theory of Life; Being the Subject of the First Two Anatomical Lectures delivered before the Royal College of Surgeons, of London*. London: Longman, Hurst, Rees, Orme, and Brown, 1814. Web. <https://archive.org/details/b28993263> (accessed 23 January 2018).

'Advice to Medical Students on their Arrival in London', *The London Medical and Physical Journal* 36 (July–December 1816): 193. Web. <https://books.google.co.uk/books?id=qUACAAAAYAAJ&printsec=frontcover&dq=london+medical+and+physical+journal++volume+36+1816&hl=en&sa=X&ved=0CCEQ6AEwAGoVChMIi_yOjIqQxgIVEy_bCh2eMwBY#v=onepage&q=Arrival&f=false> (accessed 10 November 2018).

Allard, James Robert. *Romanticism, Medicine, and the Poet's Body*. Aldershot: Ashgate, 2007.

Æsculapius [pseud.]. *The Hospital Pupil's Guide, being Oracular Communications, addressed to Students of the Medical Profession. Including Plain and Useful Directions Relative to the Best Mode of Attending to the Various Branches of Medical Study. To which is added, An Account of the Days and Hours of Attendance of the Physicians and Surgeons at St. Thomas's and Guy's Hospitals*, 1816; 2nd ed., corrected. London: E. Cox and Son, 1818.

Barnard, John. '"The Busy Time": Keats's Duties at Guy's Hospital from Autumn 1816 to March 1817', *Romanticism* 13.3 (October 2007): 199–218. DOI: <https://doi.org/10.3366/rom.2007.13.3.199>.

Barnard, John. 'First Fruits or "First Blights": A New Account of the Publishing History of Keats's *Poems* (1817)', *Romanticism* 12.2 (July 2006): 71–101. DOI: <https://doi.org/10.3366/rom.2006.12.2.71>.

Barnard, John. 'Keats, Andrew Motion's Dr Cake, and Charles Turner Thackrah', *Romanticism* 10.1 (April 2004): 1–22. DOI: <https://doi.org/10/3366/rom.2004.10.1.1>.

Barnard, John. 'Keats's "Forebodings": Margate, Spring 1817, and After', *Romanticism* 21.1 (April 2015): 1–13. DOI: <https://doi.org/10.3366/rom.2015.0206>.

Barnard, John. 'Keats's Sleepless Night: Charles Cowden Clarke's Letter of 1821', *Romanticism* 16.3 (October 2010): 267–78. DOI: <https://doi.org/10.3366/rom.2010.0102>.

Barnard, John. 'The Publication Dates of Keats's *Poems* (1817)', *Keats-Shelley Review* 28.2 (September 2014): 83–85.

Barnes, David S. *The Making of a Social Disease: Tuberculosis in Nineteenth-Century France*. Berkeley: University of California Press, 1995.

Bate, Walter Jackson. *John Keats*. Cambridge, MA: The Belknap Press of Harvard University Press/London: Oxford University Press, 1963.

Becker, Michael G., Robert J. Dilligan, and Todd K. Bender. *A Concordance to the Poems of John Keats*. New York: Garland Publishing, 1981.

Bell, John, and Charles Bell. *The Anatomy and Physiology of the Human Body. Containing The Anatomy of the Bones, Muscles, and Joints, and the Heart and Arteries, By John Bell; and The Anatomy and Physiology of the Brain and Nerves, the Organs of the Senses, and the Viscera, By Charles Bell, F.R.S.E. Surgeon to the Middlesex Hospital, and Reader of Anatomy in the Chair of Dr. Hunter, &c. &c.* 3 vols 1802–04; 4th ed. London: Longman, Hurst, Rees, Orme and Brown, and T. Cadell and W. Davies, 1816.

Bewell, Alan. *Romanticism and Colonial Disease*. Baltimore, MD/London: Johns Hopkins University Press, 1999.

Black, John, and Irving Taylor et al., eds. *Plarr's Lives of the Fellows Online*. Web. <https://livesonline.rcseng.ac.uk/client/en_GB/lives> (accessed 20 November 2018).

Blunden, Edmund. *Keats's Publisher: A Memoir of John Taylor (1781–1864)*. London: Jonathan Cape, 1936.

The British Institute of Graphologists. 'Directory of Graphologists A–Z'. Web. <www.britishgraphology.org/professional-services/directory-of-graphologists> (accessed 8 November 2018).

Brown, Charles Armitage. *Life of John Keats*. Edited by Dorothy Hyde Bodurtha and Willard Bissell Pope. London: Oxford University Press, 1937.

Brown, John. *The Elements of Medicine; or, A Translation of the Elementa Medicinæ Brunonis. With Large Notes, Illustrations and Comments. By the Author of the Original Work. In Two Volumes*. London: J. Johnson, 1788. Web. <https://data.historicaltexts.jisc.ac.uk/view?pubId=ecco-0274700701> (accessed 22 January 2018).

Brown, Sue. *Joseph Severn A Life: The Rewards of Friendship*. Oxford: Oxford University Press, 2009.

Burch, Druin. *Digging Up the Dead: The Life and Times of Astley Cooper, An Extraordinary Surgeon*. London: Chatto and Windus, 2007.

Burkey, Adam R. 'Parkinson's Shaking Palsy: The "Aspen-Malady" of John Keats', *Keats-Shelley Journal* 57 (2008): 128–37.

Burney, Fanny [Madame D'Arblay]. *France 1803–1812*. Vol. 6 of *The Journals and Letters of Fanny Burney*. Edited by Joyce Hemlow et al. Oxford: Clarendon Press, 1975.

Burton, Robert. *The Anatomy of Melancholy, What it is: With all the Kinds, Causes, Symptomes, Prognostickes, and Several Cures of It. In Three Maine Partitions with their several Sections, Members, and Subsections. Philosophically, Medicinally, Historically, Opened and Cut Up*. Edited by Holbrook Jackson. 1621; London: J. M. Dent and Sons, 1978.

Bushell, Sally. *Text as Process: Creative Composition in Wordsworth, Tennyson and Dickinson*. Charlottesville/London: University of Virginia Press, 2009.

Byron, George Gordon (Noel), Lord. *The Complete Poetical Works*. Edited by Jerome J. McGann. 7 vols. Oxford: Clarendon Press, 1980–93.

Caldwell, Janis McLarren. *Literature and Medicine in Nineteenth-Century Britain: From Mary Shelley to George Eliot*. Cambridge: Cambridge University Press, 2004.

Cameron, H. C. *Mr. Guy's Hospital 1726–1948*. London: Longman, Greens and Co., 1954.

Campbell, R. *The London Tradesman. Being An Historical Account of All the Trades, Professions, Arts, both Liberal and Mechanic, now practised in the Cities of London and Westminster. Calculated for the Instruction of Youth in their Choice of Business*; 3rd ed. London: T. Gardner, 1758.

Cazenave, [Pierre-Louis] A[lphée], and H. E. Schedel. *A Practical Synopsis of Cutaneous Diseases, from the Most Celebrated Authors, and Particularly from Documents afforded by the Clinical Lectures of Dr Biett*. Philadelphia, PA: Carey, Lea and Carey, 1829.

Chaudhuri, Sukanta. *The Metaphysics of Text*. Cambridge: Cambridge University Press, 2010.

Clarke, Charles Cowden. 'Recollections of Keats', *The Atlantic Monthly* 7.39 (January 1861): 86–101. Web. <http://ebooks.library.cornell.edu/cgi/t/text/text-idx?c=atla;cc=atla;view=toc;subview=short;idno=atla0007-1> (accessed 23 November 2018).

Clarke, Charles Cowden, and Mary Cowden Clarke. *Recollections of Writers*. London: Sampson Low, Marston, Searle, and Rivington, 1878.

Colvin, Sidney. *John Keats His Life and Poetry His Friends Critics and After-Fame*. London: Macmillan, 1917.

Colvin, Sidney. *Keats*. 1887; Cambridge/New York: Cambridge University Press, 2011.

Cooper, Astley. *The Lectures of Sir Astley Cooper, Bart., F. R. S., Surgeon to the King, &c. &c., on the Principles and Practice of Surgery; with Additional Notes and Cases*. Edited by Frederick Tyrell. 3 vols. London: Thomas and George Underwood; Simpkin and Marshall, 1824–25; 1827.

Cooper, Astley. *A Treatise of Dislocations and Fractures of the Joints*. Edited and enlarged by Bransby Blake Cooper. Philadelphia: Lea and Blanchard, 1844.

Cooper, Bransby Blake. *The Life of Astley Cooper, Bart., interspersed with Sketches from his Note-books of Distinguished Contemporary Characters*. 2 vols. London: J. W. Parker, 1843.

Coyer, Megan. *Literature and Medicine in the Nineteenth-Century Periodical Press: Blackwood's Edinburgh Magazine, 1817–1858*. Edinburgh: Edinburgh University Press, 2017.

Crosse, V. Mary. *A Surgeon in the early nineteenth-century: The Life and Times of John Green Crosse M.D., F.R.C.S., F.R.S. 1790–1850*. Foreword by Douglas Hubble. Edinburgh/London: E. and S. Livingstone, 1968.

Culpeper, Nicholas. *Culpeper's Complete Herbal, to which is now added, upwards of One Hundred Additional Herbs, with a display of their Medicinal and Occult Qualities; Physically applied to The Cure of All Disorders Incident to Mankind. To which are now first annexed his English Physician Enlarged, and Key to Physic, with Rules for Compounding Medicine according to the true System of Nature. Forming a Complete Family Dispensatory, and Natural System of Physic, to which is also added Upwards of Fifty Choice Receipts, Selected from the Author's last Legacy to his Wife*. London: Richard Evans, 1815.

Culpeper, Nicholas. *Culpeper's English Physician; and Complete Herbal. To which are now first added, Upwards of One Hundred additional Herbs, with a display of their Medicinal and Occult Properties, Physically Applied to the Cure of all Disorders incident to Mankind, to which are annexed, Rules for Compounding Medicine according to the True System of Nature: Forming a Complete Family Dispensatory, And Natural System of Physic*. Edited by Ebenezer Sibly. London: Green and Co., 1789. Web. <https://data.historicaltexts.jisc.ac.uk/view?pubId=ecco-0824600300&index=ecco&pageId=ecco-0824600300-10> (accessed 18 November 2015).

Culpeper, Nicholas. *Pharmacopœia Londinensis: or the London Dispensatory Further adorned by the Studies and Collections of the Fellows, now living of the said Colledg*. London: Printed for Peter Cole, at the Sign of the Printing-Press in Cornhil neer the Royal Exchange, 1653.

Darwin, Erasmus. *The Botanic Garden; A Poem, in Two Parts. Part I. Containing The Economy of Vegetation. Part II. The Loves of the Plants. With Philosophical Notes*. London: J. Johnson, 1791.

de Almeida, Hermione. *Romantic Medicine and John Keats*. Oxford/New York: Oxford University Press, 1991.

Debus, Allen G. *Man and Nature in the Renaissance*. Cambridge: Cambridge University Press, 1978.

Dendy, Walter Cooper. *The Philosophy of Mystery*. New York: Harper and Brothers, 1845.

Epstein, Joseph. 'The Medical Keats', *Hudson Review* 52.1 (Spring 1999): 44–64. <http://www.jstor.org/stable/3852571>.

Evans, Benjamin Ifor. 'Keats as a Medical Student'. *The Times Literary Supplement* (31 May 1934): 391.

Evans, Gareth. 'Poison Wine – John Keats and the Botanical Pharmacy', *Keats-Shelley Review* 16 (2002): 31–55.

Everett, Barbara. *Poets in Their Time: Essays on English Poetry from Donne to Larkin*. London: Faber & Faber, 1986.

Finney, Claude Lee. *The Evolution of Keats's Poetry*. New York: Russell and Russell, 1956.

Ghosh, Hrileena. '"Give Me Women Wine and Snuff": A New Account of John Keats's Poem', *Keats-Shelley Review* 30.2 (September 2016): 113–21.

Gifford, William. *The Baviad, A Paraphrastic Imitation of the First Satire of Persius*. London: R. Faulder, 1791. Web. <https://data.historicaltexts.jisc.ac.uk/view?pubId=ecco-0478701700&index=ecco&pageId=ecco-0478701700-10> (accessed 30 June 2015).

Gigante, Denise. *The Keats Brothers: The Life of John and George*. Cambridge, MA/London: The Belknap Press of Harvard University Press, 2011.

Gigante, Denise. *Life: Organic Form and Romanticism*. New Haven, CT/London: Yale University Press, 2009.

Gigante, Denise. 'The Monster in the Rainbow: Keats and the Science of Life', *PMLA* 117.3 (May 2002): 433–48. <http://www.jstor.org/stable/pdf/823143>.

Gigante, Denise. *Taste: A Literary History*. New Haven, CT/London: Yale University Press, 2005.

Gittings, Robert. *John Keats*. London: Heinemann, 1968.

Gittings, Robert. *John Keats: The Living Year 21 September 1818 to 21 September 1819*. London: William Heinemann, 1954.

Goellnicht, Donald. *The Poet-Physician: Keats and Medical Science*. Pittsburgh, PA: University of Pittsburgh Press, 1984.

Gray, Henry, and H. V. Carter. *Anatomy Descriptive and Surgical*. London: John W. Parker and Son, 1858. Commonly known as Gray's *Anatomy*.

Greetham, D. C. *Textual Scholarship: An Introduction*. New York/London: Garland, 1992.

Gregory, John. *Lectures on the Duties and Qualifications of a Physician*. London: W. Strahan and T. Cadell, 1772.

Grinnell, George C. *The Age of Hypochondria: Interpreting Romantic Health and Illness*. Basingstoke: Palgrave Macmillan, 2010.

Guillory, John. *Cultural Capital: The Problem of Literary Canon Formation*. Chicago, IL/London: University of Chicago Press, 1993.

Hagelman, Charles. 'John Keats and the Medical Profession'. PhD diss., University of Texas, 1956.

Hale-White, William. 'Keats and Guy's', Letters to the Editor. *The Times* (15 February 1921): 6.

Hale-White, William. *Keats as Doctor and Patient*. London: Oxford University Press, 1938.

Hale-White, William. 'Keats as a Medical Student', *Guy's Hospital Reports* 75 (1925): 249–62.

Hall, John E. 'Chapter 62: Cerebral Blood Flow, Cerebrospinal Fluid, and Brain Metabolism', *Guyton and Hall Textbook of Medical Physiology*; 13th ed. Philadelphia, PA: Elsevier, 2016. Web. <https://elsevierelibrary.co.uk/pdfreader/guyton-hall-textbook-medical-physiology70313> (accessed 10 November 2018).

Harvey, William. *The Circulation of Blood and Other Writings*. Translated by Kenneth J. Franklin. London: J. M. Dent/Vermont: Charles E. Tuttle, 1993.

Haydon, Benjamin Robert. *The Diary of Benjamin Robert Haydon*. Edited by W. B. Pope. 5 vols. Cambridge, MA: Harvard University Press, 1960.

Hazlitt, William. *Table-Talk: Essays on Men and Manners*. 1821–22; London/Edinburgh: Henry Frowde, 1901; reprint 1905.

Hebron, Stephen. *John Keats: A Poet and His Manuscripts*. London: British Library, 2009.

Hewlett, Dorothy. *Adonais: A Life of John Keats*. London: Hurst and Blackett, 1937; 2nd ed. 1948.

Hewlett, Dorothy. *A Life of John Keats*. Revised and Enlarged. London: Hurst and Blackett, 1949.

Holmes, Richard. *The Age of Wonder: How the Romantic Generation Discovered the Beauty and Terror of Science*. London: HarperCollins, 2008.

Holmes, Richard. *This Long Pursuit: Reflections of a Romantic Biographer*. London: William Collins, 2016.

Holstein, Michael E. 'Keats: The Poet-Healer and the Problem of Pain', *Keats-Shelley Journal* 36 (1987): 32–49. <http://www.jstor.org/stable/30210277>.

Hooper, Robert. *Lexico-Medicum; or Medical Dictionary; Containing an Explanation of the Terms in Anatomy, Chemistry, Physiology, Pharmacy, Practice of Physic, Surgery, Materia Medica, Midwifery, and the Various Branches of Natural Philosophy connected with Medicine Selected, Arranged, and Compiled from the Best Authors*; 4th ed. London: Longman, Hurst, Rees, Orme, and Co.; Scatcherd and Letterman; J. Cuthell; Cadell and Davies; Baldwin, Cradock, and Joy; Highley and Son; Cox and Son; J. Callow; T. and G. Underwood; G. and W. B. Whittaker; Ogle, Duncan, and Co.; G. Mackie; J. Anderson; Burgess and Hill; Stirling and Slade; and Edinburgh: Fairbairn and Anderson, 1822.

Hughes, Sean P. F., and Sarah Hughes, 'Keats Memorial Lecture: How Did John Keats's Medical Training Influence His Poetry?', *Keats-Shelley Review* 31.2 (September 2017): 136–46.

Hunt, James Henry Leigh. *Foliage; or, Poems Original and Translated*. London: C. and J. Ollier, 1818.

Hunt, James Henry Leigh. 'Harry Brown's Letter to His Friends: Letter VII', *The Examiner* (25 August 1816): 536–37.

Hunt, James Henry Leigh. *Lord Byron and Some of His Contemporaries with Recollections of the Author's Life, and of His Visit to Italy*. London: Henry Colburn, 1828.

Hunt, James Henry Leigh. *Poetical Works, 1801–21*. Edited by John Strachan. Vol. 5 of *The Selected Writings of Leigh Hunt*. London: Pickering and Chatto, 2003.

Hunt, James Henry Leigh. 'To Kosciusko', *The Examiner* (19 November 1815): 746.

Hunt, James Henry Leigh. 'Young Poets', *The Examiner* (1 December 1816): 759.

Hunter, John. *A Treatise on the Blood, Inflammation and Gun-Shot Wounds, to Which is Affixed, A Short Account of the Author's Life, by his Brother-in-Law, Everard Home*. London: G. Nicol, 1794.

Hunter, John. *The Works of John Hunter, F. R. S. with Notes, In Four Volumes, Illustrated by a Volume of Plates, in Quarto*. Edited by James F. Palmer. London: Longman, Rees, Orme, Brown, Green, and Longman, 1835–37.

Jack, Ian. *Keats and the Mirror of Art*. Oxford: Clarendon Press, 1967.

Jackson, Noel. *Science and Sensation in Romantic Poetry*. Cambridge: Cambridge University Press, 2008.

Jones, John Frederick Drake. *A Treatise on the Process Employed by Nature in Suppressing the Hemorrhage from Divided and Punctured Arteries, and the Use of Ligature; concluding with Observations on Secondary Hemorrhage*. 1805; Philadelphia, PA: Thomas Dobson, 1811.

Keats, John. *The Complete Poems*. Edited by John Barnard. Harmondsworth: Penguin, 1973; 3rd ed. 1988; reprint 2006.

Keats, John. *John Keats*. Edited by Elizabeth Cook. Oxford: Oxford University Press, 1990.

Keats, John. *John Keats's Anatomical and Physiological Note Book printed from the holograph in the Keats Museum Hampstead*. Edited by Maurice Buxton Forman. Oxford: Oxford University Press, 1934; reprint New York: Haskell House, 1970.

Keats, John. *The Keats Circle: Letters and Papers 1816–1878*. Edited by Hyder Edward Rollins. 2 vols. Cambridge, MA: Harvard University Press, 1948.

Keats, John. *Keats's Poetry and Prose*. Selected and edited by Jeffrey N. Cox. New York/London: W. W. Norton and Company, 2009.

Keats, John. *Lamia, Isabella, The Eve of St. Agnes, and other Poems*. London: Taylor and Hessey, 1820.

Keats, John. *The Letters of John Keats 1814–1821*. Edited by Hyder Edward Rollins. 2 vols. Cambridge, MA: Harvard University Press, 1958.

Keats, John. *The Poems of John Keats*. Edited by H. W. Garrod. Oxford: Clarendon Press, 1939.

Keats, John. *The Poems of John Keats*. Edited by Miriam Allott. London: Longman, 1970.

Keats, John. *The Poems of John Keats*. Edited by Jack Stillinger. London: Heinemann, 1978.

Keats, John. *The Poems of John Keats, Arranged in Chronological Order with a Preface by Sidney Colvin*. 2 vols. London: Chatto and Windus, 1915.

Keats, John. *The Poetical Works and Other Writings of John Keats*. Edited by Harry Buxton Forman, revised by Maurice Buxton Forman, introduced by John Masefield. 8 vols. New York: Charles Scribner's Sons, 1938–39.

Keats, John. *The Poetical Works of John Keats, Given from his own Editions and Other Authentic Sources and Collected with Many Manuscripts*. Edited by Harry Buxton Forman. London: Reeves and Turner, 1884.

Keats, John. *Selected Letters*. Edited by Robert Gittings, revised by Jon Mee. New York: Oxford University Press, 2002.

Keats, John. *Selected Letters*. Edited by John Barnard. London: Penguin, 2014.

Keats, John. *Selected Letters of John Keats*; rev. ed. Edited by Grant F. Scott, based on the texts of Hyder Edward Rollins. Cambridge, MA/London: Harvard University Press, 2002.

Knerr, Anthony D. *Shelley's* Adonais*: A Critical Edition*. New York: Columbia University Press, 1984.

Kuhn, Thomas. *The Structure of Scientific Revolutions*. Chicago, IL: Chicago University Press, 1962; 2nd ed. 1970.

Lane, Edward William, trans. *The Thousand and One Nights: The Arabian Nights' Entertainments*. Edited by Stanley Lane-Poole. 4 vols. London: George Bell and Sons, 1906.

Lawrence, Susan C. *Charitable Knowledge: Hospital Pupils and Practitioners in Eighteenth-century London*. Cambridge/New York: Cambridge University Press, 1996.

Lawrence, William. *An Introduction to Comparative Anatomy and Physiology; being the Two Introductory Lectures Delivered at the Royal College of Surgeons, On the 21st and 25th of March, 1816*. London: J. Callow, 1816.

Lee, Anthony. 'Waddington Father and Son', *Margate in Maps and Pictures*. Web. <http://margatelocalhistory.co.uk/DocRead/Waddington%20father%20 and%20 Margate.html> (accessed 14 November 2018).

Le Fanu, William R. 'Keats's Medical Notebook', review of *John Keats's Anatomical and Physiological Note Book*. Edited by Maurice Buxton Forman. *The Times Literary Supplement* (7 June 1934): 404.

Le Fanu, William R. 'Medical Manuscripts', review of *Manuscripta Medica: a Descriptive Catalogue of the Manuscripts in the Library of the Medical Society of London*, by Warren R. Dawson. *The Times Literary Supplement* (22 September 1932): 657.

Lemprière, John. *A Classical Dictionary; containing a copious account of all the proper names mentioned in ancient authors; with the value of coins, weights, and measures, used among the Greeks and Romans; and a Chronological Table*. 1788; 7th ed. London: T. Cadell and W. Davies, 1809.

Levinson, Marjorie. *Keats's Life of Allegory: The Origins of a Style*. Oxford: Basil Blackwell, 1988.

Lockhart, John Gibson ['Z']. 'Cockney School of Poetry. No. IV', *Blackwood's Edinburgh Magazine* 3.17 (August 1818): 519–24.

'London Adjourned Sessions'. *The Morning Chronicle* (23 April 1816): 3.

*The London Dissector; or, System of Dissection, Practised in the Hospitals and Lecture Rooms of the Metropolis; Explained by the Clearest Rules, for the use of Students: Comprising a Description of the Muscles, Vessels, Nerves and Viscera, of the Human Body, as they appear on Dissection; with Directions for their Demonstration*; 3rd ed. London: John Murray; J. Callow; E. Cox; T. Underwood; and Edinburgh: William Blackwood, 1811.

Loudon, Irvine. *Medical Care and the General Practitioner 1750–1850*. Oxford: Clarendon Press, 1986.

Lowell, Amy. *John Keats*. 2 vols. Boston, MA/New York: Houghton Mifflin, 1925.

McCullough, Lawrence B. *John Gregory and the Invention of Professional Medical Ethics and the Profession of Medicine*. Dordrecht: Kluwer Academic Publishers, 1998.

McFarland, Thomas. *The Masks of Keats: The Endeavour of a Poet*. Oxford: Oxford University Press, 2000.

McGann, Jerome J. *A Critique of Modern Textual Criticism*. Chicago, IL/London: Chicago University Press, 1983.

MacGillivray, J. R. *Keats: A Bibliography and Reference Guide with an Essay on Keats's Reputation*. Toronto: University of Toronto Press, 1949.

McLean, Thomas. *The Other East and Nineteenth-Century British Literature: Imagining Poland and the Russian Empire*. Basingstoke: Palgrave Macmillan, 2012.

Marshall, Tim. *Murdering to Dissect: Grave-Robbing,* Frankenstein *and the anatomy literature*. Manchester/New York: Manchester University Press, 1995.

Matthews, G. M., ed. *Keats: The Critical Heritage*. New York: Barnes and Noble, 1971.

Mellor, Anne K. *Mary Shelley: Her Life, Her Fiction, Her Monsters*. London/New York: Routledge, 1988.

Milnes, Richard Monckton. *Life, Letters, and Literary Remains, of John Keats*. 2 vols. London: Edward Moxon, 1848.

Milton, John. *Paradise Lost*. Edited by Alastair Fowler. London/New York: Longman, 1968, 1971; reprint 1992.

Mitchell, Robert. *Experimental Life: Vitalism in Romantic Science and Literature*. Baltimore, MD: Johns Hopkins University Press, 2013.

Motion, Andrew. *Keats*. London: Faber and Faber, 1997.

Munk, William, et al. *Royal College of Physicians Lives of the Fellows* [*Munk's Rolls*]. Web. <munksroll.rcplondon.ac.uk> (accessed 13 July 2018).

Murry, John Middleton. *Studies in Keats*. London: Oxford University Press, 1930.

Nussbaum, Martha C. *The Fragility of Goodness: Luck and Ethics in Greek Tragedy and Philosophy*. Cambridge: Cambridge University Press, 1986.

O'Neill, Michael, ed. *John Keats in Context*. Cambridge: Cambridge University Press, 2017.

Parkinson, James. *An Essay on the Shaking Palsy*. London: Sherwood, Neely, and Jones, 1817.

Pierpoint, William S. *The Unparallel Lives of Three Medical Students: John Keats, Henry Stephens and George Wilson Mackereth*. London: The Stephens Collection, 2010.

Plato. *Symposium and Phaedrus*. Translated by Tom Griffiths. New York/London: Alfred A. Knopf, 2000.

Pollard, David. *A Key-Word-in-Context Concordance to the Hyder E. Rollins Edition of the Complete Letters of John Keats*. Hove: Geraldson Imprints, 1989.

Porter, Roy. *The Greatest Benefit to Mankind: A Medical History of Humanity from Antiquity to the Present*. London: Harper Collins, 1997; Fontana Press, 1999.

Redpath, Theodore. *The Young Romantics and Critical Opinion 1807–1824: Poetry of Byron, Shelley, and Keats as seen by their contemporary critics*. London: George Harrap and Co., 1973.

[Reynolds], John Hamilton. *The Garden of Florence; and Other Poems*. London: John Warren, 1821.

Richardson, Alan. *British Romanticism and the Science of the Mind*. Cambridge: Cambridge University Press, 2001.

Richardson, Benjamin Ward. 'An Esculapian Poet – John Keats', in *The Asclepiad: A Book of Original Research and Observation in the Science, Art and Literature of Medicine, Preventive and Curative*: Vol. I, 138–55. London: Longmans, Green and Co., 1884.

Ricks, Christopher. *Keats and Embarrassment*. Oxford: Clarendon Press, 1974; Oxford University Press, 1976.

Ridley, M. R. *Keats' Craftsmanship: A Study in Poetic Development*. London: Oxford University Press, 1933; reprint London: Metheun, 1964.

Robinson, Janet. 'A Branch of the Jarvis Family: Daniel Jarvis 3rd', *Margate in Maps and Pictures*. Web. <http://margatelocalhistory.co.uk/DocRead/Jarvis%207%20Daniel%20Jarvis%203rd.html> (accessed 28 October 2018).

Roe, Nicholas. 'Dressing for Art: Notes from Keats in the Emergency Ward', *The Times Literary Supplement* (27 May 2015): 14–15.

Roe, Nicholas. *Fiery Heart: The First Life of Leigh Hunt*. London: Pimlico, 2005.

Roe, Nicholas. *John Keats and the Culture of Dissent*. Oxford: Clarendon Press, 1997.

Roe, Nicholas, ed. *John Keats and the Medical Imagination*. Cham: Palgrave Macmillan, 2017.

Roe, Nicholas. *John Keats: A New Life*. New Haven, CT/London: Yale University Press, 2012.

Roe, Nicholas, ed. *Keats and History*. Cambridge: Cambridge University Press, 1995.

Roe, Nicholas. 'Mr. Keats', *Essays in Criticism* 65.3 (July 2015): 274–88.

Roe, Nicholas. *The Politics of Nature: William Wordsworth and Some Contemporaries*; 2nd ed. Basingstoke: Palgrave Macmillan, 2002.

Rossetti, William Michael. *Life of John Keats*. London: Walter Scott, 1887.

Ruston, Sharon. *Creating Romanticism: Case Studies in the Literature, Science and Medicine of the 1790s*. Basingstoke: Palgrave Macmillan, 2013.

Ruston, Sharon. *Shelley and Vitality*. Basingstoke: Palgrave Macmillan, 2005.

Ryan, Ronald M., and Ronald A. Sharp, eds. *The Persistence of Poetry: Bicentenniel Essays on Keats*. Amherst: University of Massachusetts Press, 1998.

Salisbury, William. *The Botanist's Companion, or an Introduction to the Knowledge of Practical Botany, and the Uses of Plants. Either Growing Wild in Great Britain, or Cultivated for the Purposes of Agriculture, Medicine, Rural Œconomy, or the Arts*. 2 vols. London: Longman, Hurst, Rees, Orme, and Brown, 1816.

Shakespeare, William. *The Complete Works*. Edited by Stanley Wells, Gary Taylor, John Jowett, and William Montgomery. Oxford: Clarendon Press, 1986; 2nd ed. 2005; reprint 2006.

Shelley, Percy Bysshe. *Adonais: An Elegy on the Death of John Keats, Author of Endymion, Hyperion &c*. Pisa: 1821.

Shillingsburg, Peter L. *Scholarly Editing in the Computer Age: Theory and Practice*. Athens/London: University of Georgia Press, 1986.

Sinson, Janice. *John Keats and The Anatomy of Melancholy*. London: Published by the Keats-Shelley Memorial Association, 1971.

Smith, Hillas. 'The Strange Case of Mr Keats's Tuberculosis', *Clinical Infectious Diseases* 38.7 (April 2004): 991–93.

South, John Flint. *Memorials of John Flint South*. 1884; Fontwell: Centaur Press, 1970.

Sperry, Stuart. *Keats the Poet*. Princeton, NJ: Princeton University Press, 1973.

Steele, Mabel A. E. 'Three Early Manuscripts of John Keats', *Keats-Shelley Journal* 1 (January 1952): 57–63. <http://www.jstor.org/stable/30209995>

Stillinger, Jack. *The Hoodwinking of Madeline and Other Essays on Keats's Poems*. Urbana: University of Illinois Press, 1971.

Stillinger, Jack. *Romantic Complexity: Keats, Coleridge, and Wordsworth*. Urbana/Chicago, IL: University of Illinois Press, 2006.

Stillinger, Jack. *The Texts of Keats's Poems*. Cambridge, MA: Harvard University Press, 1974.

Tauber, Michael, Harry R. van Loveran, George Jallo, Alberto Romano, and Jeffrey Keller. 'The Enigmatic Foramen Lacerum', *Neurosurgery* 44.2 (February 1999): 386–91. <https://doi.org/10.1097/00006123-199902000-00083>.

Turley, Richard Marggraf. *Bright Stars: John Keats, 'Barry Cornwall' and Romantic Literary Culture*. Liverpool: Liverpool University Press, 2009.

Turley, Richard Marggraf. *Keats's Boyish Imagination*. London/New York: Routledge, 2004.

Unsigned review of *John Keats's Anatomical and Physiological Notebook printed from the holograph in the Keats Museum in Hampstead*, edited by Maurice Buxton Forman, *British Medical Journal* 1 (9 June 1934): 1040. <http://www.jstor.org/stable/25321279>.

Vendler, Helen. *The Odes of John Keats*. Cambridge, MA/London: The Belknap Press of the Harvard University Press, 1983.

Vickers, Neil. *Coleridge and the Doctors: 1795–1806*. Oxford: Oxford University Press, 2004.

Ward, Aileen. *John Keats: The Making of a Poet*. London: Secker and Warburg, 1963.

Wardrop, James. *Observations on Fungus Hæmatodes or Soft Cancer, in Several of the Most Important Organs of the Human Body: Containing also a Comparative View of the Structure of Fungus Hæmatodes and Cancer. With Cases and Dissections, Illustrated by Plates*. Edinburgh: Constable and Co., 1809.

White, R. S. *John Keats: A Literary Life*. Basingstoke: Palgrave Macmillan, 2010.

White, R. S. '"Like Esculapius of Old": Keats's Medical Training', *Keats-Shelley Review* 12 (1998): 15–49.

Williams, Helen Maria. 'Kosciusko', *The Examiner* (12 November 1815): 734.

Williams, Helen Maria. 'Kosciusko', *The Liverpool Mercury* (17 November 1815): 6.

Williams, Helen Maria. 'Koscuisko', Letter to the Editor, *The Morning Chronicle* (10 November 1815): 3.

Williams, Helen Maria. 'Kosciusko', *The Morning Post* (10 November 1815): 4.

Winston, George A. R. 'John Keats and Joshua Waddington Contemporary Students at Guy's Hospital', *Guy's Hospital Reports* 92 (1943): 101–10.

Wolfson, Susan, ed. *The Cambridge Companion to Keats*. Cambridge: Cambridge University Press, 2001.

Woof, Robert, and Stephen Hebron. *John Keats*. Grasmere: The Wordsworth Trust, 1995.

Wordsworth, William. *Poems, in Two Volumes, and Other Poems, 1800–1807*. Edited by Jared Curtis. The Cornell Wordsworth: Volume VII. Ithaca, NY: Cornell University Press, 1983.

Wright, Herbert Gladstone. 'Keats's "Isabella"', *The Times Literary Supplement* (17 April 1943): 192.

Wunder, Jennifer N. *Keats, Hermeticism and Secret Societies*. Aldershot: Ashgate, 2008.

## Nineteenth-century Journals and Newspapers

Full details of advertisements cited from the following are given in the footnotes, while details of articles cited from them appear under the 'Printed Sources' listed above.

*The Caledonian Mercury*
*The Examiner*

*The Liverpool Mercury*
*The London Medical and Physical Journal*
*The Morning Chronicle*
*The Morning Post*
*The York Herald, and General Advertiser*

# Index


Abbey, Richard 136, 138, 142, 204, 239
Abernethy, John 68, 96, 159, 162–63, 164, 165, 166
  *see also* Vitalism Debates
absorbents 24, 25, 26, 27, 28, 41, 48, 50, 55, 106, 255
  vessels 24–25, 26, 28, 37,
absorption 16, 24, 27–28, 30, 39, 54, 255
aconitum *see* wolf's-bane
*Adonais: An Elegy on the Death of John Keats see under* Shelley, Percy Bysshe
*The Aeneid* 138
'Æsculapius' (anonymous author) *see The Hospital Pupil's Guide, being Oracular Communications, addressed to Students of the Medical Profession*
albumin ('albumen') 26, 27, 39, 43, 52
Allard, James 6
Allen, William 103, 104, 162
Allott, Miriam 128n32
amara dulcis *see under* nightshade
amputation 37, 39, 66, 67
anastomosis 47, 55
'Anatomical and Surgical Lectures' *see* 'Lectures on Anatomy'
anatomy 35, 48, 91, 92, 103, 106, 113, 116, 118, 169, 202, 226
Anatomy Act of 1832 170
'Anatomy, and the Operations of Surgery' *see* 'Lectures on Anatomy'
*Anatomy Descriptive and Surgical see* Gray's *Anatomy*
*The Anatomy of Melancholy* 220–21, 256
  love-melancholy 221, 256
aneurism 20–21, 117, 178, 190
  spurious 21
aneurismal varix 23
ankle 83
Aphrodite 240
Apollo 192–93, 208, 240
Apothecaries' Act of 1815 138
apothecary 6, 103, 112, 116, 169, 223, 229, 239, 241, 260
arm 63, 64, 80, 81
arteries 20, 21, 23, 26, 29, 30, 40, 41, 45–46, 48, 50, 52, 54–55, 58, 60, 62, 71, 74, 75, 81, 84, 85, 102, 106, 117, 118, 176–78, 180, 188, 191, 192, 193, 195, 217, 220
  after death 46, 118, 192–93, 195–96
  coats of 21, 31, 46, 47, 55
  course of 31, 54–55, 106, 220
  diseases of 27, 39, 45, 46–47, 102
    *see also* aneurism
  origin 47, 191
  pulsation 45, 46, 177–78, 194, 216–17
    *see also* pulse
  temporal artery 46, 179, 216–17
  termination 22, 30, 40, 47, 55

arteriotomy 46, 179, 217
  *see also* temporal artery
*atropa belladonna see under* nightshade
Atropos 263–64

Babington, William 103, 104, 151, 157
Bailey, Benjamin 238
Barnard, John ix, xi, 1, 4, 126, 145, 206, 247
bat 34, 110, 183
Bate, Walter Jackson 112, 113–15, 117
*The Baviad see* Gifford, William
Bell, Charles 159, 257, 258, 259
  on 'the operation of attention' 257, 258, 259–60
    *see also The Eve of St Agnes and* 'Ode to a Nightingale' *under* Keats' works
  *see also* reverie
Bewell, Alan 6
bile 26, 39, 41
bittersweet *see under* nightshade
*Blackwood's Edinburgh Magazine* 130–31, 132, 135, 223, 239, 242, 246–47
  *see also* Lockhart, John Gibson
bladder 40, 44, 61
  *see also* excretory ducts
Blake, William 240
blood 10, 16, 22–23, 24, 26, 29, 30, 31, 39, 46, 48, 50, 51, 52–54, 55, 117, 118, 162–64, 166, 169, 177–79, 190, 192–93, 194, 214, 216, 219, 265
  ancient beliefs 22, 193–96
  circulation 45, 50, 51, 55, 163, 194
  red particles 52, 53, 54
  *see also* serum *and* coagulation
Blumenbach, Johann 158, 160, 192
Boccaccio, Giovanni 131
body 24, 26, 27, 30, 42, 46, 48, 52, 53, 55, 106, 163, 167–68, 196, 219, 227, 232, 269
bones 11, 12, 24, 38, 41, 42, 43, 44, 47, 48, 51, 53–54, 60, 67, 114, 115, 118, 270
  structure 51, 59
  *see also* osteology
*The Botanic Garden see* Darwin, Erasmus
*The Botanist's Companion see* Salisbury, William
botany 115, 260–63
  importance of 115, 262–65
  *see also* nineteenth century medical practice
brain *see under* nervous system
Brande, William Thomas 52, 96, 103, 159
Brawne, Frances (Fanny) 136, 250, 251
breast 35, 41
breathing 35, 38, 50, 194, 217
Brezelius, J. J. 158
*British Medical Journal* 110–11
Brown, Charles 87, 132, 135, 136, 217, 227, 237, 238, 249, 252, 253
  biography of Keats 90–91, 136
Brown, John 159, 167–68
  hypothesis of health 166–69, 214
Burney, Fanny (Madame D'Arblay) 211–12
Burton, Robert *see The Anatomy of Melancholy*
Byron, George Gordon, Lord 133–34, 137, 209, 221, 223, 225, 240

*The Caledonian Mercury* 183
cancer 28, 39, 182, 262
carbon 26, 50
Carlile, Richard 166
cartilage 15, 42, 45, 47, 48, 51, 53, 60, 77, 79, 84
catheter 40, 61
cellular membrane 21, 23, 24, 30, 32, 39, 40, 54
Chatterton, Thomas 118, 240

Cheapside 126–27, 144–46, 147, 204
Cholmeley, Henry James 46, 103, 104
chyle 24, 26, 27, 52
City of London Corporation ix, 1, 87
Clare, John 137
Clarke, Charles Cowden xiii, 91, 116, 119, 124, 139–43, 145, 205, 246–47
  formative role in Keats' poetic development 119, 139–40, 247
  letter as 'Y' 246–47
  'Recollections of Keats' xi, 91–92, 119, 141–42, 146, 247
Clarke, James 181
Clerkenwell 139, 141
Cline, Henry, Jnr. 103, 104, 105, 106, 150, 151, 153–56, 169–70, 173–74
  *see also* 'Lectures on Anatomy'
Cline, Henry, Snr. 20n2, 21, 26
coagulation 20, 46, 51–52, 53, 54, 162–63
Coleridge, Samuel Taylor 157, 218
Collins, William 240
Colvin, Sidney 2, 89, 108, 114
  *John Keats His Life and Poetry His Friends Critics and After-Fame* 2n4, 89, 107
Cooper, Astley 46, 52, 97, 102, 103, 104, 105, 106, 111, 113, 117, 118, 150, 151–56, 163, 168, 169–70, 173–74, 176–77, 178, 180–81, 183, 184, 186–87, 188, 190, 195, 214–17, 218, 254
  insistence on dissection 113, 170, 195
  lecture series
    joint lectures with Henry Cline Jnr. *see* 'Lectures on Anatomy'
    lectures on surgery *see* lectures on the 'Principles and Practice of Surgery'
    overlap between different lectures series 174, 183, 232
  medical advice 21, 23, 27, 28, 29, 31, 39, 40, 41, 43, 44, 54, 60–61, 62, 66, 67, 68, 70, 79, 148, 214–16
  as 'Mr C' 20, 21, 25, 31, 35, 35–36, 39, 42, 51, 52, 61, 68
  as pioneering surgeon 180–81, 190
Cooper, Bransby Blake 180
Cooper, George 124, 137, 158, 171
Cowper, William 240
Cox, Jane 242
Cox, Jeffrey 1
cranium 14, 32, 68, 69, 70–71
crassamentum 27, 52–53
Croker, John Wilson 131, 133, 222, 223–24, 244–45, 247
Cullen, William 159, 167
Culpeper, William 255, 261, 262, 264
Curry, James 103, 104, 151, 157, 181, 218

Darwin, Erasmus 159, 264–65
Davy, Humphry 157, 159, 162, 164
de Almeida, Hermione xiii, 5, 157, 159–60, 164, 255n99
Dean Street 125–26, 144, 147
Diana 148, 205, 222
  *see also* Diana *under* Keats' works
diastole ('dyastole') 45, 176, 188, 189, 194
Dilke, Charles 87, 91, 136, 242–43, 248
Dilke Collection 12n30, 87, 90
Dilke, Maria 248
Dilke, Sir Charles Wentworth (Dilke's grandson) 12n30, 13, 45, 87
Dionysus 240
disease 8, 167–68, 182, 224, 226, 233, 234, 237, 240, 245, 246, 248, 249, 251, 254
dog 25–26, 46, 52
doggerel rhymes 88, 129
Doubleday, W. E. 107, 108
dressers 120–21, 145
  duty dresser 121, 180
  *see also* as dresser *under* Keats, John
dropsy 27, 29, 48
dulcamara *see under* nightshade

*The Edinburgh Review* 165–66, 224
Edwards, Mary 181
  *see also* Cooper, Astley
elbow 23, 80
Elgin Marbles 140, 145–46, 208
Eros 240
Evans, Gareth 263
Everett, Barbara 189–90
*The Examiner* 97, 122, 125, 126, 134, 140, 141, 144, 145, 183, 197, 240
excretory ducts 24, 40, 48, 51, 55
  *see also* glands
exhalents 23, 28, 29, 43, 47, 55
eye 26, 34, 50, 74, 101, 110, 182–83, 216, 227, 265

face 38, 76, 77, 196, 225–27
  *see also* skull
fainting *see* syncope
fascia 38
fat 30, 39
fever 46, 159, 178–79, 189, 222, 232, 235, 237
  *see also* pulse
fibrin 26, 27, 43, 52, 53
Flajani, A. 157
follicles 40, 51
foot 35, 66, 68, 83, 115
Forman, Maurice Buxton 3, 93, 107, 111, 114
  edition xi, 1, 3, 93–97, 98–102, 111, 113, 117, 174
    accounts of 3, 110–11
    confusing 98–99, 174
    contemporary reviews 110–11
    editorial principles 93–95, 96–97, 98, 99–100, 101–02
    lack of annotations 94–95
    list of persons 95–96
    presentation of Keats' marginalia 99–101
    shifting of notes 94, 99–102
    transcription 96–97
      discrepancies with Hale-White's readings 97, 102
  'Prefatory Note' 93, 98, 108
French materialism 165–66
frog 35, 118, 197, 199
Frogley, Mary 124
Fuseli, Henry 158

Galen (Galenus Claudius) 193–95
Galignani (publishers) 134–36
  'American-Galignani' editions 134–35
gall bladder 40
Gallois, Julien Jean César ('Le Gallois') 35, 158, 183
Galvani, Luigi ('Galvano') 36, 96, 158
galvanism 183
gelatine 28, 37, 41, 42
Gifford, William 239, 247
Gigante, Denise 7
Gittings, Robert xii, 115–16, 123, 234
glands 16, 24, 25, 27, 40, 41, 47, 50, 255
  diseases of 25, 27–28, 41
  types 39–40, 51
  *see also* absorbents *and* excretory ducts
Godwin, William 141
Goellnicht, Donald xiii, 3, 156–57, 174, 231
gonorrhoea 28n35, 181
Gossett, Daniel 180
graphologist's report 109
Gray, Henry xii, 15–16
Gray's *Anatomy* 15, 19
  first edition xii, 15–16
  modern edition 15
Green, Joseph Henry 155, 168, 170
Gregory, John 159, 228–29, 230, 232
  *see also* medical ethics
Grosvenor, John 27, 96

Guy's Hospital 1, 6, 7, 103, 105, 111, 146, 148, 150, 157, 163, 169, 171, 180–81, 229–30, 232, 261
administrative records 120, 149, 151, 153
Bible-reading in wards 148–49
Christmas vacation 137–38
lecture courses 102–07, 129, 147, 153–56, 232, 254
Physical Society 155, 158–60, 166, 168
library 158–60
Minutes book of 155
professional opportunities 150
schedule of work 4, 119, 140, 145, 170
'taking-in' day 121
ward for mentally or terminally ill patients 225–26

haemorrhage 46, 55, 95–96, 180, 251
Hagelman, Charles 3, 114, 115, 254
Haighton, John 104, 105, 151
Hale-White, William 114, 156
'Keats as a Medical Student' 2, 92–93, 99, 102, 106, 107–08, 111, 112, 115, 151
*Keats as Doctor and Patient* 112, 115
Haller, Albrecht van 42, 96, 158, 159, 167
Hammond, Thomas *see under* Keats, John
Hampstead 127, 147, 204–05, 236, 238, 242, 249, 252
*see also* Keats House
Hampstead Public Library 87, 107
hand v, 64, 67, 200, 226, 269, 270
Haslam, William 248
Haydon, Benjamin Robert 126, 140, 142, 143, 145–46, 187, 206, 241, 246, 248
Hazlitt, William 132–33, 140, 141, 242
health 8, 167–68, 201, 211, 233, 234, 235, 236, 237, 259, 266
good morals as a prerequisite for 148–49
heart 21, 29, 35, 37, 45, 50, 55, 83, 85, 106, 149, 152, 156, 177–78, 184, 188, 193, 194, 222, 227, 236–37, 250–51, 253, 265
blood vessels 45, 52, 84, 85
circulation in 45, 193
situation of 84, 149
structure 12, 22, 85
hemlock 189, 190, 260, 263
henbane 260, 261–62, 265
hernia 31, 61, 121
Hessey, James 242, 244–45, 248, 252
Hewlett, Dorothy 111, 134, 174
Hewson, William 51, 52, 53, 96
hip 59n149, 81
Hippocrates 194
Holmes, Richard 4, 7
*The Hospital Pupil's Guide, being Oracular Communications, addressed to Students of the Medical Profession* 160–62, 229–30, 260
advice for students 160–61
on distractions of London 161
on importance of dissections 170
on patient welfare 230, 232
recommended further reading 160
second edition of 160, 229
Hull, Jane 6, 118, 169, 217
Hunt Circle 140–41, 142, 143, 144, 145
Hunt, James Henry Leigh 5, 97, 122, 125, 126, 127, 129, 133–34, 140, 141, 145, 146, 147, 149, 197, 204–05, 206, 213, 214–15, 241, 245, 246
*Lord Byron and Some of His Contemporaries* 5n15, 90, 134, 136
'To Kosciusko' (sonnet) 183
at the Vale of Health 142, 146–47, 204
'Young Poets' article 126, 141, 144, 145

Hunter, John 21–22, 157, 159, 162–64, 214, 217–18
experiments 25, 36, 51
theory that blood possessed vitality 51, 118, 162–64, 166, 214
teaching of 163
*A Treatise on Blood, Inflammation and Gun-Shot Wounds* ... 162–63, 214
Hunter, William 25
Hutson, Charles 180–81
*see also* Cooper, Astley

illustrations 18, 33, 49, 57, 65, 78
involuntary actions 35, 36, 50, 51, 100, 196, 226
*see also* spinal marrow *under* nervous system
Isle of Wight 123, 205–06, 219, 243–44

Jackson, Noel 8
jaw 42, 73, 79
*John Keats's Anatomical and Physiological Note Book printed from the holograph in the Keats Museum Hampstead see* edition *under* Forman, Maurice Buxton
joints 38, 44, 53, 55, 59, 63
*see also* ankle, elbow, hip, knee, shoulder, thumb *and* wrist
Jones, John Frederick Drake 46, 95–96, 192

Keats, Frances (Fanny) 187, 208, 239, 250, 251
Keats, George 125, 126, 135–36, 142, 143, 144–45, 187, 204, 235, 238, 239, 247, 248, 250, 251, 253
financial crisis 8, 252–53
Keats, Georgiana 187, 238, 248, 251
Keats House ix, 1, 12n30, 87, 91, 249

**Keats, John** 87, 97, 101, 150, 153, 218, 219
anatomical knowledge 4, 7, 8, 149, 169, 172, 199–202
biographies 2, 4, 87–90, 111–18, 134, 136
early plans for 135, 136
advertisements of 135
and Caius Cibber's statues 225
capacity for synthesis 185–88
careers, relationship between 2, 119, 129, 137–38, 140, 143–44, 145, 147–48, 149, 150, 173, 187–88, 192, 195–96, 197–98, 202, 203, 204, 214, 232, 254–67, 269–70
as chameleon poet 187
*see also* letters *under* Keats, John
Chancery case 205
and Clarke 139–40, 141, 246–47
*see also* Clarke, Charles Cowden
at Clarke's School in Enfield 90, 91, 119
congenial household 144–47
correspondence 146, 187
*see also* letters *under* Keats, John
creativity 2, 8, 148, 202
expressed in both his careers 5, 7, 269–70
fluidity of 7, 195–96, 202, 254–67
critical reception 2, 3, 4, 7, 9
focus on medical knowledge 2, 6, 111
'gendering' of Keats 132–33
*see also* poetic reputation *under* Keats, John
epitaph 132
feels besieged 243–44
finances 8, 149, 235, 249, 251–53
gambling 162
and 'Guy's Hospital' poems 2, 4, 88, 118, 119–49, 137, 171, 243, 270
analysis by location 124–27, 144–45
dates of composition 4, 121–28
phases of composition 124–30, 139–41
poetic productivity at Guy's 4, 120, 121, 127–28, 141, 144–45, 243

**Keats, John** *continued*
health 8, 219, 235, 238, 239, 244, 250–51, 253–54
confined at home 238, 239, 242, 251
death 130
dosing with mercury 243, 245, 250
final illness 112, 181–82, 232, 233, 251, 253–54
pulmonary haemorrhage 193, 251, 253
range of diagnoses 181
tuberculosis 112, 181–82, 249, 250, 265
increased risk of infection 243, 250
sore throat 242, 243, 245, 246, 247, 249, 251
imaginative engagement with the world 115, 149
interest in mythology 7, 192, 195, 202
introduction to Leigh Hunt 125, 126, 140, 141, 143, 144, 146, 147, 246
letters 140–41, 142–43, 145, 205, 235–36, 238, 242–43, 245, 248–53
on his own health 238, 242–43, 245, 250–51
indications of infection 251
individual letters
To Benjamin Bailey, 8 October 1817 203, 224
To Benjamin Bailey, 22 November 1817 260
To Benjamin Robert Haydon, 10, 11 May 1817 206
To Charles Brown, about 21 June 1820 232
To Charles Cowden Clarke, 9 October 1816 141
To Charles Dilke, 20, 21 September 1818 243–44
To Charles Dilke, June 1819 232, 251
To Frances (Fanny) Keats, 10 September 1817 208–09
To George and Georgiana Keats, October 1818 248–49
To George and Georgiana Keats, February–May 1819 187, 232, 248–49
To George and Tom Keats, 21, 27 (?) December 1817 181, 267
To James Hessey 245, 248
To John Hamilton Reynolds, 17 March 1817 204
To John Hamilton Reynolds, 17, 18 April 1817 205–06, 235–36
To John Hamilton Reynolds, 14 March 1818 235–36
To John Hamilton Reynolds, 3 May 1818 91, 149, 195, 208, 254
To John Hamilton Reynolds, 24 August 1819 233, 250–51, 268
To John Hamilton Reynolds, 21 September 1819 101
To John Taylor, 27 February 1818 254
To John Taylor, 24 April 1818 118
To John Taylor, 5 September 1819 148
To Leigh Hunt, 10 May 1817 206, 219
To Richard Woodhouse, 27 October 1818 150, 187, 247
temporal elisions in 205–06
variety in 187
living arrangements reflect intellectual commitments 4, 91, 120, 143, 144, 147, 204
'living year' 234–35, 251–68, 269–70
medical knowledge 2, 4, 15–16, 117, 156, 195–196, 208, 214, 230, 232, 234, 254, 255, 262
medical Notebook *see* Keats' Medical Notebook
medically precise vocabulary 4, 6, 8, 149, 172, 192–93, 199, 203, 215, 222, 226–27, 232, 261, 270

**Keats, John** *continued*
and medicine 4, 7, 8, 9, 91, 112, 116, 129, 147, 150–72, 202, 233, 234, 237
apprenticeship to Hammond 6, 90, 91, 103, 112, 119, 178, 179, 229, 241
as caregiver to family members 112, 235, 239, 242–44, 247, 250, 255
conscientious motives for leaving medicine 179, 217
considers return to medicine 232, 233
situation with apothecary 232, 251–52
study for physician 232
surgeon to Indiaman 232, 251
dangers of identifying too closely with patients 217, 227
engagement with medical studies 3, 111, 111–13, 114, 115, 116–18
familiarity with Hunter's theory of blood 51, 118, 163–64, 214
*see also* Hunter, John
at Guy's Hospital 1, 2, 3, 5, 6, 7, 88, 91, 110, 112, 118, 127, 129, 139, 142, 143, 149, 163–64, 168–69, 171–72, 173–202, 203, 204, 205, 218, 232, 242, 248, 254, 255, 262, 270
as dresser 89, 92, 119, 120, 124, 128, 137, 138, 140, 145, 146, 147, 149, 156, 168–69, 173, 185, 207, 230, 236, 243, 244, 255
contemporary account of 6, 118, 169, 217
duty dresser 6, 118, 146, 169, 217, 225–26
intellectual capital 5, 150
poetic ambitions mocked 140, 144
records of 93, 120, 149, 203, 204
training 102–06, 121, 150, 169–70, 202, 214, 222, 229, 262
*see also* 'Guy's Hospital' poems *under* Keats, John
last operation 91, 179, 217, 227
*see also* arteriotomy *and* temporal artery
licentiate certificate 93, 102–03, 105, 116, 138, 143, 169
licentiate examination 4, 89, 92, 93, 110–11, 117, 118, 125, 127, 129, 138, 139, 141, 143, 144, 178, 207, 229
medical career chosen for him 92
medical opinion on air quality 148
*see also* Guy's Hospital
misspellings, suggestiveness of 188
mother's death, reaction to 211, 247
negative capability 214, 266–67
*see also* letters *under* Keats, John
northern walking tour 179, 237, 238, 249–50
return to London 238–39, 269
poetry 7, 9, 150, 179, 189–90, 227, 234, 237, 239, 248, 250–51, 262, 265, 269–70
patterns of poetic composition 124–27, 129, 139–42, 143–45, 208, 248, 251, 270
enabling factors 119–20, 244, 248, 251, 268, 270
overlap between poems 204, 208
as a poet of transience 189, 201–02, 237, 267–68, 270
poetic ambitions 149, 251
poetic 'apprenticeship' 119
*see also under* Clarke, Charles Cowden
poetic development 139–40, 203, 269–70
poetic reputation 1, 130–37
myth-making 4, 130–34
as 'Adonais' 2, 131, 133–34
as apothecary poetaster 130–31
as mortally sensitive to criticism 131–34, 137
*see also* critical reception *under* Keats, John

**Keats, John,** poetry *continued*
'poetical concentrations' 5, 197, 201–02, 270
physician-poet 5, 149, 270
physiological depictions of mental states 8, 149, 193, 199–202, 208–22, 225–27, 232, 254–56, 270
relief in poetic composition 235, 237, 243–44
reluctance to publish 234, 242, 249, 252, 253
*see also* publications *and* Keats' works
politics 6, 7, 202
publications
*Endymion: A Poetic Romance* (1818) 2, 135, 221
see *also Endymion under* Keats' works
*Lamia, Isabella, The Eve of St Agnes, and other Poems* (1820) 2, 8, 232, 233–68
advertisements for 135, 233
as commentary on contemporary medicine 9, 234, 242, 254–68
composition of 232, 233–54, 247, 249, 251
biographical circumstances 8, 234–54
Keats' preoccupations during 8, 232, 233–37, 238, 251–54
publication history 8, 233–54
date of publication 233
decision to publish 9, 253–54
publishers' 'Advertisement' 233
reviews 233
*Poems, By John Keats* (1817) 119, 121–22, 126, 127, 145–46, 197
'Smith's Standard Library' volume of selected poems by Keats 137
reading 183, 213, 220–21, 254, 256, 263–64
*see also The Anatomy of Melancholy and* Lemprière's *Classical Dictionary*
risk-taking 178–81
sense of injustice 246–47
sense of verbal rhythm 2, 5, 173, 188, 197–98, 202
sleepless night 246–47
theatre 162
theme of sociality 4, 142–43
and Tom Keats 112, 237–38, 239, 247, 248
concerned for Tom's health 235–36, 257, 238
nurses dying Tom 235, 237, 239, 242–44, 247, 250
Tom's death 232, 247, 249
tomb stone 132
verbal compression 2, 173, 192–93, 196–202

**Keats' Medical Notebook** ix, xi, 1, 2, 3, 6, 19–85, 92, 97, 101, 105, 118, 120, 152, 153, 158, 169–70, 171, 173–77, 203, 217, 226, 254, 267, 269–70
accounts of 87, 88, 89, 90, 92–93, 93, 94–95, 98–99, 110, 111, 112, 113–14, 115–18
arrangement of notes 9–12, 13, 95, 117, 184–87, 190–92, 197–98
blank pages 11, 12, 16, 115, 117, 184, 186
chronology of note-taking 10, 99
logic of ordering 10–11, 12, 13, 114, 184–87
as bibliographic object 3, 12n30, 93
features 88
book plate 13, 20, 87
cleanness of 3, 89
commentary on 2, 3–9
*see also* accounts of *under* Keats' Medical Notebook

**Keats' Medical Notebook** *continued*
comparisons with Waddington 3, 5, 11–12, 105, 114, 116, 173–87, 190–92, 196–99
differences 177–79, 181–87, 190–92, 196–99
reasons for 178–79, 181–84, 184–87, 190–92, 196–99
difficulties in comparing 174–75, 192
no corresponding sections 182–83
previous attempts 173–75
reorganization of notes 5, 184–87
for bones of the skull 184–87
statistical analysis 5, 175–77
on contents 2, 7, 8, 9–12, 15, 88, 113, 138, 148, 150, 153, 171, 173, 177–87, 202, 217, 220, 226, 255–56, 269–70
case references in 20, 21, 26, 31, 32–34, 35–36, 36, 39, 46, 61, 178, 226
compact 5, 173, 176–77, 184, 196, 198
cramped 186
dating of 5, 153–56
mistakes 14
mis-numbering 11, 175
no repetitions 5, 184, 186
prefiguring poetry 5, 117, 173, 197, 198–99, 202, 269–70
use of imagery 2, 5, 35, 118, 173, 197, 199, 202
verbal compression 2, 173, 199
verbal rhythm 2, 5, 173, 188, 197–98, 202
purpose of 197–98
reorganization of notes 5, 13, 173, 175, 184–87
sketches 68
flowers 78, 79, 90, 96, 112, 114, 115, 118
foot 65, 66, 112, 115, 116
fruits 112, 114, 115, 116, 117
imaginative links to notes 115
'indicator' hand 72
skulls 13, 18, 20, 112, 116, 254
source of 5, 88, 102, 105–07, 150, 151–56, 176–77
vocabulary 6, 8, 110, 117
writing only on versos 12, 114, 184, 186
contextual information 13–14, 15
cross references 3, 5, 9, 10, 11, 13, 21, 24, 26, 48, 55, 60–61, 101, 153, 173, 175, 190–91, 198
*see also* marginalia *under* Keats' Medical Notebook
current edition 1, 9, 13, 19–85
bibliographic details 9, 13, 16, 19
as compromise 10
editorial annotations in footnotes 13–14, 15, 16, 19
aims of 13, 15
editorial interventions in text 9, 13, 16
editorial symbols used 16–17, 19
conjectural readings 16, 19
font changes 17, 19, 39, 48, 50, 51, 52, 54, 66, 68
illegibility 16, 19
Keats' deletions 16, 19
Keats' insertions 16, 19
Keats' over-writing 16, 19
Keats' page numbers 11, 16, 19, 21, 47, 51, 53
Keats' symbols 9, 16
lacunae 16, 19
page divisions 17
on text of 1, 11, 13, 16
overview of 13–17
as database *see* dynamic repository *under* Keats' Medical Notebook
dynamic repository 3, 10, 116, 175, 178, 191
handwriting 88, 107–10, 111, 186
authenticity of 88, 107–10
changes in 10, 109–10
illegible 16, 19, 96–97

**Keats' Medical Notebook** *continued*
imaginative potential of 98, 111, 117, 118, 202
*see also* on contents *under* Keats' Medical Notebook
importance of 1, 95
*see also* nineteenth-century medical practice
international outlook of 158
Keats' misspellings 16, 22
Keats' page numbers 11, 47, 51, 53
layout 9, 10, 13, 99–102, 117, 184–85, 198
location of note-taking 12, 156, 186
as manuscript 1, 2, 10, 89, 118
collotype facsimile of 93
marginalia 3, 5, 9, 10–11, 13, 16–17, 19, 39, 48, 49, 50, 51, 52, 54, 60–61, 66, 68, 72, 81, 99–101, 114, 115, 153, 175, 185, 191, 198, 216
*see also* cross references *under* Keats' Medical Notebook
misattribution of notes 106
overview 9–12, 87–118
previous edition of *see* edition *under* Maurice Buxton Forman
provenance 3, 87, 88, 93, 118
purchase price 20
rebinding 12
signature 45

**Keats' works**
'Addressed to Haydon' ['Highmindedness, a jealousy for good'] 126
'Addressed to the Same' ['Great Spirits now on earth are sojourning'] 126
'After dark vapours have oppressed our plains' 126
'Alexander fragment' (disputed) 111, 129n37
'As Hermes once took to his feathers light' 187
'Bards of passion and of mirth' *see* 'Ode' ['Bards of passion and of mirth']
'Calidore: A Fragment' 125, 129, 146
'Character of C. B.' 187
'Dear Reynolds' 237
*Endymion* 1, 7, 147, 149, 179, 203–32, 235, 243–44
anatomical descriptions 8, 149, 203, 225–27
characters
Diana 208–09, 211, 217, 218, 219, 220, 221
symptoms 209, 216–17, 221–22
Endymion 195, 208–12, 218–20, 221, 227
dream vision 210–11, 216, 220
as 'marble man' 209, 211
symptoms 209–12, 215, 216–18, 219–20, 222, 231
distraction 209, 212
dizziness 209, 220
fainting 209–10, 218
feverishness 209, 212, 215, 216, 222, 231
'fixed trance' 209–11
palpitations 209
reciprocal sympathy 216–18
recollections affected 209–11
restlessness 209, 212, 215
*see also* vocabulary used *under Endymion*
sense impressions affected 209–10, 216, 218
soliloquy on 216
Indian Maid 221
Niobe 225–27
Peona 210–11, 221, 230–32
poet-narrator 222
Venus 209, 221

**Keats' works,** *Endymion*, *continued*
circumstances of composition 203, 205–08, 219
beginnings 204–08, 219
crisis of confidence 147, 206, 219
intent to write a long poem 203, 205
prolonged gestation 204–06, 207–08, 232
*see also* recollections of *Endymion under* Stephens, Henry
critical response 8, 203, 219, 222–25
Byron, George Gordon, Lord 209, 221, 223, 225
Croker, John Wilson 131, 133, 222, 223–24, 244–45, 247
Jeffrey, Francis 224
Lockhart, John Gibson 222–23
Patmore, Peter George 222, 223
on proliferation of rhyme 223–25, 245
Scott, John (as 'J.S') 245
Shelley, Percy Bysshe 224
figures of healers 8, 203, 207, 230–32
Glaucus' Cave 227
importance of 203
love-sickness 209
*see also The Anatomy of Melancholy*
medical ethics 8, 203, 228–30, 231
*see also* figures of healers *under Endymion*
physiological depiction of passion 8, 149, 203, 208–22, 225–27, 232
plot 208–09
'Preface' 218–19, 222, 224–25, 270
sales 239, 244
vocabulary used 210, 212, 215, 222, 227
*The Eve of St Agnes* 9, 201, 208, 214, 234, 252, 256–58, 259
revisions to 252, 256–57
*see also* Bell, Charles *and* reverie
*The Eve of St Mark* 208
*The Fall of Hyperion* 5, 193, 202, 208
'physician to all men' 202, 228
'Fancy' 234, 247–48, 249
'Fill for me a brimming bowl' 162
'Give me wine, women, and snuff' 124, 129, 171
'God of the golden bow' 127, 208
'Had I a man's fair form, then might my sighs' 124, 129
'Hadst thou liv'd in days of old' 124, 129
'Happy is England! I could be content' 125, 127
'How many bards guild the lapses of time' 125, 197
*Hyperion: A Fragment* 1, 5, 101, 192–93, 195–96, 199–202, 208, 214, 234–35, 237, 243, 244, 247, 249
Apollo 192–93, 195–96, 201, 215
fallen Titans in quarantine 215, 225
Hyperion 201, 214
Oceanus' progressivism 195, 237
Saturn 195, 199–201, 214
'I am as brisk' 124, 129
'I stood tip-toe upon a little hill' 126, 146, 147–48, 204, 208, 213
mingled pleasures of minnows 212–14
*see also* Brown, John
'Imitation of Spenser' 119
*Isabella* 9, 111, 13, 172, 215, 234, 235, 236–37, 249, 252, 254–56
composition 234–35, 236–37, 249, 254, 255
excessive passion 254, 255–56
'fierce potion' 255–56
Isabella's derangement 255–56
Lorenzo's skull 172, 254–56
love-melancholy 254
*see also The Anatomy of Melancholy*
vocabulary used 215, 236–37, 256
*The Jealousies* 195

**Keats' works,** *continued*
'Keen, fitful gusts are whisp'ring here and there' 125, 142
'La Belle Dame Sans Merci' 187
*Lamia* 234–35, 252, 253
'Lines on the Mermaid Tavern' 234, 235, 249
'Nature withheld Cassandra in the skies' (translation from Ronsard) 243
'Ode' ['Bards of passion and of mirth'] 234, 247–48, 249
'Ode on a Grecian Urn' 234
'Ode on Melancholy' 9, 150, 234, 260–68
  ambiguity 262, 263–64, 266, 267–68
  heightened perceptions 260, 267
  'Keatsian' melancholy 260, 266–68
  poisons 260–66, 267
  as prescription 260, 263, 266–67
'Ode to a Nightingale' 1, 5, 9, 150, 179, 188–90, 198–99, 201, 202, 214, 234, 258–60
  anatomizes creativity 188–90
  disorientation 201, 258, 259
  intense compression 198–99
  logic of poem 190
  loss of sight 190, 214, 258–59
  reverie 258–60
    *see also* Bell, Charles
  pattern of contraction and expansion 189–90
  self-annihilation 189, 190, 201, 259
'Ode to Psyche' 187, 191–92, 234
'Oh! How I love, on a fair summer's eve' 125, 129
'On A Leander Which Miss Reynolds, My Kind Friend, Gave Me' 127
'On Fame' (two sonnets) 187
'On First Looking into Chapman's Homer' 125, 141, 142, 144
  composition of 91–92, 141, 144
'On Leaving Some Friends at an Early Hour' 126, 142
'On Receiving a Laurel Crown from Leigh Hunt' 127, 208
'On Seeing the Elgin Marbles' 127, 208
'On the Grasshopper and the Cricket' 126
'On the Sea' 123, 205, 206
'On *The Story of Rimini*' 123–24, 127, 204–05
*Otho the Great* 136
Review of Reynolds' *Peter Bell* 187
'Robin Hood' 234, 235, 249
*Sleep and Poetry* 98, 126, 146–47, 149
'Song of Four Fairies' 187
'Specimen of an Induction to a Poem' 125, 129
'This living hand, now warm and capable' 5–6, 193, 196
'This pleasant little tale is like a little copse' 127
'Time's sea hath been five years at its slow ebb' 162
'To a Friend Who Sent Me Some Roses' 125, 127, 129
'To a Young Lady Who Sent Me a Laurel Crown' 127
'To Autumn' 150, 201, 214, 235, 269
'To Charles Cowden Clarke' 119, 125, 139–40, 142, 143
'To Chatterton' 115, 118
'To G. A. W.' 126
'To George Felton Mathew' 121, 122–23, 124, 128–29, 139, 142, 143
'To Haydon with a Sonnet Written on Seeing the Elgin Marbles' 127, 208
'To Homer' 213
'To Kosciusko' 97–98, 126
'To Leigh Hunt Esq.' 127
'To My Brother George' (sonnet) 125, 127, 139, 143
'To My Brother George' (verse epistle) 125, 127, 139, 142, 143
'To My Brothers' 126, 143, 144

**Keats' works,** *continued*
'To one who has been long in city pent' 125, 129
'To Sleep' 187
'To Solitude' 122–23, 124, 125, 140, 213
'To the Ladies Who Saw Me Crown'd' 127, 208
'When they were come unto the Faery's Court' 187
'Why did I laugh tonight? No voice will tell' 187
'Women! When I behold thee flippant, vain' 122
'Written in Disgust of Vulgar Superstition' 126
'Written on the Day Mr Leigh Hunt Left Prison' 139, 205

Keats Memorial Lecture 6–7
Keats, Tom 125, 126, 142, 143, 144–45, 181, 204, 206, 235–38, 239, 243–44, 247, 248
  death 232, 247, 249
  tuberculosis 237, 243, 247, 248, 250
Key, Charles Aston 180
kidneys 40
King's College London archives ix, 151
knee 42, 44, 67, 68, 82, 226
Kosciusko, Thaddeus (Tadeusz Kościuszko) 32–34, 97, 109–10, 116, 118, 146–47, 183

lancet 23, 31, 212, 217, 269
Lawrence, William 159, 164–66
'Lectures on Anatomy' 5, 103, 104, 105, 106, 111, 150, 151, 153–56, 169–70, 173–74, 232, 254
  advertisements for 103, 104, 153–55
  contemporary accounts of 153–54
  delay to 156
  schedule for 5, 150, 151–56, 184
  *see also* Cooper, Astley *and* Cline, Henry, Jnr.
lectures on the 'Principles and Practice of Surgery' 103, 104, 105, 151–54, 174
  published as *The Lectures of Sir Astley Cooper ... on the Principles and Practice of Surgery; with Additional Notes and Cases* 174, 183
  *see also* Cooper, Astley
legs 61, 66–68, 82, 83
Lemprière's *Classical Dictionary* 194, 195, 222, 263–64
Levinson, Marjorie 6
*Lexico-Medicum; or Medical Dictionary* xii, 15
ligaments 11, 42, 43, 45, 48, 53, 68, 79–83
  diseases of 12, 44
ligature 39, 55, 180–81
  *see also* Cooper, Astley
liver 25, 29, 40, 159, 194, 265
Liverpool 238
lock jaw *see* tetanus
Lockhart, John Gibson 2, 130–31, 222–23, 239–42, 244
  'The Cockney School of Poetry No, IV' 2, 130, 222–23, 239–42
    closing advice 223, 241
    on *Endymion* 222–23
    Keats' lack of cultural capital 223, 240, 241
    Keats' medical background 223, 239, 241
    'Z' as Keatsian double 241
London as centre of intellectual activity 162–66
*The London Dissector* v, xii, 15, 170, 269
*The London Magazine* 222
*The London Medical and Physical Journal* 103–04
London teaching hospitals 1, 5, 95, 150, 156–62, 171, 228, 269
  *see also* Guy's Hospital *and* nineteenth-century medical practice

Lowell, Amy 2, 90, 114
Lowell, James Russell 226, 270
Lucas, William, Jnr. 120
lungs 29, 45, 48, 50, 83, 84, 194–95, 250–51
lymph 26, 27, 53
 *see also* serum
lymphatics 25
 *see also* lymph
*Lyrical Ballads* 157

MacFarland, Thomas 198–99, 200
MacGillivray, J. R. 4, 130, 135, 246
Mackereth, George Wilson 124, 125, 126, 138, 158, 207
mandrake 261
mania, types of 240
Marcet, Alexander 26, 103, 104, 157–58
Margate 125, 127, 139, 143, 144, 206, 219, 243–44, 270
Mathew Circle 128, 142, 143
Mathew, George Felton 88, 122–23, 128, 130, 143
 'To A Poetical Friend' 122–23
medical ethics 8, 203, 228–32
 bedside manner 229, 230, 232
 comprehensive knowledge 228, 230
 patient welfare 229–30
 personal responsibility 228, 230
 qualifications 228–29
 required reading 228
Medwin, Thomas 133
Mellor, Anne 8
'Memoir for Shelley' *see* Medwin, Thomas
mercury *see under* stimulants
metromania 239–40
Milnes, Richard Monckton 87, 88, 130, 136
Milton, John xiv, 240, 265–66
 *see also Paradise Lost*
Mitchell, Robert 7
*The Morning Chronicle* 104–05, 135, 183n39, 233, 245, 246
*The Morning Post* 154, 183
Motion, Andrew 116–17
Murry, John Middleton 122–23
muscles 36–37, 38–39, 47, 48, 51, 54, 60, 61, 63, 64, 68, 71, 74, 81, 118, 152, 163, 167, 190, 196, 217, 226
 vis tonica 38–39
the Muses 240, 241

nerves *see under* nervous system
nervous system 30, 35, 100, 101, 106, 109, 167, 176, 191, 226
 brain 6, 30, 35, 36, 48, 50, 100, 101, 109, 148, 191–92, 197, 199, 219–20, 226, 254
  circulation in 31, 55, 220
  diseases of 31
  medullary substance of 31, 191
  structures of
   cerebellum 31
   cerebrum 31
   Dura Mater 30, 31, 32, 76, 191
   Gall and Spurzheim on structure 6, 191
   Medulla oblongata 31, 50, 71, 75, 100, 101
   Medulla spinalis 31, 35, 50, 100, 101
   Pia Mater 30, 32, 191
   sinuses of 30, 48, 70, 76
 functions 32, 50, 51
 nerves 34, 35, 36, 41, 42, 50, 55, 63, 66, 67, 69, 71, 74, 75, 76, 77, 100, 101, 106, 109, 118, 163, 167, 182, 191, 196, 199–200, 217, 226
  diseases of 35–36, 77
  ganglion 32, 34, 36, 182, 191
  in brain 32, 191
  injuries to 32–34, 35, 38, 98, 109, 116, 183
  plexus 32, 191

reunion of nerves 32, 34, 109, 179, 182
sciatic nerve 32–34, 39, 81, 98, 109, 115, 183
structure 32, 191
physiology of 32–34
spinal marrow 31, 35, 56, 183, 197, 199
*see also* volition
New Historicism 6
nightshade (solanaceae) 260, 261, 262, 263–64, 265
common 262, 264
deadly 262, 263–65
woody 262, 263–64
nineteenth-century medical practice 5, 15, 150, 171, 178, 179, 181, 182, 228, 254, 260–61, 262, 266, 269
cutting for the stone 236
dependence on empirical experience 181–82
dissection v, 113, 150, 170–72, 190, 195, 255, 269, 270
history of medicine 1, 95, 110–11, 118
literary aspirations of practitioners 241–42
macabre aspects of profession 150, 171
stratification of profession 229
surgery in 168, 269, 270
training in 1, 121, 169, 171, 202, 208, 269
without anaesthesia 121, 211–12
*see also* medical ethics
nose 34, 50, 70, 77, 96, 101, 115, 118, 196, 216, 255

occiput ('os occipitis') *see under* skull
Ollier, Charles and James (publishers) 145
organs 35, 39, 168, 181
functions 50, 101, 216
types 40, 48–50
Osler, Edward 180
osteology 12, 13, 56–79, 114–15, 184, 186

Page, Ken ix, 12n30
palpitations 182, 221, 222
palsy 36
*Paradise Lost* xiv, 129, 244, 265–66
Partridge, Alderman 152–53, 154, 156
pathology 48
Patmore, Peter George 222, 223
pelvis 56, 59–60, 60–61, 81
peony 265, 267
Percival, Thomas 159, 228–29
*see also* medical ethics
pericardium 28, 83, 84
*see also* heart *and* reticular membrane
periosteum 30, 42, 53–54
peristaltic motion 38
peritoneum 24, 28, 40
*see also* reticular membrane
*The Phaedrus* 240
*Pharmacopoeia Londoniensis* 138
physiology 7, 48, 102, 103, 105, 106, 107, 114, 118, 202, 203, 214–15
pins and needles 35, 110
*see also* sensation
pleura 24, 28, 40, 83
*see also* reticular membrane
Plymouth Institution 91, 136
'poison of Venus' 28
*see also* gonorrhoea *and* syphilis
poppy 261
Proserpine 263–64
psychological effects of trauma 199–201, 211–12, 226
pulse 45, 46, 54, 158, 176, 177–79, 188, 192, 193, 194, 214–16, 221, 227, 232

*The Quarterly Review* 131, 132, 133, 165–66, 222, 223–24, 244–45, 246–47

Redding, Cyrus 134
relative bradycardia 179
*see also* fever
'Resurrection men' 171, 254
reticular membrane 14, 28–30, 39
reverie 257–60
*see also* Bell, Charles
Reynolds, John Hamilton 101, 123, 131–32, 136, 140, 142, 143, 146, 187, 204, 205, 208, 235–36, 243, 250–51, 254
*The Garden of Florence; and Other Poems* 131–32
ribs 29, 59, 60, 61, 62, 79, 84
Rice, James 236
Richardson, Alan 6, 191, 254
Richardson, Benjamin Ward *see* Stephens, Henry
rickets 67
Ricks, Christopher 188, 218, 225
Roe, Nicholas ix, xii, 4, 6, 115, 117–18, 227
discovery of contemporary account of Keats as dresser 6, 118, 169
Rollins, Hyder Edward xii, 253
rose 127, 129, 244, 265–66, 267
*see also Paradise Lost*
Rossetti, William Michael 89
Roux, Philibert Joseph 156–57
Royal College of Surgeons 162, 164–66, 229

sacculus mucosus ('saculus mucosus') 38
Salisbury, William 261–62
salivation 41, 42
*see also* glands
Saumarez, Richard 155, 159, 168
Sawrey, Solomon 181, 237, 239
sciatic nerve *see under* nerves
Scotland 87, 179, 237, 238, 249–50, 269
scrophula 28, 44–45
secreting membrane 28, 40, 51
secreting organs *see* follicles *and* glands
secretions 41, 50, 255–56
sensation 32, 34–35, 36, 50, 51, 100, 109, 226
*see also* nervous system
sensibility 37, 42, 43, 109, 116, 167
serum 27, 29, 52–53, 54
Severn, Joseph 135, 136, 142, 143, 187, 238, 248, 249–50
Shakespeare, William 240, 248–49
Sharp, Ronald 4
Shelley, Percy Bysshe 2, 108, 133, 146, 205, 241–42
*Adonais: An Elegy on the Death of John Keats* xiv, 2, 131, 133, 134
family crisis 145, 205
shoulder 62–63, 79–80, 84
Sibly, Ebenezer *see* Culpeper, William
skeleton 12, 56, 115, 190
skin 21, 23, 24, 39, 50, 55, 101, 190, 216
skull 68–76, 77, 184–87, 254
foramina 14, 15, 55, 69–70, 71–72, 73, 74–76, 220
occiput ('os occipitis') 58, 70, 73, 74, 169, 217
*see also* cranium
Smith, Horace 197
Socrates 189, 195, 240
South, John Flint xii, 106, 121, 137–38
Southampton 205
Southey, Robert 157, 241
Southwark 124–26, 207
Spallanzani, Lorenzo 34, 110, 183
sphlanchnology 12, 83–85
spinal cord 194
*see also* medulla spinalis *under* nervous system
spine 53, 56, 59, 70, 79
*see also* nervous system
St Bartholomew's Hospital 157, 162
St Thomas' Hospital 39, 91, 104, 105, 111, 121, 151–52, 157, 171

St Thomas' Street 124–25, 126, 207
Steel, Mabel 108, 114–15
Stephens, Henry 124, 125, 126, 129, 137, 138, 158, 238, 241
  conversations with Benjamin Ward Richardson 207
  recollections of *Endymion* 204, 207–08
  recollections of Keats at Guy's, written 1847 4, 88–89, 129–30, 137–38, 140n94, 144, 145, 171, 207, 242n30,
sternum 60, 61, 62
Stillinger, Jack xiii, 124n28, 126, 127, 147, 270n3
stimulants 25, 27, 41, 44, 46, 167–168, 232
  antimony 27, 255
  digitalis 27, 46, 255
  mercury 27, 41, 181, 243, 245, 250
  opium 167, 189–90, 223, 258, 260, 261
  purgatives 27, 41, 255
  snuff 41, 255
  wine 46, 167, 190, 232, 258
  *see also* pulse
stimuli 38, 41, 46, 54, 162, 166, 167–68, 196, 214, 255, 256
  *see also* secretions
Stocker, Richard 46
Störck, Anton 262
  *see also* botany
sympathy 35, 41, 50, 100, 196–97, 217, 226
  complicated sympathy 35, 196
  reciprocal sympathy 216–18
syncope 219–20, 265
syndesmology 12, 79–83
synovia ('sinovia') 43, 48
synovial membrane ('sinovial membrane') 38, 43, 44, 45
syphilis 28n35, 181
systole 45, 176, 188, 189, 194

Taylor and Hessey (publishers) 135, 137, 233, 239, 247, 252
Taylor, John 108, 135–36, 137, 148, 233, 244, 251, 252, 253, 257
tears 39, 41, 255
teeth 24, 26, 77, 104, 121
Teignmouth 235–36, 237
temporal artery *see under* arteries
tendon 36, 37, 38, 42, 48, 54, 63, 64, 68, 81
tetanus 37
Thelwall, John 158, 166–67
thoracic duct 24, 25, 27, 28
  *see also* absorbents
thorax 56, 60, 62, 83
  *see also* heart, lungs, pericardium, thymus gland
thumb v, 67, 79, 269
thymus gland 83, 84
tic douloureux 35–36, 77
*Times Literary Supplement* 88, 110, 111
toes 34, 66, 68
tongue 34, 40, 50, 75, 101, 216, 226
trachea 35, 84
trephine 70–71
tuberculosis 201, 237, 249–50
  *see also* Keats, John *and* Keats, Tom
Turley, Richard Marggraf ix, x, 6
Tyrell, Frederick 124, 137, 174

ulcerations 23, 29, 37, 40, 43, 44
ureters 40
uterus 35, 50, 55

valves 21–22, 25, 85
vasa vasorum 25, 55
Vauxhall 162
veins 21, 23, 29, 41, 47, 48, 50, 52, 76, 84, 85, 106, 176, 191, 193, 196, 198
  coats of 21, 22, 25, 48, 188
  diseases of 22, 39
    *see also* aneurismal varix
  origins 21, 48, 191

pulsation 22, 117
uniformity of contents 22, 52
valves 21–22, 85
venesection 121
vertebra 31, 32, 56–59, 62
cervical 56–58, 58–59, 78
dorsal 56, 58, 59, 60, 84
lumbar 56, 58
Vickers, Neil 168
vital principle 35, 165, 217
*see also* sympathy
Vitalism Debates 162–66
volition 35, 36, 50, 51, 100, 197, 199, 226, 267
*see also* nervous system
voluntary motion *see* volition

Waddington, Joshua 98, 105, 112, 113, 114, 116, 151–55, 158, 173, 177–79, 181–87, 190–92, 196–99
manuscript notebooks xiv, 105–06, 151–52, 153, 156, 173–75
'Lectures on Anatomy; And The Principal Operations of Surgery' 105, 106, 152, 156, 175, 176–87, 190–92, 196–99
first volume of xi, 106, 152, 176–87, 190–92, 196–99
dates for 152–54, 184
lectures on bones of the skull 184–87
'Lectures On The Principles and Practice, of Surgery' 151–52
Wakefield, Gilbert 158
Ward, Aileen 112–13, 117, 128, 141
Well Walk 127, 204–05, 238, 242
Wells, Charles 129
Wentworth Place *see* Keats House
White, R. S. x, 4, 117, 160, 230, 256n103
Whitfield, R. 71
Whytt, Robert 167
Williams, Helen Maria 183
Winston, George A. R. xii, 3, 98–99, 105, 113, 151, 152, 173–75
Wise, T. J. 107–08
wolf's-bane 260, 261, 265
Wolfson, Susan 4, 137
Woodhouse, Richard 136, 242, 245–46, 247, 252, 253, 257
Woolaston, Charles 43, 54
Wordsworth, William 123, 140, 157
'Prefatory Sonnet' ['Nuns fret not ...'] 123
wrist v, 37, 55, 63, 64–66, 67, 81, 227, 269

yew 260, 264, 265
*York Herald and General Advertiser* 183

'Z' *see* Lockhart, John Gibson